Educational Thought and Ideology in Modern Japan

Educational Thought and Ideology in Modern Japan
State Authority and Intellectual Freedom

Teruhisa Horio
edited and translated by Steven Platzer

UNIVERSITY OF TOKYO PRESS

Translation of this volume was assisted by a grant from the Ministry of Education, Science and Culture, Japan.

Contents

Author's Preface

Western scholars and educators have recently become very interested in the Japanese school system. Believing that knowledge about it will help them understand one of the most important factors underlying the growth of the Japanese economy, they, along with people in China and the countries of Southeast Asia, have eagerly consumed the information currently available about our schools. Regrettably, however, due to the fact that most of the existing knowledge about Japan and its educational system directly reflects the views officially put forward by the Japanese government, their knowledge has been altogether too one-sided or prejudiced.

Even though Japanese schools may very well appear to be outstanding when seen from the outside, from within, it is clear, I believe, that the vitality of both students and teachers is being smothered by a thoroughly oppressive set of conditions. This is testified to by the sharply rising number of incidents of bullying and the dramatically increasing number of children refusing to go to school at all. And as the level of pressure within the school system is constantly turned up, our children are being systematically denied the opportunity to develop their individuality. Thus it is no wonder that most of our youth find it impossible to sustain warm feelings about their schools even when they do manage to make good friends there, or when they study with teachers whose stimulation encourages them to want to learn.

Likewise, under the existing textbook screening system, the State's arbitrary control over the creation and dissemination of knowledge is continually tightening, and more and more uniformity is being imposed on textbook contents and forms of description. Teachers as well are being brought under an ever more pernicious system of management; in addition to their being exposed to new and more extreme forms of pressure, they are losing the freedom both to teach and to undertake educationally related research. Sadly, these pressures are being transmitted through the system in the form of physical punishments inflicted on our youth. We are seeing the emergence of a vicious circle. Thus, from my perspective, our educational system, far from presenting itself as an object deserving emulation, stands in need of the most drastic types of reform.

The character of this educational system has been strongly influenced by the nature of modern Japanese history itself.

The modern Japanese educational system got off to a late start, and even then its formation was tightly circumscribed within the framework laid down by a generation of statesmen who viewed it as an effective tool to be used to realize their own political and economic agendas. This historical tradition has been carried down to the present day; in fact, the state's manipulation of our schools is even stronger today than it was in the prewar era.

As a consequence of this, those who control education in Japan have paid scant attention to the idea that education should be organized from the perspective of human development, and they have shown little respect for the notion that the pursuit of education should be connected to the pursuit of mankind's intellectual and spiritual freedom.

However, even within the framework of this history there has been an undercurrent of educational thought aimed at the concrete realization of these humanly liberating ideas. These currents were finally allowed to rise to the surface after the war, when Japanese education was drastically reformed.

Looking at developments over the 40 years of the postwar period, we can clearly observe a struggle between those who sought to establish the foundations for a new tradition of educational practice and those who have attempted to preserve the framework within which education was considered in the past, namely as an instrument of State policy. While tracing the course of that history, this book attempts to criticize the ways education has been controlled and transformed into an instrument of State policy, and seeks to clarify the nature of the principles which are required to break the stranglehold of this way of thinking. In other words, its overriding objective is to think about Japanese education in a way which will help transform it into something designed to genuinely liberate and nurture the capacities of Japanese citizens as free human beings. In this regard, while it is a book about education in Japan, at the same time its fundamental values are those of mankind in general. It attempts to bring an international consciousness to bear upon the problems plaguing education in Japan so as to enable those scholars and general readers outside Japan who are interested in understanding our system of schooling to see the nature and depth of the problems we are currently facing. In this sense it does not rely upon or partake of the values of Japanism which are found in most of the English-language literature on Japanese education, in some cases subtly and in others not so subtly.

The editor and translator of this volume, Steven Platzer, is a young American researcher who attended my lectures at the University of Tokyo and participated in the seminars I directed there in the late 1970s and early 1980s. After reading through all of my writings, and having reached a deep understanding of my basic approach, he selected those essays which he believed would be most interesting to Western readers. Thus this is not merely a book of translations but a scrupulously undertaken work whose quality has been greatly augmented by the understanding of Japan which Mr. Platzer brought to this project. I greatly appreciate his years of hard and conscientious effort on my behalf.

Tokyo, January 1988   HORIO TERUHISA

Editor's Introduction

People in the West are increasingly intrigued by reports about the Japanese system of education. Fueled by the frequently asserted but as yet unproven claim that Japan's economic prosperity is related to the capacity of its educational system to turn out highly productive workers, these reports are giving rise to a growing sense of urgency about the need for drastic educational reforms, especially in those countries most directly affected by the growth of Japanese economic power. In the United States, for example, these accounts have generated a widely shared belief that until American children are able to match the levels of academic excellence already reached by the youth of Japan, there is simply no way to compete economically against the Japanese. Some are now even going so far as to conclude that in schooling, as in other areas of contemporary life, the Japanese have learned how to organize their efforts more effectively than the rest of us.

This wave of enthusiasm is being nurtured by a flood of recent studies which suggest that many of the educational practices seen in Japanese schools are indeed worthy of emulation. In general, however, these accounts also leave the reader with the impression that since much of what is purportedly worth emulating results from the uniqueness of Japanese culture, these achievements cannot ultimately be replicated outside of Japan. Even more perplexing is the fact that this rapid growth of knowledge has not been matched by the appearance of a critical perspective on the serious problems now plaguing the Japanese educational system and causing countless children to suffer. Those scholars whose work is underwriting these ideas are not paying sufficient attention to the ways Japan's academic standards are arbitrarily determined and bureaucratically imposed upon students and teachers alike. This is particularly troublesome because, while these standards have placed high demands upon Japanese young people, they have also seriously undermined the spirit of free thinking implanted at the core of postwar Japan's democratic social life. Thus there are good grounds for arguing that the message being conveyed by today's experts on Japanese education is at best irresponsible and at worst dangerous.

Those who want the nations of the West to strive to meet what has been called "the Japanese educational challenge" are implicitly making powerful claims about the ways in which we should be preparing our children to meet the problems of the twenty-first century. But would one listen to a doctor who showed little concern for the negative effects of the medicine he was prescribing?

The time has come for a more discriminating approach to Japanese education and the achievements which are being attributed to it. We need another perspective from which these reports can be evaluated in a more judicious light.

The translation of these essays has been undertaken in part to stimulate the kind of critical thinking presently missing from Western scholarship about Japanese education. Their author, Horio Teruhisa, professor of Educational Thought and History at the University of Tokyo and dean of the university's Faculty of Education, is one of the most interesting thinkers in the Japanese educational world today. His work, unlike those which merely skim the surfaces of Japanese schooling and recklessly sing its praises, plumbs its darkest and most disturbing truths; thus it is particularly well suited for generating an evenhanded approach to the successes now being attributed to Japanese education.

In addition to teaching in the Faculty of Education at the University of Tokyo, Professor Horio is one of the three persons chosen by Japan's educational researchers to serve as their representative on the Science Council of Japan (Nihon Gakujutsu Kaigi); chief secretary of the Japanese Society for the Study of Education (Nihon Kyōiku Gakkai Jimu Kyokuchō), a body made up of more than 3000 educational researchers; a vice-president and director of the Society for the Scientific Study of Education (Kyōiku Kagaku Kenkyūkai) and for five years editor of its prestigious journal *Kyōiku (Education)*; and a frequent contributor to many other highly respected educational journals. Furthermore, he is one of the most important critics of Japanese education within Japan itself, and a leader of those who in recent years have challenged the legitimacy of the Ministry of Education's attempt to bureaucratically dominate every aspect of Japanese educational life.

The Question of Conflict

In recent years there has been growing criticism of the clear tendency in mainstream American scholarship on Japan to overlook or minimize the highly conflictual character of that nation's modern history.[1] The

---

[1] See, for example, *Conflict: The Neglected Tradition in Modern Japanese History*, edited by Tetsuo Najita and Victor C. Koschmann (Princeton University Press, 1982).

thrust of this criticism can be directed towards much of the scholarly work recently published on Japanese education as well. An important example of the propensity to view the Japanese educational world as one essentially free of significant conflict is *Japanese Education Today* (U.S. Department of Education, 1987), a report on the results of an officially sponsored study in which most of the leading American researchers on Japanese education participated. In that report we are told, for instance, that "Japanese history and cultural values" provide a "heritage reflected in the national consensus on the importance of education," and that this "forms the invisible foundation of the contemporary education system" (p. 4). But what does this mean? What aspects of Japanese educational practice can the authors of this report actually elucidate by telling us that the values sustaining Japanese educational life are "invisible"? Does it help us understand why Japanese students study so diligently or why Japanese laborers work so hard? Or is it the admission of an unwillingness to make visible important conflicts and real sources of contention within modern Japanese life?

As will be demonstrated in Part I of the present volume, the values dominating the Japanese educational system were clearly defined and institutionalized at the end of a bitter political struggle in the 1880s over the course in which Japan's modernization should proceed. Furthermore, the tensions underscoring this struggle between the conservative forces which insisted upon the need to administer enlightenment to the people from the top down, and their progressive opponents who held that the people themselves must be the focus and center of efforts to modernize society, have continued to spark educational conflict up to the present day. Thus Horio's work has the special advantage of enabling us to grasp the highly conflictual character of education in Japan today against the background of a living intellectual history. It helps us to see, first, that those who now refuse to accept the notion that only the State's bureaucrats are in a position to determine what the Japanese people need to know are the inheritors of the values generated by the struggles of the Freedom and People's Rights Movement of the 1870s as well as the values introduced by the American Occupation reformers in the late 1940s, and, second, that those bureaucrats in the Ministry of Education who today attempt to rule Japanese educational life from their offices in Tokyo are the inheritors of the attitude of contempt for the human rights of the Japanese people which was perfected by their predecessors in the prewar Imperial State apparatus. In other words, Horio's work seriously calls into question the claim made by some scholars of Japanese education that those who today challenge the authority of the Ministry of Education are merely leftist-inspired troublemakers. A reading of this book suggests rather that their struggle in support of the spirit of intellectual freedom and liberty (in the terms set forth in the postwar Japanese Constitution) is based on values much closer to those of the liberal democratic West than we have been led to believe.

Likewise, Horio's work clearly suggests that American researchers on Japanese education have been altogether too willing to uncritically accept the ideas put forth by Japan's Ministry of Education. Instead of adopting the skeptical attitude which we should expect from professional investigators, they have failed to balance the views put forward by that Ministry with the criticisms of its opponents. One of the virtues of Horio's scholarship is that it illuminates the webs of conflict within which Japanese education is actually inscribed, and helps us to see beyond the myths of harmony and consensuality within which much of contemporary scholarship on Japan is ensconced. Thus, for example, whereas *Japanese Education Today* acknowledges the existence of "strong disagreements between the government and the teachers' union" (p. 2), but fails to either explore the nature of these disagreements or to explain the significance of their outcomes, Horio's essays do precisely that.

By avoiding such issues and the serious problems which underlie them, the current generation of American investigators of Japanese education have managed to present a view of educational control from which all signs of conflict have been eradicated. Thus, for example, they tell us that "educational policy making in Japan is systematic and consensual." While it is indeed true that educational policies are forged in an extremely systematic fashion, it is only consensual to the extent that everyone who does not share the values of the Ministry of Education is excluded from the decision-making process. The consensuality attributed to Japanese education policy making does not reflect the absence of conflict, but only the State's success in containing or suppressing it. Chapter 5 of this volume outlines some of the ways this process works.

Education, Culture, and Politics in a Democratic Society

The difficulty American investigators have in dealing with these issues results from their belief that it is possible to separate educational and cultural life from its political context. The authors of *Japanese Education Today*, for example, tell us that "Japanese education is a powerful instrument of cultural continuity and national policy" and that it imparts the "attitudes, knowledge, sensitivities and skills expected of emerging citizens of Japanese society" (p. 2). Unfortunately, however, the authors appear oblivious to the fact that in both pre- and postwar Japan, "cultural continuity" has been a social category whose meaning has been strictly defined and jealously guarded by the Ministry of Education itself. Seeing the realms of culture and knowledge as essentially different from the realms of power and politics, mainstream American thinking about Japanese education fails to see that the manipulation of culture has played an important part in the exercising of power in modern Japanese society, or that the educational system which helps make this possible has played a critically important part in the State's efforts to create an effective system of social control. These issues are taken up and explored with great sophistication in this book.

While the authors of *Japanese Education Today* speak approvingly of the role played by the national educational system in inculcating attitudes and sensitivities for citizenship, they appear untroubled by one of the most important problems Horio's analysis calls to our attention: when a society is a truly democratic one, the State should not interfere with these matters, but should leave them to the free will of its individual members. Under the system of democracy as defined by Japan's Ministry of Education, however, these matters are regarded as much too important to entrust to the people themselves; only the officials of the State can legitimately determine the values and norms appropriate for the members of society.

Likewise, unlike Horio, these scholars perceive no contradiction between the ideal of freedom as an intrinsic part of life in a liberal democracy and the reality that in Japan there is no freedom for teachers in determining what they must teach, or for students when it comes to deciding what they must learn. Moreover, they fail to provide any reasons or arguments which would justify the fundamental assumption upon which their thinking must ultimately rest if it is to have any meaning at all: the notion that the Japanese people freely yield these powers to the State. Horio's work, in contrast, explores the conditions in which this power has been taken from them, and defines the nature of the challenge which must be met by those seeking to reclaim these powers.

By neglecting to investigate the relation between education and the values, attitudes, or outlooks historically inculcated within the Japanese people, American experts of the current generation have locked themselves in a cage from within which they cannot address what Horio has called the "problem of rupture and continuity" between the pre- and postwar systems of education in Japan. Ironically, the consequence of their unwillingness to confront these issues is that they are unable to resolve one of the most important questions implicitly raised by the unabashedly laudatory tone of their own work: whether the successes they seek to document are results of the democratic reforms introduced after the war, or the historical legacy of the anti-democratic system developed during the prewar period (a system whose intellectual structure Horio analyzes very carefully in Chapter 3 of this volume, "Education and Human Cultivation in the Emperor-State"). The reader who wishes to explore the "problem of rupture and continuity" will therefore want to pay special attention to the discussion presented in Chapter 5, "Education and Law in Postwar Japan."

The Problem of Democracy in Japanese Education

Those who discuss postwar Japanese education generally frame their remarks against the background of what they take to be the meaning of its democratization. Debates over the meaning of this process have given shape to a discourse in Japan bounded on the one side by the thinking of those who believe democratization has gone too far and on the other by those who think it has not gone far enough.

Curiously, the American discourse on postwar Japanese education has proceeded largely by ignoring these conflicts and by failing to question their significance. The unfortunate consequence is that American observers have overlooked the real problems and controversies surrounding educational democratization in Japan, and have only seen its schools in terms of America's own educational problems, which are in many important but unnoticed respects actually quite different. Thus, for example, Secretary of Education William J. Bennett was led to conclude in his Epilogue to *Japanese Education Today*: "Our educational ideals are better realized on a large scale in Japan than observers have tended to realize," because "the ideas and approaches used in education in Japan can be traced to American influence four decades ago. . . . It is the American belief in the value of universal education that the Japanese have so successfully put into practice, and the American quandary over 'equality' and 'excellence' that the Japanese seem rather satisfactorily to have resolved." (p. 69).

Unfortunately, however, those who construe the educational accomplishments of postwar Japan primarily as a resolution of the "quandary over 'equality' and 'excellence'" put themselves in a position from which it is very difficult to perceive the seriousness of the problems Japanese society presently faces in attempting to balance the quest for intellectual freedom and excellence against the pursuit of social equality. Horio has been particularly concerned to call attention to the seriousness of these problems, but for the most part our Western experts, following in the footsteps of those in Japanese educational circles who totally refuse to admit that the values associated with intellectual freedom are being dangerously attacked, have been remarkably insensitive to the nature and complexity of this crisis. Thus the latter have essentially failed to consider the possibility that as long as teachers and textbook authors are not guaranteed the right to encourage the growth and development of free thinking among students, the seemingly laudable pursuit of egalitarianism in education can in fact degenerate into the promotion of an anti-democratic form of conformism.

One of the major objectives of Horio's work has been to call attention to, and propose meaningful solutions for, the paradoxical situation in which the nominal pursuit of equal opportunities for all students has in actuality seriously jeopardized the realization of a democratic form of social life in postwar Japan. This can be seen in Part II of this book, wherein he carefully examines the ways in which the values of educational freedom have been subjected to systematic assault in postwar Japan, and in Chapters 12 and 13, which take up the problem of how a number of the most important democratizing reforms of postwar Japanese education have been undermined by officially implemented policies ostensibly rooted in the values of egalitarianism.

Horio's Intellectual Development

Horio's early childhood in Kokura, Kita-Kyūshū, was like that of other young people born during the 1930s who grew up unconsciously embracing the values of Japanese militarism and ultranationalism. This is testified to by the fact that when his army veterinarian father passed away from a disease contracted at the front, the six-year-old Horio's grief was totally overshadowed by the shame he felt when in the presence of friends whose fathers had died more heroic deaths.

Following the end of the war, Horio, along with the other members of his generation, had to undergo what he has described as the "terribly painful experience of coming to terms with the fact that all the values we had been educated to accept as eternally true were thoroughly false." Thus Horio had to weather the turbulent upheavals of adolescence during a period when Japanese society was undergoing an unprecedented crisis of order. While this individual was beginning to establish himself as a human being, Japan was beginning to establish itself as a democratic society. The convergence of these two lines of development had important consequences in determining the future course of Horio's intellectual maturation.

Horio started to think about pursuing a career in education after a high school friend's failed suicide attempt. His troubled friend, the son of a deputy mayor apprehended in a case of official corruption, was driven to his desperate act by the ridicule he was forced to suffer at the hands of an insensitive teacher. This incident made a deep and lasting impression on the young Horio. Wouldn't this misfortune have been avoided, he asked himself, if the teacher had been trained to be more responsive to the needs of his students, and less concerned to assert power over them in the classroom? How, Horio started to wonder, should teachers conduct themselves so as to best fulfill their professional duties? But before acting on his desire to study education, the young Horio decided to follow in the footsteps of an older brother and pursue a more generalized course of studies in the Law School of the University of Tokyo.

During his first two years in Tokyo, Horio was not very interested in political problems, even though this was the time that the purge of communists from official positions occurred, the Korean War broke out, and the Subversive Activities Prevention Law (*habōhō*) was enacted. His concern with political problems was awakened when he began to study under the famous political scientist Maruyama Masao. In the spring of 1953, Maruyama announced that he would offer a seminar on the theme of "Nationalism and Fascism in Japan" and that any student who wanted to participate had to first submit a prospectus on the work he would do. Horio wrote what he remembers today as an unusual essay in which he challenged the view of prewar Japan then prevailing among students according to which all its social values were seen as expressions of ultranationalism and militarism. His aim was not to endorse those ideologies, or to justify the evil consequences of the activities based upon them; his point rather was to question the overly facile manner in which everything about prewar life was being uniformly rejected. At the heart of this attitude, he wrote, was a historical consciousness from which the thoughts and feelings of the individuals who had supported Japanese militarism and ultranationalism had been eliminated, and in which society was being viewed as a totality existing over and above the people who made it up. He based these criticisms on his reading of the works of existentialist thinkers like Dostoevsky, Nietzsche, Sartre, and Camus, and argued that to understand the meaning of ultranationalism or militarism for those who had served in the war like his father and older brothers, it was not good enough to rely on purely externalized, sociological categories. Maruyama was evidently impressed by the thrust of Horio's paper, for Horio was the only third-year student allowed to participate in the seminar.

As a result of his involvement with this seminar, Horio developed a deep and enduring interest in the problems posed by the study of intellectual history, and began to confront issues such as the nature of the conflict between the external authority of states and the internal freedoms of individuals. Moreover, as a result of the work he did for his project on "The Foreign View of Japanese Nationalism," Horio came into direct contact with a world of ideas and values he had previously been unaware of, and he began to reflect upon the issues which have defined the major axes of his historical thought and educational research ever since, i.e. the character of Japan's modernization and the values of human existence therein. Horio's present-day concern to approach the problems of individuals in terms of the problems of society, and the problems of society in terms of the problems of individuals, clearly began to take shape in response to the stimulation provided by his experiences in Maruyama's seminar.

As his undergraduate career at the University of Tokyo drew to a close, Horio sought out Maruyama's advice about what he should do with his life in the future. After being told by his respected professor that he was "well suited for the life of a researcher," Horio decided to pursue an academic career. But given his desire to "overcome the deep pessimism and despair generated by years of having read thinkers like Nietzsche," and his belief that work related to the concrete problems and concerns of human beings would best enable him to do so, Horio settled upon the study of education. In this spirit he consulted Professor of Education Katsuta Shūichi, who suggested that given his background in intellectual history, Horio was well prepared to do some of the very important work which then needed to be done with regard to the relations between education and politics. Accepting Katsuta's offer to work with him, Horio set off on a career in which he hoped he could integrate his intellectual and practical concerns.

Horio's graduate studies brought him into contact with many of the new ideas and methods being developed by social scientists in the West, and as he worked these into his approach to the intellectual history of modern Japanese education, he was able to uncover new problems for analysis. Construing the educational problems of individuals within Japanese society in terms of Japan's political problems and within the larger context of human history, Horio began to develop the unique approach to Japanese educational history which can be found in this book.

Horio first came to the attention of those outside the educational world through an essay he coauthored with Professor Katsuta in 1958, "The Problems Surrounding the Idea of Neutrality in National Education." This essay was written in response to a request from the editors of the highly influential intellectual journal *Shisō* for a critical comment on the textbook screening and curriculum problems which had become major issues in the mid-1950s. Asked by Katsuta to prepare an analysis of these problems, Horio realized that it was first necessary to question the proper role of the State with regard to education in light of the need to preserve its neutrality and independence. In one form or another these issues have been at the center of Horio's thought ever since; through his efforts to develop solutions to these problems he has worked out a body of extremely interesting ideas about the meaning of "educational values" and "the child's rights to develop and learn." His unique way of dealing with these issues and concerns can be seen in the essays found in Part II of this book, wherein he analyzes a number of court decisions from the standpoint of his understanding of these rights and values.

During this period in his graduate studies Horio's approach to educational research was becoming increasingly politicized, not because he had fallen under the sway of any particular ideology, but rather because he had discovered that in order to preserve the independence and neutrality of education, it was necessary to resist all attempts by the State to use its external authority to interfere with the inner freedoms of individuals. His commitment to pursue a form of educational research which would contribute to the then dawning struggle against the State's bureaucratic domination of education should therefore be grasped as part of a broadly based attempt to depoliticize education and liberate it from "all improper forms of control" (Article X of the Fundamental Law of Education [1948], which is analyzed in great depth in Chapter 4).

To deepen his understanding of these themes, Horio recognized the need for further study of Western intellectual history, and to this end he traced the growth of modern European thinking about the bonds between education, freedom, justice and the development of human character. The fruits of these investigations appeared in his doctoral dissertation, "The Structure and Intellectual Foundations of Contemporary Educational Thought" (1962), a work in which he attempted to theoretically formulate the proper character of the relationship between the State and education in a post-modern society.

Horio's desire to undertake educational research which would contribute to the substantive improvement of human social life gradually led him to broaden the scope of his theoretical interests. In the 1960s he began to investigate the scholarly literature then available on the problems of human development, in particular the works of Jean Piaget and Henri Wallon. Eventually this led him to spend a year (1969–70) at the Sorbonne, where he worked with the noted educational psychologist Maurice Debesse[2] and studied the new educational movements then taking root in France.

As a result of these new influences the focus of Horio's educational research shifted from the macro-level problems of man's historical and social development to the micro-level problems of the individual's intellectual and moral maturation. This move did not signify a decision to forsake his earlier political concerns, but was a recognition that there was much theoretical and practical pedagogic work to be done in order to guarantee that the children of a democratically revitalized Japanese society would indeed have the rights to grow and learn freely. In this context he started to think anew about the classical problems of how to balance the competing values of liberty and equality, and how to reconcile the conflicting interests of individuals and society. In turn this led Horio to recognize the need for a new interpretation of Article 26 of Japan's postwar Constitution,[3] an interpretation based on "educational values" as opposed to merely legal ones. Thus he began to work out the foundations for a new way of thinking about the tensions in Japan between education as an individual right and education as a social duty, between education as a means for cultivating the individuality of each and every member of society and education as a means for defending predetermined principles of social order and discipline.

On returning from France, Horio learned that the testimony he had given before the Tokyo High Court in a case challenging the screening and censorship of textbooks by the Ministry of Education had proved to be the decisive factor leading to a ruling that the screening system was unconstitutional.[4] In the wake of that landmark decision Horio's stature in the Japanese educational world was dramatically altered. He came to be regarded as a powerful thinker and leader of those who challenged the legitimacy of the Ministry of Education's arbitrarily imposed domination of Japanese educational life, and as a formidable

[2] Horio recently published a Japanese translation of Debesse's *Les étapes de l'éducation* (co-translator, Saitō Sawa; Iwanami Shoten, 1982).

[3] Ariticle 26 reads: "All people shall have the right to receive an equal education correspondent to their ability, as provided by law. (2) All people shall be obligated to have all boys and girls under their protection receive ordinary educations as provided for by law. Such compulsory education shall be free."

[4] This judgment is discussed in Chapter 6, "Textbook Control on Trial: The Sugimoto Decision."

opponent of those within the Ministry who had never before been humbled in such a manner. Consequently, he came to be both one of the most highly respected and vigorously reviled figures on the Japanese educational landscape.

In recent years Horio has been attempting to synthesize his macro-analyses of Japanese education from the standpoint of historical and social development with his micro-analyses of learning from the standpoint of the individual's growth as an autonomous human being. To this end he has been writing and editing a number of books on the relationship between social progress and child development, while at the same time keeping very busy in his role as a highly active critic of the serious problems besetting educational life in Japan today.

The Genesis of This Translation and the Organization of This Book

I first met Professor Horio in 1979 when I attended his lectures on the "Intellectual History of Modern Japanese Education" at the University of Tokyo. Listening to his penetrating analyses of the problems plaguing education in contemporary Japan, I was immediately struck by two of the most engaging features of Horio's thought: a refusal to rely upon the sterile categories of Japanese exceptionalism (*nihonjinron*) and the related forms of pseudo-explanation that are such a familiar part of the academic landscape in Japan today, and a deep understanding of the liberal values found in the political traditions of the West and an unflagging devotion to the most progressive ideas in modern educational thought. This initial impression was more than amply reconfirmed when I started reading Horio's texts and was able to better appreciate his not inconsiderable ability to formulate Japan's educational problems in terms of political concerns which have long troubled thinkers in the West.

Suspecting that people in the English-reading world would soon be looking for a critical approach to the successes then beginning to be reported about Japanese education, and observing that most of the works appearing in English were being written from a perspective close to, if not virtually identical with, that of Japan's Ministry of Education, I came to believe that a translation of Professor Horio's ideas would, in addition to helping satisfy the need for better ways to think about Japanese education, offer the best way to show why the view of Japanese schooling being developed in the West was so one-sided. Moreover, inasmuch as Horio's ideas are the product of years of direct involvement in a popular struggle against the Ministry of

Education's efforts to dominate Japanese educational life, a struggle
which Western scholars have remained largely oblivious to or at least
curiously silent about, it struck me that the critical insights found in
Horio's writing could exert a significant influence on the Western
world's future thinking about and understanding of Japanese education.
With this in mind I convinced Professor Horio of the need for a translation of his work, and we approached the University of Tokyo Press
in 1981 regarding the possibility of my undertaking this project.[5]

Completion of this translation was delayed a number of times. In
the intervening years, American scholars became very interested in
Japanese education, but none of the work done on this subject has
incorporated, or even revealed an awareness of, the problems analyzed
here. Thus, whereas this book was originally intended to serve as an
introduction to the study of contemporary Japanese education, it can
now be read as a rebuttal to those works or as a challenge to the
values which they represent. In this context, a decision was made to
thoroughly reorganize the structure of the book, and additional material was translated to cover some of the most recent developments in
the Japanese education world. Thus perhaps it can be said that the
delays which hindered the publication of this book have been a bless-
ing in disguise, for now it can also play an important role in the current Western discourse on the need to imitate or catch up with Japan's
educational accomplishments.

Professor Horio suggested a number of essays which he thought
would be interesting for use in this book, but the ultimate selection of
materials was left to me. As the reader will note, some of the chapters
presented here were adopted from multiple sources; in a number of
cases the result is an essay which, while fully expressive of Horio's
ideas, can nowhere be found in this exact form in his publications in
Japanese.[6] The principles underlying my taking these liberties with
his texts can be summarized as follows: (1) when and wherever possible
I tried to eliminate material that only readers who have special knowledge about Japan will be able to find comprehensible, and (2) I tried

[5] While the translation of this book was supported by a grant from the Ministry
of Education, the committee which approved the University of Tokyo's Press's request for funds was made up of scholars who respect Horio's contributions to Japanese intellectual life, and had little to do with the Ministry's support of his ideas.
Thus, in addition to the acknowledgment on the copyright page of the fact that the
Ministry of Education has underwritten the translation of this book, perhaps there
should also be a disclaimer that the Ministry does not as a result endorse the views
presented here.

[6] The List of Sources at the end of this volume gives the original titles of the essays
excerpted and translated.

to select issues and problems that would be of interest to a generalized
Western readership made up of individuals who want to comprehend
the problems confronting Japanese education from the standpoint of
a complex analytic framework, but who do not want to become bogged
down in a wealth of detailed information about Japan or Japanese
schools per se. This is of course very difficult to do, and only the reader's response to the text will determine how successful I have been
in doing so.

* * *

The essays that make up this book are most meaningful when read
in the order in which they are presented. In the first chapter, "The
Crisis in Japanese Education Today," the reader is provided with both
Horio's view of the appalling conditions surrounding the pursuit of
knowledge and learning in Japan at this time, and an introduction
to the major themes that are developed and the problems which are
analyzed in the rest of the book.

The four chapters of Part I, "The Intellectual Legacy of Japan's
Educational History," work out in great depth an analytic framework
for grasping and making sense of the problems running throughout
the development of modern Japan's educational system. The first two
examine the struggles during the prewar period between those who
saw education as a way to control and those who looked to it as a
way to liberate the Japanese people; the latter two examine the same
conflict in the context of the struggles over the meaning of the postwar
democratization of Japanese education. These essays are critically
important for an understanding of the rest of this book because
they lay out very clearly what Horio sees as the relation between
the pathology of prewar Japanese society and the severely deformed
character of its intellectual life, and the reasons why the successes and
failures of postwar education must be judged in terms of the historical
need to overcome the root causes of that pathology. Thus, while each
of these essays is a self-contained entity and can be understood in its
own right, their full force only becomes apparent when the reader systematically considers the development of his ideas in the order in which
they are presented here.

In the six chapters of Part II, "Education in the Courtroom and
Teachers' Struggles for Professional Autonomy," Horio provides the
reader with a number of penetrating insights into the ideology that
supports the system of educational control found in contemporary
Japan. Four of these critiques focus on judgments handed down by
the Japanese judiciary in a number of important legal battles over the

locus and structure of educational authority, the legality of the Ministry of Education's textbook screening system, and the propriety of
the system of secret reporting on student's behavior known as *naishinsho*. The remaining two chapters discuss the deeper agenda embedded
in, and the lasting effects of, the Ministry of Education's attempts to
institute nationwide scholastic testing in the 1960s and to impose its
own strict supervision on teachers' in-service training. These essays
contain a number of astute observations on the ways in which the
thinking that dominated educational life in prewar Japan has been
reformulated so as to appear consistent with the democratic values
introduced into Japan after the war. These essays have additional
value inasmuch as they disclose the contradictions lurking in the legal
consciousness of the Japanese courts in recent years.

Part III, "Individualism and Egalitarianism in Japanese Education:
Myths and Realities," carefully documents and analyzes the relationship between the manpower needs articulated by Japanese industry
in the 1960s as it set the foundations for policies designed to produce
high economic growth, and the subsequent subjugation of all *educational values* to predominantly *economic values*. Here Horio explains
why the high levels of academic achievement which have lately drawn
such favorable attention in the West are indeed better understood as
signs of the destruction of education in Japan. Thus the reader who
carefully considers the import of the criticisms Horio is making here
will recognize that the imposition of economic values is not merely an
unfortunate side-effect of an excellent educational system, but the very
force which drives it and makes students learn. If Japanese students
are being compelled to learn for the wrong reasons, then rather than
being concerned about how we can "replicate their successes," we
should be focussing our reformist impulses elsewhere. Horio's work
clearly suggests that there are very good reasons why the Japanese
educational system should not be looked at as a model for the other
industrially advanced nations of the world.

In the final chapter, "Conflicting Approaches to the Reform of
Japanese Schooling: Economic Liberalization versus Educational Liberation," Horio turns his critical vision upon the proposals for reforming
Japanese education formulated in the last few years by Prime Minister
Nakasone's Ad Hoc Council on Educational Reform. Here he solidly
debunks the claims made by the supporters of that Council that its
proposed reforms represent a serious attempt to create a freer environment for education in Japan. From Horio's perspective, these proposals represent rather a highly cynical attempt to tighten, under the
guise of educational liberalization, the already existing system for

rigidly controlling education. To complete the dialectic between the two opposing approaches to education which runs throughout the history of schooling in Japan over the past century, the book concludes with a statement of the philosophy underlying the program for educational reform which Horio himself advocates. By ending the book in this way I have tried to show how the system and structure of "educational control from above" established in the Meiji era is presently being reworked for Japan, and why the struggle which originated in opposition to that system is still alive and highly pertinent today.

Tokyo, March 1988   STEVEN PLATZER

Educational Thought and Ideology in Modern Japan

1 The Crisis in Japanese Education Today

In recent years education has increasingly come to be thought of as one of our most basic human rights, indeed the right by virtue of which all other modern rights ultimately derive their substance and meaning. The ascendance of this way of thinking can be tied to a growing recognition of the fact that education plays a pivotal role in the process by means of which children mature as reasoning beings and develop into responsible members of society. This enlightened approach has generally come to be accepted by educators throughout the world, and is clearly visible in Japan's postwar Constitution as well as in our Fundamental Law of Education, adopted in 1947.

Notwithstanding the fact that our school system is legally rooted in these ideals, however, the reality of present-day Japanese education is such that these values have been subverted. As the freedom of our schools is continuously eroded by the ever-increasing interference of the State's administrative machinery, as educational values fall under the domination of an ideology dominated by the one-dimensional glorification of academic competence (*nōryokushugi*), and as schools come to be seen merely as arenas for the most vicious forms of competition related to social selection and advancement, it is becoming ever more impossible to take seriously the idea that education is the sine qua non of human rights. Thus, for example, when social studies teachers ask pupils to think of education as one of their inalienable human rights, it is hardly surprising that the latter should beg to be spared from having to shoulder the weight of such an odious right.

Of course this does not mean that our schools should be reorganized to make it possible for students to pass through them without ever having learned how to actively overcome real intellectual difficulties and hardships. Ironically, however, in spite of the bitterly competitive struggles that Japanese education is well known for throughout the world, in present-day Japan the verb "to learn" is generally understood only in relation to the passive reproduction of knowledge or techniques already established by others. While the educational process is generally thought of in Japan as something individuals must negotiate *by* themselves, it is rarely thought of as something they must do *for* themselves, except in the limited sense of its relation to their per-

3

sonal social advancement and future economic well-being.

The importance of the idea of an *active* pursuit of knowledge can only become personally meaningful after one recognizes that forfeiting this right is tantamount to forfeiting the right to make the kinds of free choices which are required of all the citizens in a democratically organized nation. Unfortunately, however, in contemporary Japanese society education is organized so as to make sure that the overwhelming majority of students never grow up to become the kind of citizens who will demand much of anything, least of all their political and intellectual rights.

The Idea of Education as a Right

The notion that education is an irreplaceable human right is a recent arrival on the stage of man's intellectual history. It first appeared as an essential element of the modern bourgeois revolutions that transformed European social life from the end of the 18th century. Emerging from such fertile soil, this idea subsequently developed as a vital link in the discourse on the character of man's naturally given spiritual freedoms and was closely associated with the claim that the only just form of government is one based on the principle of popular sovereignty.

The notion that all people are endowed by nature with basic educational rights took root and matured in the field of modern pedagogic thought along with the discovery of the myriad possibilities for growth that reside in all human beings as they move from childhood to adolescence and on to adulthood. In the wake of these liberating discoveries, educators began to reorganize their institutions and instructional practices so as to give concrete form to what they understood to be the unique educational rights of the young.

The joining together of these two distinct but intimately related lines of thought has led to the idea that human beings are endowed from birth with inalienable educational rights. With time these rights have come to be viewed as an essential part of the modern child's inherent right to grow up and develop into a fully formed human being.

It was this kind of thinking that lay at the root of the attempt to remake Japanese education in the years following the end of the Pacific War. But it has not been easy for us to implant these ideas within Japanese society. As many of the totalitarian aspects of prewar educational thought were revived and reworked within the context of the modern welfare state, the prospects for a genuine educational renaissance in Japan have gradually been eroded, and the proud hopes of those who wanted to transform Japan into a democratic society have been confounded again and again.

Thus, in order to understand the depth of the crisis enveloping schooling in Japan today, it is necessary for us to reexamine the democratization of postwar education in the light both of the spiritual revolutions which transformed modern Europe and of the educational system established in prewar Japan to produce subjects loyal to the Emperor-State. Part I of this book, "The Intellectual Legacy of Japan's Educational History," analyzes the Imperial educational system and the postwar reforms designed to liberate the Japanese spirit from its subjugation to the values of ultra-nationalism and militarism.

In this introductory chapter, I want to discuss the intellectual significance of the transformations which led to the creation of modern social systems. Against that background I will then summarize some of the most serious problems plaguing Japanese education today. By proceeding in this manner I believe it is possible to demonstrate just how much trouble our educational system is really in, and why only those solutions which penetrate to the heart of the problems we face offer any real promise for the future.

The Locus of Educational Authority

The crises enveloping education in Japan today can be traced back to the deep antagonisms between those who insist that educational authority must reside in the hands of the State and those who want to affirm the autonomy of the People's educational rights. It has been almost impossible to reconcile the differences between these two camps, as the reader will see in Part II ("Education in the Courtroom and Teachers' Struggles for Professional Autonomy"), because there is still no basis upon which any form of compromise or even common understanding can be achieved regarding the proper locus of educational authority.

Ironically, these difficulties have been compounded by the fact that those who claim that educational authority properly belongs in the hands of the State can no longer argue their case, as could their counterparts in prewar Japan, with blanket assertions about the absolute priority of the State's pedagogic interests. Constrained by the democratic character of the postwar Japanese Constitution and its recognition of the People's inalienable educational rights and authority, they have attempted to shift attention away from the inviolability of these rights by stressing the administrative efficiency of the State's bureaucratic apparatus. Through their "legal arguments" that the People's educational will can only be formulated in the Diet and implemented by the Ministry of Education, they have repeatedly turned to the courts to legitimate their attempts to circumscribe the scope of the People's constitutionally guaranteed educational rights and make them fit the one-sided interpretations of educational law formulated by the Ministry of Education. Since they can no longer openly declare the State to be the one and only legitimate source of all educational rights and duties (for they could only do so by repudiating the principle of popular sovereignty at the heart of our postwar Constitution), they have chosen rather to reinterpret the essential meaning of this principle so as to eliminate the possibility of any substantive form of direct popular control.

Narrowly conceived, the problem of educational authority is related to the issue of to whom educational rights and competencies properly belong—parents, teachers, or the State; broadly conceived, it relates to the rights and duties of children, parents, and teachers in relation to the authority vested in the State and all other publicly constituted bodies. In short, this distinction leads us to reconsider the nature of the responsibilities involved in education, and the way the boundaries between the responsible parties should be drawn and defended.

The fundamental difference I want to call attention to here can be formulated as an unresolved antagonism between those who advocate the *People's educational authority* (*kokumin no kyōikuken*) and those who believe that the organization and management of learning in Japan must be conceived as an exercise of the *State's educational authority* (*kokka no kyōikuken*). The basic difference between the two becomes readily apparent when one asks, as we will have numerous occasions to do in this book, how each camp views the meaning of the child's right to learn in particular, and the citizen's right to learn in general. The underlying theoretical differences between the two opposing approaches become all the more obvious when one asks how each regards the closely related problems of who should properly guarantee the existence of these rights, and how this can best be accomplished.

The conflict between these two approaches reached a new level when those of us who contest the State's efforts to monopolize educational authority countered the efforts of government and financial leaders to implement their ideas about lifelong education by articulating new theories regarding the meaning of "the People's right to learn." On the basis of these insights we have deepened our understanding of the reasons why the right to learn must be viewed as one of the most important political rights of everyone in a democratic society, and we are now in a better position to explain why these rights must be guaranteed to all the people throughout the entire course of their lives, regardless of age, sex, or occupation. Likewise we have come to a better understanding of the reasons why the People's rights to freely inquire and pursue truth must never again be allowed to fall under the bureaucratic domination of the State. This concern to preserve and where possible extend the intellectual freedoms won by the Japanese people after the war has led us to explore an important but unexamined problem: namely, how can we define the fundamental human rights related to education in particular and culture in general which must be protected in a democratic society?

There is a great deal of discussion in Japan these days about the need to drastically reform our educational system from top to bottom, from the university right down to the nursery school. But since I am convinced that any proposal for reform is ultimately doomed to failure unless it is based on respect for each and every citizen's right to learn, I believe that all talk about improving our schools should proceed from this point. Furthermore, I want to argue, any educational transformation which is going to impart real substance to our constitutionally guaranteed right to learn must conceive this not merely as a *passive* right to receive an education but as an *active* right to learn. In other words, our current efforts to reform education in Japan must be tied to a view of "democratization" which does not construe it as something the People passively receive from the State, but rather sees it as something they actively demand and achieve through their own unwavering efforts.

To complete the reorganization of Japanese social life that began after the war when the people were finally recognized as the masters of their government, their work, their ideas, and their own destinies, it is absolutely necessary to expand our thinking about educational rights and relate it to contemporary thinking about the broader problems of human rights in general. The idea that these rights must be guaranteed in all phases of our daily lives offers us a valuable perspective from which to begin making greater efforts to more fully realize the promises unleashed by the legal reorganization of postwar Japan into a society founded on the principles of respect for the inviolable rights of individuals.

The history of the conflict between the two radically opposed approaches I have described to the organization of educational authority in modern Japanese society stretches back to the early Meiji-era struggles over the meaning of "civilization and enlightenment."[1]

Thus it is simply not true that these controversies result from recently introduced foreign ideologies which are inapplicable to Japanese conditions, as is frequently argued by those who believe that the State must take over educational authority from the Japanese people because the latter are unable to organize this authority for themselves.

These arguments also overlie another agenda: one directed at making sure that the Japanese people never become the masters of their own educational system and the free-thinking beings this would inevitably lead to. Those who attempt to dismiss direct popular control over education as an American Occupation strategy designed to weaken Japan, in spite of all their proclamations of support for democratization, still hold the Japanese people in utter contempt. Likewise, the argument that individualism violates the values of Japanese communalism and its inherent orientation towards group harmony is merely a ploy intended to retard the growth of political consciousness—the Japanese people's understanding that in postwar Japan sovereignty resides with them and not the State.

Those who believe that educational authority belongs in the hands of bureaucrats within the Ministry of Education frequently try to gain support for their position by pointing out that Japan's postwar Constitution makes no specific reference to "the People's right to learn" as such. Drawing upon these observations, Ministry officials now like to argue that any right which is not specifically stipulated by statute or law is nothing more than the cock-and-bull invention of political charlatans. However, as the constitutional scholar Takayanagi Shinichi has persuasively argued, there are indeed good historical reasons for regarding the right to learn as an expression of the spirit which makes the idea of constitutionally guaranteed liberties possible.

The Origins of Human Rights

The modern idea that all men are endowed from birth with inalienable human rights was not originally conceived only in terms of those formally guaranteed in written constitutions. Thomas Paine, for one, argued in *The Rights of Man*:

[1] Chapter 2, "The Ideological Conflict over Scholarship and Education during the Meiji Enlightenment," describes the intellectual ferment in Meiji times as it touched on education.

A constitution is a thing *antecedent* to a government, and a government is only the creature of a constitution. The constitution of a country is not the act of its government, but of the people constituting a government.

The United States Constitution did not at first contain provisions on human rights, for reasons explained by Alexander Hamilton:

Under the American Constitution, the people have not relinquished any of their rights; all are retained by the people. Therefore it is not necessary to establish specific provisions to indicate that they are retained by the people.

Here is an admirable expression of the reasons why the guarantee of human rights must not be restricted to those which are specifically stated.

For Paine the French Revolution was a seminal event in modern thought. To him its significance lay not only in the freeing of the masses from the oppression they had long been subjected to: the nobility, he pointedly noted, were "raised to the status of human beings." In that sense the Revolution represented nothing less than the "recovery of human nature." Natural rights were thereafter understood as belonging to all people simply by virtue of their existence as human beings. Thus within this new perspective the inherent connections between "all intellectual and spiritual rights" provided the necessary foundations for a new type of human society.

These beliefs were shared by thinkers like the Marquis de Condorcet, who made spiritual freedom and trust in reason the foundations of his educational thought as well. It should be noted that Condorcet naturally included among the spiritual freedoms and intellectual rights recognized as belonging to people by virtue of their humanity "the right to know the truth," "the freedom of inquiry," "the right to learn," and "educational liberty."

Not only do these principles underlie the progressive forms of modern constitutionalism; they also lie at the heart of the rights I call *the People's rights to learn*. And just as our "spiritual freedoms" can only be guaranteed when these principles are respected, so too our most important human freedoms are violated when they are abused. It can be said that the most important turning points in modern intellectual history have occurred when these principles were upheld or transgressed.

The notion that people are endowed by nature with the inalienable rights to learn enables us to grasp the inherent connections between the general principles of human rights and the politics of popular sovereignty. It teaches us that unless the People's intellectual rights are firmly safeguarded, the idea of popular sovereignty is either reduced to a mere formality or transformed into an ideology perpetrated to deprive citizens of their rights and deceive them regarding their true political condition.

The idea that all people possess the right to learn throughout the successive stages of life is rooted in a universalistic view of human nature, one that stresses the necessity of unyielding efforts to perfect our creativity, enhance the durability of our cultures, and contribute to humankind's still incomplete development. This expansive and liberating view is sharply at odds with the Japanese government's official pronouncements on lifelong education, which are rooted in an ideology that seeks rather to control the thinking of the People throughout the course of their lives.

We who oppose the government's position can trace the undercurrents of our discourse on lifelong education back to Condorcet's idea that human beings must be recognized as possessing the right to inquire and learn for themselves. Condorcet believed that through unrestrained learning and study people would be able to continually surpass themselves and develop the possibilities for a more rational form of life. Education, he argued:

> is not the mere acknowledgment of preconceived opinions. It must be approached as a process of exposing all preconceived notions to the free and rigorous examination of each new generation's insights and wisdom.

The spirit underlying Condorcet's pedagogic thought reemerged in the 1930s in arguments that education should be viewed as an endless process, one which must continue throughout the entire course of a citizen's life. The appearance of these arguments led to increasing calls for a revolution in the way schools are viewed. The philosopher Gaston Bachelard, for example, denounced the proverbial well-rounded mind (*la tête bien faite*) produced by the education offered in French schools as a closed mind (*la tête fermée*) and searched for ways to institute reforms that would parallel the advances in science and the development of contemporary thought. Based on what he described as "*le principe de la Culture continuée*," Bachelard argued for an ongoing overhaul and reconstruction of school education. Advocating a continous form of schooling to advance culture and science, he proclaimed that "sometimes the student will also instruct his teacher."

In "Rationalisme appliqué" (1949) Bachelard observed that "scientific thought itself requires an enduring pedagogy" (*pédagogie permanente*):

> All cultural philosophies must formulate their own pedagogic programs since all cultures are dependent upon their courses of study. The man who lives in a culture that has fallen under the influence of science is an eternal schoolboy [*un éternel écolier*].

These ideas about the People's need to continually educate themselves have developed and matured since the time they were originally formulated by Condorcet. In recent decades the experience of war has provided a dramatic impetus to further reflections on the need to make more headway with our educational problems.[2]

I believe there is much we in Japan can learn from these ways of thinking, particularly as we think about how to resolve the problems currently plaguing our schools. In particular, thinking about these issues from the standpoint of the People's rights to learn makes it clear that it is the People and not the State who should be the masters of scholarly and cultural creation.

The culture which Bachelard described as being locked up in the institutions of French learning has a direct corollary in Japan. Thus, to liberate our culture from the dead weight of our schools and open it up to influences from outside, it is necessary to place our trust in the inquiries and creative practices of each and every member of the nation. In the last analysis this means transforming the totality of social life into a living school.[3]

There will no doubt be some who object that these ideas are too general and abstract, so theoretical that they fail to address the "real problems" facing Japanese education today. But, I should like to reiterate, the concrete problems that are crippling learning in Japan today all stem from the abuse of the fundamental right to learn and know the truth. Thus all solutions to our educational crises which ignore this root cause are merely like the kind of medicine that is used to

[2] The history and character of these reflections in Japan after the war are taken up in Chapter 4, "Democratizing Education and Liberating the Japanese Spirit."

[3] This same idea was expressed in the 1985 Declaration on the Right to Learn of the 1985 Fourth UNESCO International Conference on Adult Education. "The right to learn," the Declaration states, "is not only an instrument of economic development; it must be recognized as one of the fundamental rights. The act of learning, lying as it does at the heart of all educational activity, changes human beings from objects at the mercy of events to subjects who create their own history."

attack the symptoms of an illness while leaving the root cause of the disease untouched. Or, to use a slightly different analogy, such solutions merely try to keep the disease-ridden patient alive and out of too much pain; unfortunately, however, they begin by assuming that the case is hopeless and beyond cure. Is this the way we want to think, or should we be thinking about the pathological state of education in Japan today? Only the worst cynics who care little about the genuine reform of education in our country can stick to such a warped outlook.

Japan's Educational Problems

I now want to call attention to some of the most distressing aspects of the crisis plaguing education in Japan today. My aim here is to demonstrate that when education is perceived as a basic human right, the many problems underlying our present-day educational difficulties appear deeply and intimately related to one another, even if they do not appear so when viewed from the conflicting standpoints of those—students, parents, and teachers—variously affected by them.

Judging from what one reads practically every day in the newspapers, Japanese children are now living in absolutely horrendous conditions. On a single recent day, for example, there were a number of particularly disturbing stories about lower secondary school students. In one of these reports we hear of a group of students who violently murdered a vagabond in Yokohama; in another we learn of two students in Osaka who violated a female teacher in the school's health office; and in still another we are introduced to a gang of wild students in Machida City who verbally tormented a teacher to the point where he pulled a knife and stabbed one of them. Recent police statistics indicate that the number of such cases is continually increasing; from this we can rightly infer that the problems which are causing such abhorrent behavior are only getting worse. This is also testified to by the persistent problems of young people committing suicide or behaving violently at home.

These behaviors result from the increasing pressures generated by our overheated school entrance examination system. They reflect nationwide trends in which delinquent forms of behavior can be seen breaking out at ever lower ages among our young men, and in unprecedented numbers among young women as well. The growth in these forms of delinquency underscores both the severity of the problems being dropped in the laps of lower and upper secondary school teachers and the worsening sense of despair and helplessness felt by more and more parents. Here we can also catch a glimpse of the circumstances in which (1) classroom violence is becoming an everyday occurrence, (2) teachers are losing the capacity to respond to conditions that are quite frankly growing out of control, (3) increased bullying is driving weaker students into deep fear and—in extreme, but widely reported, cases—suicide, and (4) ethnic discrimination is becoming more and more pronounced.[4]

Ironically, however, according to Hozumi Takanobu's recent work *Tsumiki Kuzushi* (Broken Toy Blocks, 1982), behind these socially unacceptable forms of behavior is the desperate desire of lonely young people, pushed into cutthroat competition with one another through the intensification of examination pressures,[5] to have friends and form groups they can identify with. This example has taught us that it is necessary to look behind the delinquent behavior of our misguided adolescents in order to see the distorted expressions of their desire to live socially satisfying lives. He has shown us, in other words, how important it is to recognize that within an overwhelmingly negative social environment, even patently antisocial forms of behavior may very well have a great deal of positive meaning and significance.

But there are also major distortions which result from the ways those on the "elite course" are being educated. Encouraged from early childhood to think of themselves as the victors in a race to succeed in school entrance examinations, more and more of these future leaders of society are developing thoroughly arrogant and coldhearted personalities. Moreover, these students, who are supposed to be the most intelligent young people being turned out by our society, are so thoroughly sold on themselves that they have little if any sense that we are facing very real and very serious problems. Having no critical consciousness, their very attitude belies the claims made about their supposed intelligence. In a speech he delivered at the time of his retirement from the Faculty of Economics at the University of Tokyo, the distinguished scholar Ōuchi Tsutomu declared that:

> Today's students have no historical consciousness and are thoroughly deficient when it comes to thinking critically about problems other than those they have been tutored to respond to on entrance examinations. I seriously wonder whether there is any future for scholarship in Japan.

---

[4] This refers mainly to the discrimination inflicted upon minority groups like the Koreans who have been living in Japan since the early part of this century when their forebears immigrated or were forcibly brought to Japan to provide cheap labor.

[5] See Chapter 8 for an analysis of the causes of this increased competition.

The number of teachers who have lost the capacity to understand the feelings of their students is steadily growing, and this is as true of veteran teachers as it is of new and inexperienced ones. This is testified to by the following passage from a recent work by a lower secondary school teacher named Sayama Kisaku:

> I no longer have any idea about how to make sense of the junior high school students who sit in front of me in the classroom. . . . Compared with the conditions prevailing thirty years ago, it is certainly true that Japan has become a very rich country, but if this is really so, then why is it that teaching and educating children has become such bitter and disheartening work?

Or consider the words of Uno Hajime, a high school principal with more than thirty years of experience as a teacher:

> What has been accomplished through the reform of our educational system? If our students could have developed in the ways we hoped and worked for, Japan would not be in the mess it is in today. The current state of our education makes me feel more than a little sad; I no longer have any confidence about the way we are raising our young.

The despair and irritation of experienced and skillful teachers like Messrs. Sayama and Uno leaves us wondering about the successes which our Ministry of Education bureaucrats are so eager to claim at every turn.

Indeed, as Mr. Uno noted, the conditions in which our children and adolescents are coming of age have steadily worsened since the 1960s. The list of problems stretches on and on: lower levels of academic achievement on the one hand; higher levels of truancy, delinquency, bullying, and violence at home and at school on the other. Thus it is not surprising that the crime statistics being reported for the 1980s show a sharp increase in the number of juveniles being arrested.

These conditions are also reflected in the strains distorting the physical and mental development of our youth from infancy through adolescence. Obvious signs of the former were extensively reported in the 1960s and 1970s: large numbers of children with distorted posture and weakened vision, as well as a marked proclivity towards broken bones and decreased muscle power. In the latter case we can cite an ever-growing number of anxiety-ridden children who have lost the flexibility, durability, and emotional ease generally associated with youth. These strains have been accompanied by diminished sociability on the one hand and an increasing tendency to use hackneyed language and expressions on the other. Children flock together but rarely form groups in the true sense of the term.

But more deplorable are the conditions in which our children are growing up without developing (1) any profound feelings for nature, (2) any penetrating abilities to grasp the historically determined structure of society and to think about how its rules of organization might be improved, or (3) any deep sense of purpose and direction. In short, the growth of our youth into fully developed human beings is being seriously compromised from infancy through adolescence, and the vitality of our human relationships, whether in the home, in the school, or in society in general, is being thoroughly and dangerously eroded.

In spite of our recent prosperity, the competition to enter prestigious schools is becoming more and more intense, so much so that parents now feel pressured to enroll their three- and four-year-old children in famous nursery schools, believing that this will enable them to get a head start in the race to success in our society's system of "stratification by school background" (*gakureki shakai*). As the pressures increase to get children on the academic escalator leading to social success, we find growing numbers of young people having no time or place to play, nor friends to play with. Under the pressure of their parents' expectations, and forced into endless studies intended to ensure later success in our society's entrance examination madness, our children are being robbed of their childhood.

These abuses of the child's rights to freely grow and learn result from the ideology of "over-management" which dominates contemporary Japanese society. Whether it be their hairstyle, the length of their skirts, the color of their socks, or the width of their bookbags, all aspects of our children's lives are being managed through the highly detailed rules enacted by and enforced in the nation's schools. Not only do teachers wait at the school gate to check the students' appearance when they enter the school grounds: even when children go out on their own after school hours they are required to wear their school uniforms and hats. It is particularly alarming that schools are increasingly administering physical punishment to those students who violate the school's arbitrarily determined rules of order. What kind of society are we living in that permits such flagrant infringements upon the freedom of individual expression?

It is not only students who are being made to feel the weight of this arbitrarily imposed authority. Young teachers are almost universally instructed in how to maintain this "educational philosophy" by their superiors within the administrative structure of the school; their failure to do so is met by severe disciplinary measures.

Particularly vexing from the standpoint of those concerned with stemming the erosion of human rights in our schools are the growing and related problems of corporal punishment (*taibatsu*) and bullying (*ijime*). School officials condone and encourage the administration of corporal punishment to students who violate the rules of behavior arbitrarily determined by school officials themselves. Students who are singled out for these extreme forms of "discipline" in turn pick on and abuse weaker students. Ultimately, what makes this possible is the irresponsible attitude of parents who expect teachers to provide the discipline which they themselves fail to impart to their children. Indeed, it can be argued that bullying is not simply an educational problem, but one that runs throughout Japanese society, so much so that it constitutes a major principle of social control. In this sense the abuses of human rights seen in the world of education can be thought of as an essential part of the structure of human rights abuses in general. Moreover, this is not limited to the domestic sphere. In the words of one Philippine researcher living in Japan: "Can't Japan's approach to its relations with the nations of Southeast Asia be seen as a form of bullying?"

Many Levels of Control

In addition to the highly visible infringements of fundamental human rights discussed above, it is also important to call attention to those violations of the child's right to learn which are not nearly so obvious. These can be detected for example in the textbook screening system by means of which only those teaching materials officially approved by the Ministry of Education are allowed into the nation's schools. While current "screening" practices are not as blatantly repressive as was the case with the prewar system in which all heterodox ideas were subjected to unyielding censorship, the system now in use in many ways represents a more insidious (not to mention dangerous) violation of basic human rights. Even though the Ministry of Education has tried to represent this system as a neutral attempt to eliminate politically biased opinions, or as a scientifically objective effort to correct mistaken information, it in fact constitutes nothing less than an attempt to keep out of our schools all ideas which do not fit in with the State's view of the kinds of knowledge which are both appropriate and desirable to administer to Japanese youth.[6]

Not only does this system breach the educational rights of the child; it also violates the intellectual and academic freedom of teachers and textbook authors as well, by trying to channel their thinking into the same fixed framework.

Japanese education is at present riddled with many serious problems. Those who view these problems as if they are of merely momentary importance will never be able to grasp their depths, or to make significant strides toward their resolution. The belief that all classroom problems can be entirely taken care of in the classroom, or that the responsibility for all our educational problems can be laid entirely at the doorsteps of our teachers, is an overly simplistic view of education which is extremely counterproductive and harmful. In other words, it is necessary to think about the problems involved in the organization and running of our schools in relation to the cultural consciousness of the society which supports those schools, and the problems implicit in the structure of our society. The conditions casting dark clouds over our nation's educational life—the conditions in which the work of our schools has been subordinated to the exam preparation industry, in which schools now function as the site of the struggle over social selection, and in which these days it is frequently said "As long as they know how to do well on exams, who cares whether or not they are educated?"—directly reflect the values which are impoverishing the intellectual life of our people.

* * *

Just as these practices which are sapping the vitality of education in Japan today did not suddenly spring forth out of the blue, so too they will not disappear in the dark of night and leave our schools in peace. They are the consequences—albeit in many cases unintended—of specific policies and ideas about how education should be organized and conducted. Therefore they can only be remedied by human actions specifically designed to counteract and overcome them. But in order to determine just what kinds of corrective action are now called for, it is first necessary to understand where these problems came from. This

[6] The bitter conflicts in postwar Japan over the screening of textbooks are discussed in Chapter 5 and in the Introduction to Part II. Two widely divergent court rulings handed down in response to suits challenging the legality of the Ministry of Education's suppression of one of the more controversial textbooks written in postwar Japan are discussed in Chapter 6 and Chapter 7.

requires a careful historical analysis of the intellectual environment in which the ideas and policies that produced those defective practices germinated and grew.

The essays in Part I represent an attempt to provide just such an analysis. By returning in Chapter 2 to the intellectual origins of the modern Japanese school system and attempting to recover the struggles which preceded its formulation, I endeavor to disclose in their most basic form the problems which lie at the heart of our current crisis. In Chapter 3, I show how these problems gave birth to the pathological conditions which have become the legacy of modern Japanese education. Chapters 4 and 5 discuss the efforts made after the war to eliminate and replace these distorted conditions, and analyze some of the major reasons why these strivings for reform were severely crippled, so much so that forty years of "educational democratization" have given birth to an even more pathological form of schooling and study than that which we had before the war.

The essays in Part II show how seriously aborted this educational recovery actually was, but also how sincere and valuable have been the efforts exerted by those of us struggling in the courts to secure the intellectual and academic freedoms which are absolutely crucial for establishing a form of education that respects human rights. The myths and realities of individualism and egalitarianism in postwar education analyzed in Part III reveal how much worse conditions have actually become in the past quarter-century. But even here the reader can discern the directions in which those of us who belong to the People's educational movement (*kokumin kyōiku undō*) have been moving as we attempt to formulate and win acceptance for new educational values in Japan.

Finally, in the concluding essay, the recent proposals for reforming Japanese education which have arisen from within government and industrial circles are critically examined. My aim here is to show why these proposals will, if adopted, rather than remedy our educational crisis, make it even worse. I will then propose some of my own ideas about the kinds of ideas and policies which are needed to rescue our educational system from the mess within which it has become entrapped.

Part I

The Intellectual Legacy of Japan's Educational History

Introduction to Part I

This section includes four of Professor Horio's most penetrating studies in the intellectual history of modern Japanese
education. While exposing the origins of the crisis enveloping
schooling in Japanese society today, these essays also reveal
that the educational activism of highly committed intellectuals
like Professor Horio has its roots in a carefully considered analysis of the historical problems attendant upon Japan's troubled
modernization. Thus these essays should put to rest the
popular notions that educational activism in contemporary
Japan is merely a result of the postwar infiltration of Marxist
ideology into the universities, or the consequence of a misguided infatuation with Western ideas about the meaning of
democracy, ideas which were uncritically accepted during the
early postwar period following the eradication of Japanese
fascism and ultranationalism.

"The Ideological Conflict over Scholarship and Education
during the Meiji Enlightenment" pinpoints the fundamental
disagreements between the two sides of the Meiji Enlightenment Movement as they contested for the right to fix the character of modern Japan's educational system. This essay explores the debates between those who favored an "enlightenment from above" administered by the State, and those whose
efforts to generate an "enlightenment from below" gave birth
to the Freedom and People's Rights Movement (*jiyū minken
undō*). By analyzing these struggles the author on the one hand
reveals the contradictory impulses which figured in the official
resolution of the problem of how to establish a modern educational system, and on the other points to the intellectual legacy
of those elements within Japanese society whose progressive
views on education were suppressed by the Meiji State. "Education and Human Cultivation in the Emperor-State" shows
with a great deal of sophistication how the Imperial system of
schooling that dominated educational life in Japan from the
1880s until 1945 was the outcome of the early Meiji struggle
over the meaning of National Enlightenment, and how that

form of education systematically warped both the psychological life of the Japanese masses and the intellectual life of the elites under whose guidance and control they were eventually led to the horrors of Japan's fifteen-year war. This essay falls into two parts. The first part outlines the ideology of the Imperial education system as expressed in one of the basic statements of philosophy underlying the Meiji State, the Imperial Rescript on Education, and the legal and administrative system which held it up; the second analyzes the impact of this system and its ruling ideology both upon the masses who were subjected to it in the form of compulsory education and upon the elites who received the most specialized and advanced forms of training in the prestigious Imperial universities established and supported by the Japanese State.

Through these first two essays we are able to gain a new insight into the character of education in prewar Japan, and we can begin to develop a sense of what it was that had to be reformed in Japanese education in the years following the end of World War II. Moreover, we can begin to appreciate why Professor Horio is so deeply committed to an educational system which overturns the values that dominated intellectual life in prewar Japan.

"Democratizing Education and Liberating the Japanese Spirit" examines the laws which defined the principles underlying the democratized educational system that replaced the discredited system rooted in the values of the earlier Imperial Rescript on Education. Here we are offered a way of viewing the reform of postwar education that goes far beyond summarizing the structure and mechanics of the new system, analyzing the important tranformations they in fact represented.

Finally, in "Education and Law in Postwar Japan: The Problem of Continuity and Change," we are given a history of the vicissitudes of the new democratic educational system in the years following the end of the Allied Occupation of Japan. Here the author shows how the values that underlay the democratization of Japanese education were subverted and transformed into something very different from what was originally intended by American reformers and hoped for by their liberal-minded supporters within Japanese society itself. This essay is particularly interesting inasmuch as it shows that the accomplishments of postwar Japanese education which are so widely praised in the West these days were made possible only when the values at the heart of the reform of Japanese education were shelved or repudiated, and the ideology of educational control analyzed in the earlier chapters of this section brought back in a new guise.

This history of pre- and postwar education lays the foundation for the discussion, in the remaining sections of this book, of the struggle on several fronts to create a more democratic and intellectually liberating form of education, a struggle which continues to the present day.

2 The Ideological Conflict over Scholarship and Education during the Meiji Enlightenment

I. Civilization and Enlightenment

The Meiji Restoration (1868) thoroughly transformed Japanese society and profoundly upset the ideological foundations of traditional Japanese thought. This was nowhere more true than in the closely related realms of educational thought and practice.

In the years immediately following the Restoration the leaders of the new Meiji government attempted to formulate their educational policies on the basis of *kokugaku* (nativism or national learning). However, by 1872 they had realized that it was futile to look to the nativist ideas which had earlier inspired them to overthrow the Tokugawa feudal order for concrete solutions to the problems they now faced in attempting to establish a modern political order and escape the danger of national dismemberment by the great colonialist powers of the West. This change of heart was clearly reflected in the new leaders' decision to forgo the ideology of *ōsei fukko* (restoring direct Imperial rule) and in their willingness to embrace the new philosophy of *bunmei kaika* (civilization and enlightenment). Thus, as new forms of social and political thought were mobilized in the years following the collapse of the Tokugawa *bakufu*, the privileged positions claimed by the defenders of ancient Japanese values and ideas were subjected to new and serious challenges.

In "An Outline of True Government" (*Shinsei Taii*), written in 1870, Katō Hiroyuki established his position as one of the leading champions of early Meiji Enlightenment thought when he advanced the theory that "since all men are equally endowed by nature with the right to exist, no one is therefore inherently obliged to submit to the orders of another." With this bold proclamation Katō launched an all-out attack upon the ideological foundations of traditional Confucian thought. Katō's liberalism provided the intellectual ammunition for a scathing denunciation of those who were still proclaiming the superiority of Confucian notions of a benevolently managed state.

"In an enlightened state," he argued, "the responsibility of those in government is simply to remove all impediments to the People's self-fulfillment of their own freely determined needs and desires. They have no business trying to tell the People what their needs and desires are, or should be, or how they must go about realizing them." In short, Katō argued, "the State's interference in the organization of national life should be kept to a minimum," and all political authority should be "directly entrusted to the People themselves." Thus Katō's ideas about the true nature of an enlightened state were advanced in direct opposition to the more traditional view of the state (kyōka kokka) also being advocated at that time. A truly enlightened state, he insisted, is not one in which wise leaders attempt to manage every facet of national life, but one in which they work to defend the rights of all citizens to live and work on a fair and equal basis.

Katō's early acceptance of natural-rights theory, and his commitment to public criticism of all forms of unrestricted government interference, were widely shared by the enlightened thinkers of that age who sought to transform these ideals into the concrete foundations for a modern liberal state. The advocates of these values likewise believed that the nation's future well-being ultimately depended both upon the successful development of modern forms of scholarship and upon the degree to which the nation's leaders were ultimately able to make these new forms of learning available to all the people on a fair and impartial basis.

Writing in 1875 about the true meaning of civilization, Nishimura Shigeki, a philosopher who at that time was still an enthusiastic supporter of Westernization (he was later to change his mind), drew upon the ideas of Mill and Quizot when declaring that the meaning of "civilization" should be grasped in terms of progress and development in group relations and individual human conduct and not merely in terms of wealth, ability, and power:

> Even though the nation as a whole moves towards prosperity, if the wisdom of the people has not advanced in the least, their prosperity is not to be trusted as its source is extremely unclear. . . . There is no other way to achieve this than by good education. . . . Being efficacious for good social intercourse among men, education is the factor that promotes morality, broadens knowledge, and increases the happiness of the people as a whole. . . . Moreover, nothing else can compete with the power of education in its effectiveness as the very best method for advancing the level of popular enlightenment and for bringing the conditions of social intercourse increasingly to perfection. [An Explanation of "Civilization," *Meiroku Zasshi*, Issue 36]

Mori Arinori was another early Meiji thinker who, notwithstanding his later identification with the creation of Japan's State-centered system of national education, began his career as an enthusiastic supporter of liberal values. (I will analyze the pivotal role he played in the Meiji State's consolidation of educational control in the 1880s in the next chapter.) Mori first recognized the potential importance of the contributions education could make to national development when he served as the new Meiji government's envoy to the United States between 1870 and 1872. Commenting on the relationship he had perceived between the vitality of the American spirit and the religious liberties its people enjoyed, Mori included the following observations regarding the place of education in the social life of a modern nation:

> My experiences have taught me that it is the educational system of a country which in the final analysis best guarantees the rights of its people. Thus we must raise the intellectual level of the entire Japanese nation, and for this purpose every kind of useful knowledge must be advanced. The State can facilitate the realization of these ends and therefore most effectively fulfill its educational responsibilities to the People by providing the support required to disseminate scientific and technical knowledge throughout the country. Moreover, these kinds of knowledge should not be limited to a special class or type of person, but should apply to the People as a whole. . . . Only by acting in this manner can the State eradicate the destructive influences of ignorance that invariably lead to human unhappiness, and prepare the foundations for a peaceful and enlightened form of national life.

It is important to note that the ideas Mori voiced here were not the random meditations of a solitary thinker but rather an expression of the educational consensus that was forming among the leaders of the new Meiji government. Kido Takayoshi was another of the leaders of the Meiji revolution who shared this basic outlook. "In order for our country to become independent and strong," he said, "we require both a general enlightenment and the widest possible development of human knowledge. Our schools must assume the primary responsibility for cultivating the talents and abilities thus required."

In the words of Fukuzawa Yukichi, civilization and enlightenment had to be approached as requiring nothing less than "an encouragement of the mental development of the masses." In short, these early Meiji thinkers and leaders had fully recognized that education was the cornerstone upon which the whole process of national transformation would eventually come to rest.

And as hard as it may be to believe today, the Ministry of Education was at that time in the forefront of the efforts then being made to enlighten the Japanese people. In the first issue of the *Ministry of Education Journal*, published in 1874, the argument was advanced that in order for Japan to catch up with the civilized nations of the West, education had to be made available not only to those children residing in the cities but to all those living in the undeveloped regions of the countryside as well. Moreover, even Nishimura Shigeki, who would soon distinguish himself by turning towards a conservative educational philosophy that reappropriated the traditional ideas of Confucian thought, clearly argued at this time that Japan should look to the most politically liberalized countries like England and the United States for models of a "civilized" educational system, because those nations had outdeveloped more politically reactionary societies like Russia and Prussia.

But perhaps the most important aspect of the educational discourse taking place in Japan during the early years of the Meiji era can be seen in the fact that no distinction was drawn as of yet between scholarship (*gakumon*) and education (*kyōiku*): the Meiji leaders had not yet discovered any need to view the two as different. However, as the reader will soon discover, the architects of Japan's Imperial State system (*tennōsei kokka*) would subsequently argue in the 1880s that it was indeed vitally important for the national well-being that just such a distinction be drawn and rigidly enforced. Of course the sense of necessity underscoring these claims was directly related to their attempts to generate and reproduce the kind of social order they had concluded was most desirable.

II. From the Enlightenment Movement to the People's Rights Movement

No body of ideas can take root within the social life of a nation until its advocates find the right soil into which it may be successfully transplanted. And unless the soil in which those ideas may grow is properly cultivated, the vitality of those ideas either withers away or becomes transformed into something having an altogether different nature. Keeping this in mind, we must now briefly examine the intellectual environment into which these enlightenment ideas were actually introduced, and the ways in which they subsequently took root and began to grow within Japanese society. In other words, we now need to analyze the nature of the efforts which were being exerted to realize this new "spirit of the age."

However, by no stretch of the imagination was Japanese education in the years immediately following the Meiji Restoration merely an import from the "advanced" countries of Europe. High educational standards had already been achieved during the Bakumatsu period[1] in the temple schools (*terakoya*) that were closely tied to the lives and needs of the ordinary people and in the domainal schools (*hankō*) organized by the feudal authorities to train young samurai in the military and administrative arts believed necessary for those destined to rule the nation. Thus, in the case of education, as was true in other areas of life as well, it was only natural for the leaders of the Meiji government to establish their new system by building upon the not inconsiderable accomplishments of the Tokugawa era.

It was against this background that the focus of educational and scholarly activity in Japan shifted to the enthusiastic pursuit of Western studies. As the regressive ideology of *ōsei fukko* was superseded by the progressive philosophy of civilization and enlightenment, those making educational policy were increasingly drawn to a new vision of epistemological order.

But notwithstanding the fact that the vigorous pursuit of Western learning had already been widely recognized by this time as clearly being in Japan's best interests, there were still many who believed that the nation would be better off if the impact of those studies were limited to transforming the technological dimensions of the nation's social life. This consciousness was clearly visible in slogans such as "Japanese spirit, Western skills" (*wakon yōsai*) or "Eastern morality, Western technology" (*tōyō dōtoku, seiyō gijutsu*). These slogans succinctly expressed the desires of those who were quite willing to utilize the achievements of European civilization to strengthen and improve the quality of Japanese life, but only as long as these transformations preserved the primacy of traditional forms of social thought, and as long as they did nothing to jeopardize the positions of those newly privileged in Meiji Japan.

This highly ambivalent approach to modern forms of thought and knowledge did not suddenly appear in the period following the Restoration. By the 1830s many thinkers were already arguing that the pursuit of Western studies (*yōgaku*) by no means necessarily led to

---

[1] The Bakumatsu period is the name given to the final years of the Tokugawa *bakufu*, the military government of the shoguns who ruled Japan from 1603 to 1868, i.e., the period just before the Meiji Restoration.

criticism of the existing social and political systems. In the eyes of these ideologues Western studies merely provided new ways to generate technological knowledge that wise leaders could use to supplement and strengthen the Tokugawa *baku-han* system.

This way of thinking was carried on after the Meiji Restoration by those who wanted to turn Western learning to Japan's advantage in its struggles against the colonialist powers. However, there now were also many intellectuals who, on account of their own personal involvement with Western studies, could no longer accept the distinction between the social and the technological as a viable or sustainable one. Mastering these new forms of knowledge provided this new generation of intellectual activists with methods of analysis which they subsequently used to exhaustively critique the most serious failures in the post-Restoration governance of Japan. Thus, in the new political environment in which the advocates of each position were steadily advancing within both the new government and the rapidly emerging private sector, it was inevitable that conflict would arise.

The years following the Meiji Restoration are frequently referred to as a period of enlightenment in Japan. But what does enlightenment really mean? And how was its meaning perceived during these years? According to Ernst Cassirer (*The Philosophy of Enlightenment*, 1932), the essence of enlightenment resides in an opening up of thought and in the development of an actively critical spirit. However, we must not overlook the fact that notwithstanding the flowering of new ideas, and the many attempts being made to progressively transform society, this was also the period in which the new Meiji government, through its promulgation of the Libel Law and Newspaper Regulations in 1875, tried to restrain free speech and control public discussion. These measures were particularly significant as they split the Meiji Enlightenment movement into competing factions with diametrically opposed values and objectives. On the one side we can see the emergence of a conservative approach to the problem of civilization rooted in a philosophy of "enlightenment from above"; on the other side there appeared a progressive approach which sought to transform Japanese society on the basis of a philosophy of "enlightenment from below." The struggle between these two competing ideologies has undergone a number of alterations since its original appearance in the 1870s, but it is no less important today; nor is this contestation being conducted any less vigorously now than it was in the last century. In fact, as the reader will discover in the later parts of this book, this tension can be seen at the root of all of the most important problems plaguing contemporary Japanese education.

* * *

Owing to the highly conservative character of their fundamental political agenda, the critical spirit of those pressing for enlightenment from above was very different from the critical spirit they had revealed during the Bakumatsu period when their critiques of ignorance and stupidity had led to a revolutionary crusade against the Tokugawa political and social system. In other words, in their roles as leaders of the new Meiji government, these individuals mobilized their well-developed critical powers to support the establishment of a political movement that sought to impose an entirely new form of social control upon the same Japanese people whom they had recently liberated from Tokugawa feudalism. Moreover, these "enlightened leaders" had no qualms whatsoever about using the power of the State whenever they found it necessary to forcibly quiet those who were openly critical of their policies.

Under these conditions it proved absolutely impossible for the progressivist Meiji Six Society[2] to stick to the principles enunciated in its original statement of purpose, wherein the members declared their intention to form a non-partisan, apolitical body dedicated to facilitating "the exchange of opinions, the spread and popularization of knowledge, and the development of discriminating minds." In other words, while the Society had originally been organized to promote national enlightenment through free speech and publicly organized discussions, its debates inevitably became political in nature as they became embroiled in controversies over the desirability of a popularly elected deliberative body and the growth of a nationwide movement pressing for the People's rights and liberties, and in response to increasing restrictions upon their own freedom of expression.

In response to these developments, Mori Arinori admonished the Society's members to take full stock of the seriousness of those conditions:

[2] The Meirokusha, or Meiji Six Society, was so named because its founding was proposed in the sixth year of the Meiji era (1873) by Mori Arinori. Its 33 founding members, who included eminent government officials, educators, and literary figures, saw the Society as a platform for promoting Western learning and spreading "enlightenment" among the public. Its publication, *Meiroku Zasshi*, publicized the views of its illustrious members for the better part of two years, until its members ceased publication in 1875 under the threat of censorship. The Society continued to hold meetings and lectures thereafter, but most of its impact was made in that first two-year period. See William R. Braisted (trans.), *Meiroku Zasshi: Journal of the Japanese Enlightenment* (Tokyo/Cambridge: University of Tokyo Press/Harvard University Press, 1976).

As is stated in the first article of our society's regulations, the topics to be discussed are those literary, technical, scientific, philosophical, and other matters relating wholly to education that are important for stimulating men's intellectual powers as well as for improving their conduct .... It was not originally the intention at the founding of our society, however, that the discussions would relate to contemporary political matters. Thus let us be careful in the future to avoid becoming embroiled in such controversies. [*Meiroku Zasshi*, Issue 30]

These remarks shrewdly anticipated the bitter controversy which led to the breakup of the Meiji Six Society some months later over the issue of whether the group should dedicate its efforts for the good of the government or should remain an independent body operating outside the sphere of state and politics.

In the face of restrictions on the freedom to openly publish controversial views, Fukuzawa Yukichi proposed to the other members of the Society that they cease publication of their journal. In his proposal he captured the essence of the prevailing conditions when he declared that "today's Japan is becoming not a Japan of the Japanese people, but a Japan of the Japanese government." In the tensions adhering between the positions of Mori and Fukuzawa we can see the fault line of the impending split of Meiji intellectuals into those whose support for the ideology of enlightenment from above would lead them to work to fortify the foundations of the Imperial State (*tennōsei kokka*) and those whose support for enlightenment from below would lead them to struggle on behalf of the Freedom and People's Rights Movement (*jiyū minken undō*). And as we will see in subsequent chapters of this book, we can understand the struggles over the organization of educational authority in Japan right down to the present day precisely along the lines of this split amongst enlightenment thinkers over the question of political involvement.

On the one side we find a view of the people as essentially ignorant (*gumin*), a view which underwrote the argument that enlightenment had to be administratively imposed upon the people from above. On the other side is a view of the People as the true possessors of national sovereignty, a view which saw them as the agents of any genuine form of enlightenment and which underwrote the argument that enlightenment can only proceed by awakening the reason and understanding of each and every member of the national community. In the former case enlightenment was ultimately perceived as a tactic by means of which "already enlightened bureaucrats" could continue to exercise their powers of control over the mass of the people. Here we can see that in this group's use of the word "enlightenment" there was really nothing but contempt for the true spirit of enlightenment. But in the latter case, enlightenment was perceived as a matter of both theoretical and historical necessity. And when viewed in this light it is clear that the *jiyū minken undō* was both the true inheritor of the modern spirit of enlightenment and the progenitor of our subsequent attempts to generate an educational movement in which the People, rather than passively accepting the identity which the State tries to impose upon them, actively struggle to formulate their own identities and achieve autonomy in a liberated political world.

In works such as "A Spiritual History of the Meiji Period" and "The Birth of the Modern State," the historian Irokawa Daikichi has painstakingly traced the growth of these popular struggles by focusing upon the efforts of those wealthy farmers (*gōnō*) in the provinces who led the Freedom and People's Rights Movement. Irokawa has shown us how the study circles which they formed fueled the development of popular education and contributed to the eventual organization of political parties. It is therefore particularly important for us to grasp the connections between enlightenment thought and the Freedom and People's Rights Movement. Within that movement, new knowledge was conceived not merely as an ornamental object, bestowed, as it were, on the People through the magnanimity of those above them, but as something intimately related to the everyday needs and desires of the People. In other words, pursuit of these new forms of knowledge was perceived as necessary for helping the People understand the universal principles which underscored the legitimacy of their interests and concerns.

At the time the members of the Meiji Six Society were debating the desirability of a popularly elected national assembly, Katō Hiroyuki argued that it was necessary to institute a system of national education (*kokumin kyōiku*) before such a body could be properly established. Fully aware that a system of national education could easily be transformed into a powerful means for cultivating a docile populace, one that would passively accept as true whatever the members of the assembly wanted them to, Katō insisted that the new educational system should be organized not as a form of mass propagandization, but rather on the basis of the principle that the People have the right to freely participate in the political life of the nation. Therefore, he reasoned, education should be organized to promote the development of self-consciously autonomous people who would demand the freedom and right to pursue and satisfy their desires.

From this perspective the unhindered spread of education was conceived as absolutely indispensable for the proper organization and strengthening of the People's basic political rights. Education, it was argued, should not be allowed to degenerate into a form of mass propagandization designed to secure unquestioned allegiance to, or uncritical support for, any policy formulated by the national assembly; it should function rather as the locus for cultivation of a citizenry who would make the members of that assembly responsive to their demands. And, it should be noted, it was with precisely this in mind that the overwhelming majority of teachers dedicated their efforts at that time to the aims of the Freedom and People's Rights Movement.

Drawing upon the progressive character of these enlightenment ideas, the advocates of popular sovereignty both among the wealthy farmers and within the ranks of Japan's conscientious teachers continued their struggle during the second decade of the Meiji era to guarantee to all members of the national community the opportunity to fully exercise their political rights. But, as we shall presently see, the educational system set in place during the latter half of the 1880s under the banner of Japan's Imperial institution provided powerful ideological support for the policy of "enlightenment from above," and offered its advocates a convenient pretext for tightly circumscribing the freedoms of those teachers who were pushing for the establishment of a genuine system of popular sovereignty.

III. Education as a Natural Right versus Education as a Form of Government Meddling

As the impulses fueling the calls for "enlightenment from below" gave birth to the Freedom and People's Rights Movement, it was increasingly argued that the people must be recognized as possessing a natural right to receive an education. Thus during the early period of the Japanese Enlightenment many arguments were advanced which pointed to the need for a restructuring of the Japanese educational world, a restructuring which would work to guarantee the fullest possible realization of those rights.

The *New Journal on Education* (*Kyōiku Shinshi*), established in 1877, played a major role in the propagation of this liberal *Weltanschauung* by introducing to the Japanese educational community recent trends in European pedagogic theory and practice. It was here, for example, that Japanese readers were presented with the first translation of parts of Rousseau's *Émile*. This journal provided a useful forum for the airing of a wide range of important issues during the period when there was still a great deal of uncertainty about how Japan's modern educational system should be organized and much controversy over the proper nature of compulsory education. But as the struggle between the progressive thinkers who held that the State had a responsibility to provide compulsory education to the People and the reactionary ones who insisted that compulsory education was the People's duty to the State was resolved when those who upheld the latter position grasped the reins of educational policy formulation, even this valuable journal was forced to cease publication.

The writers whose ideas appeared in *Kyōiku Shinshi* were sympathetic to the claim that "compulsory education" should be considered from the standpoint of the State, i.e., "as one of the major organs for the preservation of the State" ("The Debate on School Attendance," Issue 20). Fearing that the ignorance and illiteracy of an uneducated populace would lead to the "violent disregard of law" and the disturbance of society's peace and well-being ("Education as a Form of Government Meddling," Issue 93), they did not let their progressive inclinations stand in the way of an appreciation of the ways in which education could provide a stabilizing force within society. And since they agreed that education was vitally important for the stability of the State, they found it "perfectly natural for the government to promote and encourage universal school attendance ("Reasons for a Compulsory School Attendance Law," Issue 74). But at the same time these authors were unwavering in their support for the notion that in the last analysis education must be construed as an inalienable right of the people. From this perspective they firmly rejected the claim that the government should be completely free to intervene in any aspect of education as it unilaterally deemed necessary.

Akamatsu Tsunejirō was in the forefront of those arguing in the *New Journal on Education* against the claim that the State should be free to intervene in the workings of the educational process whenever and wherever its bureaucratic agents saw fit to do so. Declaring education to be a "unique natural right of the child," he argued that parents have a duty to make sure that this right is in fact guaranteed. However, Akamatsu was also firm in his insistence that this duty should not be construed in terms of the long-standing Confucian consciousness of the proper relationship between parents and children:

> Parents have no business interfering with their children's perfectly normal right to receive the education which they naturally require. But in our country, on account of the persistent influence of outdated forms of Confucian thought, there remains a marked

inability to understand the importance of these matters, and a very dangerous proclivity to view parental authority as essentially unlimited in its scope. As a consequence, it has been exceedingly difficult to promote the development of a modern school system built on respect for the rights of the child.

To counteract these educationally destructive conditions, it was indeed necessary for the State, Akamatsu readily acknowledged, to intervene in behalf of the child. In such cases, the State should act both to protect the child's educational rights and to help fulfill parents' educational duties. From this standpoint he reasoned that saying the State has a legitimate authority to require parents to send their children to school was entirely different from claiming this was the parents' duty to the State itself.

Akamatsu also looked to education to help the people develop the consciousness they needed to successfully press their claims for the right to fully participate in the nation's political life on an equal footing. These rights were being denied to the people during the early years of the Meiji era on the basis of a logic which declared that because they were largely uneducated, they were too ignorant to participate in the nation's political processes and should not be allowed to do so. By making education available to all the people on an equal basis, Akamatsu argued, many of the inequalities at the heart of Japanese society could thus be overcome.

These enlightening impulses within the educational world were paralleled and given additional support by the discursive efforts of activist intellectuals such as Fukuzawa Yukichi, Ueki Emori, and Nakae Chōmin.

In an essay entitled "On Popular Education" that he is believed to have written in 1877, Ueki discussed the history of education in Europe and concluded that the most fundamental meaning of education there was to "encourage and nourish the development of man's naturally given abilities in as wide a sense as possible." Ueki tied the necessity of education to the freedom of each and every individual to pursue wealth and happiness. He explained the necessity of a general course of studies required for all the People as the indispensable premise for a substantive, and not merely formal, expansion of their freedoms; he did not see compulsory education as an unwarranted violation of their rights and liberties: "Even if the heavy-handed use of law to compel school attendance appears to constitute a violation of natural rights and freedoms, this is not in fact the case." By receiving an education, he argued, the People "increase their capacity to freely pursue wealth

and happiness, and learn how to rescue themselves from disaster."
And with an eye to society's well-being, Ueki explained that education was necessary for "systematically preventing" those forms of
crime and vice which are rooted in ignorance and illiteracy. Thus the
establishment of primary schools, he insisted, was a matter of momen-
tous import for the welfare of the entire nation. And it was within this
context that Ueki invested an "expansion of the people's scientific
knowledge and a cultivation of their intellectual powers" with the
greatest possible social significance. Moreover, he reasoned, this was
absolutely essential for the success of the constitutional order whose
establishment was being proposed at that time.

It should be clear by this point that Ueki's ideas were rooted in a
political *Weltanschauung* which viewed a non-interventionist, liberal
state as providing the best form of government. Notwithstanding his
commitment to this basic orientation, Ueki agreed that it was thoroughly appropriate for the government to use its authority to establish
public schools, provided of course that they were primarily organized
to help realize the full range of human potential and to cultivate within
the minds of the nation's youth a scientifically enlightened consciousness. It was obvious from this standpoint, he declared, that the government's right to actively organize the nation's educational apparatus
by no means entitled it to arbitrarily use its political authority to dominate the inner workings of the educational process in areas, for example, such as the formulation of educational content. Thus Ueki
argued that "it is extremely important for the management of textbooks to be conducted on a local basis," and that in general "education should be administered in a free and non-coercive manner." Following this argument through to its logical conclusion, he therefore
suggested that the Ministry of Education's authority should be cur-
tailed to as great an extent as possible, and that a totally standardized
form of education should be avoided at all costs. In fact, he claimed,
nothing could be more antithetical to the aims of genuine national
enlightenment than a system of education in which the State would
uniformly determine the interests of everyone. True enlightenment,
Ueki wisely declared, meant creating a system which could tolerate
the cultivation of a wide range of people having very different spirits.
Ueki's advocacy of a liberal system of education for the new Japan
was based, in short, on a denial of the claim that the State had an inherent right to meddle with the inner workings of the nation's spiritual
and cultural life.

Ueki was dedicated to a vision in which sovereignty rested with the
People, who would thereafter act as the masters of the new Japanese

State. He spoke of their coming to possess a broadly based knowledge which would enable them to understand how to transform the ideals of popular sovereignty into the reality of liberty. The new citizenry desired by Ueki would not think only about themselves and their families, nor would they be slaves to the appearance of propriety. As a direct consequence of their enlightened consciousness, he asserted, they would acquire an eager and active interest in the most important problems of the nation and the international society of which it was a part:

> There can be no spirit of independence where there is no free-mindedness, and when the People entrust everything to their government, they come to fear it and servilely submit to the commands of its officials regardless of whether they are good and just or not. People who are not offended by things that are reprehensible, and who do not stand up in protest against things that are unconscionable, are easily satisfied, prone to become slaves to mean and unworthy leaders, and can hardly be counted upon to act as the law-abiding citizens of a virtuous state. They are indeed like corpses created by the State. ["Discourse on the People's Rights and Freedoms," 1879]

Scholarship and education, Ueki insisted, are nourished by the spirit of freedom and independence. "Freedom is more precious than order," he argued, and "a life without wisdom is more like death than life." Thus education for Ueki was crucial in the creation of a new social and political order for Japan.

Among those who were passionately committed to the establishment of a system of public schooling based on a view of education as one of the People's naturally given rights, one must not overlook the name of Nakae Chōmin. Writing in the *Tōyō Jiyū Shimbun* (*Oriental Liberal Newspaper*) in March of 1881, Nakae deployed the ideals of popular freedom and rights in formulating an incisive critique of the principles others were then relying upon to justify the government's unbridled interference in the nation's educational life:

> Our freedoms are given to us by nature. When, however, parents are lax with regard to the supervision of their children's education and do not make it possible for them to fully realize those naturally given freedoms, they must be held accountable for what is in the last analysis a violation of those rights. Even if respect is due to parents, they do not have the right to deprive their children of their naturally mandated right to be educated. Because children

have not yet reached the position from which they can fulfill their
rights by themselves, they are not able to protect themselves in
situations where their rights are being violated. In short, they can
neither educate themselves nor compel anyone else to do so. Therefore the State's educational interventions should be undertaken
precisely in order to help realize the child's rights rather than to
disturb or hinder their development.

Nakae also declared that the character of these interventions should
be tempered by the principle that the State's educational control must
be different from all its other activities:

> Therefore, when we speak of educational intervention we should
> not construe this as meaning that the State has a right or a duty
> to restrictively control the rules regulating the organization of
> educational practices and teaching materials. This should be left
> in the hands of local authorities. The State's role in this process,
> inasmuch as it has a positive or constructive one to play, must be
> to encourage parents throughout the nation to enthusiastically
> support the creation and operation of an educational system
> which will indeed make it possible to guarantee the child's nat-
> urally bestowed rights.

IV. The Early Meiji Struggle over the Meaning of Practical Learning

The conflict between those who believed that the State had to enlighten
the Japanese people "from above" and those who identified civilization
with the autonomous development of the people's authority "from
below" played itself out in the early Meiji struggle over the problem
of how to distinguish real, practical forms of knowledge from false,
totally useless ones. Thus it is not surprising that numerous attempts
were being made to redefine the nature of education and scholarship
during this highly unsettled period when the power to define the future
development of Japanese society was the object of the most intense
forms of contestation. Moreover, it is hardly surprising that each of
the new schools of learning was advancing the claim that its knowledge,
and its knowledge alone, contained the insights which were required
to lead Japan in the directions in which it should be moving. In short,
at the same time that each of the major schools of learning identified
its intellectual activities with the pursuit of genuinely practical knowledge (*jitsugaku*), it was denouncing the ideas of the others as unmis-

takable expressions of false learning (*kyogaku*). All agreed that there was only one right way to grasp the true relationship between knowledge and human existence, but each faction thought that this was best defined by its own activities. The major difference between these interpretations was that the advocates of enlightenment from above sought to separate politics from scholarship and education, while those who supported enlightenment from below tried to make scholarship and education the foundation for a new kind of politics.

But while early Meiji thinking about the true nature of practical learning was embedded within the struggle between those who advocated a tightly controlled enlightenment and their antagonists who argued that civilization had to be allowed to progress freely, it certainly did not follow that there was either unanimity of purpose or agreement on strategy within the ranks of one side or the other. Thus even if the general parameters of this discourse can be deduced theoretically, we must examine the positions of its most influential participants in some detail if we are to grasp both its complications and its evolution.

In this section I will examine the ideas of Mori Arinori, Motoda Eifu, Itō Hirobumi, and Katō Hiroyuki regarding the true nature of practical learning. My aim here is to analyze the conservative synthesis which informed the subsequent creation of the Japanese Imperial State's educational system. In the following section I will look at the ideas of Fukuzawa Yukichi, the best-known thinker on the other side of the spectrum in early Meiji Japan. And while it is true that the ideas of the conservative (or enlightenment-from-above) faction prevailed over those of their opponents, the fact that even today those of us in the People's education movement (*kokumin kyōiku undō*) are still trying to realize many of the values embedded in Fukuzawa's social philosophy certainly suggests that the defeat of progressive thinking, while the underlying cause of so much of Japan's later suffering, was certainly neither complete nor irreversible.

As already suggested above, Mori Arinori's arguments about the necessity of the State's actively liberating the people from their ignorance played an important role in the development of the Civilization and Enlightenment Movement in Meiji Japan. The immediate result of this position was to exacerbate the tensions which eventually led to a fracturing of the Meiji Six Society. Moreover, Mori's ideas about the need to keep education and scholarship separate from politics exerted a powerful influence on the development of public education in prewar Japan because it provided the agents of the new State bureaucracy (and, I might add, their postwar successors as well) with a theoretical discourse that allowed them to claim that their activities were merely intended to "preserve education's political neutrality."

It is important to note that even though the ultimate effect of this ideology was to situate the State at the center of what in effect became a national system of knowledge and learning, it was originally formulated in opposition to the views of Confucian thinkers like the Emperor's private tutor Motoda Eifu, who in 1879 called (in "The Great Principles of Education" [*Kyōgaku Taishi*]) for the establishment of a state religion and its inculcation through a system of compulsory schooling primarily given over to strict moral training. In contrast to Motoda, Mori did not believe that the demand for practical learning necessitated the State's establishing a single national religion, or its relying totally upon a special cadre of wise men who would in effect unilaterally dominate national policy formation.

Itō Hirobumi was particularly worried about the evils which would be visited upon the Japanese nation if the pursuit of education were infected by political concerns. In his "Principles of Education" (*Kyōikugi*), written in 1879, Itō argued that while "the education made available to students in the upper levels of the nation's school system should help them progress with their study of the sciences," it should also "steer them away from all politically oriented discussions" because the latter do nothing to increase what he called "national wealth and prosperity." Itō's aim of course was not to proscribe political discussion per se, but to tightly circumscribe the conditions in which it would be permitted and to specify just who would be allowed to participate:

> Since our most promising young students believe that the path to power today lies in mastering the arts of political disputation, they expend altogether too much of their intellectual energies studying those ancient Chinese classics which they vainly hope will increase their ability to speak persuasively about the most important principles of benevolent government. This fallacious confidence makes them totally incapable of undertaking the careful investigation of the real world that characterizes Western studies. And what is even worse, when they embark on studies of Western political theories, they all too frequently rush to embrace doctrines that are even more foolish than the empty Chinese ones they were previously consumed with the study of.

"To rectify these evils," Itō declared, it was necessary for these students "to begin their studies with a broadly conceived investigation of the industrial and technological arts." Only after they mastered these practical subject matters, Itō reasoned, would they be in a position to properly benefit from the pursuit of higher studies. Only then, he proclaimed, would their inquiries "increase their powers of discernment and calculation, concentrate their will and resolve, and bring their inclinations to frivolity and indignation under control."

But since Itō also understood that "the development of science is actually determined in the long run by the ebb and flow of political discourse," he recognized that it was necessary for those who would be guiding the nation's political fortunes to receive the kind of education which would adequately prepare them to discharge those responsibilities. Thus he was driven to conclude that "only those students who have demonstrated their superiority by outperforming all others in entrance examinations to the highest organs of the State's educational system should be allowed to participate in the political discourse so critical to the national welfare." In short, according to Itō, because enlightenment from above meant politics from above, the meaning of practical learning also had to be settled from above.

As we can see from even this cursory examination of the thought of "Statesman Itō" (Fujita Shōzō's term), the founding fathers of the Meiji State placed a great deal of importance on cultivating the human talents required for managing the machinery of their new State.[3] While Itō entrusted the responsibility for completing this job to Mori, his Minister of Education, he fully shared the latter's ideas about how to "create people" (*hitozukuri*). These ideas will be discussed in some detail later on in this book, but for the time being I would like to call attention to (a) the ways in which they were already beginning to be premised upon a radical separation between "scientific" and "political" discourse; and (b) the ways in which the pursuit of "practical learning" (*jitsugaku*) was already being identified with and largely restricted to technological concerns or to problems having an immediately practical focus.

In contrast to the technologically oriented "practical learning," political discourse (*seidan*) was construed within the new arrangements being settled upon by Itō as something that in the future had to be entrusted entirely to the enlightened bureaucrats the State would train to lead and rule the country. According to the guiding principles of this new *Weltanschauung*, knowledge of governance and legislation (the social sciences) would be monopolized by a small, legally trained elite which would make sure that the State developed in a steady and

---

[3] Itō was a framer of the Meiji Constitution and the first Prime Minister under the Cabinet system of government established in 1885.

well-balanced fashion. Thus it is not surprising that an Imperial ordinance issued in 1887 awarded the graduates of the legal course at Tokyo University with the special privilege of being able to directly enter the top rank of government officials. This was completely consistent with the ideas set forth in Itō's "Principles of Education" regarding the need to recruit a ruling class in a totally fair and unbiased fashion.

Katō Hiroyuki's contributions to the discourse on practical learning in the 1880s emerged from a repudiation of the ideas he had himself articulated in works such as *Shinsei Taii* (1871) and *Kokutai Shinron* (1874). In fact Katō's desire to distance himself from the liberalism of those earlier works was so great that he went so far as to have their publication discontinued, hoping that as a result they would no longer be able to influence the formulation of Japanese public opinion.

Katō's rejection of natural-rights thought was tied to his intellectual conversion (*tenkō*) from a populist philosophy of liberalism towards a state-oriented philosophy of nationalism. His particular contribution to the formulation of modern Japanese political conservatism came from his explaining this move as both an inevitable consequence and a necessary stage in the development of modern scientific thought:

> It was approximately four or five hundred years ago that European thinkers like Copernicus, Galileo, and Newton inaugurated the experimental approach to natural phenomena that in recent years enabled scientists like Darwin, Cuvier, and Lamarck to rise above the delusions dominating mankind's thought about the makeup of the material or physical world. This approach to understanding the true principles of things has enabled us to free ourselves from those abstract metaphysical theories which have dominated philosophic and political thinking for so long, and are making it possible to arrive at an understanding of the real nature of things themselves. [*Yūbin Hōchi Shimbun*, Nov. 24, 1881]

Katō feared these "delusions" at the heart of modern political liberalism and embraced the "scientific philosophy" of social Darwinism as offering the best possible remedy for the excessive concern with the rights of individuals which they unjustifiably gave rise to. In other words, his scientifically grounded criticisms of metaphysical thought provided the model for his positivistic repudiation of natural-rights discourse. Thus Katō identified "practical learning" with those forms of knowledge about the real world that enabled men to rise above empty political speculations regarding the constitution of a nonexistent, ideal world.

The identification of practical learning (*jitsugaku*) with the pursuit of modern science was a critically important move for those social philosophers who were attempting to theoretically refute the very grounds of natural-rights thought. It is important to note that notwithstanding the conservative character of their political ideas, neither Itō nor Katō was interested in denying the validity of science; their aim rather was to contrast the "truthfulness" of European science with the "empty fictions" of Chinese learning. To that extent they were indeed "children of the Enlightenment." However, inasmuch as they worked to separate science from the modern spirit of liberty that created it and attempted to thereby create a political system built upon the principle of selectively utilizing the results of scientific research to uphold a repressive social order, they were really its most dangerous enemies.

But notwithstanding their declarations of support for a philosophy based on the repudiation of metaphysical speculation, these advocates of enlightenment from above totally rejected the critical approach to "traditional" Japanese values that was being advanced by the supporters of enlightenment from below within the ranks of the Freedom and People's Rights Movement. The outlook underlying their basic philosophical attitude was clearly enunciated by Itō Hirobumi in an essay entitled "The History of the Establishment of Our Imperial Constitution":

> We cannot raise our voices loud enough in protest against the thoroughly absurd notions being spread about these days which would have us believe, for example, that there was no genuine education going on in this country or no sense of public spirit amongst our people before the country was opened up by the Western powers. Likewise we must admonish the people to reject the dangerous idea that culture only began to bloom in our country a half-century ago. These hastily conceived views of our civilization are the misconceptions of those who can only see the surfaces of things. [*Fifty Years Since the Opening of Our Country*]

Thus to repudiate the arguments of all those liberal-minded thinkers who were attempting to introduce the values of individualism and human rights, Itō portrayed them as violations of the "nobility and greatness" of Japan's traditional spiritual culture:

If there were imperfections in the character of our people in the period before the Restoration, they certainly did not result from deficiencies in the nation's spiritual and moral life, but from lack of knowledge with regard to the scientific, technological, and material problems elucidated by modern civilization. Therefore the challenges facing our nation do not reside, as foreign observers often believe, in the tasks required to transplant "civilization" into a country where it did not exist, but in appending new forms of training to an already robust and well-developed society.

Thus, at the same time that he was establishing a modern constitutional order for the new Japan, Itō was also resurrecting remnants of the feudal system of values that modern constitutionalism is designed to legally supersede. In other words, notwithstanding his careful study of European legal systems and his insightful analyses of Western legal thought, Itō was shrewd enough to realize that unless measures were adopted to limit the growth of individual rights and the closely related demands for popular sovereignty, the whole project of enlightening the Japanese people from above would be thrown into serious jeopardy. It was with this in mind that Itō declared:

The major task facing us today is inculcating within the entire populace the spirit of loyalty, devotion, and heroism (*chūyū gikyō*) that was formerly associated with the samurai class, and making these values their values. Thus we must teach the common people (*heimin*) to work and study hard for the sake of their neighborhoods and villages, and to never waver in matters that would lead to destruction of their families. Moreover, they must develop a peaceful and obedient character, show respect for the law, and demonstrate an understanding of our noble moral ideals and highly refined national sentiments.

Here we find an updated version of the earlier discourse rooted in the slogan "Japanese spirit, Western skills" (*wakon yōsai*).

At this juncture in our analysis of the formation of conservative educational thought in Meiji Japan, it is important to take account of the other major ideological current in the debate on how practical learning should properly be constituted, and to understand why the pursuit of practical learning appeared to be every bit as necessary and desirable from the more traditionalist standpoint of Confucians like Motoda Eifu as from the rationalist perspective of "enlightened" government leaders such as Itō, Katō, and Mori.

The reasons behind the Confucian turn to practical learning are not hard to grasp: it provided the best way to revitalize what had become an outdated ideology and an increasingly indefensible position. Thus, to refute the charge that Confucian approaches to contemporary problems were neither realistic nor effective, these disciples of Chinese studies attempted to turn Confucianism into a discourse on practical learning.

Motoda Eifu criticized contemporary Confucianism from the inside, in particular the tendency to "equate scholarship with discussions of poetry and prose, or with detailed analyses of fables and moral tales." He called for a return to the original teachings of Confucius and Mencius that "identified practical learning with mastery of the arts required for self-cultivation and the control of others." In short, Motoda insisted in his *Outline of Confucianism* (*Jugaku no Yō*) (1871), a revitalized Confucianism provided the best model for a form of practical learning that could be relied upon on an everyday basis.

Through his criticisms of the then fashionable forms of education based on the study of Western books in translation, Motoda attacked the empty abstractness of Western learning and the condition it gave rise to amongst its Japanese practitioners of being divorced from reality:

> The essence of education, our traditional national aim, and a watchword for all men, is to make clear the ways of benevolence, justice, loyalty, and filial piety, and to master knowledge and skill and through these to pursue the Way of Man. In recent days, people have been going to extremes. They take unto themselves a foreign civilization whose only values are fact-gathering and technique, thus violating the rules of good manners and bringing harm to our customary ways. Although we set out to take in the best features of the West and bring in new things in order to achieve the high aims of the Meiji Restoration—abandonment of the undesirable practices of the past and learning from the outside world—this procedure had a serious defect: It reduced benevolence, justice, loyalty, and filial piety to a secondary position. The danger of indiscriminate emulation of Western ways is that in the end our people will forget the great principles governing the relations between ruler and subject, and father and son. Our aim, based on our ancestral teachings, is solely the clarification of benevolence, justice, loyalty, and filial piety. For morality, the study of Confucius is the best guide. People should cultivate sincerity and moral conduct, and after that they should turn to

the cultivation of the various subjects of learning in accordance with their ability. In this way, morality and technical knowledge will fall into their proper places. [*Kyōgaku Taishi*, 1879; translated in Herbert Passin, *Society and Education in Japan*, 1965, p. 227]

Thus we can see that while Confucianists like Motoda were willing to accept criticisms directed at the abstract character of their traditional forms of learning, they were uncompromising when arguing that because Confucianism is the "science of morality" (*dōtoku no gaku*) based on the "teachings of our ancestors," it alone could best clarify "the great duties of sovereigns and subjects, parents and children," reveal the path leading to "loyalty and filial piety," and teach the "knowledge and skills" ignorance of which invariably brings "affliction" upon the entire nation.

In due time the Confucian counterattack upon the spirit of "civilization and enlightenment" achieved many of its desired results. This became particularly noticeable in the wake of the political upheaval of 1881, when government officials joined in the chorus of those voicing the long familiar Confucian moral concerns. Taking advantage of these favorable new conditions, Confucianists like Motoda abandoned their rigorous pursuit of scholarly systematicity and began to rework their ideas so as to generate exemplary moral teachings about the proper organization of everyday life. In short, they tried to represent Confucianism as the true form of practical learning.

In his now classic work "The Guiding Principles of Japan's Emperor-State System" (*Tennōsei Kokka no Shihai Genri*), Fujita Shōzō has insightfully analyzed the close ties between Confucianism and the Emperor-State ideology. Fujita has shown us how the Meiji-era Confucianists succeeded in warding off intellectual extinction by transforming the fundamental organizational principles of Confucianism into the philosophical underpinnings of the new Imperial system. By making their principles the "criteria for ordering everyday life," these Confucianists, Fujita argues, had discovered a way to make their seemingly outdated ideas into one of the driving forces behind the State's consolidation of political power in modern Japan. And from this perspective it is certainly no overstatement to claim that Motoda Eifu played a major role in restoring Confucianism's status as a form of "practical learning" by simultaneously "Japanizing" and "normalizing" its essential ingredients.

During this period the leaders of the new government enthusiastically supported the development of science and technology, but with the proviso that these pursuits should always be kept apart from political and moral concerns. As a consequence of this enforced dissociation, the "spiritual dimension of national life" was shunted off into an isolated realm. In this environment the diffusion of Confucianism "from above" as the most effective form of "practical learning" provided an extremely powerful method for controlling the pace of Japan's modernization. Thus it is no exaggeration to say that those Confucian scholars' readiness to abandon the quest for systematic purity, combined with their willingness to rededicate their efforts to concrete regulation of everyday life, played a major role in the ideological transformation of Japan from a loosely organized collection of feudal domains into a highly unified and culturally homogenized modern nation-state.

Moreover, it is clear that, notwithstanding the obvious differences between Itō's scientism and Motoda's Confucianism and the conflicts they gave rise to regarding the proper way to organize education, in the last analysis there were no real contradictions between their underlying moral / spiritual orientations. The moralism of the Confucianist Motoda was perfectly suited to supplement the nationalism of the statesman Itō. Thus when it came to developing an educational system which could turn out Imperial subjects (*teikoku shinmin*) capable of defending the Emperor-State system, it proved to be very easy to fuse the practicality of modern Western science with the virtues of Confucian moralism.

How then did the conservative architects of the Emperor-State system conceive the fundamental role of education within the new political structure they were erecting? A partial answer can be found in a speech entitled "The Principles of Education," which was delivered at the Wakayama Prefectural Normal School in 1887 by Mori Arinori, who was then serving as Japan's first Minister of Education:

> The principles of education are ultimately rooted in those principles of law which make it possible for the State to cultivate and complete the character development of children. Accordingly, it is a big mistake to think that the primary aims of education should reside in instruction in the 3 R's. . . . What kind of persons should we be relying upon our educational system to produce? The kind of person who will be the virtuous subject (*shinmin*) our Empire requires. What will these virtuous subjects be like? They will be Imperial subjects who completely fulfill their duties, which means that when called upon to do so they will willingly give their lives for the State. Thus the aim of education is to cultivate persons who can be of service to the State and nation.

The framework of Japan's national education system was set in place during the period of time between Mori's articulation of these educational principles and the proclamation of the Imperial Rescript on Education in 1890. Within that formulation, education (*kyōiku*) and scholarship (*gakumon*), which had previously been viewed as parts of a single system of learning, were thereafter presented as if they had absolutely nothing to do with one another: scholarship was marked off as a domain reserved for the nation's elite, while education was reconceived as an activity necessary for training the nation's masses. But the truth of the matter was that both of these pursuits were thoroughly subordinated to the objectives of the State. Thus learning in Japan, beginning with instruction in elementary schools and stretching all the way up to research in the universities, came to be strictly dominated by the concerns and needs of the State. It was during this period, in short, that the inequality of knowledge was officially systematized in Japan. And even though it appeared as if the new ladder system of national education generated by the structural arrangements of the Emperor-State constituted a single track which opened the path to success equally to all, in reality it provided an ingenious mechanism for reproducing a dual structure of culture by severing the ties between scholarship and education.[4]

The young Tokutomi Sohō, who, in the name of the common man, opposed this social formation of knowledge, described this state of affairs in an editorial published in the first issue of his journal, *Kokumin no Tomo* (*The People's Friend*), in 1888:

> Just as the societies of the West are democratically organized societies, so too Western civilization was born from the needs of the common man. Even though there is no reason why this calls for any special form of explanation on our part, nonetheless, because at the time when this civilization was imported into Japan, it was achieved, most regrettably, almost entirely through the agency of the aristocracy, it acquired their imprint and its benefits were largely limited to their class. Thus Western learning came to be something totally unrelated to the concerns of the People. . . . It is this unequal distribution of knowledge which we must hereafter figure out a way to remedy.

Thus it is not unwarranted to claim that at the very same time they were establishing a national system of education to enlighten the Japa-

---

[4] This subject will be developed in greater detail in the following chapter.

nese people from above, the leaders of the Meiji State were also developing a nationwide apparatus designed to make sure that an inquisitive and ultimately autonomous populace would not come into existence. By severing the bonds between education and higher learning, the Meiji statesmen were able to create a school system that functioned as a powerful tool for domesticating the Japanese people.

Conversely, to the extent that they were able to separate higher learning from the people for whose sake it should have been undertaken, they robbed it of its true power to move men and shape events. And while it is true that this educational system enabled them to inculcate within the Japanese people the skills and attitudes required for preserving the independence of the nation in an age of colonialist expansionism, it could only do so by rendering the masses incapable of using their reason without the guidance from above which only the State could provide. Thus the leaders of the Meiji State paid a high price to catch up to the great powers of the West. In this sense the Meiji educational system enabled the Imperial State to trap the Japanese people in a state of intellectual and emotional adolescence.

V. Fukuzawa Yukichi's Ideas on Education, Scholarship, and National Independence

A. The Scientific Spirit and the Spirit of Freedom

Before moving on to an analysis of education, scholarship, and human cultivation in the Japanese Imperial State, I want to draw the reader's attention to Fukuzawa Yukichi's very different ideas regarding the kind of "practical learning" Japan needed to complete its modernization.

In the first of his essays on "Encouragement of Learning," Fukuzawa called upon Japanese intellectuals to forgo the idea that being educated meant "knowing strange words or reading ancient and difficult literature, or enjoying poetry and writing verse and other such accomplishments which are of no particular use in the world." He argued that "this kind of learning without real use should be left for another day, and one's best efforts should be given to an education that is relevant to everyday use, an education based upon the study of geography, history, economics, ethics, and above all natural philosophy."[5]

---

[5] The quotations in this section are from Fukuzawa's essays on education. Unless otherwise noted, translations are by the editor/translator of this volume; however, translations of many of these essays have also been published in the following three volumes: *An Encouragement of Learning* (trans. David A. Dilworth and Umeyo

Fukuzawa's capacity to distinguish between useful and useless learning was rooted in his experiences before the Meiji Restoration as a
student of Western science. Reflecting upon the spirit shared by scholars of Western learning at the time when Japan was emerging from 250
years of self-imposed isolation, he noted that their studies had on the
one hand been dedicated to "overturning the conservatism and per-
versity of Chinese learning," while on the other they were motivated
by a desire to lead the People to an appreciation of the advantages of
this new approach to the pursuit and organization of knowledge. "It
was our deepest desire," Fukuzawa recalled, "to convey to the nation
a sense of how much more could be understood and done on the basis
of the principles of the physical universe than on the basis of the principles previously used to bring about inner discernment." Thus, for
those who had shared Fukuzawa's outlook, the development of a form
of education rooted in the methods of the natural sciences did much
more than promise better knowledge of the physical world: it offered
an opportunity to reform and remake the spiritual structure of national
life.

The historian of science Itakura Kiyonobu has described the conditions prevailing at this time in the following manner:

> Among the students of Western learning, the forerunners of scien-
> tific enlightenment like Fukuzawa were more concerned to ac-
> quire the modern scientific spirit and a new view of the natural
> world than they were to reap any immediately practical payoffs
> from their scientific investigations. . . . Working to teach the Japa-
> nese masses about the mechanistic view of nature, or the positivis-
> tic spirit of science based on Newtonian dynamics, their first
> priority was to destroy the feudalistic, Confucian view of nature."
> [*History of Science Education in Japan*]

In short, the prime concern of this early generation of Western
scholars was to disseminate the rational methods of thought which
were rooted in the practices of modern science. This was indissolubly
linked to the celebration of a new world and the as-yet-unmastered
forms of learning which would make it accessible, and at the same time
to a showdown with, and repudiation of, the old ideas and false learning (*kyogaku*) of Confucianism. Thus the real motive for the move to

---

Hirano; Sophia University, Tokyo, 1969), *An Outline of a Theory of Civilization*
(trans. David A. Dilworth and G. Cameron Hurst; Sophia University, 1973), and
Fukuzawa Yukichi on Education (trans. Eiichi Kiyooka; University of Tokyo Press,
1985).

science (in particular physics) was to influence and ultimately control the organization and growth of practical learning. In other words, those who wanted to promote the development of a scientifically re-vitalized culture perceived the eradication of Chinese learning as one of the most urgent tasks facing them at that time.

Only by scientifically uncovering the principles ruling the natural world, Fukuzawa declared, could Japanese thinkers lead the nation to a progressive form of civilization. Discovery of these principles, he continued to argue for the rest of his life, would enable the nation to bring the power of nature firmly under control. Thus, for Fukuzawa, science and practical learning were indistinguishable. "Knowledge of nature," he was fond of repeating, "is the path leading to the govern-ance of nature."

But Fukuzawa was not so naive as to think that the modern Euro-pean spirit of enlightenment could be introduced into Japan solely through formal instruction in the methods of the physical sciences. Fukuzawa had in fact himself been eagerly studying the leading Euro-pean social systems and forms of thought since the early 1860s. In the Preface to his *Conditions in the West* (*Seiyō Jijō*), written in 1866, Fukuzawa had already argued that investigations of European cul-tural life must not be limited to introducing its sciences and arts, but should be extended to include analyses of its politics and customs as well. From the standpoint of his patriotic concern with promoting Ja-panese independence, Fukuzawa resolutely called attention to Japan's critical need for research into the historical development of modern Western social life, i.e., its forms of government, finance, and arma-ments. This inquisitiveness was also closely tied to Fukuzawa's convic-tion that "an open mind" and an "enlightened society" are ultimately inseparable. And in his *Autobiography*, Fukuzawa recalled that his attempts to master Dutch learning before the Meiji Restoration[6] had opened his eyes to the need for an approach to Western studies which viewed them as intimately related to the real affairs of men in society. Thus, for example, his efforts to introduce the principles of modern

[6] During the period before Japan was opened to direct contact with the West, what knowledge its intellectuals were able to attain of the West came through the books that entered the nation from the Dutch trading outpost on Dejima Island in Naga-saki. Thus scholars like the young Fukuzawa began their studies of Western learning by mastering the Dutch language. Only later, after the country was opened up in the 1850s and 1860s, did they discover that they also had to learn other languages besides Dutch in order to truly master "Western learning." In his *Autobiography* Fukuzawa describes his amazement upon learning that Dutch was not the major language of the European world. He taught himself English by using a Dutch-Eng-lish dictionary obtained from a sailor in Yokohama.

Western political economy represented an attempt to give birth to social science in Japan, and to substitute its ideas and methods for the teachings of Confucianists regarding the organization of a benevolently managed state. Fukuzawa's *An Outline of a Theory of Civilization* (1875) was a powerful product of this new scholarly spirit.

B. Academic Liberty and a Free Nation

For Fukuzawa the inevitable outcome of modern scientific thinking was a critique of all traditional and customary obstacles to the realization of human freedom. And since, unlike those who advocated enlightenment from above, he looked to the universal dissemination of scientific method as the best way to establish the "spirit of liberty" within Japan, it is not surprising that Fukuzawa formulated his ideas about the true nature of higher learning (*gakumon*) in close relationship with his thinking about the proper organization of popular education (*kyōiku*).

Fukuzawa's new approach to scholarship and scientific inquiry emerged from his critique of the role Confucian studies had traditionally played in Japanese social life. Fukuzawa therefore redefined the aims of scholarship from the standpoint of the masses in opposition to what he perceived to be the Confucianists' identification of higher learning with the political and emotional domination of those masses. Thus whereas Confucian learning had been motivated by a desire to control other men, his own vision of an enlightened form of scholarship that made it possible to master nature and rationalize human affairs was motivated by a desire to enable the ordinary people to achieve spiritual independence and political freedom.

"The pursuit of higher learning," Fukuzawa duly noted in *An Outline of a Theory of Civilization*, "has essentially been an activity engaged in by those who have been ruling our country, an activity undertaken as one part of national administration. And notwithstanding the fact that those who have pursued such studies have done so under the aegis of different schools that are seemingly opposed to one another, in the end they have all been looking for the same thing: the best ways to control and manage the people." The development of scholarship in Japan, Fukuzawa had astutely observed, was essentially unmediated by the interests and concerns of the people.

Given the fact that higher learning had developed in Japan as the theoretical arm of political domination, it was only natural, Fukuzawa reasoned, that its propagation had previously been restricted to a tightly circumscribed number of people. Its internal logic had pre-

vented it from contributing to an equalization of the People's opportunities, and forced it to serve as a tool to keep the People ignorant and
ultimately unable to overturn the conditions within which they were
constantly being regulated. Thus scientific scholarship had not been
able to really develop in feudal Japan, Fukuzawa recognized, because
the inner dynamic between the pursuit of knowledge and the interests
of the People which had appeared in the modernizing nations of the
West had not been allowed to progress in Japan. Likewise it had been
impossible for those pursuing knowledge in Japan to clear the path
leading to what Fukuzawa had called "a free and independent spirit."

"In the nations of the West, knowledge arose among the People in
general, but in our country of Japan its growth has been firmly contained within the purview of the government." In short, the problem,
Fukuzawa declared, was that the production and dissemination of
knowledge had been thoroughly monopolized by those who held the
reins of political power.

On the other side of this ledger, Fukuzawa deplored the fact that "in
Japan there has only been a government, but as of yet no nation." The
government's monopolization of knowledge and the lack of a genuine
spirit of self-determination among the People were, in other words,
opposite sides of a single coin. Accordingly, he equated destruction
of the government's monopoly on the production of advanced forms
of knowledge and learning with the creation of both an independent
forum for scholarship and an autonomous people. For Fukuzawa the
path leading the Japanese people to become the autonomous controllers
of their own knowledge was the only path that would lead them to true
political sovereignty. Fukuzawa was fond of the proverb "Over foolish
people, there is a despotic government." It is not the case, he declared,
"that governments are despotic in and of themselves; it is foolish people rather who bring that form of government upon themselves. If the
government that rules over foolish people is despotic, then reason
requires that a government over wise people will be benign. Therefore
we have this kind of government in our country because of the way the
People are."

> Despotic government is not merely a product of the activities of
> tyrants and dishonest officials. It is also an evil that uneducated
> people bring upon themselves. . . . If the People want to throw
> off a tyrannic government, they should promptly dedicate them-
> selves to learning and elevate both their intelligence and virtue.
> Thus through the relentless pursuit of knowledge and learning

the People must raise themselves to a level in which they will by no means be inferior to our government officials. [*An Encouragement of Learning*]

Since Fukuzawa saw bad government going hand in hand with an ignorant and uneducated populace, he declared that the path leading to good government was identical with the one that could lead the People to enlightenment. But unlike other members of the Meiji Six Society such as Katō Hiroyuki or Mori Arinori, who held that this enlightenment had to be administered from the top down by wise government officials, Fukuzawa understood that this process could only be truly liberating when organized from the bottom up. Having recognized that the conservative social policies of the new government were as much designed to keep the People ignorant as they were to provide them with new forms of knowledge and intelligence, he firmly rejected the logic of his former colleagues in favor of a much more progressive approach to the modernization of Japanese society. Thus in opposition to ideologues within the government, like Katō and Itō, who wanted to limit "mass enlightenment" to a mere presentation of the facts produced by scientific investigation, Fukuzawa, who wanted to encourage the masses of people to actively demand their human and political rights, believed that this process could best be initiated by nurturing a consciousness of the modern scientific spirit itself. Thus Fukuzawa's efforts to encourage the spread of scientific learning represented a very concrete attempt to promote the creation of a politically autonomous people.

This attitude was equally evident in Fukuzawa's thinking about the way history had been written and taught in Japan. Japanese history had been conceived in most cases, he observed, as an account of the Imperial Family, the ups and downs of the nation's rulers, or as chronicles of the victories and defeats of the nation's warlords. And in those rare cases where historical narratives departed from these themes, it was only to provide tales of the "fictious accomplishments" of Buddhist priests. "Generally speaking, we have not had histories of the Japanese nation, but only histories of the governments and rulers of Japan." Not surprisingly, Fukuzawa laid the blame for this state of affairs at the doorstep of those whom he referred to as Japan's "careless scholars."

The major difference between Japan and the civilized countries of the West, Fukuzawa continually insisted, could be seen in the "overemphasis placed upon power" in Japan. The direct consequence of this way of thinking, he argued, was that everything was made to appear as if it revolved around the dubious relationship between "the ruling

family and our national strength." The results of this distorted way of
viewing the world were that "the Japanese people came out looking as if
they had nothing to do with the course of national affairs"; "scholarship was made thoroughly subservient to the interests of those in power
and contributed to the exercise of despotism"; "the power of those
holding the reins of government was made into an awesome force
always available for use to control the inner minds of the people"; and
"the practitioners of both religion and scholarship were enticed within
the spheres of those who ruled, so that in the end neither one nor the
other ever became an independent force within the life of the nation."
These observations underscored Fukuzawa's closely held convictions
that "the freedom of scholarship from authority" and the "popularization or nationalization (*kokuminka*) of learning" were absolutely indispensable for the creation of "a truly independent nation."

Fukuzawa called upon Japanese intellectuals to create a new form
of scholarship, one which would help repudiate Confucian moral
ideology and everything it stood for, i.e., the exercise of despotic governmental power. This new scholarship, he insisted, had to help create
a moral consciousness based on reason, one which would make respect
for the autonomy and value of individuals into the foundation of a
new national independence. Likewise morality, as Fukuzawa sought
to reconceive it, would no longer be something wholly subservient to
the interests of those holding political power. The ultimate expression
of this world-view was seen in Fukuzawa's claim that the bearers of
state authority had absolutely no business interfering with the values
underlying the realms of religion and education.

Fukuzawa was unyielding in his belief that the power required to
drive despotism from Japan could only be generated by the free development of human knowledge and understanding. There were no
longer any "benevolent despots" (*jinkun*) in the advanced nations of
the West, he reasoned, because the growth of knowledge and virtue
among the common people had deprived them of their *raison d'être*.
"The opportunities for exercising such absolute power had disappeared in the civilized countries of the modern world," he argued,
"following the development of private morality."

Since despotic governments can only come into being when the
masses of people live in a state of stupidity, those forms of rule would
become unnecessary in Japan, Fukuzawa reasoned, when the People
learned how to overcome their ignorance through education. The
development and diffusion of knowledge would therefore bring about
a genuine democratization and equalization of society. This enlightenment from below, he argued, was needed to bring about a complete

transformation of the ancient relationship between government and law.

> In the past, the heads of government established laws to place the People under their control, but today, in the modern nations of the world, people establish laws to prevent their governments from acting despotically. This is indeed the character of law in those countries where, along with the march of civilization, the People have gained their independence."

We can see from this passage that Fukuzawa's efforts to redefine the relationship between learning and power represented nothing less than an attempt to radically restructure the relationship between the Japanese government and the Japanese people on the basis of the modern concepts of popular sovereignty. This view of history and the constitution of power was also visible in his understanding of the Meiji Restoration. Rejecting the ideologies of restoring Imperial Rule (ōsei fukko) and national essentialism (kokutai-ron) that philosophically supported the policies of enlightenment from above, Fukuzawa portrayed the Meiji Restoration as an attempt to incite an eruption of the principles of civilization and enlightenment from below.

C. Intellectual and Moral Education

How did Fukuzawa comprehend the place of education in relation to "civilization," "scholarship," and "the People"?

Just as he was drawn to a view of scholarship which represented its fruits as necessarily belonging to all the people equally, so too he believed it necessary to think about education from the standpoint of the masses. And as for the aims of a popularly controlled system of education, Fukuzawa argued that, "rather than thinking of education as teaching people about things, it should be approached as an opportunity to remove all impediments to the development of their naturally given abilities." Likewise he advised those charged with educating children "to pay careful attention to the temperaments of those they would lead to enlightenment," and to "work to help them attain the skills and capacities heaven has endowed them with from birth."

We can see here that Fukuzawa had grasped the importance of an attitude of respect for the individuality and promise inherent in every single child, an attitude which had appeared earlier among modern European thinkers. In short, Fukuzawa had come to see that enlightenment did not only mean liberating the masses from ignorance by providing them with knowledge; it also had to lead to a blossoming of all their undeveloped possibilities. In this regard alone his thinking still occupies an important place in the history of Japanese education.

Fukuzawa was unyielding in his identification of civilizational progress with the development of human intelligence. Optimistically viewing this progress as potentially unlimited, he enthusiastically embraced a view of education that emphasized "mental training" over "moral disciplining." He tied this to a rejection of all forms of moralism that took no account of the real conditions of men in society. Arguing that abstract moralism was unworthy of a truly civilized nation, Fukuzawa valued an education that cultivated intelligence over one which provided indoctrination in officially specified virtues and fixed notions of appropriate human behavior. In this spirit he looked to the development of rational forms of thought as promising the best means for liberating mankind from the shackles of historically received traditions and from the blind forces of nature. Only when these intellectual skills are mastered, Fukuzawa insisted, would it be possible to truly acquire substantive "spiritual freedom." And in the future he trusted that this kind of education would give birth to the courage required to confront nature head-on. For Fukuzawa, therefore, the main challenge facing educators in Japan was the formulation of a moral outlook that was supported by the modern scientific spirit.

D. The Independence of Learning from Politics

Fukuzawa's vision of practical learning was not one in which the aims of education and scholarship were subordinated to the vulgar requirements of those in power, or one in which their respective values were judged solely in terms of what was immediately useful. This is particularly evident in his 1883 collection of essays entitled "The Independence of Learning."

> The efficacy of scholarship can never be measured in terms of the daily accomplishments of scholars, nor for that matter is it immediately visible in the way men actually confront the challenges they encounter in the everyday world. Thus learning should be completely separated from politics, and all efforts made to keep them from becoming entangled will prove advantageous to society as a whole, and to both politicians and scholars in particular.

As for the difference between the two:

> Even if the objectives of both are to promote the wealth and

prosperity of a nation, the work of scholars should be far removed from the immediate needs of contemporary society, while that of politicians must be given over to the everyday concerns of the People. The world of politics is an active one located on the surface of human affairs, while that of scholarship is more submerged and serene.

Thus, when the two are intermingled, he reasoned, considerable damage is done to both. Fukuzawa's formulation of these ideas emerged directly from his earlier criticisms of the role played by Chinese learning during the final years of the Tokugawa era.

Fukuzawa attempted to concretize his ideas about the separation of learning and politics, and the former's independence from the latter, through his discussion of the system of education established in Japan in relation to those found in the West:

> At the time of the Restoration, everything was being initiated anew, and no one distinguished items to be placed under government control from those to remain in private hands. Every new enterprise was under the control of the government; even minor details in industry and commerce came under its scrutiny. Therefore, it was natural that schools under the modern system were established by the Ministry of Education. However, in sixteen years, we have gradually reached a point in government organization and society where present conditions must be reconsidered from all angles and also in reference to the West. It is a very rare instance in any advanced country that the government itself establishes schools, gathers students, and requires teachers to give instruction under the direct control of government officials. This practice, I judge, has become inappropriate for Japan today.

And as for the detrimental effects of an educational system placed under the control of the government:

> The reins of governmental power will undoubtedly change hands from time to time in the future as they do in the countries of the West. Whatever form the government may take, its policies will certainly change from time to time as well. This is inevitable. Under such fluid conditions, schools and teachers throughout the nation who will be under the control of the Ministry of Education will be obliged to change their policies each time the government alters

its course. Nothing would be more unfortunate for the cause of the nation's culture and education.

On the basis of these ideas, Fukuzawa then went on to argue that just as learning and politics should be kept apart from one another, so, too, administrative and educational concerns should not be allowed to become intermingled. Not satisfied with the suggestion that "those schools now under the direct control of the Ministry of Education merely be separated" from it, Fukuzawa also proposed that laws be instituted which would stipulate the differences between cultural authority and political power. Such measures were necessary, he believed, in order to ensure that the independence of scholars and educators would not be violated. Within the framework of these legal arrangements, he argued, management of the inner workings of schools should be entrusted to persons chosen to act as the guardians of national culture.

> We should consider establishing a council of highly reputable scholars from throughout the nation who will meet on a regular basis. Since this council will act on behalf of the entire nation, it should be granted the authority to supervise without government interference the entire gamut of our cultural activities and serve as the center of learning and education in our nation. Thus its work should be to keep an eye on literary and scholastic activities, determine the most appropriate methods for study and instruction in our schools, judge books, do research on ancient history, study new theories, serve as the final authority on language usage, and edit dictionaries, etc. . . . This council shall be a kind of supreme overseer of Japan's culture.

In Fukuzawa's thinking about the constitution of this new cultural academy, we can identify the roots of what became the postwar discourse on the necessity of an independent form of educational authority.[7] But since Fukuzawa recognized that it was "necessary to administratively oversee the hundred and one items of education" related to the fiscal and personnel management of schools, and "since such supervision cannot be accomplished without the authority of the Min-

---

[7] Chapters 4 and 5 discuss the laws instituted in the early postwar years to establish this autonomous educational authority, and the subsequent controversies over the way to interpret the meaning of educational independence and neutrality within the new framework of Japanese democracy.

istry of Education," he recognized that an outright abolition of that arm of government was not desirable. In particular, he noted, compulsory education cannot be realized without the authority of the government. However, there was no doubt in Fukuzawa's mind that the government's administration of schools must be strictly limited to the external aspects of the educational process, and that its interventions should never affect decisions on matters such as "what kind of education should be provided to children, what books should be used in their instruction and what kind of books should be kept away from them, or how instruction in the classroom should actually be organized." In short, he argued, all the important decisions on learning should be left to the proposed scholars' council, while the writing of reports and other such administrative chores should be managed by the Ministry of Education.

Having distinguished between the internal and external dimensions of education in a way which called attention to the need for a clear separation between their respective spheres of activity, Fukuzawa also recognized the need to provide whatever guarantees were required to assure the independence of those educational professionals who would ultimately be responsible for the internal aspects of the learning process.

> Only those who from their early years have themselves been well trained in the sciences, are skilled in the arts of reading and writing, and actually have experience in classroom teaching are in a position to lead others along the path to education. This is why professional men of learning should be responsible for education and learning.

But in his call for the independence of scholarship and education from politics, Fukuzawa was not denying the fact there was a real need for legitimate political education.

> Politics and government are as important to the national wellbeing as are mass education and higher learning. Therefore it is vitally necessary that the science of politics progress from day to day. All of the citizens of the nation must join in political discussions and come to hold their own ideas on what constitutes good politics and good government. Citizens with no political awareness are fools, or merely the members of an undisciplined mob.... Thus the need to stimulate the growth of political awareness amongst all people is inseparable from the need to encourage learning amongst them.

Likewise he claimed that it was important for political and educational professionals to "concentrate on their respective endeavors and to never meddle in the affairs of the other."

E. Academic Freedom and National Independence

One of Fukuzawa's most important contributions to the Meiji discourse on practical learning resulted from his viewing it in relation to the problem of how to secure the nation's independence in a world dominated by the great powers of the West. Fukuzawa's perception of the "spirit of national independence" was inextricably linked to his ideas about how to create an educational system that would aid in the development of a free people, a nation of citizens who could advance the cause of civilization from below. Therefore Fukuzawa argued that not only did those who were attempting to establish a new educational system have to make the People fully aware of the dangers the nation faced in a world dominated by the Imperialist powers of the West; they also had to provide them with the skills and knowledge required to meet and overcome those dangers. Fukuzawa, the astute critic of Confucian intellectual traditions, was no less scathing when denouncing those "thoroughly vulgar Western scholars who, while remaining totally unaware of the crises facing Japan, and having nothing to offer that would contribute to their resolution, superficially introduce Western civilization" as if it contained the solution to all imaginable difficulties.

Nowadays the somewhat better-educated, reform-minded people, or those who are called "teachers of enlightenment," are constantly proclaiming the excellence of Western civilization. When one of them holds forth, ten thousand others nod their heads in approval. From teachings about knowledge and morality down to government, economics, and the minute details of daily life, there are none who do not propose emulation of the ways of the West. Even those as yet less informed about the West seem to be entirely abandoning the old in favor of the new. How superficial they are in uncritically believing things Western and doubting things Eastern!

The result of this thoughtless Westernism was that

even though it appears as if we are moving in the direction of securing the forms of civilization, we are moving further backwards everyday in the most important regard, i.e., the spiritual vitality the nation requires to be truly civilized. And without this, no matter how much progress is made towards achieving the forms of civilization, the result is merely a white elephant. Therefore we will not advance the cause of civilization by thoroughly washing away the national character in the manner being requested by today's erstwhile Western scholars.

Since Fukuzawa viewed learning as that which imparts "vitality to the People's desire for independence," it is not surprising that he identified it equally with "personal and national independence." In his "Discussion of Our National Independence" in *An Outline of a Theory of Civilization*, Fukuzawa declared:

Recently we Japanese have undergone a great transformation. The theory of human rights has flooded the land and has been universally accepted. However, equal rights does not merely mean that all men within a single country are equal. It means equality between a man from one nation and a man from any other nation, as well as between one nation and another nation; it means that, regardless of power or wealth, everyone's rights are exactly equal. . . . And although many people in society have lately been advocating the theory of equal rights, and there are some who also proclaim the necessity of realizing equal rights throughout the country, why is it that, despite the forcefulness, freshness, and attractiveness of this argument, there are so few who invoke the theory of equal rights in regard to our dealings with foreign nations? . . . Therefore, in foreign relations we Japanese do not know whether or not we are being subjected to injustice; we do not know what benefits have accrued to us; we do not know what our losses have been. And so we look on in indifference at matters connected with foreign countries. This is one reason we Japanese people have not contended for power with foreign countries. Those who know nothing of a situation cannot be expected to be concerned about it.

Thus Fukuzawa wrote *An Outline of a Theory of Civilization* in the hope that its criticisms of those "shallow thinkers who merely value the outward forms of civilization" might awaken the People to their need for an "independent national culture," one worthy of being called civilized and one capable of standing up to the great Imperialist powers of the West. After all, he reminded his readers: "It is truly appalling how heartless and cruel the British were in their administration of the East Indian provinces."

Viewing the world in this fashion, Fukuzawa concluded, only served to underscore the urgency of the challenge confronting the Japanese people at that time. Accordingly, he did not conceive the need to cultivate patriotism as part of an all-out attempt to legitimate Japanese expansionism in Asia, as was the case with those who were working to bring about enlightenment from above, but only as a means to strengthen the nation's will to resist the aggressive incursions of European imperialism. Therefore Fukuzawa was unyielding when insisting on the one hand that the nationalistic ideology of *hōkokushin* (unquestioning patriotic service) was directly opposed to the principles of universal justice, and on the other that the idea of "civilization as a means to independence" revealed a total misunderstanding of the true spirit of civilization.

Conversely, it was precisely because Fukuzawa grasped the true meaning of universal justice in this fashion that he was able to reject these early expressions of Japanese chauvinism on the grounds that they represented "a stupid and empty idealism" totally useless for confronting the real challenges underlying contemporary conditions. Only within the context of these conditions, Fukuzawa advised, would it become possible to develop the creative intelligence and subjective spirit required for overcoming the dangers lurking in the path of the new Japan.

When matters were viewed in this fashion, it was clear, Fukuzawa argued, that the People had not been a consequential factor in the framework of Japanese traditions. To correct this situation the People had to be sensitized to the meaning of human rights and independence; only then would the dream of an independent Japan become a reality. Here Fukuzawa identified the wellsprings of the spirit of commitment needed for creating an autonomous "national culture," one which would make it possible for the Japanese people to assume their rightful place in the community of modern nations, and one which would not merely be a poor imitation of the external forms of Western life.

F. Conclusion

Having grasped the intrinsic relationship between individual freedom and national independence, Fukuzawa struggled to help establish a system of education and higher learning which would enable the Japanese people to realize the untapped potential of those bonds to the greatest extent possible. On the one hand he looked to the spread of education to underwrite the steady advance of national independence and the progressive development of civilization, while on the other he envisioned scholarship and higher learning as holding the key to individual independence and spiritual freedom. For Fukuzawa the orientations of scholarship and education had to be set in accord with the values embedded in science and modern thinking about the meaning of human rights. In short, education was to provide a popularization of scholarship and lead the People to make themselves the unquestioned masters of political authority. He saw the problems which still had to be resolved as how to make scholarship available to everyone, and how to universalize its fundamental values.

These problems are still our problems. But in attempting to resolve them today, we have to deal with an additional set of difficulties: How is it possible to restore to full vitality the human nature of the Japanese people, a nature which was severely damaged by the Imperial educational system that the Meiji statesmen erected while rejecting the ideas of their former colleague Fukuzawa?

In order to appreciate the depths of the challenge facing those liberal-minded reformers who struggled to rebuild Japanese education after the Pacific War, we must first examine the character of the prewar school system, the Imperial Rescript on Education upon which its values rested, and the corruptions of the human spirit which it was responsible for producing. In doing so we must confront the fact that the appearance of Japanese militarism and ultranationalism did not represent a pathological breakdown of the educational system institutionalized by the Meiji statesmen in the 1880s and 1890s, but was its logical and necessary outcome. Only in this light can we grasp the complexity of the challenge facing educational reformers in the late 1940s, and the dangers of the counter-reforms instituted in the mid-1950s after the Allied Occupation of Japan was brought to an end.

3 Education and Human Cultivation in the Emperor-State

I. Background of the Imperial Rescript on Education

By the end of the nineteenth century it was widely understood that the growth of European imperialism and the tendency towards a colonialist division of the non-Western world were seriously jeopardizing Japan's survival as an independent nation. In light of these developments, Japan, through the Meiji Restoration, relinquished the Tokugawa system of separate feudal domains and moved towards the adoption of a new form of unified national government. The leaders of the new Meiji State were then obliged to work out the political and cultural arrangements required to mediate Japanese relations both at home and abroad. As was discussed in the previous chapter, at first this led to highly heated arguments between those who wanted to make Imperial rule the cardinal principle of national life, and those who believed that the European philosophy of civilization and enlightenment offered the most promising path for the future development of Japan as a modern nation.

As we have seen, after the early Meiji attempt to organize education and higher learning on the basis of National studies (*kokugaku*) proved unsuccessful, the ideas of the Western studies faction came to play a leading role in the establishment of Japan's first modern system of education. In particular, the ideas of Fukuzawa Yukichi exerted a powerful influence over the thought and activity of those who were working to create a new body of educational practice. His ideas about the identity of "personal and national independence" and the relation between "the spirit of civilization and the vitality of an autonomous people" were widely shared by those involved in the creation of a new educational system. For those who took these ideas to heart, popular sovereignty (*minken*) and national sovereignty (*kokken*) were seen as being in fundamental harmony. During the second decade of the Meiji era, however, Fukuzawa's beliefs were targeted by the reactionary thinkers leading the assault on Japanese liberalism. His books, which up until then had been widely read and used as textbooks, were thereafter declared unacceptable for use in the nation's schools.

In 1881 the Meiji government issued its Rules of Behavior for Primary School Teachers. In these regulations the government made it abundantly clear that it would not tolerate the participation of teachers in any politically oriented activities or discussions.[1] With the enactment of such measures it became clear that the liberal atmosphere of the early Meiji years was rapidly disintegrating, and that in its place the worn-out face of traditional Confucianism was once again rearing its ugly head.

But to fully appreciate the background of the Imperial Rescript on Education, we must take two other conditions into consideration.

The first was the widespread recognition among the leaders of the Meiji government that intellectual life in Japan had become terribly confused and chaotic. This apprehension was based on their observation of the bitter conflicts between, for example, the growing legion of Christians and the fervent adherents of Japanism (nihonshugi). This tension was most apparent in the squabbles that arose over the proper character of moral education, and was reflected in the eyes of those political leaders who feared that within that ideologically divisive environment it would soon become impossible for them to firmly fix the foundations of a universally binding and respected "national morality."

The second major factor underlying the decision to promulgate an Imperial Rescript on Education (Kyōiku Chokugo) was tied up with the problem of the unequal treaties Japan was forced to sign with the great powers of the West.[2] To revise these treaties, which the Tokugawa leadership had agreed to only when faced with the invading ships of the United States and the European powers, Japan had to take on the form of a modern state, which meant formulating a constitution and completing the erection of a legal system. In the last analysis this meant importing into Japan a modern European form of legal machinery. The problem with this, however, from the standpoint of the leaders of the Meiji State, was that it only added to their already considerable anxieties about the leveling and destruction of the traditional Japanese view of order and the principles of family organization which they wanted to make the ideological justification of their own revolutionary seizure of political power.

It was within the context of this second crisis that the Meiji leaders became aware of another serious problem that threatened their hold on power, namely the problem of what would happen when Japanese

[1] See Chapter 10, on in-service training for teachers, for a more detailed discussion of these regulations.

[2] In these treaties Japan granted the rights of extraterritoriality to the states of the West which began in the 1860s to clamor for access to Japan.

society was provided with a modern civil code. Modern civil codes, they fully recognized, constituted the backbones of societies in which individuals could assert their independence and demand the privileges accruing from their rights to live within society as private citizens. The problem with this from the standpoint of the Meiji statesmen was of course that these rights could be asserted in opposition to the collective obligations and requirements of all the members of national society as determined *for the People by the State*. These shrewd political operatives took advantage of the incompatibility between a modern civil code and the traditional family system dominated by a virtually all-powerful father. By establishing an Imperial Rescript on Education, which would ideologically override the "mere legalisms" of a civil code, the founding fathers of the modern Japanese State attempted to foreclose on the unlimited possibilities for new forms of creative human engagement which a society based on respect for the values of individuals and individualism implicitly made conceivable.

It was only to be expected that a bitter conflict would arise between the supporters of Japan's traditional family system and those who were working out a modern legal order based on the principles of natural law. As Hozumi Yatsuka put it: "Civil law leads to the ruin of loyalty and filial piety." In other words, even though the leaders of the new State recognized that implementation of a modern civil code was unavoidable, they were exceedingly uneasy about the likelihood of its setting in motion a chain of events which would result in a leveling of the established principles of social control which they drew upon when exercising their political power. Thus, to placate those who wanted effective counter-measures to minimize the damage which they feared would be done by a new civil code, the government began to think about how it could use the new national system of education to realize its objectives.

In order to give credence to the claim that they were indeed modernizing Japan and successfully convince the Western powers to revise the unequal treaties in ways that would be favorable to Japan, the Meiji statesmen had to give the appearance that they were themselves at the forefront of those leading the social transformation of the nation. To this end they found it necessary to present themselves as thoroughly imbued with the moral sensibilities, habits, and customs of the modern West. Having framed their actions in this manner, these leaders therefore had to accept full responsibility for the confusion which was then plaguing Japanese life. Thus, in response to the ever louder chorus of protest from local officials who felt the strain of the times most acutely, the leaders of the Meiji State decided in 1890 to take firm measures designed to stem the rising tide of "public confusion, moral decay, and laxity in social discipline."

It was against this background that the Imperial Rescript on Education was drafted and promulgated in October of 1890. Modelled after the Imperial Rescript to Soldiers and Sailors (1882), its purpose was to impart the same spirit of selfless dedication to the State through the nation's educational institutions.

To today's eye the Rescript appears as a series of piously vague statements about the duties of loyal Imperial subjects; in the context in which it was written, however, it was a masterful formulation of the moral base created to mandate the switch in people's loyalties from family and clan to Emperor and nation.[3]

How did its authors see the essential nature of a desirable national character? Their approach to this problem arose from the contemporary debates concerning the true nature of moral training, debates wherein it had been claimed that the Japanese masses had nothing to provide them with a moral foundation the way Christianity did for the European masses. To fill this void the Meiji leaders decided to make the Emperor the foundation of a new national morality, and to this end they transformed the ancient mythic beliefs in "a single line of Emperors from time immemorial" (*bansei ikkei*) and the "essential national polity" (*kokutai*) into the foundations of a modern reactionary ideology. Thus the Emperor-State was created and education made into one of its most important structural elements.

II. Characteristics of the Imperial Education Apparatus

A. The National Polity as Fountainhead of Education

The ideology of the Japanese Imperial State rested upon the special relationships "between the Emperor and His subjects" as they were proclaimed by the Imperial Constitution (1889), the Imperial Rescript on Education (*Kyōiku Chokugo*) (1890), and the Imperial Rescript to Soldiers and Sailors (1882). Therein we find that while "His August Reverence" was the "sole source of sovereignty" and the "ultimate wielder of political power," he was also the living manifestation of all the spiritual values and moral tenets directly inherited from his Imperial ancestors.

The idea of locating the emperor at the center of national morality

[3] The full text of the Imperial Rescript on Education will be found in Appendix I, page 399.

(*kokumin dōtoku*) and national education (*kokumin kyōiku*) represented the Meiji political leaders' resolution of the problem of how to create
a populace imbued with a consciousness of themselves "as loyal Japanese." The idea of using education to solidify the Japanese people
under the banner of an Imperial State became particularly appealing
and was adopted at the moment when, in the face of the populist
arguments of the Popular Rights Movement (*jiyū minken undō*), an
impasse had been reached in the attempts to balance individual liberty
and State independence on the one hand and popular sovereignty and
State authority on the other. Adoption of an ideology that allowed
education to be dominated by the Imperial State signaled the Meiji
leaders' resolve to reject the claims of those who had been insisting
that individual liberty and popular sovereignty were fitting goals for
social life in the new Japan of the late nineteenth century.

Mori Arinori, the first Minister of Education, was in the forefront
of the efforts to realize this "spirit" of the times. Upon receiving his
appointment from Prime Minister Itō Hirobumi, Mori instituted an
elaborate system of School Edicts (*Gakkōrei*) that fortified the foundations of national education. Mori conceived the task of national
education to be "the cultivation and development of the national
will and resolve." He located the source of this "will" in the essential
national polity (*kokutai*) and described it as follows:

> The Japanese Emperor and the *kokutai* will continue on without
> end since it has never been and will never be humiliated by the
> acts of foreign nations. Since the beginning of our history the
> Japanese people have protected the nation by being brave, loyal,
> and obedient. They have always been cultivated to think and
> act this way. This is the superb treasure of the Japanese nation
> which is unmatched by any other people. It contains the secret
> power by means of which Japan will become rich, strong, and
> without peers in the community of nations. Based on this unique
> spiritual inheritance, our educational system must strive to keep
> the character of our people moving forward and upward.
>
> Education produces good subjects when the proper discipline
> is provided by teachers. The principle of education shall hereafter
> be to cultivate persons who will be the faithful subjects required
> by the Empire, subjects who will do their utmost to discharge
> their duties to the Empire. And what does it mean to discharge
> these duties? It means being firm in one's resolve to work for the
> State as befits one's position and station in life.

The Imperial Constitution also recognized the foundation of the Japanese State's existence in the national polity as apotheosized in the slogan *bansei ikkei*: "a single line of Emperors unbroken for all ages eternally." The author of the Imperial Constitution, Itō Hirobumi, clarified the meaning of this unparalleled authority when he wrote in his *Commentary on the Constitution* (1888):

> In our classical texts we are instructed that Amaterasu Ōmikami [the first god in the Japanese pantheon] said, "Japan shall be ruled by my descendants continuously; therefore my descendants shall go there and govern the people.

In Itō's formulation, a national polity of eternal Imperial rule led to an inescapable demand for total allegiance to the values mandated by the Imperial system of government. The Imperial Rescript on Education, promulgated shortly thereafter, was put forth as the fountainhead of Japan's national education. Inoue Tetsujirō, Professor of Philosophy at the Imperial University in Tokyo and one of the most powerful ideologues of the Imperial system, wrote in his officially authorized and influential *Commentary on the Imperial Rescript* (1891) that the Rescript encompassed all the wisdom of the myths of the national foundation (*chōkoku*) extending from Niniginomikoto (the first spirit in the myths of Japan's creation) to Jimmu Tennō (the first emperor according to legend). As can be readily understood from this conception of education centered on the primacy of the Imperial Rescript, the function of teaching was to instill in the Japanese people the spirit of loyalty and patriotism. Beginning from the myths of national foundation, the overriding task of this educational enterprise was therefore to internalize the consciousness of being a loyal Imperial subject at the center of a publicly mandated and universally shared value system.

Minister of Education Yoshikawa Akimasa gave expression to the spirit informing this program of national education through public schooling when he wrote, on the occasion of the distribution of copies of the Rescript:

> All educators should never lose sight of the need to cultivate themselves by relying upon the spirit of the Emperor as revealed in this Rescript. On ceremonial days and on other convenient occasions students shall be assembled, especially in schools, read the Rescript, taught how to properly recite it, and given the proper explanation in an easy-to-understand manner.

Thus in the Meiji State the ideology of the national polity (*kokutai*) occupied the premier position in the inculcation of a national morality (*kokumin dōtoku*). Already by the end of the first decade of Meiji rule the problem of how to organize moral education had become a focal point of much heated controversy. For conservative-minded thinkers like Nishimura Shigeki the problem took the form of creating a source of authority that could fulfill the role played in the civilization of the European countries by Christianity. Officially given the responsibility of compiling textbooks for courses in morality (*shūshin*), Nishimura adopted a Confucian perspective and explained the meaning of the Imperial Rescript:

> In the various European countries Christianity provides the foundations of national morality. In Prussia the Kaiser is also the supreme religious figure, and the people believe in him deeply and obey him. Thus in some of the most powerful countries in the world even today people are governed by imperial despots who control both politics and religion. . . . In Japan, even though we have an unequalled Imperial system, it is not yet understood that the Emperor system must be the foundation of moral education. Our educators do not yet understand this, and public opinion still searches wildly for the proper foundations of moral education. This is an unforgivable mistake. We must make the Imperial Throne the fountainhead of morality itself, and in our schools the Throne must directly control moral education. The Ministry of Education should be limited to regulating intellectual and physical education. When our system is so corrected, the Japanese Empire will increasingly flourish.

Whether (as in Nishimura's formulation) the Emperor was the "fountainhead of morality" or (as in Mori Arinori's) the *kokutai* was the "source of an unparalleled moral capital," the basic motif of cultivating Imperial Japan's national morality occupied the central position in the thinking of those responsible for formulating the State's educational agenda. It is important to recognize that the Imperial Rescript on Education was not merely an expression of Imperial beneficence, as even today some like to think, but was an expression of the supreme standard of education in prewar Japan. This is testified to in part by the famous prewar constitutional scholar Hozumi Yatsuka, who described its essence in his "Address on the National Morality":

> It should go without saying that the essence of education resides

in the Imperial Rescript. However, there are some people who mistakenly think that the character of the Rescript is like the teachings of wise men of the past, and they don't understand its efficacy as a national law. It should be made clear in the first place that this Rescript has been created by an act of the Emperor's political will and gives us the supreme principle for our education. Therefore it is impudent to even compare this exalted Rescript with the mere writings of wise men.

The Imperial Rescript was designed to preside over the inner life of the nation, and was legally explained as an exercise of the Emperor's inherent powers of supreme control. It was criticized in the constitutional thought of the times: some legal scholars opined that, because it was neither a law nor an ordinance, the people were not obligated to obey the Rescript as if it were a law. However, while the Rescript did not take the form of a legal stipulation, its contents possessed a binding power which was repeatedly manifested in other Imperial mandates and decrees.

B. Academic and Educational Freedom

In Japan, "academic freedom" had a very different lineage from that in the West, where it emerged as the outgrowth of a deep concern with civil liberties. In Japan academic and educational freedom was always associated with special privileges.

In the Japanese Imperial State there was no room for academic or educational freedom. In his *Commentary* Itō Hirobumi offered the following explanation for the failure to provide for these freedoms in the Imperial Constitution:

> Academic and educational freedoms are indeed clearly spelled out in the constitutions of many countries. . . . However, if we endorse the same liberties, we will in the future, without fail, be visited by every imaginable sort of disputation (*giron*), with the result that the Government's authority will be severely impaired.

What about the freedoms of thought and belief? Article 28 of the Meiji Constitution recognized religious freedom, with the provision:

> This [freedom] is limited to beliefs which do not disturb public order and which do not counsel violation of the duties properly expected of Imperial subjects.

Furthermore, while Shintoism was declared to have a nonreligious status—an indispensable move in the creation of the dialectic of the *kokutai*—it was actually afforded the standing of an official State religion. In effect this meant that the Imperial Japanese State was constructed as a pseudo-religious entity whose spiritual values were rooted in the closely related existence of the Emperor and the *kokutai*. This led to a restriction of the freedoms of thought, belief, speech, and education, in the name of the State's authority. The suppression of thought and the undermining of education were not, as some like to argue, excessive abnormalities arising during the period of Japan's militaristic fascism. They were not signs of the pathological breakdown of the Imperial State; they were the very principles by means of which it sustained itself.

Let us consider the Uchimura Kanzō Incident (1891) in this light. Uchimura, who refused to bow before the Imperial Rescript because of his Christian beliefs, was dismissed from his teaching position at the First Higher School in Tokyo. Similar incidents took place in Nagoya and Kumamoto. These were the first cases of heresy in the Imperial State, and the refusal of the government to yield led to a clash between education and religion.

These incidents and the controversies surrounding them are instructive because they reveal the structural relations between the forces of authority and the cries for freedom in the prewar Imperial State. Moreover, as symbols of the usurpation of freedom of thought and belief, they are benchmarks in Japanese intellectual history.

In the forefront of those making capital out of these incidents was Imperial University Professor of Philosophy Inoue Tetsujirō, who bitterly attacked Christianity as an ideology in opposition to the *kokutai* in his essay "The Collision between Education and Religion" (*Kyōiku Jiron*, November 1891).

The counterattacks on Inoue launched by Uchimura's defenders reveal a clear grasp of the relation between political power and religious ethics under the tightening grip of the Imperial State structure. The principles of intellectual freedom evidenced here occupy an important position in the intellectual legacy of Meiji Japan. The main defenders of Uchimura, the prominent Meiji-era Christians Oshikawa Katayoshi and Uemura Masahisa, charged in their joint declaration:

The idea that the Emperor is a god and that he must be religiously worshipped is equivalent to putting shackles on a person's conscience, and means the usurpation of the individual's freedom to serve his own chosen god.

Kanamori Tsūrin wrote in the *Christian Newspaper*:

Even if it [the Imperial Rescript] were a government-issued ordinance, it would be impossible to obey without violating one's own conscience.

In response to Inoue Tetsujirō, Uchimura declared in "Current Arguments on Religion and Morality" (*Nihon Hyōron*, nos. 49–51):

The political monarch must not violate the individual's conscience, and he must not trespass on the sacred domains that belong exclusively to the Creator.

Here we can see an impassioned insistence upon the need to demarcate the boundaries between worldly authority and a privatized space in which freedom of conscience would be recognized as legitimate.

Ōnishi Hajime, a professor at the Christian-founded Dōshisha University, argued in "The Problem of Christianity" (*Kyōiku Jiron*, June 1891) that the principles of ethics should not be advocated behind the shield of the Imperial Rescript, but should be "freely investigated." He also insisted that the freedoms of learning and religion must not be prohibited under the guise of preserving the "security and peaceful order of the State" (*kokka no annei*).

In Kashiwagi Gi'en's refutation of Inoue, we find a harsh indictment of the State-centered ideology of nationalism:

If the State becomes the only spiritual center, and the individual's conscience and reason have no standing against the State, the people will be made into slaves of the State, its mere instruments. Christianity, from its very beginnings, has been incompatible with this type of thinking. . . . If it is the spirit of the Imperial Rescript to suggest such a state of affairs, then it is most certainly an unconstitutional document.

The current-day proclamations of loyalty and filial piety [*chūkō*] are nothing other than an excuse for obstructing freedom of thought, for suppressing man's reason, and a tool for the self-embellishment of hypocrites. ["The Imperial Rescript and Christianity," *Dōshisha Bungaku*, nos. 59–60]

In the Imperial State, however, there were no principles of tolerance which would allow such precious declarations to receive official recognition and a proper response. Indeed, as political scientist Maruyama Masao has said:

Through the promulgation of the Imperial Rescript, the Japanese State served notice of the fact of its own intrinsic ethical character, and that thereafter it would monopolize and officially determine the contents of all values. [*Gendai Seiji no Shisō to Kōdō*, 1964; published in English by Oxford University Press as *Thought and Behavior in Modern Japanese Politics*]

The problem of the clash between education and religion only served to make this all the more clear.

These incidents reveal in unmistakable outline the essence of the Imperial system and its vision of the *kokutai*. With the Emperor as both the supreme political and the supreme spiritual authority, this system was directly opposed to Christianity's very existence since it both legitimated and demanded the invasion of any corner of inner space (and the freedom and values implied therein) by the bearers of political authority. This Imperial system taught its administrative elite to severely restrict the freedoms of belief and scholarship and, when that proved insufficient, legitimated their exorcising of all undesirable heresies.

The Imperial educational system made the cultivation of the national ideology (*kokutai kannen*) and the teaching of the morality of the harmony of loyalty and filial piety (*chūkō itchi*) its central tasks, and crowned itself with the Imperial Rescript at its apex. Moreover, the separation of scholarship and education provided the grounds for the restriction of educational freedom. The principle of this separation became an accepted tenet after being formulated by Minister of Education Mori. In an address to the heads of local government and local education at the Miyagi Prefectural Office in 1887, Mori criticized previous educational edicts precisely because they had failed to make this distinction, and set forth what he perceived to be the necessary nature of this separation:

Education is the enterprise which gives intellectual, moral, and physical guidance to children. In the final analysis it should not be undertaken in response to the demands of the child himself, but must be moved entirely by the directions of others. As for scholarship, it is specialized academic work conducted on the basis of individual choice. Others can only give direction concerning its methods. The Imperial University is the locus of scholarship; the primary and lower middle school is the locus of education. In particular, the upper middle school belongs to the category of half scholarly, half educational enterprise.

The distinction between scholarship and education was rooted in the imperative to make schools the locus for the creation of national morality. For this reason, it was thought quite permissible to distort scholarly truths in the schools. In addition, the school system was an apparatus for assigning talented people to their "proper place" in society—in other words, a means for creating social order. The distinction between scholarship and education corresponded to the distinction between educational objectives at the various levels in the school system. Mori defined the character of the various schools:

> The primary and ordinary [*jinjō*] middle schools are places whose objectives are to give education in practically useful things, and . . . their graduates will upon graduation immediately either enter the working world or take up specialized studies of a decidedly practical nature. The higher middle schools are for those who are fit to enter the top levels of society. They are places designed to cultivate those who will wield the most decisive influence over the mental life of society. If they enter government they will be the highest-ranking officials, if they enter the commercial world they will be its top managerial class, and if they enter the academic world they will become the specialists leading the development of our arts and sciences.

Following the higher middle school was the Imperial University, which, according to Article I of Mori's Imperial University Edict, was commissioned to investigate abstract principles and metaphysical propositions (*unnō*) and to offer instruction designed to produce an elite educated in the fine points of law, technology, medicine, and other "arts and sciences" necessary for the State's development.

In short, the university was to be a place for the creation of the highly talented people who would serve the interests of the Imperial Japanese State.

Responding to the furor stirred up by the Seven Professors Incident (Teidai Nana Hakushi Jiken),[4] Inoue Tetsujirō wrote an essay entitled

---

[4] At the time of the conclusion of the Russo-Japanese War, in 1905, seven professors at the Tokyo Imperial University issued a manifesto demanding that the government not acquiesce in the humiliating conditions provided for by the impending cessation of hostilities. In response the government declared that professors at the Imperial University had no right to criticize the policies of the government. The seven—one of whom was Inoue Tetsujirō—countered that they in fact had this right within the context of university autonomy. Although the militarist-nationalist views of the professors in this case were in contrast to those of many academics today, the case marked the beginning of the struggle for university autonomy in Japan.

"Teikoku Daigaku Ron" ["On the Imperial Universities"], which appeared in the January 1906 issue of the journal *Taiyō*. Inoue argued for the necessity of keeping the Imperial universities independent from the political power of the State. As the Imperial universities had already established their curriculum, and since they were completely different from the privately organized technical and professional schools which to Inoue were little more than "quick training schools," he argued that the special privilege of autonomy should be awarded only to the State-sponsored institutions. Inoue's theory that university independence was a special preserve of the Imperial institutions was opposed to the understanding of scholarship that was being propounded by schools such as Tokyo Senmon Gakkō, the forerunner of today's private Waseda University.

The foundations of a system of national education were laid by the end of the 1880s along the elitist lines articulated by Inoue. In the later years of the Meiji era, textbooks were nationalized and instruction in morals (*shūshin*) was made the premier subject in the official curriculum. All textbooks were, according to a Ministry of Education directive, to be compiled so as to realize the purposes set forth in the Imperial Rescript on Education. In response to the Lèse-Majesté Incident in 1910 and the Northern and Southern Dynasties controversy in 1911,[5] a National Morality Movement (Kokumin Dōtoku Undō) was initiated which led to a reaffirmation of the separation between scholarship and education: the fixed point for making all educational decisions—on, for example, the content of education or the composition of textbooks—was to be found in the perspective of national morality. In this context, it came to be seen as only natural to distort any inconvenient truth or reality.

Inoue Tetsujirō, at the time of the controversy over the Northern and Southern Dynasties, declared:

When doing research and making judgments on one and the same historical reality, there are of course two attitudes we can take. First, with regard to reality as reality, we must conduct our inquiries in a scientific manner, without sticking to questions of right and wrong, good and bad. In the other case we are obliged to pursue our researches and make our judgments from the viewpoint of the national morality. In other words, I am talking about placing the major focus on the issue of what is good or bad for

---

[5] In the Lèse-Majesté Incident (Taigyaku Jiken), a group of anarchists and communists were accused of plotting to assassinate the Meiji Emperor. In the Northern and Southern Dynasties controversy, over the legitimacy of the Imperial succession, claims to primacy were made for two branches of the Imperial family.

the State. And it should go without saying that in the case of our National Textbooks, the principle of selection is not to be found in the first of these attitudes.

Thus we find the separation of scholarship and education mandated by the demands inherent in the dissemination of the *kokutai* ideology. This separation was a necessary part of the program by means of which the *kokutai* ideology was injected into the national life through the tightly controlled system of national education. It was also at this time that Uesugi Shinkichi started to launch his attacks on Minobe Tatsukichi's Emperor-as-organ-of-the-State theory.[6]

During a brief period in the Taishō era (1912–1926) ideas about a democratized society were widely aired, and a movement for a freer education took off under the leadership of a number of artists and educators at private schools. However, as Japan started down the road leading to war in the early Shōwa era (1926–1989), the possibility for expressing the kinds of freedoms embodied in these movements was smothered.

The total ascendancy of the policy of using education for the unabashed instilling of *kokutai* ideology is seen in the National Schools Edict (Kokumin Gakkōrei) of March 1, 1941, in which the educational apparatus was recomposed for total national unity under wartime conditions. Its declared objective—"The National Schools shall conduct primary education in accordance with the teachings of the Imperial Way, and shall provide the fundamental training required for Imperial subjects"—left no room for confusion about the work of the schools. Regulations Concerning the Enforcement of the National Schools Edict further specified:

(1) In all its endeavors education must work, in reverent acceptance of the principles bestowed in the Imperial Rescript on Education, to give training in the Way of the Imperial State, and in particular to deepen faith and conviction in the *kokutai*.

(2) Along with a clarification of the special character of our Na-

[6] Minobe Tatsukichi, a constitutional scholar and professor at Tokyo Imperial University, contended that sovereign power rested with the State and that the Emperor's power derived from his position as an organ of the State under the Constitution. Needless to say, this theory, although it enjoyed ascendancy during the Taishō years (1912–1926), was not popular with nationalists, and at the latter gained power during the late 1920s, the Emperor-as-organ theory was denounced as *lèse-majesté*; in 1935 Minobe was denounced and forced to resign all his public posts. Uesugi Shinkichi, a fellow professor at the Imperial University Faculty of Law, was an exponent of the *kokutai* theory of constitutionalism and an early opponent of Minobe.

tional Culture, education must strive to enrich the temperament and quality of the Empire's servants, based on an awareness of the Imperial State's position and destiny within both Asia and the world at large.

This document went on to define the objectives of the course in national studies (*kokuminka*):

This course will yield mastery in the areas of our National Morality, National Language, History, Geography, National Strength, and, through clarification of the brilliance of the *kokutai*, cultivate the National Spirit and help develop the proper consciousness of our Imperial Destiny.

Even the universities did not remain free from the spellbinding power of nationalism. It had already been declared in the University Edict of 1886 that scholarly inquiries were to be directed towards "practical sciences" in response to the "needs of the State." The Edict of 1918 mandated that "attention should be paid to the cultivation of National Thought [*kokka shisō*]," and in 1937, when the government had come under the control of the fascistic militarists, the universities were urged anew to function as "seats of learning for the important needs of the State and to help realize in concrete form the Cardinal Principles of the National Polity" (*Kokutai no Hongi*, 1937).[7]

The educational authorities reiterated at this time that "a clear distinction exists between scholarly research and what should be taught to students," and that "instruction must not be offered in either inappropriate or unperfected doctrines." The theory of the separation of scholarship and education, which had originally made it possible to place education under the State's control, at last destroyed all traces of academic freedom, and scholarship was itself drawn into the web of State control. Even the elitist theories of people like economist Kawai Eijirō (who introduced the English Hegelian Thomas Hill Green's thought to Japan and who argued that even if there was no freedom in society at large, freedom should be guaranteed in the universities) eventually lost their efficacy.

Thus in Japan's education before and during the war, from primary school right on up to the university, truth was hidden and perverted, the individuality of children and adolescents was negated, and human

---

[7] *Kokutai no Hongi*, authored and published by the Ministry of Education, played an important role in ideological mobilization for war.

nature itself was abused. "Education" was nothing but a "domestication" of the Japanese people designed to render them instruments of the State and fit them into the desired mold of an exalted Imperial community.

The path that eventually led to Japan's devastation in war inevitably followed in the wake of the process by means of which the bonds between scholarship and education were severed. Once again I should like to make it clear that, far from being a pathological breakdown of the Imperial system, this was the unavoidable consequence of its very essence.

C. The Concept of Compulsory Education

Japan's modern educational system was initiated in 1872 with the proclamation of the *Gaku-Sei* (Basic Code of Education), and, through Minister of Education Mori's various School Edicts (*gakkōrei*) of the late 1880s, the basic prewar model was essentially articulated. The centrality of the position occupied by the educational apparatus within the grand scheme of the Japanese Imperial State was reaffirmed by the Imperial Rescript on Education (1890) and subsequent revisions of the Primary School Edict (*Shōgakkōrei*).

Although the *Gaku-Sei* and the 1879 Educational Edict (*Kyōikurei*) encouraged universal school enrollment, the systems they inaugurated were not obligatory in any legally binding sense. The systematic organization of compulsory education on a strictly enforced legal basis dates rather from Mori's Primary School Edict of 1888.

The legal character of the prewar school system was explained by Kobayashi Utakichi in his *Law of Educational Administration* (1900) as follows:

Education is not simply the development of the individual's abilities, nor should its main principles be derived in accord with the requirements and demands of the individual. Its primary aim is to cultivate Imperial subjects (*shinmin*) for the benefit of the State, citizens who will contribute to its existence and survival. To produce subjects truly worthy of our Empire, in what directions should this cultivation be carried out? The answer lies quite simply in the production of subjects who will be loyal to the Throne and who will aid and support the Eternal Imperial Destiny. Beginning with the cultivation of subjects who are loyal to the Throne, it will become possible to fashion a vision of the State's continued existence and prosperity.

The internal criteria for compelling our subjects to make their children receive an education come from a consideration of the conditions in which the State finds itself and its subjects, and the external ones are based on the needs of our country in its intercourse with other nations. In both instances the primary need is to guarantee our State's survival.

Thus the duty to enroll a child in school was conceived not as a responsibility of the parent to the child, but as the former's responsibility to the State, ultimately enforceable by the power of public law:

This duty is not based on a notion of individual rights and responsibilities, but is something demanded by the State, and something which it is the business of all loyal subjects to faithfully submit to. This obligation is not to the child, but is borne entirely with respect to the State.

This interpretation of the child's guardian's duty to the State may be viewed as a classic expression of the thinking which underlay the system of compulsory education in the Imperial Japanese State.

The Civil Code Controversy

The significance of this conception in the social life of Meiji Japan is highlighted by the controversy over the place of education within the framework of a Civil Code.

A group of scholars led by the Frenchman Gustave Boissonade, an invited advisor to the government, drew up in 1890 the first draft of a Japanese Civil Code based on the Civil Code of France. At the heart of this document was a concept of human rights based on natural law which supported the following interpretation of parental rights regarding education:

Parental rights should not be given for the sake of the parent, but for the benefit of the child. The child's education is the parents' responsibility, not their right. All rights belong to the child; the parent only has the responsibility to guarantee their fulfillment.

However, this proposed Civil Code was viciously attacked on the grounds that it was irreconcilable with the spirit expressed in the Imperial Constitution:

Our Constitution declares the Monarch (*kunshu*) to be the very essence of sovereignty, and without His mandate all laws lose their very ground of being. . . . In direct violation of that spirit, this Civil Code seeks to validate the doctrines of natural law which claim that all men are endowed from birth with inalienable rights. In short, it is diametrically opposed to the basic idea and spirit of our *kokutai.*

Because this Civil Law draft advanced the notion that education is a natural right, it pointed out the internal contradiction between the spirit of education and the idea of education as part of the *kokutai* ideology. In this sense it did indeed contain the embryonic beginnings of a challenge to the legitimacy of the Imperial education system. In the end, however, the idea of a nationalistically oriented education proved so overwhelmingly strong that there was no room left for the successful germination of these ideas about education as a basic human right.

The "contradiction between civil law and education" reflected the same fundamental conflict I already analyzed in discussing the "clash between religion and education." In short, the inviolability of the State-centered system of education was used as a pretext for crushing both the freedom of conscience implied by the existence of religion and the concept of human rights implicitly contained in these attempts to formulate a Civil Code. Of course this "education" was nothing more than a form of indoctrination that was conducive to the Imperial system and the requirements of its nationalistic ideology. Using the pretense of Imperial authority, the agents of the State assumed the right to totally monopolize and control the world of education. This was most clearly manifested in a view of education that saw it as the best means for "settling in advance" all potentially threatening issues. In this fashion the progressive idea of education as a right was effectively smashed while still in an embryonic stage by being linked to publicly unacceptable ideas of religion and civil law.

This controversy ended with a victory for the anti-natural-law faction and the Civil Code being redrafted.[8] Its Article 820 finally defined parental authority in terms of the parent's right to custody of the child, but subordinated this to their responsibilities to the State, for example the duty to make sure the child was educated. This reveals the enormous obstacles put in the path of those who tried to establish a discourse in Japan on the idea of children's rights.

Within the context of the semi-feudal social relations of the family-

[8] The French law-inspired draft was dropped in 1892; the revised Code, modeled on German law, went into effect in 1898.

State (*kazoku kokka*) ideology of Imperial Japan, the development of a body of civil law represented one of the most anguishing phases of our country's modernization. During the proceedings conducted by the Committee Investigating a Civil Code, doubts were raised concerning the stipulation of parental powers. Hozumi Yatsuka declared:

> Let's exclude mention of the responsibilities that the parent has to the child. . . . After all, the child's custody and education are the parent's privilege.

And even Ozaki Saburō, a legal scholar who leaned towards democratic interpretations, said:

> Custody and education of the child are obligations to the State. . . . It is therefore the height of insolence to even consider the child being given rights to demand anything.

These remarks clearly reflect the officially mandated position of the child in the Japanese family. There was no room whatsoever, from this perspective, for the idea that children have any rights. In fact, the very idea of such rights was seen as a sign of disloyalty to the State and as a lack of obedience and duty to the parent.

Even in the works of Hozumi Shigetō, who is today highly regarded for his early advocacy of the nuclear family and its legal legitimacy, the notion of children's rights was rejected. In his main work, *Family Law (Shinzokuhō)* (1933), Hozumi argued:

> Up to now, parental power has been viewed from the side of the parent's rights, but I think it would be preferable from this time on to see this as a parental obligation. Of course there may be those who immediately object that this leads to an undesirable advocacy of the child's right to receive an education, but this criticism is based on the fallacy that the beneficiary of an obligation automatically has a right to its receipt. However, this is not so. The parent's obligation to see that his child is educated is not one to the child, but should be construed as an obligation to State-society (*kokumin kokutai*).

It is important to note that this conceptualization of parental obligation was based on the notion that all responsibilities were to the State. It showed absolutely no respect at all for the idea of the rights of children. This was an inseparable element in the network of rights and responsibilities required to uphold the ideology of the family-state.

Interpretations of parental powers such as Hozumi's that denied the existence of the child's rights were in fact the commonly accepted ones. According to a widely consulted educational dictionary of the time:

> The obligation [of compulsory education] is one the State requires from the child's guardian by public law so that the State can realize its own purposes. It does not have any standing in private law as an expression of the guardian's obligation to the child.

It was also firmly declared that arguments such as those voiced in foreign countries which presented this obligation as the parent's duty towards the child had no validity whatsoever in Japan.[9] Thus what people in other modern nations viewed as essentially a problem of private law was expropriated by the Imperial State for its own single-minded interests.

Dissenting Views

Of course it does not follow that there was no discourse at all in prewar Japan on the child's rights in general, or the child's rights to an education in particular.

These concerns, as we have seen, first appeared in the Meiji *Keimō* (Enlightenment) Movement and the Freedom and People's Rights Movement led by Ueki Emori. (For example, see the *New Education Journal* [*Kyōiku Shinshi*] established in 1878).

The program of Japan's first socialist party, the Shakai Minshu Tō (1901), stated the following position: "Education is the fountainhead of human activity, and all citizens have a right to receive an education provided at the public's expense." And even in the earlier dispute over parental powers in the Committee Investigating a Civil Code, scholar of French law and Boissonade disciple Ume Kenjirō argued in opposition to Hozumi Yatsuka: "Parents have an inescapable obligation to see to their children's education. This obligation is not to the State but to the child." The original (but ultimately rejected) draft of the Civil Code firmly insisted: "All rights belong to the child. Mothers and fathers only have obligations."

Against the background of democratic thought and the flourishing labor and educational movements of the Taishō era (1912–1926) Shi-

---

[9] Here is an example of the use of tradition as a pretext for keeping politically destabilizing influences from working within Japanese society.

monaka Yasaburō declared, "Receiving an education is not a duty of the members of society but their right."[10] In *Reconstruction of Education* (1921), Shimonaka argued for a total organization of national education focused on the "right to learn" (*gakushūken*), viewing it as "one part of mankind's right to existence." In response to the extension of compulsory education taking place at that time, he charged, "This is merely a strengthening of the system of forced education from the perspective of nationalism." However, these claims must be recognized as merely exceptions to the overwhelmingly powerful currents of thought legitimated by the ideology of the Imperial educational system.

Even today the prewar mode of thinking persists, in spite of the fact that our Constitution clearly affirms the child's right to an education. For example, Professor Wagatsuma Sakae of the University of Tokyo Faculty of Law writes, "The nurturing, custody and educating of children is one of the most important responsibilities the parent bears towards State-society." And Aoyama Michio has declared, "I would like to think that, just as Hozumi Shigetō advocated, the obligation to provide care and education for their children is the parent's obligation to the State." Thus we see that this ideology continues to wield a strong influence over the commentaries and interpretations of civil law by the leading scholars in this field of law. These interpretations of parental powers have stood as major obstacles to the realization of both the general idea of children's rights and the specific idea of education as a human right. In order for these ideas to truly take root in Japan, it is imperative for us to do battle with the remnants of this conception of compulsory education.

Unfortunately, however, it is all too clear that the prewar conception of compulsory education still exerts a powerful influence over the educational thinking of the Japanese people. Moreover, the idea of the parent's obligation to the Imperial State has been redesigned in the postwar environment to mean an obligation to the welfare state and the ideology of the collective public good. This concept of the welfare state has given new life to the prewar sense of obligation and has provided a potent theoretical weapon for the use of those who wish to vitiate the central ideas of the postwar Constitution.

D. The Special Character of Educational Administration

Under the Meiji Constitution, education was categorized as one of

[10] Shimonaka Yasaburō was a teacher who organized the Keimeikai, Japan's first teachers' union, in 1918. He was the first to use the term "right to learn" (*gakushūken*) with reference to the child.

the Imperial prerogatives, and through the formula "State=Emperor" the actual control of education fell into the hands of the State bureaucracy. The purpose of education, as I have noted, was the formation of national morality in accord with the dictates of the Imperial Rescript. Within the framework of this ideology, the concrete determination of educational policy was placed beyond the reach of all duly constituted legislative bodies, and was presented in the form of Imperial Decrees (*chokurei*). Thus, for example, the Primary School or University Edicts, which determined the fundamental objectives for their respective educational organs, did not emerge as pieces of legislation ratified by the Japanese Diet, but were promulgated in the name of the Emperor. Of course these Imperial Orders were nothing more than legal fictions; in reality they were all issued by the Imperial bureaucracy in collaboration with the military and the elder statesmen (*genrō*) who ruled Meiji Japan in collegial fashion.

The use of Imperial Decrees in the dissemination of educational policy reveals that education had fallen under the total control and direction of the bureaucracy. The principle of control by decree was supported by the fact that the Imperial Constitution contained no provisions whatsoever regarding the regulation of education. This was reaffirmed in 1890 during discussions on regular revision of the Primary School Edict. At that time the formal mechanism of the Imperial Decree was triumphantly reasserted as the one and only legitimate means for issuing educational policy, and all arguments that these issues be submitted to the deliberative process of the legislature were resoundingly turned back.

The notion of what constituted the proper procedures of educational administration also fell under the sway of the ideology of State authority, in particular as one part of the Home Ministry's[11] program for the preservation of peace and public order.[12] There was also a strong tendency to think of the schools themselves as one part of the State's administrative apparatus. Thus from the point of view of legal theory no distinction was made between education and educational administration, and the commonly accepted view saw school education as an agency of State authority. Theories like those of Minobe Tatsukichi,

---

[11] The *Naimushō* was the ministry (1873–1947) that controlled the police in prewar Japan, and also had authority over many aspects of social policy, including education.

[12] In the name of preserving peace and public order (*chian*), several repressive legal measures curtailing free speech and organization were implemented early in the twentieth century. The best known of these was the Peace Preservation Law (Chian Iji Hō), passed in 1925 and rescinded in October 1945.

which demonstrated that this was an abuse of the concept of authority, were dismissed as being merely divergent opinions.

The system developed for administratively controlling the inner workings of the educational process had its own unique character as well. Matters pertaining to the content of the curriculum were placed under the direct jurisdiction of the State in the name of the Emperor, while the day-to-day management of schools was entrusted to local government officials. The school itself was subject to administrative management as a public building (*eizōbutsu*). Within the school, special power relationships ensured that the teacher had to submit to the control of the principal, who in turn was made totally submissive to the Ministry of Education's school inspectors. The entire process of control was extra-legal from beginning to end. Even though it was all legally legitimated under the auspices of the State, which made educational control one part of administrative law, there was no room whatsoever in this conception for the existence of a system of educational law based on the logic and intrinsic values of education.

In short, under the educational administration of the Japanese Imperial State, the spiritual freedom of the individual was treated as if it were worth nothing. The diverse possibilities of each individual human were held back, and in most cases prevented from seeing the light of day. Such was the reality of the national polity of our Imperial rulers.

III. Human Cultivation in Prewar Japan

I would now like to examine the two distinct forms of human cultivation authorized by the educational system of Japan's Emperor-State: that of an educated elite who would rule, and that of the obedient masses who would follow.

A. The Ideology of Culturalism (*Kyōyōshugi*)

After the forced opening of our country and the initial "European shock," the subsequent Japanese response to Europe was characterized by a widely shared fascination with these foreign cultures but at the same time an overwhelming credulity and impoverished understanding of them. What we had was a posture of accepting enlightenment delivered, as it were, from on high. Fukuzawa Yukichi sharply criticized the absence of self-confidence that marked the response to the European style of learning. In his *Outline of a Theory of Civilization* (1875), he had argued persuasively that it was necessary to grasp European civilization in terms of its fundamental spirit. Accordingly, he insisted, there had to be a thoroughgoing transformation in the "ethos of the Japanese people." This viewpoint, however, definitely remained that of the minority of those concerned with Japan's modernization.

Erwin von Baelz, who was intimately aware of the conditions of Japan's modernization through his work as a lecturer at Tokyo Imperial University, made the following observations on the historical consciousness of those cultivated souls (*kyōyōjin*) who were leading Japan's march into the future:

> The strange thing is that today's Japanese wish to know nothing about their own past. Even so-called men of culture display an inferiority complex when it comes to their past.

In response to Baelz's questioning, these men of learning denied the importance of Japan's own past by dismissing it as "barbaric." "Our history begins from today," they told him.

When we combine Fukuzawa's criticisms with Baelz's observations, the distorted aspect of modern Japanese culturalism (*kyōyōshugi*) is clearly revealed. It was all too easily forgotten that culture must have its roots firmly embedded in historical actualities. What we observe when looking back at this period is little more than a childish pawing at the surfaces of European civilization.

However, after the first phase of vulgar Westernization, a very different face revealed itself.

The Meiji statesman Itō Hirobumi left the following recollection of the character of students during the period when the discourse on popular rights was at its height, and the "learned societies" of the time discussed the teachings of Rousseau and Burke:

> Beginning in the universities and extending to all types of higher schools, students were reciting these works and arguing with one another. However, even if students were discussing these books in school, when they returned home they didn't have the courage to chatter on about Burke's theory of the family in front of their conservative elders.

Indeed, the discourse on popular rights was never very successful beyond the gates of the academies of new learning. Theories of popular sovereignty did not generate the kind of support which would cause the Meiji rulers to seriously fear them. After all, the possessors of the new knowledge that gave rise to such ideas in most cases returned home to become the inheritors of the traditional ethos.

Beginning with Katō Hiroyuki, who later became the first president of Tokyo Imperial University, the leaders of the Meiji Enlightenment very rapidly underwent an about-face that was representative of the culturalist drift of the times. These conversions, inasmuch as they were rooted in the desire for power, were tied to a vulgar utilitarianism. Seen in this light, the spirit which ultimately dominated the Meiji Enlightenment cannot be valued as a truly enlightening one, but should be seen rather as having been utterly steeped in the spiritual void of culturalism (kyōyōshugi)—the ideology of culturalism.

Natsume Sōseki, the novelist and professor of English literature, characterized the civilizing impact of Japan's Enlightenment:

> In a nutshell, the Enlightenment of contemporary Japan has settled on a superficial and vulgar type of civilizing. The Enlightenment we have witnessed is symbolized by the person at a banquet who samples the many dishes laid out in front of him and who, without pausing long enough to appreciate what he has already tasted, quickly goes on to yet another table. How empty are the sensitivities of the people who have been influenced by this Enlightenment. Their hearts must be burdened with heavy frustrations and great uneasiness. ["Gendai Nihon no Kaika," 1911]

As this thoroughly superficial form of enlightenment made further encroachments upon the Japanese spirit, it transformed the fabric of our culture. However, as it still lacked a firm footing, its advocates continued to avoid a radical confrontation with traditional Japanese culture. During the Taishō period (1912–1926) the intelligentsia's absence of contact with social realities worsened to the point that the idea of culturalism became interiorized, abstract, and capricious.

As suggested in the previous chapter, the Meiji leaders' notion of enlightenment from above, in spite of its obvious shortcomings and politically reactionary character, inspired those leaders to believe they had a mission to reform Japanese society by hook or by crook and to lead it into the modern world. In short, their understanding of enlightenment was colored by perceptions of their own political requirements. But after the difficult period that followed the Lèse-Majesté Incident, Taishō culturalism was severed even from these political concerns and became an anti-political meditation on the abstract values of cultural transcendence.

Reflecting the shock produced by the Lèse-Majesté Incident, the novelist Nagai Kafū wrote in his 1912 Kōcha no Ato (After Tea):

For the time being there is nothing else for us to do but write harmless historical dramas replete with beautiful images under the pretext of *l'art pour l'art*. . . . "Harmless" means that it must neither be noxious nor pleasing. These two conditions are not limited only to the world of the arts. To the extent that this haunts every aspect of present-day Japanese life, we are burdened by the handicap of having to resign ourselves to acting by stealth and speaking in whispers. I despair for our future.

In these words of self-scorn we see both Kafū's change of artistic direction (he adopted a pointedly apolitical stance as a writer) and a whole generation of cultured individuals' renunciation of their earlier concerns with social reality in turning towards more meditative interests.

The philosopher Miki Kiyoshi traced the roots of the "culturalism" of these years:

The ideology of culturalism arose in the Taishō period as a reaction to the Meiji Enlightenment. Herein resides the significance of the word *kyōyō* in the history of our country.[13]

The poet Ishikawa Takuboku also drew out, in his essay "Jidai Heisoku no Genjō" ("The Causes of Our Current Silence"), the negative mediations that tied the Meiji Enlightenment to Taishō culturalism and the "dead-end" atmosphere of the time.

According to the philosopher Raphael von Koeber, the "ideology of culturalism" was planted at this time and in this soil. Through his teachings the eyes of Japanese intellectuals were opened to the realm of an inner self and the classics of the West's cultural storehouse.

By the time of von Koeber's arrival in Japan the philosopher Watsuji Tetsurō had already declared his revulsion with "the frivolity and irresponsibility of learned institutions in our country." Sensing this unease, von Koeber dedicated his efforts to the clearing of a path that would lead "to an independent world of scientific research, one that would make possible the spiritual growth and freedom of the Japanese people." In pursuit of these ends von Koeber continuously argued that Japanese intellectuals needed to engage in "classical research and *Philologische Bildung*." He criticized what he saw as the Japanese intellectuals' lack of subjective independence and the way he saw them

---

[13] "My Intellectual History" ("Dokusho Henreki"), *Bungei*, June 1941. A specialist in German idealism and Marxist theory, Miki was imprisoned during the war years for leftist inclinations, and died in prison in 1945.

passively following in the footsteps of the West. He spoke of Japan as a country "caught in the drag nets of Western culture." The severity of Koeber's criticism can still be felt in his remark that the Japanese were not walking about wearing frock coats; rather, he said, frock coats were wearing the Japanese.

The spokesmen for the ideology of culturalism who insisted that it was possible to absorb the spirit of Europe simply through the study of its classics inadvertently revealed a deep sense of despair which drove them to renounce all concerns with "current problems." Yet hidden within the pretense of transcending these problems there lay concealed a very definite anxiety regarding the course that events were taking in the contemporary world.

Sardonically dismissing European theories of "the yellow peril" as so much nonsense, von Koeber was however troubled by what he saw as "Japan's red peril." He expressed his hope that "the interiorized aristocratism of Japanese intellectuals will not be easily agitated by the dreary clamoring for democracy that comes from the newsroom." Thus we can see that Koeberian culturalism and spiritual aristocratism were already being used to formulate styles for opposing democracy and socialism.

It is commonly thought that Koeber's disciple Abe Jirō and the latter's work *Santarō no Nikki* (*Santarō's Diary*) are representative of Taishō culturalism. However, in confused adherence to von Koeber's teaching "Rather than broaden yourself, deepen yourself!" Santarō thought that Christ, Shinran, Nietzsche, and Tolstoy all shared a common set of values. Furthermore, unconscious of his own dilettantism, he lacked the self-confidence necessary for choosing between "this" and "that." Suffering from the conceit of a cosmopolite who fooled himself into believing that he can have "both this and that," Santarō revealed the intellectual and moral poverty of the Taishō man of culture.

Questioning the attitude towards social realities that was shared by those in his milieu, Santarō opined:

> Since what we must concentrate our energies on today is our own selves, I believe our general attitude must be one in which we avoid the complications and dissension that mark actual society.

This attitude led directly to an ideology of personalism and reflected Abe's own response to the political realities of the time. At the time of the Morito Incident[14] he set forth his views in this way:

---

[14] Morito Tatsuo, an assistant professor of economics at Tokyo University, in

Even if I had the ability to discuss the problems raised by these events, there is no freedom to openly discuss them.

From his self-proclaimed "ethical" standpoint, Abe could therefore offer nothing more than noncommittal comments on the affairs of the day.

The discovery of an inner world and the glare of self-fixation that it engendered resulted in the bittersweet works of Tōkoku and Sōseki.[15] Their works are part of the precious intellectual inheritance that entered Japanese life through the discovery of an inner world and the personalities that inhabit it. However, this interior world, severed from everyday actualities and directed away from real-life concerns, was nothing more than a delusion that had already anticipated all possible objections to itself. Obsession with this inner world led to a careless relaxation and loss of mental focus, which manifested itself most clearly in the highbrow dilettantism of the time. The "boundless embrace" of ideas, combined with the absence of a clearly defined center or focus, produced an attitude towards intellectual pursuits that the philosopher Maruyama Masao has called "the construction of the miscellaneous."

The tensions of the Taishō period were mediated on the one hand by postwar prosperity and on the other by heightened worker unrest and the resurrection of a socialist movement. The tendency towards intellectual eclecticism that Taishō culturalism supported was further spurred on by the superficial "liberty" and "democracy" that were widely proclaimed as the ideological mood of the times. In this sense Abe's Santarō was certainly a character who represented Taishō culture and its ideology of elite culturalism. I suspect that even such individuals subjectively struggled to be independent in the world despite their refusal to immerse themselves in it. However, independence implies self-consciousness in matters of choice and judgment about the actions one must take in the social world. In short, independence must be decisively distinguished from mere internalized subjectivity. Thus the very idea of an independent realm of selfhood in which relations with the actual world are severed was the worst kind of willful dissimu-

---

1920 wrote an essay on the Russian anarchist Peter Kropotkin; as a result he lost his academic position and (along with the editor of the journal that published his article) was tried and sentenced to three months in prison. The case became a focal point for discussion of academic and intellectual freedom.

[15] Kitamura Tōkoku was a Meiji-era thinker who focused on the problems of love and selfhood. Natsume Sōseki, the renowned novelist of the Meiji-Taishō eras, wrote a series of novels with the individual and the modern world as an underlying theme.

lation. This could not help but lead to the ultimate forfeiture of self since the quest to consciously unify the self as a self-in-itself (*an sich*) resulted in the loss of any mediative tension. In this sense, the followers of Taishō culturalism, just like Santarō, while subjectively working to develop their individuality, could not help but become dilettantes who expressed limitless interest in a wildly heterogeneous body of things.

Karaki Junzō, who wrote on the spiritual history of Japan as seen through its literature, compared the Taishō ideology of culturalism with traditional Japanese thought about moral and mental culturalism (*shūyō*) and concluded that "style has been lost." For Karaki this represented a treacherous transgression of the Japanese spirit and the exalted status it had awarded to teachers. The attitude which was so offensive to thinkers like Karaki was also visible in the attempt to substitute books for human teachers, for it led to a forfeiture of Japan's own classical tradition. The modern method of asking and answering one's own questions as a way to further inquire into oneself was seen by Karaki as a clear prelude to discarding the inherited forms of culturalism, in which one apprenticed oneself to a teacher and learned by listening to the teacher. Gone was the beauty of training in strict adherence to a fixed form and the experience of instantaneous comprehension (*satori*) that came from following a strictly regimented path to salvation. The ideology of culturalism was thus decried on account of the insufferable intellectuals it gave birth to; their cultural snobbism and contempt for the real world made them totally unfit for all forms of political action except aristocratism. Karaki associated the self-proclaimed superiority of the 1920s "Taishō culturalists" with their attempts to escape from reality and the willful falsifications this required.

In his memoirs Miki Kiyoshi adroitly recreated the intellectual atmosphere of the Taishō period:

At the same time that we encountered the colossal impact of the First World War we were absolutely uninterested in politics. Or perhaps I should say we were *able* to become indifferent. What ruled us rather was the ideology of *kyōyō* [culturalism]. Our contempt for the politicization and valorization of the cultural revealed an anti-political and unpolitical bias.

For the novelist Kafū there were bittersweet rewards associated with an attitude of dissociation from social realities. For one whose ideal was the confluence of artistic and social existence, choosing "an attitude of secession from society" was a form of resistance to the official demand for a type of art that would serve as handmaiden to politics. When the anarchist Ōsugi Sakae and the socialists Arahata Kanson and Sakai Toshiaki began publication of *Kindai Shisō* (*Modern Thought*) in 1912 they were being truthful to the passion for revenge that arose from having been forced to submit to the distortions of the age. Ōsugi described the conditions at the time that he and his colleagues initiated their journal:

> In the aftermath of the so-called Lèse-Majesté Incident we were deprived of all freedoms to openly express our political and economic demands. We were forced to hide our liberal ideas behind scientific, literary, or philosophical banners.

However, the ideology of culturalism that reflected the prosperity of the postwar period, and that made its objective the creation of anti-political selves, was ultimately betrayed by the pride its adherents took in their own activities.

In the end Ōsugi turned out a scathing critique of the culturalist tendencies promoted in this political space:

> To flee from the struggles of life, and to set about devising ways to perfect oneself through addiction to purely meditative concerns or through forms of self-examination unmediated by external reality, is to live a make-believe life of deliberate falsehoods. It provides nothing more than a temporary escape from the real struggles of this world. [*Kindai Shisō*, Vol. 2, No. 12, January 1918]

Commitment to notions of "self-perfection" or the "enrichment of one's soul" obliged the upholders of these ideas to deny anything in the surrounding environment which was deleterious to their solipsistic agendas for refinement. Even Ōsugi Sakae, who barely managed to keep *Kindai Shisō* afloat during the years of transition from Meiji to Taishō rule, declared it in the end to be nothing more than "intellectual masturbation" and ceased its publication.

The social crises of the Shōwa years heavily influenced the emerging character of culturalism. This was nowhere more apparent than in the case of the 1925 Peace Preservation Law and the way it legitimated opposition to the resurgent socialist movement. The turn towards fascism was swiftly expedited on the heels of this well-orchestrated repression. In the aftermath of the fascist triumphs culturalist ideology came to almost completely dominate the consciousness of Japan's youth. I mean this in a most literal sense, for it was culturalism that captured youth rather than they who chose it.

This expanded scope for culturalist refinement was of course part and parcel of the ruling elite's efforts to protect Japanese youth from Marxism. The official policy of "giving proper guidance to public thought" (*shisō zendō*) was based on the foundations already well established by culturalist ideology.

One of the leaders of this drive, Kawai Eijirō,[16] wrote as follows about the motives that had led him in 1936 to edit a book entitled *Gakusei to Kyōyō* (*Students and Cultivation*):

> The ideology which previously commanded the consciousness of our youth led them to objectively dissect and analyze the phenomena they directly encountered. This led them to experience great concern and impatience with the problems of reforming society. ... However, when they actually encounter all the various disturbances and agitations found in the real world of politics and society, they are unable to maintain themselves as beings who are dauntless and unshakable.

For Kawai the challenge facing educators was not how to encourage the development of independent beings who were able to change existing reality, but rather how to cultivate selves who would remain unaffected by transformations in the political and social environments within which they lived. Kawai unabashedly identified "the hope for our future" with a transformation of the accepted understanding of what constituted human culturalism:

> We must change our perspective on education from one concerned with objectivity to one concerned with the culturalism of subjectivity [a sense of self as being in control of one's own fate]. Thus we must lead our youth away from their fumbling and lack of discrimination, and out of the darkness they have wandered into.

It was the duty of educators, Kawai pointedly remarked, to actively engineer and supervise this transformation (*tenkō*).

The passion fueling the claim that what was really needed was a purely "subjective" self led to the wish to deny all forms of independent

---

[16] Kawai was a professor of economics who specialized in the history of social thought. An anti-Marxist liberalist, he had a great influence on many Japanese students of the 1920s and 1930s but became an object of official criticism during the years when fascism was ascendant in Japan.

action in response to actual problems. It also legitimated deep-seated feelings of contempt towards labor. Kawai borrowed the liberal internationalist Nitobe Inazō's distinction between "to do" and "to be" and set them in opposition to each other. For Kawai it went without saying that "to be" was of infinitely greater value:

> The development of character is of far greater value than the pursuit of fame, riches, scholarly knowledge, or the ability to carry through bold undertakings.

One is immediately struck by the extent to which the contents of action (the "to do") are deprived of any real substance. This reflects the emptiness of the culturalist ideology of character in its state of radical severance from the concrete world of doing and acting. But the question "What is a human being?" cannot be answered apart from the question "What does a human being do?" or "What is a human being capable of doing?" I am convinced that it is only when the "to do" and the "to be" are in fact joined that human cultivation becomes truly possible.

Rōyama Masamichi, political scientist at Tokyo Imperial University and one of the authors whose work was included in Kawai's *Students and Cultivation*, argued from a humanistic standpoint that was in opposition to both Marxism and fascism. His aim was "to reconstitute social science itself as a form of culturalism." For Rōyama this meant transforming it from a practical social movement into a form of personal and cultural edification. Thus, under the pretext of "investigating the philosophy and basic problems lying behind modern social ideologies," Rōyama sought to defuse the activist humanism of youth and reconstitute it as a contemplative humanism. These forms of advocacy of "individualized cultural refinement" were tied to an anti-intellectualism which was eminently anti-democratic in character:

> If knowledge is made democratically available to the masses, it will jeopardize the stability of our history, traditions, and authority. The equalization of Japanese life will level all its distinctive features and destroy all our privileges.

Rōyama had a definite prescription for countering these threatening possibilities:

> It is absolutely crucial that the essence of culturalism be rooted in ethical, aesthetic, and sentimental concerns. What should be

officially recognized as intelligence must be controlled by the objectives designated for cultivation. They must generally arise from interests far removed from the concerns of actual social life.

But no matter how earnestly or frequently it was proclaimed that the aims of culturalism were "self-development" and "individual enlightenment," because this aesthetic, philosophical, and meditative culturalism was cut off from all genuine social concerns, it remained fundamentally opposed to all substantive intellectual interests. It could never lead to anything more than a vain and empty form of expectation, and was inevitably degraded into a shallow dilettantism lacking unity, a confused and incoherent field of knowledge. In the volume Kawai edited was an essay by the philosopher Kuwaki Genyoku entitled "Kyōyō toshite no Tetsugaku" ("Philosophy as Cultivation"), in which we can see the full implications of this spurious form of refinement:

> The strength of modern culturalism in comparison with traditional forms of training is that there is no strict obligation to act within a framework of consciousness such as that narrowly and formally expounded by Confucian teachers. The distinctions between purity and impurity or between good and bad are swallowed up in our present practices of culturalism. The point is that in thinking of philosophy as a form of culturalism we must provide wider and more varied types of knowledge rather than foster the powers of discrimination.

In Kuwaki's understanding of culturalism we find the corrupted form of education that inevitably followed from the failure to produce autonomous individuals possessing the capacity to organize and control their knowledge—in short, individuals who could operate on the basis of their own practical wisdom.

While there were differences of nuance and emphasis in the articulations of the ideology of culturalism provided by Kawai, Rōyama, and Kuwaki, their philosophic and contemplative posturing had in common an anti-intellectual and anti-existential character.

Karl Löwith, a philosopher who spent these years in Japan as an invited professor at Tohoku University, offered a most trenchant evaluation of the Japanese students he encountered. While readily acknowledging the diligence with which they studied European writings and their apparent understanding thereof, Löwith remained troubled by what he described as their failure "to extract anything that could enrich the Japanese components of their selfhood." Löwith saw his students living in a two-storied edifice, the top floor of which was appointed in a neatly arranged fashion with elegant scholarship ranging from Platonic to Heideggerian disquisitions, while life on the ground floor preserved the traditional forms of "thinking and feeling in a Japanese way." Löwith was particularly appalled by the total absence of any "ladder" that could connect the two. The attitude towards scholarship promoted by the ideology of culturalism clearly reinforced the tendency towards severance that made thought and action discontinuous. Miscellaneous fragments of knowledge were isolated from one another as discrete instances of insight, and no attempt was made to nurture independent thinkers who could unify this discordant epistemological environment. Accordingly, knowledge was not a living, working force within the bounds of everyday life and praxis. Rather, it was appropriately extracted in response to a particular requirement, in response to utilitarian motives. This was nothing more than a way of showing off one's learning—or, one might say, making sport of it.

The dialectic of thought and action was thus suppressed. As concepts went unmediated by contact with actuality, it became increasingly impossible to test the value of ideas by submitting them to incorporation within a deliberate body of concrete practices. Ultimately, this resulted in a failure to produce either a creative or a practical form of intelligence. The natural consequence of this intellectual malnourishment was the appearance of dilettantes who took pride in their highly ornamental and contemplative knowledge. Concurrently this authorized a simplistic return to those traditional attitudes towards life in which primary importance was given to a form of passivity which amounted to little more than following in the wake of convenience.

Thus the distinguishing features of the ideology of culturalism can be summarized in terms of a tragically unmediated contradiction. On the one side we see the rapid importation of preconceived ideas of foreign origin and their utilitarian application, while on the other it is clear that the consciousness of those who proclaimed these ideologies remained buried within the traditional Japanese approach to the world. This duality also characterized the pathetic condition of Japan's cultural life.

B. The Separation of Scholarship and Education

As culturalism (*kyōyō*) was monopolized by one segment of society and became internalized in the form of a cultural *Weltanschauung* isolated from all realities outside itself, it provided the basis for a mistaken worldview; or, alternatively, exploited by clever commercialism, it was popularly vulgarized. The education of the masses of Japanese people, at the same time, took place in complete isolation from the products of science and scholarship. The chasm that separated these two worlds was extremely difficult to bridge.

If the result of Japan's so-called cultural modernization was a form of cultural indigestion produced by superficial and unmediated encounters with European learning and culture, then education was the process of tying up the remaining loose ends. The 1890 Imperial Rescript on Education certainly had this character. As Hozumi Yatsuka observed, "Civil law leads to the ruin of loyalty and filial piety." For the leaders of late Meiji Japan this was accepted to a certain extent as an inevitable concomitant of modernization. But in order to limit the potentially disruptive ramifications of this legal liberalization, educational institutions were mobilized to keep a firm lid on the forces threatening the Meiji system of political control. This use of education, as was suggested at the beginning of this chapter, represented a concerted effort to preserve what remained of the traditional value system and social order inherited by the leaders of the post-Restoration government.

This way of thinking was dredged up every time a major structural crisis appeared, and policies were formulated to reestablish the foundations of control. This can be seen for example in the Boshin Rescript of 1908 and the Rescript to Promote the National Spirit (Kokumin Seishin Sakkō) of 1923, both of which centered on movements of mass propagandization.[17] The same strategy was invoked in 1935 in the Movement to Clarify the Kokutai (Kokutai Meichō Undō), which was organized by the government as part of its mobilization for total war.

By means of such measures, the intimate relationship between education and scholarship was severed, and the former was made to serve a social function radically opposed to the discovery and transmission of truth.

As has often been observed, ever since Minister of Education Mori Arinori first enunciated the principle that scholarship and education must be separated, it has been extremely difficult to synthesize educational content and scientific endeavors. In the words of Mori:

[17] The Boshin Rescript was an Imperial proclamation issued after the Russo-Japanese War that supplemented the Imperial Rescript on Education in terms of the new situation in which Japan found itself after the war. The Rescript to Promote the National Spirit was issued after World War I with the aim of countering the influence among young people of the liberal currents of thought of the times, known collectively as Taishō Democracy.

Education in the Japanese State is not intended to create people accomplished in the techniques of the arts and sciences, but rather to manufacture the persons required by the State. Rather than proceeding in accord with Western principles and methods, we should carefully follow the rules developed in the schools for training army officers. . . . In short, education must be approached in basic conformity with the spirit of *chūkun aikoku* [loyalty and patriotism].

The idea of separating education and scholarship was closely connected with the privileged position given to military interests in Japan's modernizing development. According to the Meiji leader Kido Takayoshi: "Neither our educational nor military systems should be allowed to function free from the most rigorous forms of control."

Unfortunately, the ideology which made education a possession of the State was not totally eradicated by Japan's defeat in the war, and even today we have not escaped from its underlying intellectual framework. In the modern liberal states of the West, the principles of freedom of thought, belief, and education were established as an outcome of the strained relations between state authority and morality (religion). It has been quite different in Japan, where, as a consequence of the "collision between education and religion," education was made to function both as a substitute for religion and as a manifestation of state power. The same forces that gave rise to the convergence of religion and education were also able to manipulate the radical severance of relations between scholarship and education.

Beginning in 1892 with the dismissal of the eminent historian Kume Kunitake from his Imperial University post,[18] there occurred a series of incidents in which scholars who advanced theories or expressed opinions judged deviant or undesirable from the national-morality point of view were criticized and their work denounced as heretical.

In the so-called Northern and Southern Dynasties controversy, over the lineage of the Imperial Family, historians were pressured to adhere to the officially approved version of a single line of descent for the Imperial Household. Inoue Tetsujirō, the philosopher and defender of the *kokutai*, while acknowledging the historian's right to adopt either of the two conflicting theories in the controversy, was

---

[18] Kume, professor of Japanese history at Tokyo Imperial University, had served as official recorder on the 1871 Iwakura Mission to North America and Europe. In 1891 he published an essay suggesting the fallibility of Shintoist doctrine, and in short order was removed from his university post. (He spent the rest of his academic career on the faculty of Waseda University, a private institution.)

quite blunt about the attitude required of textbook authors:

> Books that are to be used at the compulsory levels of national education must of course be based solely on the foundations provided by our national morality.

It should be noted that those who were responsible for the writing of textbooks did not try to unify their contents with the results of scholarly inquiry. One of those having responsibility for educational content, Mikami Sanji, professor of Japanese history at Tokyo Imperial University, wrote with regard to the dynastic controversy:

> Historical disputes should be contained within the boundaries of historical discourse and should have no bearing whatsoever on history as it is generally taught in the nation's schools. I therefore think it is wholly appropriate that no instruction be given in the lower schools regarding the problem of legitimate and illegitimate dynastic claims.

At the same time the legalist Uesugi Shinkichi was beginning to become exasperated with Minobe Tatsukichi's theory of the Emperor as an organ of the State[19] and its widespread acceptance. Uesugi, a self-appointed defender of the *kokutai*, was particularly troubled by Minobe's being called to lecture at the Ministry of Education-sponsored summer training sessions for middle-school teachers. In an essay entitled "A Dissenting Opinion on the *Kokutai*," he wrote:

> If those who follow the calling of education derive their authority from this understanding of the *kokutai*, the consequences will be extremely grave. It is one thing for scholars to manipulate these theories and be proud of their clear-mindedness in their offices, but quite another when our teachers fool with dangerous ideas.

And a book Uesugi authored in 1911 for use in the national education system, *Kokumin Kyōiku: Teikoku Kenpō Kōgi* (*An Explanation of the Imperial Constitution for Use in National Education*), clearly proclaimed on the cover:

> This is reference material for those who work in the field of com-

---

[19] Chapter 5 further discusses the Emperor-as-organ-of-the-State theory and the controversy between Minobe and Uesugi, both professors in the Faculty of Law at Tokyo Imperial University.

mon, universal education. It is to be read as providing resources for nurturing and training the average citizen's love of the State.

The Okamura Incident of the same year, 1911, showed the extent to which the State would go in punishing those who were thought to have violated the separation between education and scholarship. Okamura Tsukasa, professor of civil law at Kyoto Imperial University, criticized the traditional Japanese family system in front of an audience of school teachers, and was officially reprimanded.

In the aftermath of the Lèse-Majesté Incident, the debates on national morality became superheated, and the exasperation of the authorities was seen in the fury of their propaganda campaigns. The taboo against nonofficial pronouncements on the *kokutai* (particularly in the context of national education) became more rigid, and it was declared "appropriate" to impose "educational rectification" in "cases where unwholesome influences are exerted on the State and the ideological convictions of the masses."

The detachment of education from scholarship was not only a problem in the teaching of history. In science courses, too, an ideology that disavowed genuine scientific learning came to permeate the world of national education.

As a result of the annexing of education by the State, the People were given at best a fragmentary knowledge which had value only in matters of practical application. To borrow Löwith's metaphor, there was no "ladder" between education and scholarship. The causes of this condition were the same as those which brought about the previously described rupture between thought and action among intellectuals. This reflects the original perversion that set Japan on the course of its contorted modernization.

C. Propagandization of the Masses and Cultivation of the Elite

As an inevitable consequence of this way of thinking, a dual cultural structure was established. On one side were the masses, who were the objects of State propaganda, and on the other was an elite which was given special privileges. The dichotomy echoed traditional social attitudes. Thus academic freedom in our country, taking advantage of the separation of scholarship from education, created its own discourse on university autonomy at the expense of educational freedom for the masses. In the end it just barely managed to survive.

Writing in 1938, Kawai Eijirō argued for the special privileges he believed university people were entitled to:

Even if in society at large freedom of thought and expression is prohibited, in the university, as a specially designated sphere for free research, freedom should be unconstrained. . . . Even if the expression of dangerous ideas be forbidden outside of the university, these "dangerous ideologies" must be permitted in the university.

In fact "dangerous ideologies" *were* permitted in the universities. The historian Aida Yūji has provided us with a very revealing recollection of life in the world of prewar higher education:

The ideal of the university in the old days was akin to esoteric learning. When we entered the world of the higher school during the early years of the Shōwa era, we were immediately taught about the Jinshin Rebellion.[20] Never having heard that this was a strategy of Emperor Temmu, it came as quite a surprise to learn that *bansei ikkei* [the unbroken line of Emperors] was completely fallacious. What were our feelings when our teachers shocked us with this new knowledge? . . . Having such an important truth revealed to us proved that we were truly elite. Even though we now understood this important truth, it remained something that others must not be allowed to know about. . . . This was the crux of our elite consciousness. [*Jiyū*, July 1966]

It is certainly true that academic freedom existed within the arena of elite education. However, this was not a freedom bolstered by a "critical spirit." Quite to the contrary, in fact, it represented a renunciation of critical spirit. The freedoms one found in the elite institutions had meaning only inasmuch as they were tied to the path that led to membership in Japan's ruling elite.

Political control in Japan remained secure to the extent that reality was monopolized by the ruling class. The freedoms permitted in the prewar higher schools established the foundations of that most noxious form of control.

As the shock waves of the Great Depression spread through Japanese society in the late 1920s and early 1930s, leftist-leaning students appeared even within these organs of higher learning. Amidst worsening economic conditions, university graduates found it increasingly

---

[20] A war of succession over the throne took place in 671–72, after the death of Emperor Tenji; Tenji's son was killed and the throne usurped by his uncle, who became Emperor Temmu.

difficult to find work, and the "culturalism" provided in these institutions of elite training became dangerously dysfunctional. After the 1931 Manchurian Incident, which resulted in Japan's occupation of Manchuria and eventually led to war with China, the nation drifted towards fascism with increasing speed; freedom was usurped in the universities, and truth was driven into exile. This was made manifestly clear by attacks on liberal scholars in the 1930s.

In 1933, the Minister of Education demanded the resignation of Kyoto Imperial University law professor Takigawa Yukitoki, on grounds that he had been unpatriotic in his lectures. A number of faculty members resigned in the ensuing uproar. Minobe Tatsukichi, whose theory that the Emperor was an organ of the State had once been widely accepted, was forced to resign from the House of Peers and to give up other honors; his books were banned in 1935, and in 1936 he was wounded in an assassination attempt.

Mikami Sanji captured the spirit of the times regarding the division between scholarship and education in 1936 when he addressed the Council on Educational Reorganization (Kyōgaku Sasshin Hyōgikai), which had been established to meet the needs of a nation preparing for war:

> The notion that scholarly research should be absolutely free comes mainly from the world of natural science. However, a clear distinction should be drawn regarding research and the education of students in the natural and spiritual sciences. Take for example the proposition that this is the 2600th year since the national foundation (*kigen*). From the standpoint of scientifically validated historical research there is ample room for doubting the veracity of this proposition. However, when it comes to giving instruction on such matters, it should be expected that teachers will refrain from discussing these doubts.

The theory long since employed in the sphere of national education to legitimate the separation of scholarship and education was also introduced at this time into the world of higher learning to regulate the relationship between research and instruction. The denial of professorial freedoms inevitably led to a shackling of the freedom to conduct research. The State was then able to eliminate theories that had already come to be commonly accepted within the academic world. This was the background for the "ethical," anti-scientific character of *kyōyōshugi* as it triumphantly emerged during the years of mobilization for Japan's total war.

Under the pretext of the division between education and scholarship, academic freedom in Japan continued to exist for a time in one sphere. However, the radical removal of scholarly truths from educational praxis allowed one part of Japanese society to monopolize scholarship. This meant that, more than simply keeping the truth from the people, education came to be used to propagate "the big lie." This system of making education a means to propagate falsehood in the end turned scholarship itself into a lie. The world of scholarship, which had passively stood by while education was separated from it and had just barely managed to preserve its own narrow band of authority, destroyed itself in the end for precisely those reasons.

In the previously cited words of Kawai Eijirō, we can recognize resistance to the encroaching destruction of freedom even within the university in the wake of the controversy surrounding Minobe's Emperor-as-organ-of-the-State theory. However, Kawai's claims that even if freedoms were being denied in a wholesale fashion, they should be guaranteed at least in the universities, were no more than echoes of an impotent elitist consciousness. From the viewpoint of the everyday lives of the masses, these claims were nothing more than self-serving chatter. This reveals the essential impotence of prewar culturalism. In the end this view of scholarship had a poisonous effect on Japanese society.

The hope that universities would be allowed special freedoms that were denied other social and educational institutions was from the beginning negated by its own inherent impossibility. Even if some freedoms were possible, academic theories would only be allowed free expressions to the extent that their dangerous qualities were defused. Dangerous theories are for some people and in certain circumstances not dangerous, as we saw in the recollections of Aida Yūji. His example does not constitute proof of the existence of academic freedom in the university. Rather it merely shows that there are certain conditions in which dangerous thoughts and ideologies can be made to lose their upsetting qualities. Indeed even Marxist theory recognizes that under certain specified conditions it is possible to take advantage of dangerous ideas for purposes of more effective political control.

4 Democratizing Education and Liberating the Japanese Spirit

I. The Road to a Democratized Japan

Among the inevitable results of the August 15, 1945, acceptance of the Potsdam Declaration, with its demands for an end to Japanese militarism and the construction of a democratic political system, were the destruction of the Meiji constitutional order and the collapse of the Imperial educational apparatus which had served as the primary agency for its social reproduction and legitimization. In short, the end of the war necessitated a radical reform of the values which upheld the Imperial system of education and a major structural transformation which would bring education into harmony with the ideals being proposed for a new constitutional order.

A. The Quest for a New Direction

At the outset of the Occupation period, the Supreme Commander for the Allied Powers, General Douglas MacArthur, called for an inquiry that would lead to the creation of a new constitution to replace the one promulgated some fifty years earlier by the Meiji government. Subsequently he issued Four Directives Regarding Education, which swept away in one broad stroke the ultranationalistic and militaristic practices which had been a major part of education in Japan prior to that time. The Ministry of Education followed suit by issuing its own Directive Concerning the Treatment of Imperial Rescripts and Edicts, wherein it was officially acknowledged that the Imperial Rescript on Education had lost the power to stand as "the one and only fountainhead for education in our country." This directive further declared that public recitation of the Rescript was no longer to be included in the list of required activities for holidays, and explained that the Rescript should not be treated as a divine revelation. Then, with the Emperor's declaration of his humanity on January 1, 1946, the Imperial education system was shaken to its very roots.

The March 1946 visit of the U.S. Education Mission to Japan and the publication of its proposals for reform provided powerful encouragement to those who were already working within Japanese society for the liberalization and democratization of education. The committee organized to cooperate with the Mission inherited the strivings for reform which had already begun to appear in the prewar environment and, taking advantage of the new conditions brought on by the end of the war, gave direction to these long-suppressed strivings in the Report of the Educators' Committee. This group eventually developed into the Education Reform Committee, which, in light of the deliberations going on at that time regarding the establishment of a new constitutional order, laid the foundations for a new basic law for education to replace the Imperial Rescript. The work of this group subsequently provided the nucleus of Japan's Fundamental Law of Education.

At the opening session of this committee's proceedings, Minister of State Shidehara Kijūrō,[1] acting as spokesman for Prime Minister Yoshida Shigeru, gave the following greeting:

> If we boil down to their roots the causes of the war which brought on Japan's recent defeat, we must call attention to our misbegotten educational system. The imperialistic, ultra-patriotic formalism which hitherto characterized our education cannot provide a basis for cultivating the youth who will be responsible for the future of Japan. Let us abandon our mistaken ideals and establish in their place an education which respects truth, human character, and peace. In this way we must demonstrate our respect for the true dignity of an education that is indeed worthy of the name.

These remarks were followed by those of Minister of Education Tanaka Kōtarō, who implored the committee to define the objective of educational reform as "the establishment of a democratic system of education that finds its values in the ideals of truth and peace."

The First Special Committee of the Educational Reform Council (responsible for conducting inquiries on the implementation of a new basic educational law to replace the Imperial Rescript) issued its General Plan for a Fundamental Law of Education at its thirteenth session (Nov. 29, 1946). In its preface we can see how the new thinking about education was informed by deep reflection on the errors of the past:

> Education must be carried out with the expectation that it will

---

[1] Shidehara, a prewar diplomat who had been forced out of office because of his opposition to hard-line militarism, would become Japan's second postwar prime minister, cooperating with the Americans in the reform of legal and political institutions. In charge of drafting the Constitution, he was reported to have taken the initiative in drafting Article 9, the renunciation-of-war clause.

bring about the cultivation of truth and the perfection of human character. Up until now education in our country has made light of the true scientific spirit and shown no respect for religious sentiments. Moral training was denigrated to a mere formalism, and education was deprived of any autonomy. This certainly helped to pave the road which led to the ascendancy of militarism and extreme nationalism. To rectify these grievous blunders we must reconceive our education right down to its roots.

Thus the search for new educational ideals centered in the activities of the Educational Reform Committee was carried out on the basis of a deep and penetrating examination of the dangerously defective system of prewar education.

B. The Constitution and the Fundamental Law of Education

In the Preamble of the Fundamental Law of Education one can find the dual roots of postwar Japanese idealism, its democratic and pacifistic values:

The members of the Diet have already ratified the Constitution of Japan, and in order to construct a democratic, cultured state, have shown our determination to contribute to world peace and human welfare. . . . For the complete realization of these ideals, we must in the last analysis wait for the power of education to reap these fruits.

From these words we can begin to appreciate the magnitude of the role education was envisioned as necessarily playing in the re-creation of Japan as a peaceful society and democratic state. In this vein the preamble concludes:

Following the spirit of the [new] Constitution of Japan, we herein declare the objectives of a new system of Japanese education, and we establish this law in order to confirm its legal foundations.

The import of this declaration is further reflected in Minister of Education Takahashi Seiichirō's explanation of the reasons for the proposed legislation which was submitted to the Lower House of the Diet on March 13, 1947:

In order to establish both the political and legal foundations of democracy and pacifism, we have already carried out epoch-making revisions in the field of constitutional law. But the realization of a truly democratic and civilized Japanese State which will contribute to the development of a more peaceful world depends upon the nation's willingness to constantly make creative efforts to fulfill these ends. And it is by no means an exaggeration to claim that the realization of these ideals depends in large measure upon the power of education.

To achieve these ends, we must resolutely execute a fundamental reform of education, based on faith in the absolute necessity of carrying out these objectives.... This Fundamental Law of Education gives public recognition to the necessity of concretely amplifying the spirit in those passages of our new Constitution pertaining to education in terms of clear educational principles.

The minister went on to clarify the special character of the Fundamental Law of Education as follows:

In the sense that this law is a declaration of educational ideals, we may well think of it as having the status of an "educational declaration." And in the sense that it *defines the standards for the whole range of educational laws* which must be enacted hereafter, I believe it can be said to possess the character of an absolutely indispensable law [*konponhō*] with regard to educational matters. Therefore this proposed law is in essence different from the ordinary run of laws.[2]

As is clear from Minister Takahashi's explanation of the proposed legislation, the Fundamental Law of Education was at one and the same time a declaration of new educational ideals to replace the Imperial Rescript, and a basic principle designed to give direction to the future course of educational law. In the words of the administrative law scholar Tanaka Jirō, it was "the central law within the body of educational law, an Educational Constitution." In other words, because it embodies the spirit of our democratic Constitution, the Fundamental Law of Education should be thought of as a vehicle designed to facilitate the realization of those constitutional ideals in the realm of education. Thus, in addition to representing a concrete expression of educational goals, it was also intended to set the directions for a new system of educational practice and administration.

[2] This interpretation differs from that of today's Ministry of Education officials, who view this law as no different from others.

These ideals are unambiguously expounded upon in the Preamble to the Constitution:

> We, the Japanese people . . . resolved that never again shall we be visited with the horrors of war through the action of government, do proclaim that sovereign power resides with the people and do firmly establish this Constitution.

The Constitution goes on to call democracy a "universal principle of mankind," and, recognizing that "all peoples of the world have the right to live in peace," declares that its basic principles are respect for fundamental human rights, democracy, and the pursuit of peace. On the subject of human rights, Article 97 declares:

> The fundamental human rights by this Constitution guaranteed to the people of Japan are fruits of the age-old struggle of man to be free; they have survived the many exacting tests for durability and are conferred upon this and future generations in trust, to be held for all time inviolable.

I wish to stress the fact that these rights were put forth as universal and inviolable because this constitutes an important dimension of our subsequent educational struggles against those elements within Japanese society which have constantly fallen back on notions of Japanese exceptionalism as the basis for their attempts to repudiate the progressive values of democracy. Let me also call attention to Article 12, found in the section on the rights and duties of the People:

> The freedoms and rights guaranteed to the people by this Constitution shall be maintained by the constant endeavor of the people.

The Constitution unhesitatingly calls on the People to always take whatever measures are necessary to fully realize their human rights and liberties. The People, through their everyday activities, and educators, through their everyday teaching, were thereby given a mandate to continuously strive to create this new society. Article 26 of the Constitution clearly stipulates that the People have the right to receive an education, and this has led us to argue that the members of a democratic society should also be guaranteed the freedom to inquire and learn. Furthermore, it is important to note, these rights are not merely an enfranchisement to liberty, but are inseparably related to the citizen's basic rights to live and work. The Constitution also recognizes the People's rights to pursue happiness and wealth, to freely formulate and express their thoughts and beliefs, as well as to enjoy academic freedom. Along with the rights to inquire and to know the truth, this has quite reasonably been interpreted as a recognition of the People's basic spiritual freedoms. Takayanagi Shinichi, for one, has very properly called this the field of "constitutional liberties."

In summing up these developments, it can well be said that the idea of education promoted by the postwar Constitution is decisively different from that seen in the prewar Imperial system, in which education was one of the Imperial subject's cardinal duties along with military service and the obligation to pay taxes.

C. The Ideals for a New Educational Administration

There was a widespread recognition at this time that in order to fully realize these new educational values, it was absolutely necessary to assure the independence of education from the bearers of political power at any given time. This required the creation of an administrative apparatus which would respect all of the ideals and values implied by the notion of educational autonomy. Those who attempted to formulate the outlines of this new system spoke in terms of an "independent educational authority," an idea reminiscent of Fukuzawa Yukichi's proposal for an autonomous cultural council. Tanaka Kōtarō, for example, frequently mentioned an autonomously structured educational authority. He advised the Educational Reform Committee to consider the following points most carefully:

What we should be thinking about and aiming for is a system which first eliminates and then prevents all of the impediments to a genuine educational practice that arise from forces outside the educational world. . . . In particular, I would like you to think about issues such as how school administration should be conducted, or how academic freedom and educational liberty can best be guaranteed. In general, I hope you will concern yourselves with the problem of how to establish an administrative system which will generate the conditions necessary for the fulfillment of our new educational objectives.

Here we can already detect the spirit of independence underlying Article X of the Fundamental Law of Education, the spirit in which the bureaucratic control of education that stood at the heart of the old system was abolished and the duties of educational administration were limited to providing the overall management of educational conditions needed to guarantee education's much-needed autonomy.

In the Ministry of Education's own *Commentary on the Fundamental Law of Education* (written by Tanaka Jirō and Tsujita Tsutomu), the prewar system of centrally controlled educational administration was vigorously criticized as follows:

> The spirit of domination found at the core of this system made it possible for educational administrators to penetrate right down into and interfere with the innermost workings of the educational enterprise. It was a spirit that finally led our schools to become totally subservient to the political powers of the time. This was a system which made it possible for the nation's leaders to control even thought and scholarship in the service of an ultranational and militaristic ideology. Moreover, local school administration was made an organ of the Ministry of Home Affairs's general administrative apparatus, and education came to be directed by that ministry's clique of officials, who had neither an understanding of, nor any real or sufficient experience with regard to, education. This kind of educational administration made it exceedingly difficult for a lively, animated, free, and autonomous form of education to be created in prewar Japan.

Thus even the Ministry of Education, which had itself played a major role in smothering the development of educational freedom in prewar Japan, recognized its own mistaken ways at this juncture and stressed the importance of the new arrangements outlined in Article X of the Fundamental Law of Education, which officially guaranteed educational freedom and autonomy.

As the preceding remarks should make abundantly clear, the ideals for a new system of educational administration were conceived as a rejection of the central government's mechanisms for bureaucratic over-control. These principles had the negative aim of preventing direct governmental interference and guaranteeing education's autonomy from political pressure. And, in a positive vein, they were intended to contribute to the establishment of an educational system which would be responsive to the particular conditions in each part of the country.

D. From Imperial Decree to Public Legislation

Ratification of a Fundamental Law of Education based on the idea of "education as a citizen's right" drastically altered the relation between education and the State in Japan. This new concept signaled a repudiation of the hitherto existing arrangements which were legitimated by the Imperial Rescript on Education and maintained through a wide range of Imperial decrees. In the previously quoted *Explanation of the Proposed Legislation for a Fundamental Law of Education*, Minister of Education Takahashi Seiichirō spoke directly to these issues:

> In our attempt to establish this law we are seeking to repudiate the use of Imperial rescripts and ordinances which have provided the very form of educational control in effect up until now. Thus, in the place of orders unilaterally imposed from above, we propose the institutionalization of decision-making procedures which will mobilize the will of the People in assemblies composed of their duly chosen representatives. This law is designed to provide an appropriate basis for the discussion and resolution of educational issues in accord with the spirit embodied in our new Constitution. It is appropriate and, I think, vitally necessary for education in the new Japan.

Both the form and content of educational activities, it was declared, were from that time to be liberated from the grip of Imperial control and relocated in a sphere of law reflecting the popular will as expressed in accordance with the spirit of the Constitution. This awareness was amply reflected in a newspaper editorial from the March 5, 1947, edition of the *Asahi Shimbun*:

> The purpose of the Fundamental Law of Education proposed to the Diet is to make it possible to discuss the basic issues and problems of education in our country, and to resolve them by a consensus of the People's duly elected representatives. Henceforth the ideals and directions of our education will not be unilaterally bequeathed from above, as expressions of the Imperial will, but will be democratically formulated manifestations of the People's will. Thus even if the Fundamental Law of Education is a piece of legislation, in actuality it is the self-proclaimed "Educational Declaration" of the People for our new Japan. It is without doubt one of the most important links in our ongoing democratic revolution.

Enactment of a democratic Constitution and the establishment of a system grounded in the Fundamental Law of Education made it inevitable that the Imperial Rescript on Education would lose its efficacy. As clearly stipulated in the Constitution, "... no law, ordinance, imperial rescript or other act of government, or part thereof, contrary to the provisions hereof, shall have legal force or validity" (Article 98). (I will turn in the next chapter to an examination of the legal measures that were subsequently implemented to invalidate the Imperial Rescript on Education in particular.)

It is also important to point out that initially the Ministry of Education was very positive regarding the significance of the reforms rooted in the passage of the Fundamental Law of Education:

> In addition to affirming the values of free thinking encouraged by the Fundamental Law of Education, we also recognize the real promise it holds for completely transforming the worst traditions of modern Japanese education. [*Monbushō Hōkokusho*, August 1949]

Thus it can be unambiguously stated that the Fundamental Law of Education was designed to make sure that education in Japan would never again fall under the control of those who would abuse it for the narrowly conceived aims of ultranationalism or militarism. In short, by stipulating the legal foundations and intellectual principles required to ensure the continued development of democratic values in Japanese society, this law gave voice to an irrevocable departure from the educational traditions of prewar Japan and set forth the role it was hoped education would play in the reformation of Japanese national life.

II. Key Provisions in the Fundamental Law of Education

I would now like to analyze some of the most important principles enunciated in the text of the Fundamental Law of Education in order to clarify the ways in which the basic spirit of reform discussed above was concretely embodied in law.

In Article I, on the "Aim of Education," we find a list of objectives that now seem thoroughly commonsensical, so much so that when read by today's youth they appear totally unexceptional. But at the time this law was actually drafted these goals were anything but; indeed they were antithetical to everything that Japanese educational system had long stood for.

Article I's declaration of support for "the full development of personality," its "esteem for the individual," and its commitment to the rearing of people who will "love truth and justice" and "have a deep sense of responsibility" constituted nothing short of a stunning indictment of the prewar education system and its *raison d'être*. After

all, this evolution towards an educational system based on the Kantian notion of treating man not merely as a means to an end but as
an end-in-himself represented the clearest possible repudiation of the
prewar educational apparatus and its attempt to fit the "Emperor's
subjects" into the mold of a "national morality" revolving around
the values of *chūkun aikoku* (loyalty and patriotism). In other words,
the objectives stipulated in Article I were based on an attitude of reverent respect for the important human values which the Imperial
education system had first denied and then tried to destroy. This article's explicitly stated veneration of truth stood in clear opposition to
the forms of falsehood demanded by the Imperial bureaucracy and
legitimated in the name of the Emperor. Within the new framework
authorized by the Fundamental Law of Education, ideas and beliefs
were no longer to be monopolized by a totalitarian State; they were
designated as an essential element of the inalienable intellectual freedoms that properly belong to all individuals in a democratic society.[3]

In Article II, on "Educational Principles," we find it stated that
academic freedom must be respected in order to guarantee the realization of these objectives. Moreover, in its insistence that these aims
must "be realized on all occasions and in all places," the Fundamental
Law declares that its values should not be limited to school education,
but should be extended to all forms of social education including that
provided within industry. In other words, its stated spirit of respect
for men, women, and children as individuals, and its dedication to the
pursuit of truth and peace, were nothing short of total.

Here again we can see that the Fundamental Law of Education was
fashioned in direct opposition to the values which perverted educational life in prewar Japan. As was discussed in the previous chapter,
the values which underwrote the organization of higher and lower
education were in clear opposition, even though in the end both were
thoroughly subordinated to the objectives of the State. Thus in its
rejection of the long-standing practices by means of which the aims of
scholarship and education were separated, this article renounced the
State's use of education as a tool for creating and inculcating a national morality. Furthermore, to the extent that it dispensed with
the idea that academic freedom belongs only to those working in universities, it served notice that schoolteachers were being liberated
from the despotic system of control under which they had been forced

---

[3] It is worth noting that the objectives set forth in the Fundamental Law of
Education were also enunciated the following year (1948) in the United Nations
Declaration of Human Rights.

to operate while trying to provide their students with knowledge and insights into the character of life in the modern world.

In Article III, on the equality of educational opportunity, and again in Article IV, on compulsory education, the new character of the relationship between individual and State in democratic Japan is clearly set forth. The first addresses the nature of the "right to receive an education in accord with one's ability" that is guaranteed by Article 26 of the Constitution. By adding the additional proviso that all citizens must be given the opportunity of "receiving education according to their ability," the authors of the Fundamental Law shrewdly anticipated and attempted to forestall the efforts made in recent years by those who have grabbed control of our educational system to limit this right to those who are judged to have the abilities deemed desirable.[4] (This problem is taken up and examined in great detail in Chapters 12 and 13.)

Like the other articles of the Fundamental Law of Education, this one was grounded in reflection on the flawed character of education in prewar Japan. While it is indeed true that modern Japanese education had outpaced the European systems in terms of realizing the ideal of equal educational opportunity at the lower levels of the educational ladder, inasmuch as there was no system of middle-level education which led directly to the Imperial universities at the apex of the national educational system, the possibilities for advancement were severely restricted for the masses. The post-primary education which was made available to them in the form of vocational schools (*jiitsugyō gakkō*) was structured not in accordance with their needs and abilities but on the basis rather of the needs and requirements of Japan's Imperial State.

This was directly tied to the problematic character of compulsory education as discussed in the previous chapter. As pointed out there, the duty involved was conceived not in terms of the need to guarantee the rights of the child, but rather in terms of the Imperial State's need to make sure that parents complied with the obligation to submit their children to the kind of education which the State's bureaucracy deemed necessary. In this light the drafting of Article IV of the Fundamental Law of Education represented a major turning point in Japanese edu-

---

[4] It is important to note that in the languages of Europe the notion of educational rights is expressed as "right *to* education," "*Recht* auf *Erziehung*" or "*droit* à *l'enseignement*. In all these cases the right in question is not a passive one, i.e., the right merely to be educated, but an active one, i.e., the right to demand an education, to enjoy an education, or to reject what is taught when and where the individual who bears this right determines rejection to be appropriate.

cational history because the responsibility involved was conceived in terms of the need to guarantee the child's right to receive an education in accord with his or her own requirements. Likewise, Article V, by declaring that schooling in Japan would thereafter be coeducational, reiterated the idea that the focus on education would thereafter be on what was fair from the standpoint of the individual and not the totality as defined and interpreted by the State.

Article VI on "School Education" formulates an important new perspective for thinking about the "public nature" of public education when recognizing that not only schools established by "the State and local public bodies," but even private institutions established by "juridical persons" have this character. In other words, it acknowledged that the very act of setting up and operating a school is indeed a public one and that therefore the quality of being public is not something which can be monopolized by the various kinds of governmental bodies.

In fact, Tanaka Kōtarō, speaking for the Ministry of Education in the House of Peers on September 19, 1946, went so far as to observe that while schools originally developed in modern Europe and North America as privately established public organs, the exact opposite had been true in modern Japan, where only the State was recognized as legitimately having the authority required to establish schools. The democratization of Japanese educational life, Tanaka insisted, demanded the inversion of this way of thinking: thereafter the State's proper role should be limited to encouraging the development of private education. It was in precisely this spirit that the Fundamental Law of Education sought to prevent the State from interfering with the inner workings of the educational process. Under the new framework it established, the public character of education was to emerge from the needs and requirements of individuals, rather than being uniformly imposed from above by the State; the role of the latter was reduced to supplying from the public treasury the funds required to make this new kind of education possible.

Likewise, this new way of thinking also helped the framers of the Fundamental Law of Education to re-envision the public character of scholarship and culture so that they would no longer be dominated by the State acting solely in accord with its self-determined interests. One of the direct corollaries of this new approach to the relationship between the People and the public character of their cultural and intellectual life was a new definition of the responsibilities of schoolteachers. The second clause of Article VI addresses this by declaring that those who teach in the schools "prescribed by law shall be servants of the whole community" and "conscious of their mission." What I find particularly significant about this passage is the fact that in its definition of the public character of education it does not construe the beneficiaries of the teacher's efforts as the Emperor or the State, as was true in the prewar system. Nor does it declare that the primary responsibilities of public school teachers should be mandated in terms of the interests and requirements of a particular social class or political party; it represents these responsibilities always and only in relation to the People as a whole. Thus this article was unwavering in its support for the professional autonomy of the teacher, seeing it as the best means of guaranteeing the fullest possible flowering of the free spirit of children.

Recognizing learning to be an activity which continues during the whole course of a human life, Article VII of the Fundamental Law declares that the citizens of Japan have the right to enjoy the use of publicly supported educational facilities even after their formal schooling comes to an end. It places the financial burden of establishing and maintaining libraries, museums, and other institutions on the various types of governmental bodies. But having done so in order to promote the rebirth of Japan as a democratic nation, this article makes it clear that the People themselves are the only legitimate masters of these organs of social education. Thus, in contrast to the organs of social education organized in the prewar period as means to propagandize the masses and unify them into a powerful national weapon, the Fundamental Law re-envisioned the existence of these institutions in terms of popular sovereignty and the human right to receive an education regardless of one's age and station in life.

Finally we come to two of the most important provisions in the Fundamental Law of Education, Article VIII on "Political Education" and Article IX on "Religious Education." The first of these addresses itself to the biggest defect in prewar Japanese education, the failure to cultivate the political knowledge required to promote intelligent citizenship. The second seeks to remedy a closely related problem generated by the prewar educational system, the failure to respect the beliefs and conscience of individuals.

Under the 1889 Imperial Constitution, all sovereignty resided in the Emperor, and since the Japanese people were merely Imperial subjects (shinmin), their education was ultimately designed to make them both loyal and obedient to Emperor and State. And while this system of national moral formation was constantly drumming the spirit of selfless patriotic service (messhi hōkō) into them, it was also dedicated to the goals of driving the spirit of concern with and criticism of national policy entirely out of them.

Against the background of the international drive towards democracy during the Taishō era, demands for the right to vote were voiced for a brief period of time. And while this was realized in 1925 with the establishment of a system of universal male suffrage (women were excluded), the right to participate in national politics did not mean that the People had become the rulers of the nation. This was reconfirmed by the simultaneous passage of the Peace Preservation Law (Chian Iji Hō) and the establishment of a program designed to carefully monitor and where necessary correct popular thought. Reforms in the educational system introduced at this time were clearly designed to make sure that the newly established system of univeral suffrage did not seriously disturb the existing constellation of power. Transformations of society made during the 1930s by the Imperial Rule Assistance Organization (Yokusan Taisei) as part of the preparation for total war included the demand for an educational renovation which would produce youth who were not the least bit skeptical about the things the nation's leaders told them and who faithfully followed whatever orders they were given.

In this sense it is clear that the opportunities for learning about or studying society and politics were severely restricted in prewar Japan. In fact it is certainly no exaggeration to claim that one of the aims of national education was to produce what the political philosopher Sigmund Neumann described in his analysis of Nazi Germany as "political illiteracy."

Against this background it is not hard to see why Article VIII of the Fundamental Law of Education's insistence upon the need to cultivate a politically knowledgeable citizenry is so vitally important to the national well-being. If we are to live within a constitutional order founded upon the principle of popular sovereignty, then it is absolutely crucial that the People be provided with the kind of education that enables them to fully understand just what is required of and from them, if they are to make the idea of democracy something more than a merely formal or abstract point of reference.

By declaring that education must display an attitude of respect and tolerance towards religion, Article IX resolutely repudiated the prewar Imperial State's disregard for the freedoms of thought and belief, and firmly established the principle of separation between church and state. While it is true that the Imperial Constitution had formally recognized the existence of these freedoms, through its declaration that "Shintoism is not a religion" it had, in reality, laid the foundations for reconstituting it as a State religion, a religion that was imposed on the Japanese people through the nation's schools.

The separation of state and religion is one of the major principles of the modern state. It is rooted in a fundamental distinction between the kind of authority which derives from the possession of political power (kenryoku) and the kind of authority which is only made possible by the possession of moral dignity (ken'i). This necessarily leads to the proposition that because the state is a secular entity, it must neither possess nor attempt to inculcate religious doctrines and dogmas. In other words, this principle was included in the Fundamental Law of Education in order to make sure that the Japanese State would never again be able to use its political authority to violate the sanctity of those inner realms of belief which should properly be entrusted to the dignity of individuals. And by virtue of its adoption of this principle, the Fundamental Law undercut the pseudo-religious character of the prewar Emperor-State.

But of all the articles in the Fundamental Law of Education, the most controversial—and most important—is Article X on "Educational Administration."

Under the arrangements legitimated by the Meiji Constitution and reinforced by the Imperial Rescript on Education, the State monopolized the administration of education as one part of its domestic governance. Thus the bureaucrats in the Ministries of Education and Home Affairs who exercised this control in a centrally coordinated manner paid no attention to differences in regional conditions or to the needs of local communities. In short, the independence of education was thoroughly trampled because the State saw educational administration as an essential part of its police power.

To remedy this deplorable state of affairs, Article X of the Fundamental Law of Education formally guaranteed the independence of education and the freedom of educators. By declaring that the State must never again be allowed to force teachers to yield to its extra-educational authority, this article sought to encourage them to autonomously establish new forms of creative educational practice. Thus the first clause of this article takes educational authority away from the State and places it directly in the hands of the People; likewise, its second clause limits the work of educational administrators to the "adjustment and establishment of the various conditions" required to realize the aims of education.

What specifically did the drafters of this article have in mind when they declared that education must never again be subjected to "improper" forms of control, and that it "shall be directly responsible to the whole people"? It is important to consider these points very carefully because they have become the central issues in many of the legal controversies surrounding Japanese education in the postwar period, controversies which I will examine in great detail in the second section of this book.

The Ministry of Education has in recent years defined "improper control" as referring mainly to the activities of the Japan Teachers' Union. It is true that at the time this legislation was enacted, the notion of "improper control" was conceived in a way which made it possible to include teachers' unions and other interest groups among those parties which might violate the sanctity of education; in fact, however, according to the then Minister of Education, Tanaka Kōtarō, the primary focus of concern was the administrative activities of the government itself. In particular, it was feared that future governments might attempt to use the administrative power of the State to interfere with the formulation of educational content.

In order to properly grasp the meaning of educational institutions' being "directly responsible to the People as a whole," it is necessary to think about Article X in relation to Article VI's declaration that "teachers . . . shall be servants of the whole community." From this perspective it becomes clear that the best way to guarantee a form of educational administration in which the State cannot improperly control what goes on in schools is by making teachers directly responsible to the People themselves.

Today, however, we find this article's insistence upon direct responsibility to the People being interpreted in two widely divergent fashions. On the one side is the view put forward by the Ministry of Education, according to which the practice of education is identical with the administration of education. This view derives from a particular understanding of the relation between educational policy formation and implementation within the framework of a parliamentary democracy. Here the argument is put forward that the educational will of the People as a whole can only be determined by a majority in the Diet. Likewise, it is maintained, this national educational will can only be executed by the Ministry of Education when it fixes the content of education and formulates regulations for the supervision of teachers. The import of this interpretation, in short, is to redefine the concept of "improper control" over education so that the activities of the Ministry of Education can never be criticized or challenged as improper.

In an alternative view, the notion that education should be organized and supervised so that it will be directly responsible to the People has been interpreted to mean that teachers themselves, rather than the Ministry of Education, should take the leading role in making education responsive to the desires of the People. This view is closely related to the principle enunciated above which states that the autonomy and independence of teachers must be firmly protected. And as the reader will soon see, this teacher-oriented interpretation of educational democratization plays a central role in the discourse of those of us outside government who want to assert the People's educational rights (*kokumin no kyōikuken*) over those claimed by the State (*kokka no kyōikuken*).

This teacher-centered approach to the democratization of education is a direct corollary of Fukuzawa Yukichi's ideas regarding the independence of learning from politics and the distinction he drew between the internal and external dimensions of education (see Chapter 2, Section V). According to the logic underlying this distinction, matters pertaining to the content of education or the forms in which teaching is organized should be thought of as internal aspects of the educational process, while matters related to the financing of instruction or the construction of schools should be regarded as external aspects of education. According to the values formulated in terms of this distinction, problems related to the former must be entrusted to the discretion of teachers and their autonomously established professional organizations; conversely, those related to the latter are best dealt with when entrusted to the administrative expertise of educational bureaucrats.

The importance of this distinction was underscored in the report issued by the members of the U.S. Education Mission to Japan in March 1946: "The best capacities of teachers flourish only in an atmosphere of freedom. It is the business of the administrator to furnish this, not its opposite."

However, simply because they insisted upon the need to distinguish between the internal and external dimensions of education, it certainly does not follow that the architects of postwar Japanese education believed it necessary to sever all ties between teachers and administrators. In fact, quite to the contrary, they fully understood how important it was to establish mutually reinforcing relations between these two sides of educational life. The kind of education teachers are able to provide is indivisible, in other words, from the kind of working environment that educational administrators arrange for them. Therefore it is critically important that educational administrators make it their business to satisfy the demands, both quantitative and qualitative, that educators formulate from the standpoint of their concern for the internal aspects of education.

Unfortunately, however, for historical reasons I will discuss in the next chapter, the reality of contemporary Japanese education is exactly the opposite. Thus, notwithstanding the very real efforts which were exerted to liberate education in postwar Japan, external concerns have once again come to dominate the inner workings of the nation's educational process.

III. The Legal Foundations of a New Educational System

Having reflected deeply and carefully on the dehumanizing character of prewar Japan's ruling educational ideology, the authors of the Constitution and the Fundamental Law of Education cleared the ground for the creation of a thoroughly revitalized educational system. No longer viewed as a duty to the State, education was now redefined as an inalienable right of the Japanese people. Its objectives were liberated from the militaristic values of the Imperial State and rededicated to the creation of a democratic and pacifistic society. Thus the ultimate aim of education was no longer conceived as producing loyal, passive subjects, but as cultivating the kind of human beings who would never waver in their commitment to pursue truth and demand justice in their social relations. In short, the declaration of new principles for Japanese education went hand in hand with the desire to nourish the development of autonomous individuals and the values of human dignity.

Enacting these new legal arrangements profoundly altered the hitherto prevailing relationship between the State and education. Henceforth, the State, it was declared, would be obliged to respect equally the academic freedom of those doing research in the universities and those teaching in the nation's lower-level educational organs. Accordingly, the standards of truth and reality could no longer be subjugated to the ideological agenda of the State, nor could the State's agents arbitrarily determine what knowledge is necessary for the People, because the purpose of education was no longer to control the thought and activity of Japan's "Imperial subjects." To preserve the integrity of the struggle to fulfill education's new mandate, educators, it was likewise insisted, must never again be forced to submit to improper—i.e., extraeducational—control. Educational responsibility, it was therefore reasoned, had to be understood as falling directly on the shoulders of the People themselves; the State was now obliged to respect the independence and autonomy of education. Teachers were encouraged to strive, through their own studies and research, to further the child's right to learn, and expected to live up to the unparalleled trust invested in them by the People.[5] And finally, these new legal standards strictly limited the realm of educational administration to those activities, and only

[5] This point is discussed in detail in Chapter 10.

those activities, which were deemed necessary for securing the conditions required for the successful realization of these new educational objectives.

Taken as a whole, these constitutional reforms were intended to free the postwar educational enterprise from the multitude of restrictions that had been imposed on the system built upon the values and priorities encapsulated in the Imperial Rescript.

The significance of these reforms did not reside, however, only in the transformation of Japanese education from a system dedicated to inculcating the moralism of the family-State (*kazoku kokka*) ideology to one designed to nurture the development of citizens who would actively and autonomously pursue truth and justice in their daily lives. At its very heart this reconstruction also represented a total repudiation of the constellation of values which had made it possible for Japanese educational life to be subjugated to the program of national formation (*kokumin keisei*) rooted in the ideology that declared the Imperial Rescript on Education to have been divinely bestowed on the People. It was, in other words, a complete and total rejection of the thoroughly anti-intellectual dimensions of the Imperial Rescript. Thus the establishment of the Fundamental Law of Education represented no less than an attempt to radically reconceive the underlying political and moral dimensions of Japanese pedagogic life.

What, then, was the real meaning of the prewar system's declaration that education must be conducted on the basis of the Imperial will as it was revealed in the Imperial Rescript? It was merely a way to legitimate the bureaucracy's unlimited power to intervene in the spiritual life of the people and mediate the very formation of their inner values and personal consciousness. The bureaucratic manipulation of this nebulous "Imperial authority" represented a sustained attempt to compel the Japanese people to adopt the unified value system publicly mandated by the State itself. Drawing upon this "divine mandate," it was relatively easy to deny academic and educational freedom and systematically repress all forms of thought and belief deemed to be heterodox.

The postwar environment made possible by the Fundamental Law of Education nullified the Imperial Rescript (in Chapter 5 I will discuss the ways in which this was accomplished), and effectively eliminated the mechanisms of control by Imperial decree. As revealed by the fact that the concrete aspects of educational organization were now determined through particular pieces of legislation such as the Fundamental Law of Education, the School Education Law, and the Board of Education Law, the ground for educational activities was shifted away from the Imperial will and towards the will of the People. Formulation of these laws provided the most tangible evidence of the profoundly important shift in postwar Japan's educational world from Imperial domination to popular sovereignty.

In the following chapter I will examine in some detail the depths and extent to which these new values and legal arrangements were actually able to transform the foundations of our nation's educational life. But before turning to those problems I want to discuss one of the most troublesome issues accompanying the shift from a totalitarian educational system, one whose fundamental policies were determined in the name of the Imperial will, to a democratic system, one whose policies are determined on the basis of a popularly reached consensus. Is it permissible to impose educational objectives and materials on the People that are directly opposed to the spirit embodied in the Constitution and the Fundamental Law of Education, as long as this is done on the basis of legislation that passes through the Diet? This issue may be defined as the conflict between legality (*gōhōsei*) and legitimacy (*seitōsei*).

In thinking about this it is important to observe that both the Constitution and the Fundamental Law of Education explicitly state that academic and spiritual freedom must not be abused even by laws that are legal in the procedural sense (i.e., that are passed by the Diet). In particular, Article X of the Fundamental Law, in order to guarantee educational autonomy, clearly imposes limits on the authority and jurisdiction of educational administrators. It was formulated to circumscribe the limits within which educational problems could be settled by legislative means. Therefore, while it is true that on the one hand establishment of the principle of publicly formulated law as the basis for educational decision-making signaled a departure from the principle of control through Imperial edicts, on the other it was also intended to give expression to the principle that educational autonomy should not be violated by improper forms of legislative interference. In short, it was based on the concept that legislators should exhibit self-restraint regarding matters that pertain to the inner workings of the educational process.

By guaranteeing the independence of education from the State, the new system founded on the Constitution and the Fundamental Law of Education clearly sought to vest educational authority and responsibility directly in the hands of the People. But inasmuch as the Fundamental Law of Education itself sets the general objectives of education, can't it be said to be self-contradictory? This problem can only be resolved by grasping the doubly reflexive relationship between the

Constitution and the Fundamental Law of Education.

The Fundamental Law of Education was conceived in conformity with the constitutional ideal of a democratic and cultural state. Its Preamble declares: "The realization of this ideal shall depend fundamentally on the power of education." It was formulated, in short, to further the values and ideals set forth in the Constitution. And whereas the postwar Constitution guarantees the Japanese people's right to an education and ensures their freedoms of belief and conscience, Article X of the Fundamental Law of Education seeks to guarantee education's independence from the State by setting limits upon the extent of the government's administrative authority in the realm of educational matters. Thus the Constitution and Fundamental Law of Education created a legal framework designed to impose strict limits upon the legality and desirability of those legislative actions which set the objectives of educational practice.[6]

The reasons for the erection of this new legal framework are not hard to understand: it was articulated on the basis of a well-founded fear that, given the opportunity to legislatively formulate educational policy, the holders of governmental power might be tempted to interfere with the work of educators for their own narrowly conceived political interests.

Here again, however, we run into an unavoidable contradiction between this prohibition and the fact that the Fundamental Law of Education itself defines the ideals and objectives of education. There were many who were already fully aware of this difficulty at the time the Constitution was being established. The then Minister of Education, Tanaka Kōtarō, argued as follows in response to the opinion that a chapter relating to education should be included in the Constitution:

The Constitution is essentially a piece of political legislation. Accordingly, if education is construed as an undertaking that the Constitution makes extensive provision for, it too will become highly politicized. Thus I think it highly inappropriate to include moral and educational principles in this Constitution.

On the basis of this persuasive logic Tanaka and his supporters were able to reject the calls then being made for an authoritative constitu-

[6] This interpretation of the meaning of Article X (stating that education "shall be directly responsible to the whole people") is widely at odds with that which has been advanced in recent years by the Ministry of Education and the ruling Liberal Democratic Party. This will become much clearer in later chapters.

tional definition of the nature and scope of educational activities. In a work written a number of years later, Tanaka further clarified the point at issue here:

> I personally believe that it is close to impossible for the State, on the basis of legislation, to elucidate the objectives of education. Educational activities are essentially based on the creativeness of individuals; they are cultural, not political, undertakings. When we realize that they take place outside the world in which law can properly intervene, it becomes incumbent upon us to acknowledge that there must be limits on the extent to which the Constitution or any other law makes specific provisions for education.

When we think about this in conjunction with Tanaka's arguments on educational independence, his logic appears to be most reasonable:

> Education must not be compelled to submit to improper administrative control at the hands of the State. Education should be freely carried out by educators who themselves are free and independent.

This being the case, it is indeed correct and proper to argue, as Tanaka often did, that to guarantee the autonomy of education, legislators should refrain from using their authority to control educational activities.

Thus we must keep the following points in mind when thinking about the issue of whether the Constitution and the Fundamental Law of Education exceed these limits and infringe upon the autonomy of education. The principles that breathe life and vitality into the Constitution are based on an unshakable belief in the inviolability of human rights and popular sovereignty. These are universal principles, the fruits of mankind's age-old struggles against injustice and despotism. In the case of Japan, these values have been tied to the nation's deeply felt desires for peace and the renunciation of war, desires rooted in the suffering and sacrifices the People were compelled to make for the haughty rulers of the Imperial State. These ideals, universally applicable and clearly oriented towards the future, are becoming more and more highly valued in our current historical context, and we must continue to hold out great expectations for their further development. The Constitution is, then, uncompromising towards and intolerant of the politics and politicians who disregard the sanctity of these principles.

Furthermore, it is absolutely crucial that, in order to realize these ideals, freedoms of thought and conscience as well as academic and educational liberty must be guaranteed. The necessity of such guarantees is underscored by the fact that academic and educational freedom are the *sine qua non* for the activities of creative inquiry required to make the defense of peace and the actualization of a democratic social life possible. Thus the Constitution, by not stipulating any specific provisions for education, and the Fundamental Law of Education, by clearly fixing the limits of educational administration, attempted to formally guarantee the independence of education from State control.

This means that there is a need to clearly prohibit politically based and therefore arbitrarily enforced educational control. It was recognized at that time that educational authority had to be liberated from the grasp of the Imperial bureaucracy and put into the hands of the People. These measures also revealed a well-justified fear of the dangers which would arise if educational autonomy came to be plundered under the guise of procedural legality. This was closely tied to an appeal to the People that, to preserve this precious independence, they had to take the direct responsibility for education. It is therefore no exaggeration to claim that the educational system grounded in the Constitution and the Fundamental Law of Education was designed to provide checks against the State's attempts to improperly control education in the future in the manner in which it had done so in the past.

I would also like to call attention to the idea that education must be independently organized as an activity possessing its own unique human values and ideals. This is the other side of the principle which declares that just as the State must not be allowed to use its powers to interfere in the domain of culture, neither should the People tolerate such impositions of State authority and the forms of intellectual control that accompany it. In this light it is clear that the basic problem of educational administration and educational law these days is how to define the conditions which are necessary for fostering the development of education's essential attributes—i.e., what are the conditions that will inspire and not impede the highly desirable flowering of the child's human potential? In short, what exactly is it that should be legally guaranteed to the People, and what must be denied to the government?

Only after we discern the basic nature of education and think about *its* unique laws and values can we objectively identify the grounds for erecting a system of *educational law*, a system genuinely responsive to the needs of human development and not merely a practical application of the more general principles of administrative law. In this regard it must also be recognized that the prewar system, dominated as it was by the narrowly nationalistic values embedded in the Imperial Rescript on Education, could neither tolerate nor support the development of those values which I want to distinguish as essentially educational in character, and it most certainly did not allow any room for the growth of an *educationally* meaningful system of educational law.

It is therefore exceedingly important to recognize that the postwar reforms of education are only truly meaningful when grasped as the outcome of a radical criticism of the principles that informed the system which was based on the Imperial Rescript. In this sense we can see why these reforms erected an image of a democratic and pacifistic human being in opposition to the image of a militaristic and nationalistic human being, and why the aim of this new education had to be the cultivation of people who love truth and respect independence. Moreover, it should now be clear why the basic principles of educational administration in this new setup were defined as the elimination of bureaucratic control over education, the eradication of State interference in the inner workings of the educational apparatus, and the confirmation of educational autonomy so as to ensure the growth of the teacher's creative educational practice. Thus we must not lose sight of the significance of the fact that ideas such as "popular sovereignty" or "education as a citizen's right" are completely different from the ideas of "Imperial sovereignty" and the notion that education is one of the Imperial subject's basic duties.

In conclusion, then, let me reiterate that the shift from an educational system based on the Imperial Rescript to one resting atop the Fundamental Law of Education was not limited, as some want to think, merely to a redefinition of the nation's educational objectives. It signified, rather, a complete transformation of the entire structure of Japan's educational enterprise. To the extent that it repudiated the basic orientation of the Imperial educational system, the Fundamental Law of Education was indeed a *new constitution* for education. Thus there is no way whatsoever to legitimate the calls frequently put forth for a democratic Imperial Rescript (see Chapter 5). Democratization meant that Japanese thought in general was liberated from the framework of the *kokutai* ideology, and education in particular was liberated from the dehumanizing fetters of the Imperial education system. This could only lead to the establishment of a system that entrusts educational authority to the independence and creativity of the People.

5 Education and Law in Postwar Japan: The Problem of Continuity and Change

I. The Process of Reform: Continuity and Rupture

A. Disposing of the Imperial Rescript on Education

The ideals informing the postwar reform of Japanese education did not redefine its reality simply by virtue of their inherent rightness; nor were they unanimously endorsed at all levels of society. Because they represented a thoroughgoing repudiation of long-cherished ideals, it was inevitable that those elements in Japanese society which still valued prewar notions would dress them up in new guises to save them from complete eradication.

Since history is propelled by the contradictions between the actual and the ideal, or the new and the old, in order to grasp the problematic character of postwar Japanese education it is necessary to more fully explore the continuities and ruptures between schooling in prewar Japan and that in the postwar years in terms of the relations between education and educational law.

Shifting sovereignty from the Emperor to the People represented a clear and unambiguous rupture. Its political origins are to be found in what the constitutional law scholar Miyazawa Toshiyoshi has called the August 15 Revolution. However, even within this apparent rupture we can identify disturbing continuities between prewar and postwar political processes and social predispositions.

It is relatively easy to trace these continuities back to the efforts of the ruling elites, who struggled in whatever way they could to resist an open declaration of popular sovereignty in the Constitution and fought tenaciously to preserve the existence of the Imperial system. It is no exaggeration to say that their efforts paid off in the form of the retention of the Emperor as a symbol, and that by the end of the Occupation period they had regained their grip on the reins of power in Japan.

The system founded on the Imperial Rescript on Education could not be swept away in one broad stroke by the early postwar educational reforms. As testified to by the controversies surrounding the problem of how to dispose of the Imperial Rescript, there was great confusion and bewilderment and much searching for ways that would neutralize or at least minimize the psychosocial dislocation these transformations brought on.

When we consider these matters carefully it becomes clear that the Imperial system and the Imperial Rescript on Education were inseparable. Thus, no matter what claims are made about "Japanese-style democracy" or "a democratic Imperial Rescript," we must be especially wary of the real objectives of those political actors within Japan's ruling elite who have repeatedly sought to reintroduce into the postwar political environment the ideologies of "preserving the national entity" (*kokutai no goji*) and "defending the Imperial system" (*tennōsei no yōgo*). We must also pay special attention to the consequences of the Allies' decision to overlook the Emperor's war responsibility and use the Imperial institution to further the aims of the Occupation. By allowing the Emperor to escape culpability for the tragic war fought in his name, and deciding to restore him as a symbol of national unification, the Americans were able to depoliticize the Imperial institution and use it as an effective tool for achieving political control.

Based on the paradoxically convergent interests of the Occupation authorities and Japan's own ruling class, a number of directives were issued in rapid-fire succession between the time of the surrender and the issuance in March 1946 of the U.S. Education Mission report—the "negative measures" that repudiated ultranationalistic and militaristic educational ideologies and their influences upon the determination of teachers' qualifications, the selection of classroom materials, and educational administration in general.

While these measures effectively dissolved the knot that held the State and Shintoism together, no official action was taken with regard to the Imperial Rescript. Not surprisingly, the U.S. Education Mission's report did criticize the process of control through the issuance of the Imperial Rescripts:

> The observance of ceremonies in the reading of the Imperial Rescript and obeisances to the Imperial Portrait in the schools are regarded as undesirable.

But the report went no further than this, and it displayed an extremely cautious attitude towards the Imperial Rescript on Education.

On the Japanese side, too, there was a great deal of circumspection with regard to the problem of how to preserve the Imperial institution and how best to dispose of the Imperial Rescript on Education. We can classify these responses into four distinct types.

The first was an open advocacy of the Imperial Rescript's continued validity. The liberalist Maeda Tamon, who as Minister of Education from October 1945 until January 1946 was the first person directly charged with responsibility for overseeing the postwar educational reforms, gave a radio address on September 9, 1945, entitled "A Proclamation to Youth and Students," which succinctly reveals the thinking of Japan's leaders in the weeks immediately following the war's end:

> I am quite sure that even at this most unfortunate time in our history, as we are feeling the effects of the recent Imperial edict, all of you still appreciate the beneficence of the *kokutai*. To show our respect for the Imperial decision, let us cast aside all differences of standpoint and opinion, and let all of us, acting in a common spirit, display our resolve to humbly accept this Imperial mandate.

In an address presented on October 15 concerning the "Directions for a New Japanese Education," Maeda argued that the educational world should be purged of all forms of militarism and extremely narrow-minded nationalism, and should rededicate itself to the promotion of "our exalted moral principles":

> Let us once again respectfully read the Imperial Rescript on Education and endeavor in our hearts to carry out the teachings of its exalted instruction.

Maeda Tamon's successor as Minister of Education, Abe Yoshishige (January–May 1946), proclaimed to an assembly of local governors that "there are many doubts afloat in the world today, but there is no basis for changing our respect for the Imperial Rescript on Education as the standard of our daily morality." And in a nationally broadcast radio speech he declared:

> The Imperial Household [*kōshitsu*] is the nucleus of our national life. Let us, in these dark days following the end of the war, worship the Imperial Rescript on the New Year, and extol the Imperial will as it endeavors to construct a new State.

Abe was followed as education minister by Tanaka Kōtarō (May

1946–January 1947), who also maintained that the Imperial Rescript on Education was still valid and on this basis rejected the efforts then being made to petition the Emperor for a new Imperial Rescript. Tanaka expressed his thinking in a speech before the Ninetieth Session of the Imperial Diet:

> The Imperial Rescript has existed for all historical time as the infallible, inviolable, and cardinal principle of Japanese ethics.

In what must be seen as a rather remarkable statement, Tanaka further insisted that because the virtues expounded by the Imperial Rescript on Education are essentially based on natural law, it would be meaningless to revoke them.

Amano Teiyū, a famous Kantian, spoke on September 25, 1946, at the second meeting of the First Special Committee of the Educational Reform Council, which was considering the problem of how to handle the fundamental ideals of education as they related to the Imperial Rescript:

> As the standard of Japanese morality, the Imperial Rescript is indeed a superb thing, and there is absolutely no basis for abandoning it.

From this point of view, it was useless, Amano maintained, to even think about calling upon the Emperor to proclaim a new Imperial Rescript on Education.

The second response to the problem of what to do about the Imperial Rescript took the form of an argument which called on the Diet to petition the Emperor for a new Rescript on Education that would be better suited to the requirements of a new age. Representative of this position was the Committee of Japanese Educators that was formed to cooperate with the U.S. Education Mission. In its report it expressed the following opinion concerning the Imperial Rescript:

> As a manifestation of the principles of universal justice [*tenchi no kōdō*], the hitherto existing Imperial Rescript on Education was certainly not mistaken in its teachings, but, along with the change of the times, let us be honored with the receipt of a new Imperial edict that hereafter will give appropriate direction to the spiritual lives of our people, and let it be based on the ideals of pacifism that will constitute the nucleus for the construction of a new Japan. This new Imperial edict should clarify the fundamental

policies for our new national education as well as for our re-conceived national spiritual life and being. . . . This new decree should avoid enumerating specific virtues . . . and stay clear of giving the appearance of using words that directly suggest an order from the Emperor himself. . . . What we have in mind rather is an expression of the Emperor's worries over the nation's future and his concern for the well-being of the People that will muster their absolute trust with regard to education and fully permeate their thinking. . . . As for its compositional style, it is preferable for it to be extremely plain and simple, with a deeply intimate form, and if possible in a colloquial style [kōgo buntai].

This Committee of Japanese Educators was made up of representative intellectuals of the day, with the President of the University of Tokyo, Nambara Shigeru, as its head. It did not directly follow the wishes of the Occupation authorities, aiming instead for a reform of Japanese education that could grapple with the problem of the independence (shutaisei) of the Japanese people.

Ashida Hitoshi, who in 1948 would become Japan's fifth postwar prime minister, also expounded on the necessity of a new Imperial Rescript at a meeting of the First Special Committee of the Educational Reform Council in September 1946:

I recognize the status of the Emperor as the symbol of the national unification of the Japanese people, in particular his power to provide spiritual leadership. Seen as an expression emanating from the spiritual center of Japanese life, the bestowal of a new Imperial Rescript would not violate the spirit of our new Constitution.

But Ashida's real contempt for the Japanese people was revealed by his next statement:

Because the Japanese people are incapable of understanding the Constitution, it will enter their heads better if presented to them in the form of an Imperial Rescript written in the simplest of language. Because the Emperor is the most popular figure in Japan, there will be no difficulties whatsoever in utilizing this format.

This argument, which saw no contradiction between the meaning of the new democratic Constitution and the call for a new Imperial

Rescript, showed an essentially anti-democratic and anti-constitutional bias predicated on a view of the People as basically ignorant (*guminkan*); this is an old but familiar motif in Japanese political thought, one repeatedly used to legitimate despotism.

The third approach to this problem called for a new Imperial Rescript to declare that the 1890 Imperial Rescript on Education was no longer valid. For example, Morito Tatsuo, who would be Minister of Education from May 1947 to October 1948, in the Katayama and Ashida Cabinets, argued that the contents of the existing Rescript were based on "feudalistic principles" and that it was "in its basic spirit totally inappropriate to the construction of a democratic State." In a speech to the first meeting of the First Special Committee of the Council on Educational Reform, he criticized the Imperial Rescript on Education, saying that the important tasks of education should be formulated and decided upon through the supreme will of the People in conformity with the Constitution.

However, because Morito's thinking was only directed to the problem of "weakening the power which the conservative strata of society exert over education," he was quite prepared to petition for a new Rescript, one suited to the educational needs of the time. In short, he only wanted a document that would negate the hitherto existing one:

> It would be most troublesome if we receive a Rescript like the previous one. If we receive a clear statement in this new Rescript that education must be based on the new conditions in Japan, then it will not be necessary to say whether the former one was either good or bad. Isn't putting forth a new one in this manner the best way?

While it is beyond doubt that Morito, along with Mutai Risaku, played a very important part in the efforts to democratize education in the meetings of the Educational Reform Council, it is clear that even such supporters and advocates of democracy were themselves not free from the mystique of Imperial Rescripts.

In response to a question posed to him during the course of the deliberations over the Fundamental Law of Education concerning the relationship between it and the Imperial Rescript on Education, Minister of Education Takahashi Seiichirō argued:

> I think there is no basis whatsoever for charging that there is an essential contradiction between the two of them. However, moral

teachings change along with the tendencies of the times. And since the hitherto existing Imperial Rescript was misinterpreted and abused, it has been decided not to reverently read it in the schools any longer. However, I do not hold the belief that the thinking which enriched and glorified the Rescript was absolutely mistaken; nor is the Fundamental Law of Education in any sense its replacement, nor could it ever even aspire to be.

The minister's rather vague opinion on the Imperial Rescript is diametrically opposed to his explanation of the proposed Fundamental Law of Education, in which he argued for a system of education based on the will of the People. The obvious contradictions in the government's own position regarding what to do about the Imperial Rescript reflect the widely divergent thinking of the day. Those directly charged with the responsibility for reforming Japanese education accepted as an unavoidable premise the notion of an educational system based on the People's will as expressed in the Diet, which they thought of as the supreme organ of State authority. Nonetheless, even though they rejected the patently contradictory call for a new Imperial Rescript, they still sought to preserve the grounds for the existence of the Imperial will. Even if the Rescript on Education lost its formal validity, they wanted to be able to minimize the damage to the institution of Imperial Rescripts.

The fourth response to this problem was embodied in the historian Hani Gorō's address to the Upper House of the Japanese Diet, on May 27, 1948, entitled "On the Abolition of the Imperial Rescript." Hani's remarks were in clear opposition to the thinking of both Japan's ruling class and leading intellectuals because they were free from the thinking that supported the Imperial Rescript; they even implied a radical criticism of it. Hani insisted that the Imperial Rescript should not be treated in a passive way as it had been up to that time, but should be straightforwardly disposed of by means of a legal directive that unambiguously repealed it. This, he argued, required a detailed explanation to the public of exactly how the Imperial Rescript had been injurious and detrimental to the nation:

The fundamental problem with the Imperial Rescript on Education lay in the fact that it sought to impose solutions to all moral problems and issues through one-sided commandments of the sovereign. Some people think that there are aspects of the Rescript which it is not necessary to oppose, but that isn't the real issue. For example, even if the Rescript stated what is absolutely true, this is unacceptable because it would be forcibly ordered on the basis of an Imperial mandate. Even if there were not a single flaw in it, and even if it gave expression to unchallengeable verities, it would be mistaken simply because it was an order forced on the citizenry by a despotic regime.

The argument advocated by Hani was ultimately upheld, and on June 19, 1948, the Lower House adopted a Resolution Eliminating the Imperial Rescript on Education and Related Rescripts, which emphasized that to construct a democratic and peaceful State, it is necessary to work for the "promotion and renovation of education in accordance with the Fundamental Law of Education":

> Because the hitherto existing administrative apparatus has been unsatisfactory, we have been improperly burdened with a body of Imperial mandates, ranging from the Rescript on Education to that for Soldiers and Sailors, that have essentially corrupted the work of education. Furthermore, it is misleading to make the claim that these documents can continue to serve as the guiding principles of our national morality. . . . Because the basic ideals expressed in these Imperial mandates reside in notions of monarchical sovereignty and of a mythical *kokutai*, they are oppressive to human rights, and violate the principles of international justice. In accordance with the intent of Article 98 of the Constitution, this House of Representatives eliminates all of these Imperial mandates, and declares that their guiding principles are no longer recognized. The government is hereby ordered to collect all copies of them, and must take whatever steps are required to ensure that they are removed from national life.

On the same day, the Upper House, in addition to its adoption of the resolution declaring the Imperial Rescript null and void, passed a measure "designed to establish the true dignity of education and further the national morality by imploring the entire nation to struggle to realize the uncompromising principles stated in the Fundamental Law of Education."

Based on these parliamentary resolutions, the Ministry of Education issued a directive "On the Treatment of the Imperial Rescript on Education" (June 25, 1948), which ordered that all copies of this document be removed from the schools. In this way the Imperial Rescript on Education actually disappeared from the schools of Japan, and its annulment was finally confirmed.

Curiously enough, even though the new Constitution had already been in effect for a year, and Imperial sovereignty had been replaced by popular sovereignty, until a special resolution of the Japanese Diet was passed in 1948, the Imperial Rescript on Education could not be—and in fact was not—officially repudiated. Here we find striking evidence both of the persistent reluctance of Japan's leaders to renounce the Imperial Rescript and of the difficulties the Japanese people had to overcome to establish a genuine democracy. Finally we can begin here to intuit the earliest signs of the forces that would later on be organized to emasculate the Fundamental Law of Education and replace it with a postwar variant of the discredited Imperial Rescript.

B. Assigning Value to the Principle of Local Autonomy

Prewar educational administration had been placed under the general administrative control of the Imperial State's centralized bureaucracy. The postwar educational reforms sought to completely redefine the standards and procedures available to the central government and to substitute the principle of local autonomy. Accordingly, it was hoped that the tasks of educational administration would no longer be envisioned as a matter of single-minded direction and supervision, but would be seen rather in terms of providing the best possible professional advice and guidance.

The principle of local autonomy, as stipulated in Article 92 of the Constitution, was established to redefine the foundations for administrative activities in general. The Home Ministry, whose bureaucrats haughtily occupied the premier position of authority in the prewar Japanese administrative system, was dissolved, and the jurisdiction of locally constituted self-governing bodies was strengthened. Educational administration, which along with police administration had played an important role in maintaining order in Imperial Japan, was restructured so as to be responsive to the will of the residents of the various localities. To facilitate the realization of these ends, publicly elected boards of education were instituted.

The thinking behind this system of governance was formulated in accordance with the principles of the modern democratic state. As Thomas Paine said, "The Constitution takes precedence over the State, and the People take precedence over the Constitution." In other words, the principles of human rights were conceived prior to those underwriting the existence of the modern state, and the organization of the State was therefore based on the principle of respect for human rights. Accordingly, when it is perceived that these rights are in danger of being violated, it is the responsibility of the State to defend them. In an analogous way, the rights to regional or local autonomy were conceived as having an inviolable status which the State is obligated to respect. Thus regional autonomy is not granted by the State, nor should the mechanisms of self-rule depend for their existence upon the prior existence of the State. Local authority (*pouvoir municipal*) and the manner in which it was conceived as something inherently belonging to the people of a particular locale were accentuated by the bourgeois revolutions that took place in various countries and affected the composition of the governments that these upheavals gave rise to. It is not wrong, then, to declare that, in a historical sense, regional and municipal self-government precedes the existence of the modern State.

It is thus quite reasonable to regard the modern State as having a duty to respect the principle of local autonomy. It is also entirely appropriate to think of the Japanese Constitution (which belongs among the modern constitutions that guarantee human rights) as authorizing an administrative system premised on the idea of local autonomy.

However, this principle, no matter how natural or appropriate it may seem, was not adopted easily during the course of the Constitution's formulation. Provisions for local autonomy failed to appear in either the government-sponsored draft or those that were drawn up by various private parties. It first appeared in the February 13, 1946, Draft for a Constitution prepared by the American military authorities in the Occupation's General Headquarters. That document states:

> The inhabitants of the capital area, cities and towns are, . . . within the boundaries of law, guaranteed the right to draw up their own charters.

However, in the final version of the Constitution, as it exists today, the term "inhabitants" was replaced by the phrase "locally constituted public bodies," and the word "charter" was altered to read "ordinances and regulations." As the political scientist Tsuji Kiyoaki has pointed out:

> The most important objective behind this thinking, the desire to make local residents the real bearers of local autonomy, was thus made to disappear from the main text of the document in a blink of the eye.

Furthermore, as revealed by this linguistic turn, local autonomy was based in the end, not on respect for the idea that these powers are inherent in the existence of a locale, but on the theory that these powers are ultimately handed down by the State. Here we can see just how deeply postwar thinking was influenced by the administrative consciousness developed in prewar Japan. In this regard it is worth looking at Minobe Tatsukichi's theory of administrative power, a theory which is commonly accepted as having defined for prewar Japanese legal consciousness the nature of regional authority and the extent of its jurisdictional discretion:

> Because the local self-governing body comes into existence only after the State grants it recognition, it can have no existence prior to that of the State. Therefore the duties of the self-governing body are only those which are entrusted to it by the State, and there is no justification whatsoever for its taking the initiative in declaring its own realm of affairs. Thus, even though one may think of these duties as belonging to the local body, in the end they are nothing other than those delegated to it by the State. Any attempt to distinguish between the self-governing body's inherent and entrusted powers has no basis in reality as its authority is always rooted in the prior existence of the State.

Tsuji Kiyoaki points out that Minobe's theory was the commonly accepted one among the majority of prewar scholars of public law. Furthermore, he notes, strictly from the point of view of legal relations, the greater number of scholars of public law even in the postwar present still uphold Minobe's theory of delegated powers.

Tanaka Jirō, a major authority in the field of administrative law, also recognized this feature of postwar thinking about the legal character of administration:

> The postwar reforms of our legal system were extremely profound. However, in spite of all the alterations, owing to the lack of forcefulness in our research—or, perhaps I should say, to our neglect— there has not yet come into being a firm and rigorous, commonly accepted theory which can claim to have taken the place of Minobe's theory. . . . Up to the present day, revisions of administrative law have only been partial, theoretical interpretations, even though we have reached the point at which we should be witnessing a theoretical recomposition of the total body of administrative law.

Here we see a reconfirmation of Otto Meyer's maxim, "Even if the Constitution is changed, administrative law does not change." And, even more significantly, behind this theory of public law we can detect the persistent influence of the theory that the State exists as the nation's ultimate juridical entity.

This theory, according to political scientist Matsushita Kei'ichi,

> was a concoction of nineteenth-century German thinking about the State which sought to reconcile the political opposition between monarchical and popular sovereignty by making each into a separate organ and sublating them under the notion of an abstracted State sovereignty. . . . Postwar constitutional scholarship, beginning with the official *Commentary on the Constitution*,[1] has accomplished nothing more than substituting the citizenry for the Emperor as the supreme organ of the State. In effect, the legal technology of prewar Japan continued unscathed in the discourse on the State as ultimate juridical entity. In the prewar debates on the Constitution, the point of controversy was whether the Emperor was the subjective nucleus [*shutai*] of the State or its organ, whereas in the postwar environment it has shifted to the question of whether the citizenry is the nucleus of the State or its organ.

By converting the theory of the Emperor as organ of the State into a theory of the citizenry as supreme State organ, postwar constitutional thought has made it impossible to articulate a theory of the State based on genuine popular sovereignty. This way of thinking has in many regards totally emasculated the new Constitution and transformed it into merely an empty shell of the early reformers' intentions.

An identical pattern is visible with respect to the "conversion" of postwar Japan's new educational ideals and the basic organizational arrangements that support them. Article 23's stipulation of academic freedom and Article 26's provision for the right to receive an education were enunciated in clear opposition to the prewar usurpation of the People's freedoms of thought and belief. Notwithstanding this sharp break with the past, at the level of legal interpretation, as represented by the *Commentary on the Constitution*, these provisions were interpreted to mean that the State must work to fully guarantee compulsory education. The argument that there is no difference at the level of compulsory education between the State's and the People's

---

[1] The *Commentary on the Constitution* was an authoritative, authorized interpretation of the postwar Constitution by the Hōgaku Kyōkai, a group of eminent legal scholars mostly from the University of Tokyo Faculty of Law.

control reveals a shocking lack of understanding of the historical significance of the constitutional provision for the right to receive an education, and demonstrates precisely how prewar educational thought governs conditions even today.

The same problems can be detected with regard to the critically important issues of educational autonomy and the decentralization of educational authority as well. Thus, notwithstanding the Fundamental Law of Education's clear stipulation in Article X of the limits and responsibilities of educational administration, the agencies of central educational administration continue to bureaucratically control local educational administration and employ the authority of the State to interfere with the inner workings of the educational process. As we shall presently see, the 1956 repeal of the 1948 Board of Education Law, which had guaranteed the local self-control of education and the citizens' basic educational rights, and its subsequent replacement by a law which provided for appointed boards of education (the Law Pertaining to the Organization and Management of Local Education) was the most open expression of this shift in the postwar educational environment.

II. Reconstituting Postwar Education: Undermining the Fundamental Law of Education

A. The Abstractness of the Postwar Reforms

It was by no means easy for the ideals of the postwar educational reform to take root in Japanese society. Attempts to carry out significant democratic reforms were opposed at every turn, and the reformers had to stand firm and hold their ground in the face of countless obstacles and rearguard attacks. To understand these challenges, we must not overlook the profound changes taking place in the international political environment or the disheartening alterations in the liberalizing policies of the Occupation authorities. In particular, the outbreak of the Korean War gave a new lease on life to the opponents of the ideal of Japan as a pacifist state, and provided them with an opportunity to regain many of their prewar powers. Under these conditions, as Japan took the first steps down the path to remilitarization, the early postwar dedication to the goals of "peace education" was subjected to doubt and re-examination. The signing of the San Francisco Peace Treaty and ratification of the U.S.-Japan Security Treaty sparked intense debate concerning the meaning of "national independence" and "love for the homeland." In turn, this prompted severe criticisms of Japan's "new education" and its stated objectives.

In response to these dangerous trends, Uehara Senroku and Munakata Seiya engaged in 1951 in a series of discussions collected and published under the title *The Creation of the Japanese People* (Tōyō Shokan, 1952). This discourse was extremely important because it helped to foster a new concern with reformulating the most essential tasks of a humanely liberating form of education.

Uehara Senroku construed these issues in relation to the problem of how to reconstruct the foundations required for an enduring form of natural community. "How is it possible," he asked,

> to rediscover the destiny of the Japanese nation and properly fashion our future? I believe that the answer lies in an inquiry into the relations between the various meanings of our existence as independent individuals, as citizens of the Japanese nation, and as members of the human community. In short, it is precisely in this manner that we can positively respond to the demand for educational ideals that will contribute to the "formation of the new Japanese."

Munakata Seiya agreed that the educational objectives of the Fundamental Law of Education were "basically correct," but argued that he couldn't help but feel that somehow or other they were too abstract. To replace the destructive ideology that dominated prewar education, he insisted:

> We must depict and delineate the new objectives of education in more vivid and concrete terms. If we do not, it will prove impossible to truly dissociate ourselves from the ideas and methods that have controlled our educational practices up to now. In essence I feel that we should be trying our hardest to relate the new educational objectives we desire to a more concrete image of man, for our careful investigations have revealed that a clear image of what a Japanese person should be has yet to appear—a new image that could be shared and upheld by the common man.

In this spirit Munakata called for a new representation of human beings as students, one that did not stop at the level of a coldly distant ideology or of abstract educational objectives. It was only, he said, when questions like "how do and how should children express their emotions, behave and carry themselves, speak, etc.," are raised that the new educational ideals might become living forces in Japanese society.

Consciousness of the importance of these issues was widely shared by the many teachers who unselfishly struggled for independence and peace and sought through their teaching to further the goals of a democratic form of education. At the end of 1951 the First General Meeting on Educational Research sponsored by Nikkyōso, the Japan Teachers' Union, was held, and initial steps were taken towards investigating the problems of peace and national independence as issues intimately related to the formulation of educational practice. It was also at this time that nongovernmental, independent educational research groups began to criticize the abstractness and false optimism of the new education being imposed from above by the Ministry of Education. It is important to note that by this time those criticisms were being made by teachers based on their own classroom experiences.

For example, the Society of History Teachers (Rekikyōkyō) was formed in July 1949 for the purpose of fostering a scientific approach to historical education. This group attacked both the ultranationalism of prewar history education and the amorphous and pointedly non-nationalistic character of the history instruction offered in the early postwar period. In the Society's Articles of Association we find this expressed as follows:

We hereby affirm the principle of unlimited love for our homeland as the foundation for a proper form of historical education. But in making this the basis for our work we recognize that a genuinely scientific form of historical education is as incompatible with nationalism as it is with a cosmopolitanism that is devoid of any concept of the importance of homeland. Thus it is our conviction that the best type of historical education is one which nourishes both a healthy form of national self-confidence and a consciousness of the importance of the spirit of internationalism, because in the end both theory and the realities of history teach us that a nation's independence and autonomy must ultimately be premised on true respect for the principles of internationalism. Accordingly, historical education must be strictly based on the fruits of historical scholarship and practiced with regard to the best lessons that educational theory has to teach us. In other words, it must be conducted in a manner that is free from all forms of pressure grounded in principles that exist outside the realm of scholarly and educational truth.

Since the time of its organization, Rekikyōkyō has therefore worked to scientifically clarify the "challenge of nationhood" and has continued to insist that it is only through a well-articulated program of research and education in history that genuine "national independence" is in fact achievable. This approach, its members have repeatedly argued, is indispensable to the realization of peace and democracy.

Similarly, the Society for the Scientific Study of Education (Kyōkaken), in its declaration of intentions at the time of its rehabilitation in 1952,[2] stated:

> We seek to expedite the development of a democratic and pacifist form of education in Japan in accord with the ideals expressed in the Constitution and the Fundamental Law of Education. It is in this spirit that we fervently want to contribute to the work of constructing the foundations of an independent nation.

And, on the goals of education:

> We believe it is critically important to educate Japanese children so that they will acquire the knowledge and intellectual skills [gakuryoku] necessary for the citizens of a state based on the principles of popular sovereignty—in other words, so that they can grow up to become members of society who are autonomous agents living within the framework of a group and its activities. With these goals firmly in mind, we dedicate our activities to discovery of the best ways to guide children in their education so that they can mature as individuals who (1) are replete with the spirit of respect for human rights, (2) possess richly expressive emotions, and (3) see, think, and act rationally. In essence, we seek to instill in them the strength to overcome the bad influences in today's society and to have a hopeful outlook for the future.

In this way the members of Kyōkaken opened the way for an organization that would allow teachers, parents, and young people to talk with one another and work within an organized framework to create a "substantive People's education."

In addition to these groups we should also mention the establishment of the Joint Association of Independent Educational Research

---

[2] This group had originally been established in 1937 but was disbanded by the government in 1941. The author has been an active member and has served as editor of its journal, Kyōiku (Education). See Chapter 12 for a more detailed discussion of this and other groups concerned with educational reform.

Groups (Minkyōren), in which a wide spectrum of research bodies participated and worked to awaken the nation's consciousness to the tasks required in each academic subject and educational area in order to create a democratic state and the educational infrastructure necessary for upholding it and helping it to mature.

C. Correcting the "Excesses of Democratization"

On the other side of the Japanese political spectrum—the side of the ruling elite—a campaign was launched in 1951 to "correct the excesses" of postwar democratization through the creation of the Committee for the Investigation of Governmental Decree Revision (Seirei Kaisei Shimon Iinkai). The newly inaugurated school system came under this committee's fire and became a highly visible focus of the revisionism leading to the "reverse course" or retreat from the early postwar democratic reforms. One of the most conspicuous features of this campaign was the call for the resurrection of what was then (and is still) heralded as "patriotic" education.

In November 1951 Minister of Education Amano Teiyū drew up a program called "An Outline for National Moral Practice" ("Kokumin Jissen Yōryō") and planned to distribute it to the schools under the direct control of the Ministry of Education. Amano explained his reasons for composing this document as follows:

> Nowadays, as a result of too much emphasis being placed on the "individual" and the "world at large," there has arisen a marked tendency to weaken the ground of the State's existence. This can be neither excused nor thought of as an impartial or unbiased development in Japanese thought.

Amano's plan was designed to provide a new criterion for a national morality based upon and centered around love and respect (*keiai*) for the Emperor. According to "An Outline for National Moral Practice":

> The State is the womb of our existence, the ethical and cultural core of our collective existence and activities. Therefore the very life of the nation depends on those activities which the individual willingly performs so as to contribute to the well-being of the State.

Unfortunately for Amano, his plan was exposed to severe criticism in the various committees of the Diet and publicly ridiculed as "Amano's Imperial Rescript."[3] Amano was obliged to withdraw his plan but after he left office in 1953 published it as the opinion of a private citizen.

It was just around this time that Prime Minister Yoshida Shigeru made the following statement in an address to the Diet:

> In addition to re-examining the educational reforms enacted at the end of the war, we must work, in the light of the current conditions prevailing in our country, to promote the cultivation of patriotism, which is the keystone of our national independence.

Through these words Yoshida expressed his government's intention to alter the path of educational reform and signaled the directions in which this would subsequently be carried out.

The discussions held the next year (1953) between Ikeda Hayato, head of the Liberal Party's Policy Research Committee (he would become prime minister in 1960), and American Assistant Secretary of State Robertson resulted in a repudiation of the goals of peace education and a strong insistence upon the necessity of patriotic education as part of a program designed to propel Japan's remilitarization. Of course this gave rise to the contradiction, still visible in Japanese life today, of a form of patriotism that is subordinated to American global interests.

According to a joint memo issued after these discussions:

> During the eight years of the Occupation, Japanese children received an education which taught them that no matter what might happen, they should never take up arms. Those who were most affected by this "education" are precisely the youth who must now assume the responsibility of safeguarding the Japanese nation.

The political and social difficulties standing in the way of remilitarization were analyzed in this coldhearted manner and the ideals which had given direction and substance to the postwar reform of Japanese education were sacrificed on the altar of expediency. The joint statement continued:

> As a consequence of peace education, the number of conscientious youth entering the Peace Preservation Corps has fallen dramat-

---

[3] The humor in this ridicule rested in part on the fact that the characters for Amano's name can also be read "Tennō," or "Emperor."

ically. However, we cannot very well allow riffraff and rabble into the corps to which the security of the country is entrusted. Moreover, there is also a danger that as a result of the hastily conducted augmentation of the Peace Preservation Corps, it will be difficult to prevent the infiltration of intellectually inferior elements of society. These dangers are compounded by the fact that this stratum of society is ill-equipped to protect us from the military threats posed by the communists, or guard against their attempts to pry into our secrets.

Here we see a typical expression of the opinion that a sudden rapid remilitarization in the case of an emergency would be very dangerous, and an affirmation of the idea that it was necessary to remove the obstacles created by peace education in order to respond to American demands for Japan's remilitarization. Memoranda were exchanged that stated:

The parties to these discussions are in fundamental agreement that it is vitally necessary to bring about changes in the Japanese social environment that will increase the citizenry's sense of responsibility for national defense. Thus the first responsibility of the Japanese government is to make sure that education and the various media are used to nourish and propagate the spirits of patriotism and self-defense throughout society.

Thus patriotic education was resuscitated with the backing of the American government, and the repudiation of peace education was used to provide a vital link in the process leading to Japan's remilitarization.

At about the same time, the then Vice-President of the United States, Richard M. Nixon, declared on an official visit to Japan that the Peace Constitution represented a major "mistake" in America's postwar policy for the reconstruction of Japan. Thus peace education was conceived of by both American and Japanese leaders as an obstacle to constitutional revision and remilitarization. Patriotic education was strongly advocated as the most desirable way to correct what were then being spoken of as the "excesses of democratization." Through their calls for a new emphasis on patriotism the anti-pacifist, anti-socialist, pro-American elements in Japanese society had found a new way to revive the prewar *kokutai* ideology and reassert what were ultimately anti-democratic values.

The following year new legislation was enacted concerning educational neutrality which provided an opportunity for those in power to legitimate a radical change in the relationship between education and the State. In the immediate postwar environment the political neutrality of education had originally been conceived as an expression of the principle of educational autonomy that was guaranteed by the Constitution and the Fundamental Law of Education. Those documents proclaimed that the State should neither hold nor advocate any political doctrines of its own with regard to education, and that it must maintain a neutral position with regard to all questions or problems of social values. The new legislation, however, reconceived the State as the sole defender and protector of educational fairness and impartiality with regard to education. With the passage of this law it was now the State's responsibility to judge precisely what constituted a departure from or violation of the fairness and impartiality of education. This opening made it possible to utilize the mechanisms of educational administration to resurrect the ideologies of nationalism and the structure of an "administratively managed State" (*kanri tōseishugi*). This has effectively emasculated the spirit of the Constitution and the values embodied in the Fundamental Law of Education.

In 1955 three pieces of educational legislation were proposed to the Diet: the Law Concerning the Management and Operation of Local Educational Administration; the Textbook Law; and the Law Establishing an Extraordinary Deliberative Council on the Educational System. The shared aim of all three of these was to bring about substantive reforms that would cut the heart out of the system set in place by the Fundamental Law of Education. In raising the issue of the need "for a re-examination of the Fundamental Law of Education," the then Minister of Education, Kiyose Ichirō, attempted to clarify the reasons why reforms were necessary and the directions in which they should be carried out:

> It is simply not good enough to speak about the rights that accrue to individuals as the members of a democratic society; we must also make as concerted an effort as possible to advocate and nurture among our students feelings of loyalty and devotion to the State. These deficiencies are particularly evident in the existing Course of Study [*gakushū shidō yōryō*] and the way it has been constructed in accord with the Fundamental Law of Education.[4]

Kiyose insisted upon the necessity of clarifying the "State's respon-

---

[4] See a more detailed discussion of the Course of Study in Chapters 8 and 9.

sibility" with regard to the content of education, which, he argued, should not be constrained by the liberalizing objectives laid out in the Fundamental Law of Education, but should be revised to redirect the aims of national education to meet the critical need for citizens who would be loyal and thoroughly devoted to the aims of the State.

The three proposed pieces of legislation were designed primarily to alter the Fundamental Law of Education, in particular its sections on educational objectives (Article I) and on educational autonomy and the stipulation of limits on educational administration (Article X). These legislative proposals aroused severe criticism, spearheaded by a joint declaration of ten university presidents including Yanaihara Tadao of the University of Tokyo, Ōuchi Hyōe of Hosei University, and Uehara Senroku of Hitotsubashi University.

Yanaihara Tadao, speaking to a joint meeting of the Cabinet and the Upper House's Educational Policy Committee, declared:

> The most critical part of the agenda provided us by the Fundamental Law of Education is the cultivation of individuals having personalities suited to life in a democratically organized society. In opposition to those who are attempting to remake our new educational system to ensure that it produces obedience in parents and loyalty to the State, I want to argue that these characteristics of a healthy human personality will emerge naturally from a democratic form of education without any special measures being implemented to guarantee the appearance of these values.

Rebutting Kiyose Ichirō's call for "democracy, plus something else," Yanaihara went on to charge that the ugly face of prewar Japanese nationalism was once again emerging from the shadows in which it had gone into hiding. In response to this "extreme danger," Yanaihara declared his total opposition to all such attempts to alter the ideals which had made the Fundamental Law of Education possible.

In the face of numerous counterattacks launched from many corners of Japanese society, only the Law Concerning the Management and Operation of Local Educational Administration was able to pass the Diet by a narrow margin; the other two were soundly rejected. Moreover, the Law on Local Administration could only be passed with the protection of the Special Task Force (Kidōtai), a group of police guards brought into the Diet to maintain order during the tumultuous debate. Nullifying the hitherto existing Board of Education Law, this law replaced the publicly elected boards with appointed ones. This signaled a renunciation of the principle of decentralized educational control, and made it possible for local educational administrations to be subordinated to the administrative apparatus of the central government. Thus the bureaucratic control of education was reintroduced as the most desirable mode of operation. It is very important to point out here that in the wake of this "reform," Article 1 of the old Board of Education Law was totally eradicated.[5]

Along with the two laws that perverted the meaning of educational neutrality, the Law on Local Administration clearly signified an emasculation of the system rooted in the values proclaimed by the Fundamental Law of Education. The very next year, a system for the evaluation of teachers' performance[6] was put into effect, in accord with these new ideas about democracy, and a re-centralization of educational administration was pushed through in the name of educational "normalization."

In 1958 the Course of Study was revised and given a legally binding power that flew in the face of the whole earlier effort to remove the State from the business of prescribing the contents of education. This measure changed the very character of the educational process by removing a great deal of the freedom that had been built into the system put into operation after the war, in which responsibility for making decisions about the curriculum had been entrusted to the teachers. Originally the Course of Study was designed to serve as nothing more than a reference plan, not as something teachers were legally obliged to follow. Yet, after the Ministry of Education unilaterally redefined the status of the Course of Study, it suddenly became illegal to teach anything other than what it prescribed, or to provide instruction in a manner other than that which its authors mandated.

At the same time, the rigorousness of textbook inspection was increased and brought into line with the spirit already seen in the previously cited remarks of Minister of Education Kiyose Ichirō. Up to that time, it was unconditionally stated that the process of textbook certification must be "in strict accord with the Fundamental Law of Education and the School Educational Law and must not be conducted in violation of the spirit thereof." Inasmuch as specific guidelines were given for evaluating textbooks, they had been limited:

Is there, for example, anything that is contrary to educational

---

[5] Article 1 stated that education should not be submitted to improper control, and that the responsibility for carrying it out falls upon the entire populace, through elected boards of education that would fairly express the popular will and conduct educational administration in response to the particular conditions of the locales.

[6] Chapter 10 contains a more detailed discussion of teacher evaluation.

objectives such as cultivating the spirit of peace, respect for truth and justice, respect for individual values, attaching importance to work and responsibility and the spirit of autonomy?

However, in the wake of these 1958 revisions, all the "for example" passages disappeared and were replaced by a vague reference to textbook material that went "against the Fundamental Law of Education." This meant that in effect the Fundamental Law of Education had been shelved. The aims of the Textbook Law which had been defeated only a year earlier could now be realized through the Ministry of Education's "unilaterally imposed administrative guidelines."

D. "The Image of the Desired Japanese"

As Japan entered the 1960s new forms of educational planning were implemented as essential parts of the comprehensive national policy designed to promote high economic growth. It was at precisely this juncture that the government's spokesmen began to introduce the ideology of academic competency (nōryokushugi) in relation to the principle of school diversification (which was really a euphemism for discrimination).[7] Public education was transformed into a system for competition and social selection, and through the formulation and implementation of an official "Image of the Desired Japanese," a substantive transformation of postwar educational objectives was enacted which sought to make education subservient to the wishes of governmental and industrial powers.

From the standpoint of these leaders of society, the educational system based upon the Constitution and the Fundamental Law of Education was little more than an obstacle to the policy of rapid economic growth made possible by the framework of the Japan-U.S. Security Treaty. On August 19, 1960, at the Extraordinary Joint Meeting of the Heads of the Prefectural Boards of Education and Educational Superintendents, the Minister of Education in the first Ikeda Cabinet, Araki Masuo, made these most revealing remarks:

If we accept as our point of departure the notion that the basic aims of our educational system should reside in the cultivation of people whose praiseworthiness is a function of their Japaneseness, then we cannot avoid recognizing that the system grounded in the ideals embodied in the Fundamental Law of Education is deficient in a number of important regards.

[7] See Chapter 13 for a more detailed discussion of academic competency and diversification.

On October 15 of the same year, speaking to the Education and Culture Committee of the Upper House, Araki directly addressed the issue of the necessity of revising the Constitution and the Fundamental Law of Education:

> The American Occupation Policy directly after the war was rooted in the desire to ensure that Japan would never rise and threaten the U.S. again. The currently existing Constitution was forced on us based on this way of thinking, and the Fundamental Law of Education merely reconfirmed these values. Thus it can hardly be claimed in good faith that either of them is a clear expression of the thought and free will of the Japanese people. The Constitutional Investigation Committee has been reappraising the Constitution for almost four years now, and after the upcoming general election, I would like to gather a group of men of wide learning and experience and begin a reappraisal of the Fundamental Law of Education. [*Asahi Shimbun*, Oct. 16, 1960]

Minister of Education Araki, following up on this "public pledge," put the issue of reforming Japan's educational objectives before the Central Educational Council and charged the Council (which was entrusted by the Ministry of Education with the formulation of educational policy) with the responsibility to undertake an inquiry directed at defining "the Image of the Desired Japanese."

In 1961 a nationwide academic achievement test was forcibly administered,[8] and under the banner of "normalizing education" various measures were devised by the government to destroy the teachers' unions in various areas of the country. One of these measures was the strengthening of control over what was supposed to be the teachers' autonomously organized programs for in-service training.[9] During this period the inspection of textbooks by the Ministry of Education was intensified, and even in textbook selection and adoption at the local level, "hidden" administrative guidance was measurably strengthened.

Finally, in 1964, an interim draft of "The Image of the Desired Japanese" was issued, and the next year a definite plan was published. What did this portend for the *system* of education rooted in the Fundamental Law of Education? A partial answer to this can be seen in the reasons for its publication given by Kōsaka Masaaki,[10] the chief

[8] The achievement test is discussed in Chapter 8.

[9] In-service training is the subject of Chapter 10.

[10] Kōsaka Masaaki, a professor of philosophy at Kyoto University before the war and a member of the rightist Kyoto School (*gakuha*) which formulated the

investigator for the committee that issued the "Image":

> While based on the fundamental ideals of the Japanese Constitu-
> tion and the Fundamental Law of Education, it is intended to
> ground this spirit in a more Japanese setting [*fūdo*], and to sup-
> plement the deficiencies of the Fundamental Law. These are the
> motives which have informed the activities of those of us who
> have brought this new statement of ideals to life.

In reality, however, "based on" meant shelving, and "supplement-
ing" meant a series of stages for retrogressively revising the democratic values of postwar Japanese education. And from the previously
cited declaration of Education Minister Araki we can see how inseparably connected the investigation leading to "the Image of the Desired
Japanese" was with the movement to destroy the Fundamental Law
of Education.

The majority opinion in the Report of the Constitutional Investigation Committee published just prior (1964) to the appearance of the
"Desired Japanese" insisted that a Constitution appropriate to Japan

> should, along with the principles of universal humanity, be in
> conformity with Japan's unique history, traditions, and national
> character.

Furthermore, as stated in the Joint Declaration of Intent by the
seventeen individuals who made up the advance guard of the constitutional revision faction within the investigative committee:

> We must devise measures which will successfully preserve Japan's
> long traditions and which are appropriate to Japan's spiritual
> uniqueness. Only when we proceed on the basis of the feelings
> of love the Japanese hold for their homeland, independence, and
> traditions will it become possible to construct for the first time a
> Constitution of the Japanese people, by the Japanese people, and
> for the Japanese people.

These notions were supplemented by the strong opinions of people

---

famous "Philosophy of Total War," had been an important figure in the State's
wartime program of mobilizing intellectuals. He was purged after the war but
returned to academic life in the 1950s. In 1960 he was appointed president of Tokyo
Gakugei University, the leading teacher-training college under the control of the
Ministry of Education.

like Kyoto University Professor Ōishi Yoshio (an advocate of Constitutional revision) concerning the enduring characteristics of Japan's Imperial system:

> The most fundamental problem with our Constitution is that there is nowhere to be found within it the spiritual foundations of the Japanese State. Thus, the Imperial system, which has been established over the long course of the history of the Japanese race, has lost its authority to provide the center of national unification and control. . . . Because the Occupation policies destroyed the spiritual foundations of Japan, the first reason for a thoroughgoing reappraisal of the existing Constitution lies in the imperative we face of re-establishing our spiritual center.

Of course there were many differences of opinion concerning the points to be emphasized; however, it was a shared concern of the constitutional reform advocates to set the Emperor as the centerpiece of national unification. This can be clearly seen in the 1964 report of the Constitution Investigation Committee itself.

The same intellectual grounds that informed the work of the Constitution Investigation Committee can be observed in the criticisms of the educational ideals and objectives of the Fundamental Law of Education and the cries for reform that appeared in "The Image of the Desired Japanese Who Emphasizes His Consciousness as a Japanese."

Among the seventeen people who issued the Joint Declaration of Intent I want to call attention to the name of Aichi Kiichi, one of the leaders in organizing the group's activities. At the time the Interim Report on "The Image of the Desired Japanese" was published, Aichi, then serving as Minister of Education, declared that the "Image" was issued as a substitute for the prewar Imperial Rescript on Education (*Monbu Kōhō* No. 393). He is reported to have officially avowed, "I want to establish an educational charter on the basis of the final report on the Image of the Desired Japanese," and promised that he would work to revise the Fundamental Law of Education (*Tokyo Shimbun*, January 11, 1965).

Kōsaka Masaaki is reported to have said, when asked what "The Image of the Desired Japanese" was based on, that he constructed it after having referred to the Gokajō no Seimon (Charter Oath) of 1868 and the Gunjin Chokugo (Imperial Rescript to Soldiers and Sailors) of 1882. According to the published proceedings of the Special Committee which produced this document, at the time the "Image" was being debated, the first issue taken up was the Imperial Rescript on Education. The chief investigator of the committee even went so far as to liken himself to the Meiji statesman Inoue Kowashi when the latter was drafting the Imperial Rescript on Education ("Personal Views on the Image of the Desired Japanese").[11]

In "The Image of the Desired Japanese" we can see a reflection of its drafters' consciousness of the difference between pre- and postwar Japan.

> As a result of World War II great changes were effected in the structure of the Japanese State and society as well as in the way the Japanese people think. In particular, the reality of our wretched defeat has given rise to the hallucination that the ways of Japan and the Japanese in the past were, almost without exception, mistaken and wrong. This has produced a tendency to disregard Japanese history and the unique character of the Japanese people.

What is obliquely referred to here as "the past" is of course the totality of prewar Japan. For these people, the postwar period—i.e., the history of our democratic accomplishments and the struggles through which they were achieved—is merely a disgusting stain on the purity of the true, Japanese form of experience.

The historical consciousness of those who were involved in the creation of "The Image of the Desired Japanese" is important to consider when attempting to understand the political character of this document. Morito Tatsuo, who had earlier played a progressive role in the democratization of Japanese education during the period of reform immediately following the war, was in 1964 the chairman of the Central Council on Education. Arguing in support of this report, Morito charged that it was now necessary to "reform the postwar reforms":

> What is the basic direction and along what lines should the "re-reforms" be carried out? In regard to this point I think it is desirable to call to mind the very similar conditions that prevailed during the middle of the Meiji period when the new educational system was reformed. [This refers to the creation of the system based on the Imperial Rescript on Education.] The three features of that reform—modernization; Japanese spirit, Western skills;

---

[11] The two imperial declarations of the Meiji era stressed loyalty to the Emperor as the basis for all activities, political, cultural, and military. The Imperial Rescript on Education, which is translated as Appendix A to this volume, is discussed in detail in Chapter 3.

rich country, strong army—were very appropriate for the national policy of that time. It is only natural then to see the strong demands for a recovery of Japan's national autonomy [*shutaisei*] which informs our efforts to re-reform postwar education as essentially similar to the efforts exerted for the reform of education in the middle period of Meiji, which sought to protect the spirit of the Japanese people from the temptations of the Civilization and Enlightenment [Bunmei Kaika] Movement. [*Monbu Jihō* No. 1072]

Chairman Morito's remarks at the time this document was published clearly convey this intention. In his explanation of the construction of "The Image of the Desired Japanese," Morito called special attention to its Section 2, Chapter 4.

I would very much like to see people think about our ideas on what should constitute the qualities desired from the citizens of Japan as members of a state-society. In particular, I want them to carefully read the sections on what constitutes proper patriotism, what constitutes an attitude of respect and affection for the symbols of our national existence, and how to carry forward and further develop our superb national character. (*Monbu Kōhō* No. 432)

Morito spoke even more straightforwardly concerning the aims embodied in "The Image of the Desired Japanese":

Isn't it vitally necessary for us to be fully prepared to defend ourselves in case of an emergency? At such a time, mustn't we possess the resolve to protect our fatherland with every last drop of power we can exert? If we think in this way, I believe that it is most necessary for us to reflect deeply upon the ways of thinking that gained popularity after the war, such as "pacifist country" and "peace education," and correct the policies that issued forth from them. [*Monbu Jihō* No. 1072]

It is interesting to observe that in this report the focus of the qualities which are said to make up the desired Japanese as citizen is located in the "possession of a spirit of respect and affection for symbols." Of course the symbol referred to here is the Emperor, and it is very telling that this is the only place in "The Image of the Desired Japanese" where there is a quote from the Constitution. In an explanation no doubt intended to deceive people concerning this "symbol," it is argued:

If we inquire into what is contained in the idea of respecting and loving the Emperor, we discover that this is an idea which leads to love and respect for the country of Japan. In the final analysis this is because *loving and respecting the Emperor*, who is the proper symbol of Japan itself, leads to *love and respect for the essence of what makes Japan truly Japanese.*

The foundation upholding "The Image of the Desired Japanese" is one and the same as that informing the discourse on revising the Constitution; it is an attempt to create feelings of warmth and nostalgia for the Imperial system and the educational apparatus legitimated by the Imperial Rescript on Education. However, we must not lose sight of the fact that at the same time coercive restraints are imposed upon the scientific depiction of ancient Japanese history through the textbook screening system. Similarly, we must not lose sight of the real aims of those who call for a revival of the Kigensetsu (National Foundation Day, or Anniversary of the Emperor Jimmu's Accession to the Throne) as a national holiday. These impulses are in basic conformity with the thinking which underlies "The Image of the Desired Japanese."

However, we must not comprehend these trends simply as an expression of the reactionary, anachronistic demands of the restorationists (*fukkoshugisha*) or the imperialists (*tennōshugisha*) on the right. If we look at the total picture it becomes quite clear that what is involved here is no simple-minded restorationism. Quite the contrary, the thinking which supported "The Image of the Desired Japanese" is bound up with the American demands for Japan's remilitarization and is solidly connected with the policies of Japan's economic elites designed to make manipulation of the labor force more effective.

Chairman Morito explained at the time of the final report on "The Image of the Desired Japanese" that:

We now possess a dual, perhaps even three-levelled, economic structure, and in response to social demands for a diversified work force suited to these conditions, it is necessary to diversify the latter part of secondary education. The guiding ideals for the reform of educational content in response to this economic imperative is provided for us in "The Image of the Desired Japanese." [*Monbu Kōhō*]

From the viewpoint of a manpower policy designed to meet the demands of the economic sector, we can say that the cultivation of a patriotic self-consciousness along the lines set out in "The Image of the Desired Japanese" on the basis of esteem for the Emperor was highly desirable: in addition to making possible the control of national values (*kokumin no kachikan*), it facilitated the production of a nation of people who would consciously perceive themselves as members of society in terms of the satisfactions they derive from being "totally absorbed in work" (Section 2, Chapter 3 of "The Image"). If we look at this text in this way, it is not possible to lightly dismiss the insistence in "The Image" on esteem for the Emperor and revival of the National Foundation Day as an anachronism on the part of the reactionary elements within Japanese society, or as simply expressions of the cultural and political values that necessarily accompany such outdated forms of thought.

It is true that having been redefined as a symbol, the Emperor was in one sense liberated from his political function in Japanese society. However, this apoliticality was made into a pretext both for parrying the criticisms of the progressive factions within society and for strengthening a sense of psychological stability in the Japanese masses. Thus, rather than serving as a focal point for national unification, the symbol of the Emperor was made into a signifier that could play an ideologically cementing role by forcibly linking together essentially different and conflicting quarters of the national consciousness.

"The Image of the Desired Japanese," in other words, provided an ideologically charged series of representations which legitimized the values of the welfare state in the stage of monopolistic capitalism by appealing to the idea of "being uniquely Japanese." That this is in fundamental opposition to the ideas of popular sovereignty and the People's right to education, as well as being in contradiction with the Constitution and the Fundamental Law of Education, is all too clear. While this version of the Imperial system does have similarities with its prewar predecessor, we must acknowledge that it possesses an essentially different structure and function. This imperialism does not simply reflect the desires of Japan's reactionary groups, because the success of this policy has been a crucial issue for the advocates of the ideology of economic rationalism. In short, "The Image of the Desired Japanese" was in part an ideological camouflage in the plan for reforming senior high school education to meet the demands of the economic world. The warm welcome it received from the head of the Keidanren (Federation of Economic Organizations), Maeda Hajime, only serves to underline this point.

The educational policy of the 1960s, then, was built upon two pillars, each of which drew its life from the idea of "creating people" (*hitozukuri*) as symbolized in "The Image of the Desired Japanese." The first pillar was the policy of diversifying the school system, which we shall later examine more closely as *nōryokushugi* ("ability-first") education (see Chapter 13). The second pillar was the policy of strengthening the State's control over education.

E. Education on Trial

As Japan entered the 1970s, the various strands of revision that had been under consideration during the sixties were consolidated and embossed under the 1971 slogan "The Third Reform of Education." This slogan was intended to give formal notice of the revisions to be imposed on the postwar educational reforms.[12]

Successive Japanese governments, notwithstanding their responsibility to uphold and defend the ideals embodied in the Constitution and the Fundamental Law of Education, have on the one hand attempted to attack in bold fashion the very spirit of those laws, and on the other hand sought by a series of deceptive steps to in fact eradicate the influence of those laws from Japanese educational life.

However, beginning at precisely this time a legal counterattack was launched by the citizenry at large, and Japan's teachers in particular, reflecting the degree to which the spirit of the Constitution and the Fundamental Law of Education had taken root among the People. Let me now briefly turn to an examination of the legal challenges made to the authority of the Ministry of Education in the courts of Japan.

The process of reorganizing the reformed educational system that began in earnest around 1955 engendered so much controversy that it was inevitable for resistance to control imposed from above to break out within the educational world. As these tensions became increasingly pronounced, the conflicts they led to often found their way into the nation's courtrooms. As a result of these prolonged judicial struggles, a unified body of thought concerning "educational rights" has come into existence. The formation in 1970 of the Society for the Study of Educational Law, a group made up of parents and teachers as well as a number of scholars from several disciplines, gave added impetus to the active pursuit of these rights.

Controversies over the efficiency rating system for teachers (see Chapter 10), academic achievement tests (see Chapter 8), and the textbook authorization process (see Chapters 6 and 7) provided the focus for a number of important educational lawsuits (*kyōiku saiban*).

---

[12] In this schema, the first reform was that of the Meiji era; the second, that which had followed World War II.

The courtroom battles waged over these issues have played a very significant role both in the struggle to establish the fundamental working rights of teachers and in the attempt to clarify the meaning of "educational rights" and "educational authority" within the framework of postwar educational law. In this context, the textbook and academic achievement test cases have grown into vigorously contested disputes about the nature of educational power, and have raised new questions about the meaning of our democratic Constitution. We will turn to a more detailed examination of these issues in Part III of this book.

F. The Development of a Nationwide Citizens' Education Movement

The history of postwar Japanese education is not a one-sided story of reaction and of attempts to reverse the course of democratization. It is also the history of the progress and achievements made by an educational movement that has attempted to strengthen and carry forward the spirit of the Constitution and the Fundamental Law of Education. In the course of these struggles, consciousness of the historical importance of human rights has been significantly deepened, and efforts to gain support for these rights through new legal interpretations have continually been intensified. In response to these efforts, the forces of reaction have increased, and greater pressures have been applied to openly destroy the system of education based on the Fundamental Law of Education.

When we speak about a nationwide citizens' educational movement, we must call attention to the diversity and depth it has already achieved. In fact, there are a number of distinct movements, including the teachers' movement for professional autonomy, the parents' movement for participation in the educational decision-making process, city and rural residents' study movements, and a number of workers' self-education movements.

The core of these movements can well be thought of as residing in the efforts schoolteachers have made to improve their everyday teaching practices by supporting their autonomous research and study; these efforts have led to the development of teacher-administered in-service training programs (*kenshū*) (see Chapter 10 for a detailed discussion). In the last analysis, it has been the countless study circles and research organizations both inside and outside the schools, with their exchanges of ideas and teaching practices, their mutual criticism and encouragement, that have made our education movement possible and provided it with intellectual support.

These teachers' movements were intended from the outset to promote cooperation and communication between parents and teachers, and to proceed onward and upward from the firm foundations thus laid for positive action. In fact, it was on the basis of deepening parental concern about education, the democratizing reform of local PTA activities, and regional round-table discussions that criticisms of textbooks and a wide variety of demands (for the right to have a voice in the selection of textbooks, for the building of more upper secondary schools, etc.) became clarified and vocalized in the concrete form of a nation-wide citizens' education movement.

On another level, political alliances against pollution and the exploitation of the natural environment afforded a chance for citizens to further educate themselves. In tandem with workers' on-the-job self-education (as opposed to training administered by the State or by industry), consciousness of the right to *self*-education throughout the whole course of life profoundly contributed to the energies fueling a nationwide education movement. Thus, through an ever-expanding sense of solidarity among teachers, parents, and workers, a wide range of urgent demands have coalesced into a unified whole.

Here we find a most positive and promising response to the Constitution's dual invitation to the Japanese people to give their unceasing efforts to self-information and to accept responsibility for the education of the younger generation: in short, here we find signs of the development of a movement that is indeed worthy of a democratic people.

III. The Special Characteristics of Law and Education in Postwar Japan

Let me now attempt to briefly summarize the relationship between law and education in postwar Japan. The unfolding realities of education during the thirty years of the postwar era have a markedly two-sided nature that closely parallels developments regarding the ideals embodied in the Constitution. On the one hand we have seen these ideals taking firm root in the imagination of the Japanese people, while on the other we have witnessed the government's concerted efforts to emasculate them and rob them of all meaningful content. The history of education in this period can be grasped as the history of the way these opposing forces have advanced in relation to each other.

While the ideals of the Fundamental Law of Education have become fixed in the consciousness of the citizenry and have provided both the foundation for a widely based People's Education Movement and the justification for our struggles to give real meaning to the idea that the People have both the right and the authority to control education, these ideals have also become the target of repeated government efforts to render them impotent.

This multi-faceted relationship among the Constitution, the People, and the government was already hinted at in my discussions of the process through which the Constitution and the postwar reforms came into being. The Constitution was born in a political environment in which the government was hostile and the People were sympathetic. As the civil law scholar Watanabe Yōzō has remarked, this is "extremely strange" when we consider the fact that constitutions are basically designed to protect and guarantee the stability of systems of control and give them clear order and regularity. Furthermore, notwithstanding the fact that the Constitution is the basic law of the existing regime, revising it has been the goal of successive Liberal-Democratic Party governments. On the other side of this equation we have a citizenry which criticizes the government and struggles to protect and further cultivate this Constitution. Here is one of the most telling features of legal life in contemporary Japan.

In the field of education as well, as revealed by the changes in the relations between the State and education and the modifications imposed upon the system grounded in the Fundamental Law of Education (which is basically a guarantee of the citizenry's educational rights and authority and a guarantee of professional educational autonomy), one can clearly detect vestiges of prewar thinking about the application and interpretation of educational law. These previously discredited modes of thought have been remobilized through the discourse on the modern welfare state, a discourse that has in effect relegitimated the prewar ideology of selfless patriotic service (*messhi hōkō*). We may well say that the attempt to confuse and legislate out of existence the concept of the People's educational rights under the banner of a nationalistic system of public education is characteristic of the ideology which is being used to fuse education to the State in present-day Japan.

The carefully orchestrated, step-by-step revisions and violations of the essential integrity of the Fundamental Law of Education enacted by the government, the Ministry of Education, and the various regional boards of education reveal the peculiar nature of the relations between education and the law. As I previously mentioned, through lower-order laws (*kaihō*) which transgress the spirit of the Fundamental Law of Education, our system of educational law has become entwined in contradictions and internal inconsistencies. This is most apparent in the two laws on educational neutrality, the Law Con-

cerning the Management and Operation of Local Education Administration, the awarding of legally binding power to the Ministry of
Education's Course of Study, and the legislative systematization of
the Head Teacher System: all of these measures have substantively
violated the higher-order status which should be recognized as residing in the Fundamental Law of Education. In all of these cases it was
maintained that the legal character of the Fundamental Law of Education is the same as that of these ordinary laws. In short, the principle
of the rule of law (*hōchishugi*) has been used to destroy the foundations of the postwar reforms of education and educational law.

The second characteristic I wish to emphasize concerns cases in
which proposed legislation has been turned down due to the opposition of public opinion or to strong protest within the Diet, but the
aims of such legislation were effectively realized anyway through the
procedural mechanism of revising the Ministry of Education Law or
through the application of official "administrative guidance." Here
we find the principle of the rule of law reduced to a mere matter of
convenience.

In 1956, for example, the government and the Ministry of Education submitted the draft of a law on textbooks that was designed to
strengthen the government's control over the contents of education.
This particular plan was aborted due to the intense criticism leveled
against it both inside and outside the Diet. Yet thereafter, through an
administrative measure (*gyōsei sochi*), the original aims of this draft
(altering the machinery for textbook certification and authorization,
revising the criteria for authorization, and conferring legally binding
power on the Course of Study) were actually realized. Another example
is found in the 1973 "legalization" of the Head Teacher System, which
had already effectively been put into operation through a ministerial
order back in 1957.

Here, then, we see the way in which the government works its will:
first it fulfills its own intentions by an extra-legal mechanism, and then
it formalizes them through legislation when political conditions make
it possible to do so. The Ministry of Education's order concerning the
school's internal supervisory system (*shuninsei*) in 1976 reveals the
same pattern of action.

The third characteristic is the strengthening of control by means
of the outright abuse of administrative authority. For example, the
administering of a nationwide, all-inclusive Lower Secondary School
Scholastic Achievement Test, beginning in 1961, is an act of malfeasance which exceeds the Ministry of Education's legitimate authority
to make surveys. In its judgment on the controversies arising out of

the administration of an achievement test, the Supreme Court itself said that the principle of local control of education is one of the basic principles of educational administration and that the Ministry of Education does not have the authority to carry out such testing on its own, nor does it have the authority to force local boards of education to do so. However, the court stated in its decision that as long as these exams are carried out on the basis of the local board of education's autonomous judgment, then such tests are procedurally legal. In this truly unfortunate decision, we can see just how serious the problem of the Ministry of Education's central administrative control really is and how willingly the courts have played into it.

Another example is provided by the in-service training system (also known as administrative in-service training or ministerial teaching and research). This system is of no value in heightening the teacher's abilities as a teacher; it is nothing other than an attempt to fit the teacher's vision of education and educational practice into a Ministry of Education-approved framework. In response to teachers' independently organized study and in-service training programs (for example, the activities of private educational research groups and circles, or the research activities of the Japan Teachers' Union), not only has the ministry failed to recognize these activities as appropriate study for teachers: it has used them as an excuse for declaring teachers to have acted in violation of their principals' orders. This has provided justification for disciplinary punishment, dismissal, and pay cuts to teachers, mechanisms for developing criteria for negatively evaluating teachers on their efficiency rating reports, and legitimation for transferring "problem" (i.e., independent-minded) teachers. These blatant forms of repression are by no means rare.

Thus, under the guise of "normalizing education," and through the shady guidance practices of the educational administration authorities, many devices for forcing teachers to withdraw from their union—simple union-busting—have been put into effect. This has resulted in severe pressures being applied to those teachers' research movements which were designed to promote creative teaching practices, and represents a wide-ranging effort to curtail their intrinsic professional freedoms.

The fourth feature deserving our attention is the fact that under these legal and administrative conditions, educational strife has come to be focused in the courtroom, to the extent that a significant body of decisions has already been handed down. However, as will be discussed further in Part II, there are a great many discrepancies among court decisions pertaining to essentially similar cases, and even with regard to the same case the decisions of the higher and lower courts have been markedly divided.[13] The general tendency has been for the lower courts to rule conscientiously on the basis of the Constitution and the Fundamental Law of Education, while the upper courts have become increasingly reactionary. We may well see here a reflection of the generally unstable judicial conditions in Japan at the present time.

However, there is one more tendency worthy of our notice, a result of the efforts of concerned lawyers to develop arguments touching on the nature and logic of education. These efforts have begun to pay off inasmuch as their arguments have come to be reflected in the lower courts' interpretations of educational law, and in a deepening of many judges' understanding of the relations between education and law. These arguments have also succeeded in freeing educational law from the facile ways of thinking that view it as merely one practical branch of administrative law. Inasmuch as the nature and logic of education are being rendered into linguistic problems in the courtroom setting, a great deal of progress can indeed be said to have been made.

The Citizens' Education Movement and teachers' educational activities have changed the general standards of educational consciousness and understanding. Through the joint efforts of legal and educational scholars, a more logical approach that is in basic conformity with the essence of education has been reflected in some of the legal interpretations of the lower courts. Generally speaking, these efforts to construct a concrete discourse on the People's educational rights and powers have forced a re-examination of long-established and uncritically accepted theories in the legal world, and have helped to formulate a new interpretation of the Constitution's educational stipulations (Articles 23 and 26) as the basis for new theoretical thinking about the relations between education and law.

Even the Supreme Court's decision on the Scholastic Achievement Test issue (see Chapter 9), handed down as a constitutional judgment, could not neglect the new discourse on the People's educational rights and powers. Focused on the "child's right to learn," it adopted a method of synthesizing the responsibilities and powers of those involved in education. Through it the judges finally entered the same arena as those who have been advocating the position that the People's educational rights and powers take precedence over those of the State. Here we can see the degree to which the citizens' education movement and the discourse on the People's educational sovereignty have affected Japan's educational consciousness.

[13] The chapters in Part II provide a detailed look at some of the important cases and rulings.

From the perspective of the legal consciousness long accepted by the majority of the Japanese people, these issues may well be difficult to understand, but these interpretations of the law are very different from those that have been conceived in the ivory towers of academia. They reveal the development of a "living law" that seeks to clear a path to a new reality.

Within the various citizen-based movements that include the anti-pollution and education movements, new positions are being articulated, on the basis of the principles of human rights and self-government, that have the potential to overturn the traditional ideologies which have legitimated bureaucratic domination. The education movement in particular, in addition to developing a discourse on the logic of education, has aimed to erect an autonomous system of educational law free from the domination of administrative law. This has not been confined to the pursuit of a theory of educational law which strives to deepen the roots of the idea of human rights among the Japanese people; it seeks to renew and invigorate the People's constitutional consciousness and to deepen their appreciation of the important role the Constitution should be recognized as playing in structuring Japanese social life.

Education in the Courtroom and Teachers' Struggles for Professional Autonomy

Introduction to Part II

The essays included in this section employ the principles and values already set forth to examine some of the most vexing and conflict-generating issues in postwar Japanese educational life: the screening and approval of textbooks, the evaluation of students and teachers, curriculum control, and the training and retraining of teachers. Most of these conflicts were crystallized in the form of lawsuits that pitted the Ministry of Education against teachers, students, and textbook authors. The chapters that constitute Part II of this book discuss and analyze the rulings of Japan's courts in a number of the most important of these cases. These essays frame the basic issues involved in terms of the problems focused upon in Part I, such as the separation of education and scholarship, and the question of whether the power to control education should be vested in the government or in the People.

The educational system in prewar Japan was one uniformly controlled from above. At the end of the war it was decided that a better way to organize education was called for, and an attempt was made to launch a new system from below built upon the efforts of all the People. It was in this spirit that the Course of Study (Gakushū Shidō Yōryō) was conceived in 1947 to serve as reference material for teachers preparing their teaching plans. It was intended as "a guide to help teachers complete their inquiries" into the problems they encountered when attempting to fashion a curriculum which would be responsive to the related demands for a new kind of society and a new kind of child.

The Course of Study was divided into separate volumes that covered the different subjects taught from the first year of primary school to the last year of upper secondary school. Thus, for example, for the benefit of a teacher entrusted with the responsibility of giving instruction in social studies to sixth graders, it provided a series of recommendations pertaining to the things the teacher might want to pay attention to when thinking about how to select and organize the materials he or she would teach. But in all cases these suggestions were of a very general nature and merely intended to be used by teachers as reference materials.

After 1958, however, when the revised Course of Study was published in the official Government Register, its character changed dramatically: it was endowed with legally binding power. The Ministry of Education argued that it was no longer appropriate to think of the Course of Study as something to be freely consulted by teachers; rather it was something which they had to strictly follow when preparing and giving instruction. Moreover, the Ministry firmly insisted, textbooks now had to be written to conform with the "standards" set forth in the Course of Study.

I. Textbook Screening

At the same time that the Course of Study was being thus transformed, major changes were being enacted in the standards employed in the screening of textbooks. Prior to 1958 the inviolable standard for textbook screening had been formulated in the following manner: "Does the text in question violate the Fundamental Law of Education, for example its insistence upon the spirit of peace and respect for truth and justice?" The import of the changes imposed by the Ministry of Education in 1958 is amply symbolized by its deletion of the second part of this passage—of phrases such as "the spirit of peace" and "respect for truth and justice." In short, the Fundamental Law of Education was preserved as the absolute standard for textbooks in name only.

To give concrete form to the spirit of this transformation, the Ministry of Education increased the number of textbook inspectors it employed; this enabled the Ministry to intensify the severity of the screening process.

These efforts did not begin suddenly in the late 1950s. Prior to the 1955 consolidation of the Liberal and Democratic parties into the Liberal Democratic Party (which has controlled the government ever since that time), the Democratic Party issued a pamphlet entitled "Deplorable Textbooks," which denounced all texts that emphasized the values embraced by the Peace Education Movement.[1] In particular, this pamphlet attacked

---

[1] Advocates of Peace Education select teaching materials that promote the values

a number of textbooks written in the postwar years by first-rank researchers and scholars, on the grounds that their texts were biased. In the wake of this campaign we witnessed revisions in the Course of Study and an intensification of the textbook screening system. As a consequence of this "screening" process, we are today faced with a situation in which any textbook that does not share the values mandated by the Ministry of Education must either be revised to satisfy the Ministry's inspectors or be judged unfit for use in Japanese schools.

In response to these unsettling developments there arose within the Japanese intellectual world a recognition of the need to counteract these infringements upon the constitutionally guaranteed freedoms of thought and expression. The growing consciousness of this imperative was galvanized when the eminent historian Ienaga Saburō, mindful of the harm being done to the authors of social studies textbooks in general and to those (like himself) of history textbooks in particular, brought suit against the Ministry of Education on the grounds that its textbook screening system violated his constitutionally guaranteed rights of expression and academic freedom. Two of the court rulings on his case are discussed in Chapters 6 and 7. As a brief consideration of conditions at that time makes quite clear, however, the textbook screening problem was not limited to social studies texts. It is no doubt true that because textbook screening is entangled with a wide range of ideological problems, social studies texts are the most obvious targets of ministerial interference. However, they have not been the only ones: texts written for use in courses on the Japanese language as well as mathematics, the physical sciences, music, and art have also been subjected to the meddling of Education Ministry inspectors. It is important to observe that these unjustified interventions into the educational process constitute one of the most serious problems plaguing postwar Japanese education.

A. Some Examples of Textbook Screening

One of the most telling examples of the extent to which the Ministry of Education has been willing to go to ensure that the uniformity of its control over teaching materials is pre-

---

of peace and nonviolence, international cooperation, and racial and cultural equality.

served is found in the case of the response of its censors to the physics textbook written by Nobel Prize laureate Tomonaga Shin'ichirō for use in upper secondary schools. In writing his textbook Tomonaga attempted to develop a new style for getting students to think about physics. But in response to this the textbook inspectors in the Ministry of Education declared that his book was not a textbook. To be a text appropriate for use in schools, they asserted, a book must be written in a form in which correct knowledge is presented in a predetermined and exact style. Any work which does not adopt this approach or conform to its underlying view of education cannot, in other words, be considered for approval as a textbook regardless of the pedagogic aims of its author. As it was precisely Tomonaga's desire to develop more thought-provoking teaching materials, in the end he had no choice but to abandon his attempt to creatively reform the composition of science textbooks.

Another typical example of the Ministry of Education's fundamental approach to the certification of textbooks is found in its response to a poem included in a Japanese language textbook intended for use by sixth graders in elementary school. In this poem, entitled "The River," there was a great deal of onomatopoetic play on the sounds made by a rushing river. The Ministry's textbook inspectors rejected the use of this poem on the grounds that in standard Japanese (that is to say, Japanese as it is officially defined by the Ministry itself) the onomatopoetic words corresponding to the sound of a river are slightly different from those found in this poem. Therefore the textbook in which the poem was included was deemed inappropriate for elementary-school children. We can only conclude from this that the Ministry's inspectors feared that children might get the idea that it was all right to play with the national language in ways which would encourage them to think of it as something belonging *to them* rather than as something whose use is controlled by the State *for them*.

In a different case the Education Ministry's inspector declared that it was not permissible to use the word *kenka* (fight, brawl, squabble) in a Japanese language textbook. The author of this text was told that to be acceptable, the story he was relating had to be reworked so that the phrase "they went to the next village to rumble with the boys there" could be replaced with "they went to the next village to have a sumō match with the boys there." Are the Ministry of Education's textbook inspectors really so foolish as to think that simply by proscribing the word *kenka* they can safeguard the harmoniousness which they want to represent as the essence of Japaneseness? This simplistic moralism is most unsuitable for the education of a people who are supposed to be free.

These kinds of alterations not only impoverish the teaching materials in question; traditional stories which children have heard as toddlers are revised, with the result that children are often shocked and led to think that what their mothers had read or told them was simply wrong. Fortunately, in the case of a text in which traditional stories were officially rewritten, the work was allowed to be published, almost—but not quite— in its original form in response to the complaints of the textbook author and to criticisms from many corners of Japanese society. How in the world can Ministry of Education officials claim that their textbook screening does not constitute a form of censorship and that the Ministry completely respects the principle of free expression when they will not even permit the direct quotation of poems and other literary works in the way they were originally created?

In the case of history textbooks, the Ministry's inspectors have been uncompromising in their desire to constrain the freedom of authors with regard to a number of important issues, such as the way Japanese antiquity is represented. This is reminiscent of the attitudes displayed in the early part of this century with regard to the problem of the Northern and Southern Houses of the Japanese Imperial Family (see Chapter 3). Moreover, the Ministry has been quite meddlesome with regard to the language used for example in describing Japan's modernization, the Imperial Constitution of 1889, the Imperial Rescript on Education, Japan's repeated warmaking, and the daily lives of the masses of ordinary people. We have also seen that the Ministry is not at all willing to trust the free judgment of textbook authors when it comes to issues such as the postwar reform of Japanese political life, the Japan-U.S. Security Treaty, the stationing of American troops in Japan, the continuing buildup of Japan's Self-Defense Forces, and the presence of the Soviet soldiers occupying the Northern Territories which, the government insists, must be returned to Japanese sovereignty.

With regard to issues it is particularly concerned about, the

Ministry of Education now sends a list to all of the textbook publishing companies instructing them how it expects certain issues to be dealt with. In fact, its inspectors now even go so far as to advise them in terms such as: "Write about that like this," "Please rethink this as follows," or "Rewrite as follows."

The screening system that has been instituted by the Ministry has two designated categories for textbooks that are judged to require revisions. The first is an "opinion regarding correction" (*shūsei iken*) and the second, an "opinion regarding improvement" (*kaizen iken*). In the case of the former, the Ministry inspectors demand that the proposed textbook be rewritten according to the specifications they mandate; in the latter case, if the textbook author still has a different opinion after reading the criticisms of the Ministry inspector, he or she can submit a rebuttal and once again submit the work for certification. In those cases where the Ministry's inspectors merely ask authors to rethink their position, we can still say that some respect is being shown for the free judgment of the textbook's author, but when it is specifically spelled out that failure to rewrite according to ministerial direction will result in failure to receive textbook certification, we cannot help but think it strange to call such a system a "screening system." In truth, this is nothing other than censorship, which is in fact forbidden by Article 21 of our postwar Constitution. My own experiences as the author of a social studies textbook have taught me just to what extent the Ministry of Education is willing to go to suppress political viewpoints different from its own.

As these examples more than amply demonstrate, the view of textbooks dominant among those who certify them in Japan is not one which places value upon their capacity to stimulate the intellectual powers of students; this educational philosophy measures the value of a textbook solely in terms of how faithfully it reproduces knowledge which has already been officially certified as "truthful." This points to one of the biggest problems running through education in Japan today: an educational philosophy which, rather than exposing children to the play of different constructions of knowledge and allowing them to work out the conflicts and disparities on the basis of their own comprehension of the world, seeks to instill in them an allegiance to a single, systematized body of knowledge about the world. Underlying this philosophy we can detect an updated version of the ideology at the heart of the prewar system of nationalized textbooks which attempted to control from above the People's access to and assimilation of knowledge in order both to deepen their intellectual reliance upon the State's superior wisdom and to intensify their emotional commitment to the goals set for the nation by the State's bureaucracy. And as the tragedies caused by Japan's involvement in World War II so poignantly revealed, implementation of this educational philosophy had rendered the Japanese people willing agents of the Imperial State's destructive expansionism in Asia and the Pacific region. When we bear this in mind it is obvious that the postwar Ministry of Education's attempt to intensify its control over textbooks represents a very serious and indeed ominous problem both for the Japanese people and our Asian neighbors.[2]

B. The Ienaga Cases

Realizing that the spiritual freedom of the Japanese people would once again be ensnared within dangerous webs of State-defined truths unless something was done to counteract the worsening conditions in which textbooks were being censored, the historian Ienaga Saburō brought three lawsuits challenging the constitutional legality of the screening system to which his own textbooks had been subjected. The first of these suits was initiated in 1965; its aim was to secure the payment of damages for the suffering Ienaga claimed he was needlessly forced to endure by having to submit his texts to the relentless interference of the Ministry of Education's textbook examiners. The second suit was filed two years later; it sought a revocation of the changes forced upon his upper secondary school Japanese history book in 1966 and a restoration of its original text. This case grew out of Professor Ienaga's argument that the Ministry of Education's opinions regarding the accuracy of his textbook were totally inappropriate. In pressing this case Ienaga rejected the arguments advanced by Ministry of Education officials that the textbook screening system is nothing more than a normal form of administrative management, and therefore well within the legal authority of the Ministry. The third suit was initiated in 1984 in response to the new

[2] As described below, changes required by the Ministry in 1982 in history textbooks covering the Pacific War were in fact questioned and protested by the governments of other Asian countries.

campaign begun in the 1980s in which a group of educators and commentators charged that the textbooks used in Japanese schools were terribly biased.

Let me now review the course of these three suits and the decisions that were handed down by the various courts which sat in judgment on them. The first verdict came from the Tokyo District Court in response to the second of these cases; issued in 1970, it was authored by Justice Sugimoto Ryōkichi. (This decision is taken up in detail in Chapter 6.). Although it did not go so far as to declare that the screening system is unconstitutional in itself, it handed down a ruling that was extremely favorable to Professor Ienaga's contentions by declaring that the system as it was administered at the time violated the Constitution's prohibition of censorship and upholding of the freedom of expression in Article 21 and its guarantee of academic freedom in Article 23, and Article X of the Fundamental Law of Education's prohibition against the "unreasonable control of education." The Ministry of Education, not surprisingly, found this decision unsatisfactory and appealed it to the Tokyo Higher Court.

The second verdict in this case, handed down in 1975, was authored by Judge Azegami, head justice of the Tokyo Higher Court. In this decision the textbook screening system was found to lack consistency and to be administered in a thoroughly arbitrary fashion; in short, the system was ruled to be unfair.

While the Sugimoto decision approached the problem of the textbook screening system head-on from the perspective of the Constitution and the Fundamental Law of Education, in particular developing a new interpretation of Article 26 of the Constitution ("All people shall have the right to receive an equal education correspondent to their ability"), the Azegami decision, although a victory for Ienaga's side, did not have the same theoretical importance because it did not break new judicial ground as an interpretation of the People's constitutionally guaranteed educational freedoms. The Sugimoto decision, however, was clearly a landmark decision whose significance resulted from its reformulation of the accepted understanding of the child's rights to learn. And by articulating this view of the rights to learn within the larger framework of the People's educational freedoms, the Sugimoto decision produced an exceedingly conscientious statement of the proper relations between the State and education in a democratically organized society.

The Ministry of Education was thoroughly dissatisfied with the Azegami decision and appealed it to the Supreme Court, which handed down its ruling in 1982. Unfortunately, however, the Supreme Court's decision in the case was an extremely odd one. In essence it went like this: since the issue at the heart of this controversy was rooted in the textbook screening system in effect during the 1960s, and because the Course of Study had subsequently been revised, all textbooks, not just Ienaga's, had to be rewritten to conform with the new standards decreed by the Ministry of Education. Therefore, it followed, Ienaga's suit no longer had any concrete basis; even a ruling in his favor would be meaningless. (This of course was precisely the position advocated before the court by the Ministry of Education.) Having handed down this essentially evasive ruling, the Supreme Court nevertheless sent the case back to the Tokyo Higher Court for further adjudication, thereby covering over its attempt to avoid ruling on the constitutional problems raised by the Sugimoto decision.

In 1974, the first ruling in the other case brought by Professor Ienaga (actually the first suit, initiated in 1965, seeking payment of damages for the suffering he underwent as a result of the textbook screening) was finally handed down by Justice Takatsu of the Tokyo District Court. While this decision ostensibly constituted a recognition of Ienaga's charges and ordered the Ministry of Education to pay the historian damages totaling ¥100,000, it affirmed the propriety of the State's role in the screening and approval of textbooks, which it found to be ultimately legitimate. (This judgment is the subject of Chapter 7.) Notwithstanding the fact that its practices were fundamentally approved of, the Ministry of Education still found this judgment unacceptable and initiated an appeal. Likewise, even though he had ostensibly won the case, Professor Ienaga found this decision's interpretation of the constitutional issues at stake fundamentally unacceptable and began his own appeal. These appeals are still being considered by the Tokyo Higher Court. The fact that today, more than twenty years after this suit was first launched, it is still only in the second phase of adjudication is a sorry reminder of the snail's pace of justice in postwar Japan.

Before we can examine the suit brought by Professor Ienaga

against the State in 1984, it is first necessary to examine the historical context in which it came about. The 1970 Sugimoto decision caused the Ministry of Education a considerable loss of face; even though that decision was only the first round in what would be a lengthy legal process, it had already achieved for Ienaga's cause a great deal of respectability and publicly acknowledged legitimacy. Consequently, the Ministry of Education recognized that it had to exercise much more discretion in the administration of its textbook screening system. Within this new environment more and more people were inspired to write textbooks, and within a few years better and better ones started to appear. In the wake of these liberalizing developments the conservative elements within both the Ministry and the ruling Liberal Democratic Party became increasingly disturbed, and in the early 1980s they set about launching a new barrage of attacks on the textbooks used in Japanese schools.

It was in this context that during the early 1980s we saw the Ministry of Education order the authors of history textbooks treating the 1930s and 1940s to change the word "invasion" (*shinryaku*) to "advance" (*shinshutsu*); the latter, it was declared, is the only appropriate word to employ when describing Japanese actions in Asia during the last war. Even though this caused a disruptive diplomatic incident in which Japan was bitterly criticized by Chinese and Koreans who still remembered the brutal atrocities committed by Japan's "advancing" troops, the Ministry of Education stubbornly held to the position that the word "invasion" was absolutely unacceptable for use in textbooks read by Japanese young people. In the end the Ministry was forced to partially revise this stance under the weight of intense political pressure, and it allowed limited use of the word "invasion." But in general, it has been extremely severe in its censorship of textbooks that take a critical stance towards Japan's role in the war. Ienaga's 1984 suit challenged these developments. It, too, is still being adjudicated.

II. The Scholastic Achievement Test

Having unilaterally transformed the character of the Course of Study in the late 1950s, the Ministry of Education then decided in 1961 to institute a new form of student testing, a Scholastic Achievement Test which would be conducted on an all-inclusive nationwide basis. The aims of this testing were (1) to determine the extent to which textbooks were being used in conformity with the goals set forth in the official Course of Study, and (2) to determine the attitudes and opinions conveyed to the students through the instruction provided by their teachers. This testing was designed to serve as an important link in the policies the Ministry had implemented as part of its attempt to impose greater control over the contents of education, the production of textbooks, and the organization of classroom instruction.

In response to these new efforts by the Ministry of Education to violate Article X of the Fundamental Law of Education's injunction against "improper educational control," many members of the Japan Teachers' Union recognized the urgent need for effective countermeasures. This took the form of a collective protest in which teachers in all regions of the nation refused to distribute the prepared answer sheets or refused to admit the testers into their classrooms on the day the testing was scheduled to be conducted. In response, the Ministry of Education, through the regional boards of education which it controls, brought suit against those teachers who refused to cooperate, charging that they had failed to execute their proper educational duties.

In adjudicating these cases the lower courts handed down a number of conflicting decisions regarding the legality of the Scholastic Achievement Test. But as time went on it became clear that the lower courts were inclined to interpret Article X of the Fundamental Law of Education as supporting the autonomy of the teacher's educational authority and requiring limits upon the State's intervention in the educational process. In 1962 the Kumamoto District Court, and in 1963 the Kōchi District Court, ruled that the Scholastic Achievement Test was legal, but the following year the Kokura Branch of the Fukuoka District Court ruled that the testing was illegal. In succeeding years both kinds of decisions were handed down; by the time of the Supreme Court's ruling in 1976, the Scholastic Achievement Test had been deemed legal in seven cases and illegal in ten others. The Supreme Court's ruling on the Scholastic Achievement Test, which is analyzed in detail in Chapter 9, came in response to the Asahikawa (Hokkaido) Incident and the Iwate Prefecture Teachers' Union Incident. In the first of these cases, the Asahikawa District Court in

May of 1966, and the Sapporo Higher Court in June of 1968, ruled that administration of the Scholastic Achievement Test was illegal. In the second of these cases, the Morioka District Court in July of 1966 found the testing legal, but the Sendai court reversed this ruling in February of 1969.

The decision handed down by the Morioka District Court declared that the Scholastic Achievement Test "was a legitimate exercise of administrative management having clear legal foundations." The following reasons were giving to support this finding:

> In the final analysis it must be said that the People, through their representatives in the Diet, entrust the State with the power to execute their general educational will. In this context it is only natural that the central government have the responsibility for determining appropriate national standards and making sure that they are upheld. Thus education should be conducted so as to be in conformity with the nationwide standards determined by the State's educational administrators.

Accordingly, the Morioka court ruled, since the State's administrative control of education does not fall into the category of the "improper control" forbidden by Article X of the Fundamental Law of Education, the authority to organize the curricula used in the nation's schools "belongs in the first instance exclusively to the Minister of Education," and therefore the official Course of Study "has the force and efficacy that belongs to all laws, regulations, decrees, and directives." Moreover, this court ruled, teachers "must faithfully follow the official orders of their superiors" within the administrative hierarchy of the educational system. As the basis for this argument the court relied upon the prewar theory that construed the school as "a public building" (*eizōbutsu*) subject to the same administrative regulations that cover all publicly controlled institutions.

We can see in this decision a startling failure to distinguish between education and educational administration, at one level, and between educational administration and public administration at another. The decision was a typical example of an interpretation of educational law based on the ideology of total administrative supremacy.

The Sendai Higher Court rescinded the findings of the lower court and found that the teachers who had refused to administer the Scholastic Achievement Test were not guilty of any crimes. However, there are serious flaws in the logic underlying this decision, particularly with regard to the issue of educational authority and its interpretation of "improper educational control"; this resulted from reliance on the same theories regarding the nature of "administrative control" in a system of representative government that were seen in the lower court's decision. Nevertheless, the Sendai Higher Court gave this argument a somewhat different reading by concluding that the State's administrative control should be subject to "reasonable limits." Indeed, this decision invented a totally new and contradictory logic to define the nature of administrative control.

While this decision acknowledged that the authority to control education inherently belongs to the People, it also went on to declare that under the framework of parliamentary democracy "the general educational will of the People" can only be expressed in the national assembly (Diet). Therefore, the judges concluded, "the general educational will of the People can only be manifested in the form of legislation enacted therein, and nowhere else." This decision then went on to insist that

> Even if administrative management has legal foundations, this does not mean that it is always lawful. This is particularly true in the case of educational administration, which should observe reasonable restraints with regard to those aspects of education that impinge upon the internality of human character or the professionalism of teachers. Granting the propriety of this argument, it then becomes critically important to take the necessary measures to ensure that neither legislation nor administrative management is allowed to impart the appearance of legality to violations of the liberties required by educational practice.

The decision went on to interpret Article X of the Fundamental Law of Education from the standpoint of the thought of its drafters:

> This article was rooted in a severe criticism of the prewar

184 INTRODUCTION TO PART II

State's bureaucratic domination of education. In particular, it sought to eliminate the "improper control" of education by the agents of the State's authority. With this in mind, the drafters of the Fundamental Law of Education attempted to clarify the responsibilities of educational administration and the restraints which should be imposed upon it. As a result they produced an unambiguous affirmation of the principle that the independence and autonomy of education must be guaranteed.

Based on this interpretation of the logic underlying Article X of the Fundamental Law of Education, the Sendai Higher Court rejected the theory, advanced in the first decision on this case by the Morioka District Court, that the authority to organize the educational process and its curricula belongs to the Minister of Education, arguing instead that "this authority basically belongs to local public bodies."

It is only proper that the authority to concretely organize the educational process should reside in the schools which have the direct responsibility for carrying out those educational activities. . . . [The Course of Study] establishes the yardsticks for organizing the educational process, but the authority to control compilation of the curricula used in the nation's schools does not belong to the Minister of Education.

In direct contrast to this finding, both the district and higher court rulings on the Asahikawa Scholastic Achievement Test Incident ruled that the orders issued to teachers to execute this testing deviated from the realm of activities properly demarcated for educational administration and therefore constituted an illegal abuse of administrative authority. The rulings of both these courts defended the educational authority of the teacher.

In the first decision handed down in this case, the Asahikawa District Court concluded that the Fundamental Law of Education was established on the basis of "deep reflections on the centralized, standardized, and formalized controls which were imposed on education" during the prewar and wartime years. Therefore, the court argued, its Article X in particular was intended to curb the "State's attempts to use its not inconsiderable administrative powers to intervene in the formulation of educational content." Moreover, the judges on the Asahikawa district bench argued, this article was "based on the ideals of ensuring the independence of educational activities, and of respecting the teacher's free, creative, and autonomous professional practices." Thus, the court reaffirmed the validity of the interpretation of this article which limited the duties of educational administrators to "establishing educational institutions and equipping them with the facilities required to make teaching possible." Proceeding from this basic position, the Asahikawa court reached a similiar conclusion regarding the authority to organize the educational process, and in doing so rejected the claim that the Minister of Education has complete and total authority in these matters.

> It is clearly the case that neither the Fundamental Law of Education nor the School Education Law was enacted to make it possible for the Ministry of Education to establish detailed regulations regarding the contents and methods of school education; nor were these laws passed to give the Education Ministry the legal authority to restrict the educational activities of teachers.

From this perspective the Asahikawa District Court drew the conclusion that the Minister of Education's authority with regard to formulation of the contents of education should be limited to the establishment of very generalized standards; as for the Course of Study,

> those items which go beyond the scope of providing very broadly conceived guidelines have no legally binding power, and should not be thought of as anything more than helpful suggestions, advice, or guidance which teachers are free to accept or reject as they themselves see fit.

The second ruling in this case was handed down by the Sapporo Higher Court, which upheld the finding of the district court in Asahikawa and reiterated that the teachers against whom charges had been brought were not guilty of any crimes. The intent of the framers of the Fundamental Law of Education played a big part in this ruling as well, particularly since it was seen as based on a reflection upon the dangers of the State's domination of national education. Thus the Sapporo Higher Court reaffirmed the principle that education "must not be subjected to any improper political influences, and should be conducted in an autonomous fashion." Furthermore, this decision clearly distinguished between "education and educational administration," and declared that education "should be entrusted to the free creativity and resourcefulness of teachers, and not be subjugated to interference and domination by the agents of national educational administration." The organs of educational administration, it declared, "should have as their objective the arrangement of those conditions required for the realization of education, and should not go beyond this." Within the realm of compulsory education, the authority of the Minister of Education should be limited to "establishing to the minimal degree necessary the general standards required for upholding the uniformity of education on a nationwide basis." Apart from this, the Ministry's activities should be limited to providing "guidance, advice, and support as long as they are understood as having no legally binding power."

Thus, when viewed from this perspective, the existing Course of Study appeared to the Sapporo Higher Court as having exceeded the framework of "establishing in general terms national standards with regard to the contents of the educational process." Accordingly, the court reasoned, implementation of the Scholastic Achievement Test based on the then existing Course of Study "clearly went far beyond the legitimate authority of the Ministry of Education" and "violated the existing system of educational laws beginning with the Fundamental Law of Education."

In the wake of the confusion generated by these conflicting rulings regarding the legality of the Scholastic Achievement Test and the illegality of the Asahikawa and Iwate teachers' refusal to administer it, and in response to the appeals submitted to it, the Supreme Court was obliged to hand down a definitive constitutional judgment. Both sides in this long drawn-out controversy anxiously awaited the Supreme Court's decision, and many others eagerly looked forward to this decision in the belief that it would have an important impact on the ongoing textbook trials. Unfortunately, the decision of the Supreme Court affirmed the legality of the Scholastic Achievement Test and dismissed the original judgments which found it to be illegal. This did not come as a big surprise, as we have already learned what to expect from the legal consciousness of our highest-ranking jurists and the judicial system in operation in Japan today. This decision is examined in detail in Chapter 9.

Nonetheless it is very important to note that while the Supreme Court's decision ostensibly legitimated the administrative activities and authority of the Ministry of Education, a careful examination of the reasons provided in the text of this judgment reveals that even the Supreme Court could not completely reject the principle, affirmed in the earlier decisions, that because educational authority rests with the People, the independence of education should be respected. In this light the court's verdict recognized the rights to learn of the citizenry in general, and of children in particular. Based on its affirmation of these rights to learn, the court declared that because educational administration can indeed constitute "a form of improper control," the Ministry of Education's interventions should be constrained within "a necessary and reasonable framework." Moreover, it declared that there are real problems with the use of the Scholastic Achievement Test and the Course of Study as instruments of educational policy, and that it is important for the government to reconsider the way such matters are handled. Thus, while this verdict affirmed the Ministry's claim that the Scholastic Achievement Test represented a legal exercise of administrative authority, it also served notice on our Education Ministry bureaucrats that they have to be more circumspect in their handling of such matters. In this respect the Supreme Court's decision, regrettable as it may be in the last analysis, can still be seen to have real value.

III. Other Issues

"The Struggle to Control Teachers' In-Service Training" explores another one of the most important dimensions of the contestation in postwar Japan over the appropriate character of the democratically organized system of schooling and instruction. The essay examines the clash between those in the Japan Teachers' Union and their allies in university departments of education who have sought to reshape education on the basis of respect for the values of professional autonomy, and those individuals, both in and aligned with the Ministry of Education, who have consistently sought to subordinate the activities of teachers to bureaucratically defined and supervised objectives. We are able to see how the tensions underlying the prewar struggle between those who believed in "enlightenement from above" and those who believed in "enlightenment from below" were reconstituted as one of the central issues in the ongoing debate in postwar Japanese educational circles over the appropriate relation between knowledge and power in a democratic society. Thus this essay highlights from one more perspective both the continuities and the ruptures between prewar and postwar educational thought and practices.

The final essay in Part II, "Student Evaluation and Personal Control: The *Naishinso* Decision," analyzes the problems of freedom and human rights as they arise at still another level of postwar Japanese educational life. While analyzing the logic underlying the rulings handed down by the Japanese courts in a well-known and controversial suit that challenged the legality of the administratively mandated system of secret reporting by means of which teachers are required to keep tabs on students' behavior, it opens up the problem of student evaluation and presents a powerful argument calling for the introduction of a different system of values as the basis for judging both the personal and the academic performances of Japanese youth.

6 Textbook Control on Trial: The Sugimoto Decision

The Sugimoto decision was handed down in response to Professor Ienaga Saburō's suit challenging the constitutional legality of the textbook screening system and the process by means of which the Ministry of Education withdrew the certification of his Japanese history textbook for upper secondary school use. This outstanding judgment has directly addressed the critically important problems of where educational authority (*kyōikuken*) should properly reside and how the educational enterprise should be organized. By approaching these fundamental issues head-on, Justice Sugimoto has inquired scrupulously into the essence of education. Basing his decision on a thoroughgoing investigation of the historical development of education in a number of other modern nations, the currently accepted international understanding of educational standards, and the thinking of the legislators who gave us our Fundamental Law of Education, Justice Sugimoto has handed down an epoch-making theory that recognizes the related concepts of the People's educational rights and the People's educational freedoms. His decision is the first to interpret Articles 23 and 26 of the Constitution from the perspective of the People's right to know the truth. In doing so he has dauntlessly invoked the authority of the judicial system to reaffirm the constitutional guarantee of "academic freedom" and its logical corollary, "educational independence," thereby imposing limits on the activities of the State's educational administration. This judgment is all the more significant because it represents the first time our judiciary has adopted the ideas developed by those thinkers in Japanese society who are concerned with the integrity of an autonomous body of educational law.

I

At the beginning of this ruling we find a very important interpretation of Article 26 of the Constitution that states the fundamental point of view running throughout the decision. Herein the idea that the People have the "right to receive an education" is formulated as an expression on the cultural plane of the fundamental right to existence.

189

Justice Sugimoto reasoned as follows regarding the People's right to receive an education:

> A democratic State is premised on the existence of a citizenry each and every one of whose members is a fully self-conscious being. Therefore, it is the task of education to cultivate the new generation who will subsequently bear the responsibilities of such a society. Thus the educative process is of interest to all of the People. But more than anything else, education is a *right of the child based on his or her own needs and requirements* [italics Horio's].

In addition to seeing the child as the bearer, or subject, of the basic human right to receive an education, this judgment calls attention to the special character of the human rights children possess by virtue of their existence as beings having "inherent potentiality in and possibilities for the future." Accordingly, Justice Sugimoto recognized the "child's rights to grow and learn" as "innate rights" grounded in natural law.

> In order to guarantee the child's rights to learn, it is necessary for the People as a whole to take an active interest in and show a serious concern for the tasks of education. It is with this in mind that the Constitution guarantees the People's—and in particular the child's—right to receive an education.

The interpretation of the right to receive an education based on the idea that the child has a right to grow and develop also appears in the detailed exposition of this decision and forms its nucleus, being repeated over and over again. Thus it may rightly be argued that the notion of the child's rights to grow and learn in a manner befitting a free human being indeed constitutes the crux of this decision's logical structure.

The relationship between the responsibilities of the educator and his or her educational freedoms is also theoretically formulated in accord with this notion of the "child's rights." The decision states:

> In light of this view of the nature of education, it should be clear that the primary responsibility for educating the child and guaranteeing his or her right to learn falls upon the People as a whole, and upon parents in particular.

However, because these educational obligations are realized for the most part through the work of the teacher, the latter's professional duties are grasped as responsibilities to society that are entrusted to him or her by the child's parents. Accordingly the teacher is,

> on the one hand, with respect to the child, the person bearing the official responsibility to fully nurture the right to learn; at the same time the teacher bears a responsibility to accept the parents' and the People as a whole's ideas about education, and to undertake to provide an education based thereon.

The bases for the teacher's intrinsic freedoms are located within the general framework of these professional responsibilities. These freedoms are thus by no stretch of the imagination unlimited in their scope. Accordingly, the Sugimoto decision envisions education as

> a high-level mental activity undertaken for the purpose of drawing out the child's possibilities. Through his or her interventions in the educational process, the teacher should work to deepen the student's understanding of the fruits of scholarship and research. Because these activities should nourish all the intellectual and creative powers the child needs in order to think about the myriad phenomena encountered in the world, it is indispensable that the teacher be guaranteed academic freedom.
>
> To scientifically ascertain the particular needs of a mentally and physically developing child and to respond to them in an educationally effective way, teachers require deep affection and a rich body of experiences. When teachers' work is viewed from this perspective, it is obvious that their educational and instructional freedom must be respected.

As for the nature of this freedom, the Sugimoto judgment declares that "it is a freedom attendant upon the profession of the teacher."

> Since these freedoms are required by the professional and scientific nature of the educational enterprise, they are essentially different from what are termed natural freedoms.

The freedoms of the teacher are based upon the trust of parents and citizens. They are rights granted in accord with the fundamental professional responsibilities of the teacher, primarily the obligation to guarantee the child's (the new generation's) right to a humane growth and development through a substantial and meaningful realization of the right to learn (*gakushūken*). Furthermore, the Sugimoto decision declares that with regard to educational activities, which are in their truest nature free and creative undertakings,

> the intervention of State authority must be vigorously averted. Educational "neutrality" is a personal responsibility of the teacher, and its autonomy must be guaranteed.

Not limited to freedoms guaranteed by judicial precedents, the educational freedom upheld by this decision includes "freedom of educational thought" and "freedom in the formulation of educational policy."

> In the last analysis, the teacher's educational and instructional liberties are understood here as being guaranteed by Article 23 of the Constitution's provision for academic freedom.

It is especially worth noting that this is not a simple-minded interpretation of Article 23 which confines it to a one-dimensional guarantee of the professor's freedom to publish the results of his or her research. Rather we find a deep awareness of the fact that both academic and educational freedom are—and must be—deeply rooted in the very existence and practice of education itself.

The Sugimoto decision views education as a means for substantiating the child's constitutionally guaranteed rights to learn and know. Inasmuch as this ruling finds that the educational tasks of "cultivating a citizenry that demands justice and cherishes truth" are indivisible from the political goals of constructing a "peaceful democratic State," it reaffirms the necessity of a "truthful education" as the basic principle of our entire pedagogic undertaking. Consequently, the teacher is envisioned both as the person primarily responsible for providing a truthful education and as the individual chiefly entrusted with the responsibility to conduct the scientific research required to uphold the veracity of the contents of education. On these accounts the decision argues that the academic freedom of the schoolteacher must be firmly guaranteed.

Moreover, the basis for insisting upon the necessity of the teacher's academic freedom is not limited merely to this point. The teacher is conceived in Justice Sugimoto's ruling as both a researcher *in* and a practitioner *of* the science of education. In this regard, no less than in those mentioned above, the teacher's academic freedom must be unwaveringly secured against any and all forms of infringement. The Sugimoto decision recognizes this as meaning that it is necessary for a special "educational consideration" to be given to children as beings still in the process of developing:

> In order to properly exercise the required educational considera-tion, scientific understanding of the child's physical and mental development and psychological and social environments is ab-solutely indispensable. Pedagogy is the science which affords this understanding. In other words, since the proper execution of these educational considerations is itself one form of academic practice, scholarship and teaching are essentially inseparable.

The term "educational consideration" as employed here is nothing other than the sensitivity made possible by the free practice of educa-tional science. Its usage here is directly opposed to that which the Ministry of Education has in mind when it uses the same term as a pretense for justifying its one-sided attempts to thoroughly control national educational life. Thus, the Sugimoto decision supports the foundations for an enduring form of educational freedom by recogniz-ing professionalism as something that properly adheres to the teaching occupation, and by acknowledging the teacher's freedom to carry out his or her own work-related research.

The legal logic developed in this judgment must be seen as an espe-cially valuable one for all those involved with the day-by-day practice of education. Inasmuch as teachers are obliged to provide truthful and scientifically valid lessons, they must have the freedom to carefully research what they teach, and this freedom must be scrupulously pro-tected. Conversely, to fulfill their duties to society and its still-develop-ing members, teachers must cultivate within their own activities a scientific understanding of the close relations between children's en-vironmental conditions and their potential for intellectual, moral, and physical growth. We are fortunate to have within our judiciary a judge who has been able to understand that this is an indispensable condi-tion for the performance of the teacher's professional responsibilities.

By grasping the exercise of "educational consideration" as a form of "scholarly practice" that should inform the full range of the teacher's everyday pedagogic activities, the Sugimoto decision reveals a deep appreciation of the special character of contemporary educational science. This is succinctly expressed in Justice Sugimoto's recognition of the "essential unity and indivisibility of scholarship and education."

This landmark case has itself contributed to the structured develop-ment of educational science by introducing in a judicial forum the foundation for a new form of legal thinking about the nature of education. By not viewing the teacher's freedoms simply as a corollary of Article 23 of the Constitution's stipulation of academic freedom but, rather, connecting educational freedom to academic freedom vis-a-vis the citizenry's comprehensive rights to know the truth, Justice Sugimoto has imparted a deeper significance to the already accepted notion of academic freedom and the guarantees it requires. Thus, while readily acknowledging the obvious differences between scholarship and education, the ruling recognizes theii indivisibility by focusing on their common grounding in the People's right to pursue and know the truth. This indivisibility is most forcefully manifested in the court's awareness that educational praxis is itself a vitally important form of scholarly praxis, and that the two freedoms can only exist by mutually reinforcing one another.

The Sugimoto decision offers a clear sign that the courts are beginning to recognize that both educational and scholarly freedoms are equally founded on Article 23 of the Constitution: "Academic freedom is guaranteed." Accordingly, "academic freedom" is not narrowly interpreted as a special privilege of university scholars, but as itself one aspect of the larger right of the People to know the truth. Therefore the lasting accomplishment of the Sugimoto decision has been to breathe fresh life into the original meaning of Article 23 by equating academic freedom with educational freedom.

II

The arguments in the text of this decision concerning "educational considerations" are very different from those previously put forward to restrict freedom within the framework of differentiated stages of schooling—arguments that were really nothing more than an excuse for anti-scientific, politically based values. Once the concept of "educational consideration" is used to reduce educational freedom to instructional freedom, the development of real educational freedom is severely restricted. Thus the Sugimoto decision deserves a great deal of praise as a theoretical development of the position that seeks to expand pedagogic freedom from the point of view of the nature of education; its argument derives its driving force from the dynamic interplay of educational practice and educational research. It demands our highest respect as an interpretation of the Constitution that is based on the standpoints of the People's intellectual liberties and the essential logic of education. Premised on the idea that the People have a fundamental political right to know the truth, it assigns to the teacher's freedoms of research and education a position between the child's right to an education (Article 26) and the People's right to scholarship (Article 23). In this way the Sugimoto decision can be said to indicate the direction for a new and unified interpretation of both of these articles of the Constitution.

What demands does this new standpoint make with regard to the process by which the contents of education are administered? Because it is premised on the freedoms required to support an "educationally meaningful point of view," it demands that teachers be respected as the recipients of a national trust, and that their professionalism should function as the dominant force in educational life. The text of the decision declares, with regard to the teacher's educational and instructional freedoms:

> It must be recognized that the teacher is in the best position to judge the most appropriate teaching materials and methods for educating the child. And because the teacher should be given the leading role in the selection and adoption of textbooks [as recommended by UNESCO], it must be said that such activities of the State as the one-sided imposition on teachers of a duty to use textbooks, the limiting of their participation in the selection of textbooks, and the restriction of the teacher's freedom in the schools by giving the Course of Study legally binding power are inappropriate in the light of the educational logic outlined above.

This is a radical criticism of the existing system of textbook administration and the fundamental way of thinking that supports it. It expresses agreement with the idea that guaranteeing the autonomy and truthfulness of education is the responsibility of the individual teacher. Furthermore, in its interpretation of Article X of the Fundamental Law of Education, it rejects "improper control" by "the State's administrative authorities"; in addition to limiting the State's duties to the external matters of education, it reaffirms the direct responsibility of the People to guarantee the child's right to learn as it is entrusted to the teacher.

III

Of course the judgment is not without its problems. One of these concerns the relationship between the People's educational rights and the freedoms of textbook authors. In response to the claim of the plaintiff that "the textbook screening system infringes on educational liberties," the court found:

The authoring and publication of textbooks has no direct relationship to either the child's right to receive an education or the educational liberties of the teacher. Accordingly, the incident under consideration in this case does not constitute a violation of Article 26 of the Constitution.

However, is it not the case that guaranteeing the researcher's freedom to author textbooks, along with being a matter of the "author's benefit," is also indispensable for guaranteeing the citizenry's educational rights? Must we not say that infringing on the freedoms of scholarship and expression constitutes a violation of the People's right to know the truth? Doesn't this also constitute a transgression of *its* foundation, the child's right to a "truthful education?"

Even though the Sugimoto decision is flawed in these regards, its importance cannot be minimized as it for the first time gives judicial standing to the conception of the People's educational liberties in opposition to the theory of the State's total control over education. Basing its decision on the notion of the child's rights, and recognizing both the responsibilities of parents, citizens, and teachers with respect to those rights and the fundamental unity between teachers' academic and educational freedoms, the Sugimoto court has handed down a truly remarkable judgment. While recognizing the constructive responsibilities of the State (as well as other public organs) with regard to the financing of education, it also expresses the idea that in order to guarantee educational autonomy there must be limits to the exercising of educational administration.

IV

The decisive power that led to a legal victory for the plaintiff actually came from the People's Educational Movement organized to give real meaning to the notion of the People's educational rights as well as to defend "educational freedom." Within the train of events that saw educational freedom being systematically denied and education being swallowed up by the mechanisms of the State, a movement (centered around Professor Ienaga's case) came into being with the express purpose of resisting these abuses and securing freedom for education. Through everyday educational praxis and research activities designed to support it, this movement has struggled to defend education's autonomy while creating a functioning concept of the People's educational rights. These efforts to both quantitatively and qualitatively elevate educational and scholarly praxis impressed the court, and helped to affirm on the legal plane our resistance to the State's attempts to monopolize educational life.

The postwar educational research and practice movements (conjointly with the movement to create a citizen-based education) have developed in a striking manner, and the accomplishments of the teacher as researcher and practitioner have been tied to these efforts to develop basic awareness of teaching as a form of scholarly praxis. Moreover, subject matter education and research have posed a number of important problems in related academic fields, and contributed to the development of those fields of learning. At the same time, teachers, inasmuch as they are especially well situated to contribute to an understanding of the principles of instruction and learning, have assumed a major responsibility in the development of a new science of education. In particular, the teacher who participates in an independent research movement, and who, on his own initiative, takes a leading role in the activities of that movement, is at one and the same time a practitioner *and* a researcher. Or we can say that it is only through being a researcher that he can guarantee the quality of his praxis and raise his consciousness of the professional nature of his enterprise.

The Sugimoto court has taken a close look at the actual accomplishments of many teachers and their impressive practice and research activities. It has endorsed the theoretical findings of those studying educational law and other fields of education. Setting Article 26 in the forefront of its thinking, the court is widely thought to have contributed to the development of the legal logic behind the People's educational rights and teachers' educational freedoms. As I suggested above, in this the court is in accord with the thinking of the legislators who drafted the Fundamental Law of Education. It also reveals a universality and objectivity that is at one with the spirit driving the development of modern educational thought, as seen for instance in the Universal Declaration of Human Rights and the International Labor Organization's 1964 Recommendation on the Status of Teachers. Accordingly, this decision should not be dismissed as a mere reflection of the presiding judge's individual viewpoint, as the Ministry of Education claims, but should be seen and appreciated for its important contribution to the human struggle for freedom and dignity.

Likewise we should note that the movement to support this lawsuit has not merely been one of support for Professor Ienaga and his complaint; it has grasped the issues involved as pertaining to the basic human rights of each and every Japanese citizen. In particular, this is true of the teacher who, through his efforts to raise the quality of everyday educational praxis, and supported by the fruits of research, seeks to strengthen his ties with his pupils' parents. Efforts to create a citizen-based education have been the major force upholding this movement. By questioning the quality and foundations of educational praxis, this movement has sought to deepen and cultivate the roots of democracy in Japan. It can also be understood as an intellectual movement to create a nationwide citizen-based foundation for education. Thus the need for continuous attempts to consciously reconceive our praxis can never be stressed enough.

7 Textbook Authors on Trial: The Takatsu Decision

I

The ruling of the Tokyo Superior Court on Ienaga Saburō's suit against the government, in which Professor Ienaga sought compensation for damages suffered on account of the Ministry of Education's decertification of his high school history textbook, is a terribly disappointing and highly deceptive decision. Its ulterior motives are very disquieting. It was hard to believe that such a judgment would be rendered in this extremely important case that seeks to educe the judiciary's support for the constitutionally guaranteed right to freedom of expression.

A careful reading of this decision reveals that the justices sitting on the bench in the case were, notwithstanding their granting of damages to author Ienaga, totally taken with the logic revealed in the legal briefs submitted by the defendant in the controversy, the Ministry of Education. The language used in the decision suggests, moreover, that the judges in this case did not even make an effort to understand what Professor Ienaga's lawyers and witnesses tried to argue about the meaning of pedagogic theory, educational practice, and the need for an autonomous body of educational law. This is the only conclusion that can be properly drawn from Justice Takatsu's impertinent pronouncements on issues that are still matters of spirited historical debate as well as his judgments on the propriety of teaching methods and materials for use in our nation's schools. Consider this passage, for example:

The following understanding of "the People who uphold history"[1] is the proper one. In the first place, the word "uphold" is generally used to mean the supporting of a corporeal object by something from underneath. The words "upholding history" are by no means clear or precise. . . . For upper secondary school students this is

[1] This phrase was used by Ienaga in his discussion of Japan's history; in rejecting it, both the Ministry of Education censors and the Takatsu court express the conviction that the populist orientation it symbolizes is inappropriate for Japanese democratic education.

difficult to understand. . . . *In the light of the developmental stage of high school students,* upper secondary school textbooks should not be based on words like "history" or rigid concepts drawn from philosophizing about the meaning of history. The court finds that expressions which have a common-sense obviousness, like "the force propelling history," or "the work of our ancestors," which have a common-sense usability, are easier to understand . . . and therefore more desirable. Furthermore, on the title page of each chapter of this textbook there are illustrations and explanatory descriptions which reflect the creativity and ingenuity of the plaintiff, but as there is a fear that these will support a highly biased view of history, and *for reasons pertaining to educational method as well,* the court holds them to be suspicious [italics Horio's].

How, we must wonder, did the justices become authoritative scholars of history, and where did they develop their expertise on the problems of education? These judges' notions of "educational considerations" are visible in other places as well. They pronounce photos of a political demonstration and quotes from Kiyosawa's wartime diary "undesirable" from an educational point of view;[2] moreover, they declare, "the educational consideration shown by the Ministry of Education's textbook screeners is thoroughly appropriate and quite legitimate."

Not satisfied to limit himself to supporting the government's censors, Judge Takatsu goes on to add his own criticisms of Professor Ienaga's textbook.

In response to the Ienaga textbook's definition of primitive society as anarchic: "This is a mark of the lack of discretion shown with regard to the proper terminology for use in a high school textbook."

Concerning the descriptions of the position of women as courtesans in the aristocratic society of pre-modern Japan: "Isn't this difficult for high school students to properly understand?"

With regard to the characterization of the Constitution of the Imperial Japanese State as "backward": "To preserve the proper balance of the book as a textbook, the constructive qualities of the Imperial Constitution should be touched upon to an equal degree as is its 'backwardness,' and 'educational consideration' should also be given to the problems involved in studying history."

---

[2] Kiyosawa Kiyoshi's *Ankoku Nikki,* a diary begun by the journalist before the start of the Pacific War and continued during the war years, took a pacifist tone and criticized the haughty demeanor of Japanese military officers.

Even in response to the term "(American) military base," which was deemed unacceptable by the textbook screening authorities: "Because it is more easily understood by students, in view of *educational considerations* it is appropriate for inclusion in a textbook."[3]

The question I want to raise in regard to this legal ruling is: Are these the kinds of matters the judiciary should be passing judgment on? In other words, I would like to suggest that the problem is not whether the justices' understanding of "educational considerations" is right or wrong; the mere fact of the court's making judgments about educational considerations is a flagrant transgression of the proper limits of its powers and responsibilities. The court, which should have declared the Ministry of Education's screening system to be extralegal, has itself exceeded the boundaries of judicial prudence and involved itself in issues with regard to which it does not properly possess competence. The one and *only* thing that the court should have done was hand down a ruling reaffirming the principle that "the State must not have or profess its own academic theories."

There is a striking difference between the Takatsu decision and the Sugimoto decision (discussed in Chapter 6). Commenting on the government's claim that the heading "The People Who Uphold History" is not suitable for use in a history textbook, Justice Sugimoto found that those arguments "violate the plaintiff's way of viewing history and his ideas about the nature of historical education." Concerning the State's charge that Professor Ienaga's treatment of ancient texts such as the *Kojiki* and *Nihonshoki* as myths rather than as historically accurate texts is unacceptable, Sugimoto found that such claims are "tantamount to a violation of the plaintiff's consciousness of historical facts, as well as his understanding of what constitutes educational considerations." In response to the government's criticism of Professor Ienaga's interpretation of specific historical events, the Sugimoto court held that the government was in effect denying the plaintiff's rights to interpret historical facts and evaluate them on the basis of his own scholarship, simply because his conclusions were contrary to the positions officially taken by the government in regard to the same issues.[4] This is equivalent to prior censorship of the contents of a textbook writer's scholarly opinion, and is clearly in violation of

---

[3] The implication here is that "educational consideration" (*kyōiku-teki hairyo*) is no more than a code word for "political consideration."—Trans.

[4] For example, the Japanese Ministry of Education's official position on the 1941 Russo-Japanese Neutrality Pact has been that the Soviets acted in such a way as to violate it, thus forcing Japan to invade Manchuria. Ienaga was critical of this one-sided interpretation in his textbook.

Article 21 of the Constitution, as well as Article X of the Fundamental Law of Education. What is of particular importance here is that the Sugimoto court declared that the administrative branch of the government (the Ministry of Education) must not be allowed to interfere with issues such as the appropriateness of historical scholarship or with the educational philosophy of the textbook author. Once we contrast these two judicial rulings, it becomes remarkably clear how each of the presiding justices conceived the nature and shape of his exercise of judicial authority.

II

When we take a careful look at the Takatsu decision, it becomes clear that this regrettable instance of judicial malfeasance was by no means accidental. The theory of the State which supports this judgment is a distorted type of "welfare-state" theory that gives the existence of the State precedence over the welfare of the People. Hence it validates to a shocking degree the legitimacy of the State's participation in the organization of education.

In his ruling, Justice Takatsu reveals some awareness of the Sugimoto decision and its landmark interpretation of Article 26 of the Constitution. In the first place, Takatsu argues:

> Education is the process in which the abilities that define the promise of the child unfold and develop on all fronts. In other words, it is an enterprise carried out to complete the maturation of the child's character.

While then stating that the "child's right to learn" is a "natural right," this decision goes on to reason that, as the "modern state is a welfare state,"

> the dissemination of education is critically important to maintenance of the public welfare. Thus, in addition to declaring the ideals of the welfare state, the Japanese Constitution guarantees as one of the basic rights of men and women in a democratic society the right of the citizen to receive an education. In order to fully realize these rights so important to preservation of the public welfare, the Constitution empowers the State to provide the People with the education they require.... Public education in today's society has abandoned the purely private, personal qualities that characterized education in an earlier time. Having transcended

the individual-oriented character of education, it was only natural that the members of society would entrust the State with the responsibility and authority to fulfill this collectively experienced need by administering public education for the common benefit of all.

Thus, while ostensibly recognizing the child's natural right to learn, the Takatsu decision substantially denies the child's freedom to learn by relying upon theories about the role of the system of public education within the modern welfare state.

The foundation of the textbook screening system is also approached from this dangerously State-centered perspective:

> The State has a responsibility to carry out textbook screening in order to maintain the equality of educational opportunity and to continually raise the level of educational standards in accord with the appropriate developmental stage of the student. Thus, even if, as a consequence of the process of textbook screening, the author's freedoms to write and have his textbook published are limited or restricted, this is something which must be endured as a restraint imposed for the sake of the public welfare.
>
> In modern societies the State determines the kind of education that is necessary for students, on the basis of its understanding of what kind of knowledge is appropriate for children to possess. Accordingly, the Minister of Education has the authority to screen textbooks in order to uphold the quality of educational standards and to promote the equality of educational opportunity. Thus, in this limited realm of activity, the freedoms of expression which are otherwise guaranteed to citizens must necessarily be withdrawn.

Because the foundation for this "officially authorized" (kōkenteki) interpretation of the right to receive an education is the connection between the State and politics, it is most certainly not based on the nature or logic of education itself. Therefore, even while this decision formally recognizes the right to receive an education as something inherently belonging to the People, in reality it supports the State's claim of its right to dominate educational administration. The right to receive an education, according to this logic, only exists as something that the People are obliged to hand over to the State for safekeeping. This concept of the "welfare state" is based on a fictitious representation of the public good in which the personal nature of education is abandoned and the legitimate rights of the People are discarded. The State is thereby authorized to administer education from "its own standpoint" and single-handedly determine what constitutes proper "educational considerations." We do not find the naked expression "State control of education" (*kokka no kyōikuken*) used in these formulations as it was in prewar Japan, but in actuality the claim being made is that the State should possess the authority to dominate the world of education.

It is worth noting in this context that the logic of public education that leads to a "discarding of the view of education as a personal affair" actually leads to an abandonment of the spirit of education itself, degrading education into a type of indoctrination.

If, however, we grasp the People's right to education from the outset in terms of the principle of realizing the right to learn (*gakushūken*), then education appears as a series of interactions among teachers, teaching materials, and students; in short, it is something that can only be realized on a day-to-day basis. Since this is an active process in which learning equals education, if the spiritual freedom of both teachers and students is not guaranteed to the highest possible degree, then education in the true sense of the word cannot possibly come into being. Even if the People possess the right to receive an education, in the absence of the freedoms necessarily demanded by this process, an "education administered by the State" in accord with preconceived standards created by the State is nothing short of a usurpation of the teacher's spiritual creativity and inquisitiveness and a crushing of the student's freedom and right to learn. The Takatsu decision gives vivid proof of this reality.

III

The Takatsu decision offers the following interpretation of the stipulation in Article X of the Fundamental Law of Education, which states that "direct responsibility for education rests with the People as a whole":

> Within a parliamentary democracy the collective will of the nation is reflected in the laws issued by the national assembly. Thus the State, in compliance with these laws, has both the responsibility and the authority to administer public education. Conversely, only the State is in a position to bear direct responsibility to the People as a whole.

It is extremely important for us to analyze these ideas in order to understand the thinking that dominates the Japanese educational world today. In support of the position it adopted, the Takatsu decision quotes from the Explanation of the Proposed Legislation for a Fundamental Law of Education drawn up in 1947:

> The idea that the People are directly responsible for their education means that there must not be any improper, foreign elements inserted between the People and their education. The People's will regarding the general administration of education is to be expressed through the Diet, but this does not mean an outright rejection of the government's educational responsibility, particularly that of the Ministry of Education, to execute the will of the People's duly constituted assembly.

The Takatsu decision draws heavily upon this passage to justify its rather perplexing conclusion that *only the State* is in a position to directly realize the desires of the People as a whole. As should be clear, however, even from a brief reflection on the meaning of the paragraph quoted above, this is a thoroughly unwarranted conclusion. Furthermore, even the Ministry of Education itself made this point clear at the time of the enactment of the Fundamental Law of Education when it stressed the difference between politics and education in its own interpretation of the significance of Article X:

> Even though politics and education are similar in that they both are built on relations of responsibility to the People as a whole, it must be recognized that there is a fundamental difference between them. In order to express this point, Article X states that "education will not be subjected to improper control," and that "it is the direct responsibility of the People." "Directly" means that the will of the People and education are to be directly connected. For this reason, in contrast with mechanisms developed for determining the actual political will of the People, it is necessary to construct a system which will make it possible to capture and reflect the People's will concerning education. [Interpretation of the Fundamental Law of Education, p. 130; Study Group on Educational Statutes, 1947]

In short, even in the Ministry of Education's own understanding of Article X at the time of its inception, the expression "This is not a rejection of the State's responsibilities" was thought of as meaning only that the State was naturally expected to take responsibility for financing education. The conclusion reached in the Takatsu decision, that the State is the one and only legitimate bearer of direct responsibility for education in general, is a dangerously distorted interpretation that totally lacks a solid legal and intellectual foundation.

IV

In this judicial decision's interpretation of the meaning of academic and educational freedoms (Article 23 of the Constitution), there seems to be a pronounced ignorance regarding the important body of research in recent years on constitutional and educational law. Moreover, by remaining silent on the points that were at the heart of the Sugimoto decision, the Takatsu court adhered to the anti-educational view of academic freedom that characterized judicial thought prior to the appearance of that landmark ruling. Thus it bluntly states: "Academic freedom does not include educational freedom in the lower-level educational organs."

Justice Takatsu based this finding on the German view of academic freedom regarding the "unity of research and instruction" in universities and argued that "reasons for this way of thinking can also be found in the nature of the education offered in the organs of lower-level education."

> This separation is inexorably demanded by the need to guarantee the neutrality of education and uniformity of the contents, materials, and methods of instruction.
>
> Because children do not sufficiently possess the ability to criticize what they are taught, it is necessary to exercise great discretion and educational consideration appropriate to the stage of their intellectual development. By no means should we allow the classroom to become a forum for teachers' exposition of their own theories or for their insistence upon the correctness of the results of their own inquiries. This imperative is one of the most important reasons why we must impose limitations or restrictions on the educational freedom of teachers and textbook authors. Thus this court finds that the lower the level of the educational organ, the stronger the degree of restrictiveness must be.

The point of view expounded here is exactly the same as that found in the interpretation of Article 23 in the *Commentary on the Constitution of Japan* edited by the Society for the Study of Law (Hōgaku Kyōkai), which insists that the lower the level of the educational organ, "from the nature of education itself," the more its freedom must be limited. There is nothing mysterious about the source of this claim: the only question we must ask is why its advocates are so absolutely ignorant of, or unconcerned with, the guarantees which are required to ensure the conditions necessary for the creative pursuit of education.

It should go without saying that when we speak about educational liberty we are not talking about the freedom to give one-sided exegeses of sophisticated doctrines while recklessly ignoring the developmental level and needs of the child. The crux of the problem—if I may be so bold as to use the same words as those in the Takatsu decision—is: *By whom* and *in what manner* should "appropriate educational consideration and discretion be exercised in response to the child's developmental level?" It seems perfectly clear to me, at least, that those in the best position to carry out these tasks are not the agents of the State (the Ministry of Education and the courts) but classroom teachers and scholars in their role as authors of textbooks. In particular, it is the teacher who is the expert with regard to these matters, and in order to raise this competence to the level of a specialized skill, it is necessary for teachers to unendingly conduct research on a wide range of problems related to children, teaching materials, and instructional practices. It is precisely here that we should find the basis for the teacher's professional liberties: research and the freedom of praxis concretely backed up by rigorous research.[5]

Educational freedom is demanded by the very nature of education itself, particularly considering the "nature of education" in the "lower-level educational organs" themselves. This is patently clear if we follow the pattern of the child's intellectual and moral development from infancy. Arguments like that found in the Takatsu decision, which claim that the younger the child the more need there is to restrict educational freedom and impose unified educational content, are flagrantly unscientific and irrational. They can only be expounded by people who are ignorant of the conditions and logic of human development. For example, if a completely standardized format is forcibly imposed on nursery school education, the small child's spirit of curiosity will suffer seriously. In order to guarantee an education that matches the child's individuality and shows respect for the tempo of his particular maturation, even at the most basic stages of development, a highly diversified education is called for. This in turn necessitates guaranteeing the freedom of scholarly research and educational praxis required for

[5] See Chapter 10, on in-service training, for a more detailed discussion of this issue.

realizing these objectives. When we speak of the "nature of education" in this sense, it should be clear that the demand for freedom must be treated as inviolable. Moreover, in accord with Article 23's guarantee of academic freedom, the teacher's educational research on teaching materials, on child development, and on instruction must be firmly secured. Thus "educational considerations," the logic of the Takatsu decision notwithstanding, can be nothing other than pedagogic considerations. If these educational inquiries are not duly recognized as being themselves a form of scholarly research, then pedagogy can be neither understood nor practiced as a professional discipline. Accordingly, this court decision constitutes nothing less than a major challenge to the very character of the science of education itself.

The notion that educational freedom should be based on the nature of education itself is therefore not a wantonly arbitrary one. Similarly, the necessity of these freedoms is set by the intrinsic responsibility of the educator to guarantee the child's development and right to learn. It is only when this freedom has been secured that it in fact becomes possible to create and guarantee the conditions within which the child's spirit can truly be set free.

The Sugimoto decision incorporated this understanding when it addressed the question of what properly constitutes an "educational consideration." After pointing out that education should be "truthful education based on the results of scholarly research," Justice Sugimoto argued:

It is obviously not appropriate to give the results of scholarly research in an undigested form. This must always be understood, rather, as part of an education that is organized in conformity with the stage of the child's mental and physical development. The author of a textbook must therefore endeavor to shape these findings in such a way that the child can understand the truth of what is being taught, and can autonomously utilize these findings in pursuit of his or her own human development. Furthermore, the teaching methods employed in the classroom must be of such a nature that they help children to think critically about the world they encounter and to obtain a consciousness of it as a complex totality. This is what we should properly think of as "educational consideration." In order to accurately realize these educational considerations, it is necessary to achieve a scientific understanding of the interrelations between a child's physical and mental development and the psychological and social environment. It is pedagogy which indeed constitutes this science. In other words, the very exercise of these educational considerations is one type of scholarly praxis. Thus it must be recognized that by their very nature scholarship and education form an indivisible unity.

The Takatsu decision, regrettably, revealed no understanding of these points as they were argued by those on the plaintiff's side in this case; in fact, we may well say that it tried to obliterate the Sugimoto decision by simply ignoring it. On this count alone many in the education movement are inclined to lose faith in the courts once again. The judiciary has inflicted yet another wound upon itself by thus transgressing the proper limits within which it should be functioning.

V

The most prominent characteristics of this decision are its nearly total lack of awareness of the historical significance of modern ideas about human rights and its utter ignorance about education. It shamelessly camouflages a prewar legal consciousness under the guise of a discourse on the welfare state. Thus it legitimates both the abandonment of "education's personal nature" and the imposition of restraints on "educational freedom," all the while claiming to do so for the public good. What is even more frightening is that the arguments it uses to justify State intervention in education as a necessary part of the welfare state are not limited to validating the authority of the Ministry of Education, but also advocate empowering the judiciary on its own authority to interfere with the art of history and the science of education.

This situation, in which the court, which should be passing judgment on the malfeasance of the Ministry of Education's activities, actually meddles in the content of and theories about education, is nothing less than abominable. Here we see the distinctive character of the crisis in Japan's present system for the administration of justice. This logic of the welfare state and the various forms of State involvement may be designated the judiciary's "self-consciousness" of the power in its own mode of activity. The Ministry of Education censors textbooks, the prime minister makes pronouncements on morality,[6] and the judiciary passes judgment on the propriety of various doctrines and theories. There is clearly a shared tendency here. This also reveals just to what extent the exercise of judicial authority has become one

[6] This is an oblique reference to Tanaka Kakuei, who was fond of pronouncing on morality during his term in office as prime minister. Tanaka was later charged with unethical behavior for accepting bribes.—Trans.

plank in the edifice upholding State power. Furthermore, it leaves the People with no means whatsoever to appeal the government's overstepping of its proper authority. In these conditions we should remember that it will be necessary in future appeals of this case to denounce the abuses perpetrated both by the Ministry of Education and by the judiciary itself.

In addition to the grave problems already mentioned, there are a number of delusions and contradictions in this decision which must not be overlooked. For example, the decision quotes from the Report of the Organization for Economic Cooperation and Development on Japanese education, commenting that there is value in listening carefully to it. Among the points made in the OECD report are:

(1) The goal of the Japanese government is "to sacrifice diversity and emphasize uniformity."

(2) The Course of Study restricts the teacher's freedom.

(3) In the case of textbook screening in subjects like history, "there is a clear danger of forcibly compelling standardized political values."

(4) "Centralization and standardization" interfere with the "innovative practices and experiments" designed to improve the "contents and methods" of education.

Clearly, the diagnosis presented here is a scathingly critical one. Yet after the Takatsu decision goes to the trouble of quoting from these sections of the OECD report, it concludes by stating that the report "does not possess the character requisite to give advice or counsel concerning the improvement" of Japanese education. In spite of the fact that the report reflects internationally accepted common sense about education, the justices on the Takatsu court do not have the good sense to take these findings to heart.

An example of this internal inconsistency is the recognition on the one hand of the "child's right to learn" as a natural right combined at the same time with an insistence on the "abandonment of the personal nature" of modern public education. The claim that "improper control sometimes does and sometimes does not include improper administrative activities" is another example of the Takatsu decision's evasiveness.

The understanding of the concept of "freedom of expression" revealed in the Takatsu decision also deserves our attention:

> Freedom of expression is an important and basic right of the citizenry; it may even be said to constitute the nucleus of a democratic system of governance. It cannot be denied that inasmuch as the prewar textbook screening system constituted one link in

the State's thought-control apparatus, and because it was designed to serve as a tool in the policy of standardizing education, it showed no concern for the principle of freedom of expression. Even textbooks under the existing system, particularly history texts beginning with Japanese history, reveal a striking contentiousness with regard to historical views and doctrines arising from disagreements over political ideologies and values. Accordingly, the textbook screening authorities make a principle of strict neutrality, and from the outset should be sternly warned not to act arbitrarily or in a manner that would in excess of necessity restrict the freedom of expression of the textbook author or go beyond enforcing the proper measure of educational consideration. Since the textbook screening system is essentially intended to exclude books that are inappropriate for use as textbooks, it should be non-aggressive in its orientation and maintain an attitude of humility towards those situations in which freedom of expression is problematic.

However, this judicial decision is itself, as we have already seen, completely ensconced within the logic of the "modern welfare state," and has thereby abandoned the "attitude of humility" towards spiritual freedom in general and towards the freedom of thought and expression, scholarship, and education in particular. In fact, quite to the contrary, it has taken a lenient view of a wide range of State interventions. This should be made the crucial point of dispute in future courtroom pursuits.

VI

This decision provides an opportunity to reiterate the basic problem of the textbook trials by returning to the original issue of the litigation. At this time, it is critically important for us to rededicate our efforts and resolve to carefully study the nature and logic of education.

The issue which originally triggered the dispute underlying the textbook trials is the State's establishing itself as the arbiter of reality and truth in our textbooks. Through violations of the author's academic freedom and freedom of expression, this has led to an encroachment upon the rights of children—the new generation of citizens—to learn and know the truth. The significance of Professor Ienaga's litigation lies in the fact that, while resisting the infringements on his own rights, he has also sought to defend the child's right to learn and know the truth by denouncing the screening system and the attitude underlying its ill-begotten application. Thus the key issues raised by this case are: How does the teacher's educational research and praxis further the child's right to learn? and How should teachers' professional autonomy be guaranteed so as to help realize these ends? Renewed dedication to the resolution of these problems should be the new point of departure for our movement.

Educators committed to the goals of the democratic education movement should continue to investigate the nature of education and ask how best to realize genuinely educational values. This requires the willingness to wage the struggle necessary for creating a form of everyday educational praxis that is as creative as it is autonomous, and which is rigorously supported by the results of careful scientific research. The lawyers among us, proceeding from the nature and logic of education (*kyōiku no jōri*, in the words of the legal scholar Kaneko Masashi) must struggle to preserve educational freedom and autonomy as constitutional liberties. Collectively we must make our best efforts to awaken popular consciousness to the importance of thinking about education as the human right that makes all others possible. In this way we can strengthen and deepen the support which has been given to the authors' point of view in these textbook trials.

Victories and defeats in the courtroom are not the ultimate source of our joys and sorrows. By working to further realize the People's right to learn through honest and inquisitive educational praxis, we will gain the intellectual and political strength needed to win a succession of long-overdue victories in our nation's courts.

8 The Ministry of Education's Scholastic Achievement Test: Economic Growth and the Destruction of Education

I. The Issue before the Supreme Court

The decision of the Supreme Court concerning the Scholastic Achievement Test is close at hand. It will be delivered in the form of rulings on two cases, from Asahikawa (Hokkaido) and Iwate Prefecture, that were argued before the Grand Bench (Daihōtei) of the Supreme Court.[1]

In the Asahikawa case, the court will rule on the charge that when, in defiance of their principals' orders, teachers sought cancellation of the test on the day it was supposed to be administered, their action constituted a violation of the law prohibiting interference with the execution of official school business.

In the Iwate case we are awaiting a ruling regarding the charge that the local teachers' refusal to administer the Scholastic Achievement Test and their decision to conduct normally scheduled instruction instead, was an illegal political strike because it constituted an impermissible criticism of the government's official education policy.

To arrive at a definitive ruling in these cases, the justices must resolve the issue of whether or not these kinds of protest criminally obstruct execution of the public's business. Moreover, the court must address itself to the related issues of whether the so-called public business in these instances—the testing—was legitimate or not, and whether or not the teacher's decision to conduct normal instruction can be construed as constituting a politically motivated act that violates the legally guaranteed neutrality of education. On the other side of the ledger, the court must come to grips with the question of whether or not this testing represented an attempt on the part of educational administrators to improperly control education (in violation of Article X of the Fundamental Law of Education), in which they exceeded the limits of their responsibilities.

It is clear that the Supreme Court has found itself compelled to pass judgment on the propriety of the Ministry of Education-sponsored Scholastic Achievement Test. If this were not the case, there would

---

[1] See the Introduction to Part II, pages 180–187, for a detailed review of these cases, and Chapter 9 for an analysis of the Supreme Court's subsequent ruling.

213

have been no reason for the court to deliberate as long as it did: a decision could have been reached simply with regard to the charge brought against the teachers that by criticizing government policy they obstructed official public business and violated the Local Public Employees Law. If the Court's decision avoids clarifying both the appropriate limits of the authority of our educational administrators and the fundamental nature of the Scholastic Achievement Test, choosing rather to render nothing more than a token decision without real substance, then it will have to answer to the judgment of the citizenry. There will also no doubt be much criticism of the manifestly political ends served by having delayed handing down this decision for so long.

Since the occurrence of these incidents in 1961, an unreasonably long period of fourteen years has elapsed. In the history of postwar Japan, the 1960s were a period of special importance. During this time the Japanese economy, under the umbrella of the new Japan-U.S. Security Treaty, attracted the attention of the world as a major force to be contended with. The shift from "postwar recovery" to "high-level economic growth" had important ramifications in both the spiritual and the material life of the nation. On the one hand we heard the euphoric slogan "At last the postwar period is over!" while on the other we saw widespread pollution brought on by the increasing industrialization of the country. The fragility of the government's policies for high economic growth was demonstrated by the oil crisis of the early 1970s, when the psychological toll of those policies was brought home with stunning poignancy.

II. Social Background at the Time of the Testing

The Scholastic Achievement Test was primarily designed to serve an important function in the implementation of these industrialization policies by tightening the State's control over the educational apparatus and by making it more responsive to the manpower requirements of Japan's economy and industry. Constructed to measure the extent to which the Course of Study (Gakushū Shidō Yōryō)—which had been revised and given legally binding power in 1958[2]—had actually penetrated into the lower secondary schools, this test's underlying objectives were to strengthen the Ministry of Education's control over the

---

[2] Although a 1956 attempt to give the Ministry of Education power to control textbook content in a manner reminiscent of prewar practices had failed, the Ministry was able to reclaim a form of this power in 1958 when it declared that the Course of Study would thereafter be published in the official Government Register and it would therefore have legally binding power.

intellectual growth of Japanese children and to test the loyalty and commitment of teachers to the aims and values which the State sought to impose under the guise of its administrative expertise. Thus, in addition to providing a way to measure the extent to which teachers were actually following the government-mandated curriculum, it also provided a way to test their loyalty to the Ministry in general. In other words, the teacher's attitude to the testing provided a source of very useful data for the Teacher Evaluation System.[3]

Thus through the Scholastic Achievement Test the Ministry of Education sought to put the finishing touches on the system it had earlier erected to control the contents of education through a reconstituted Course of Study and an intensified program of textbook screening bordering on censorship. Now, through this new mechanism for controlling teachers, the Ministry attempted to bring the remaining loose ends of educational freedom within the purview of its administrative control.

The second major objective of this testing was to forge a new relation between education and the manpower training policies desired by the leaders of Japan's economy in the 1960s in line with their attempts to promote and sustain rapid economic growth. These efforts were initiated by the government's call for a doubling of national income. Concordant with these objectives it was decided that long-term labor power planning was called for, and this in turn was interpreted as requiring a precise measurement of the nationwide distribution of talent that would provide the data required for the establishment of an effective manpower policy. In this light it was determined that the talent available for mobilization by the nation's economic planners was best measured in terms of academic achievement.

The Ministry of Education publicly declared its objectives right from the beginning:

A broadly based policy to develop human talent is required to support the long-term economic planning which will lead to a doubling of the national income. To this end it is critically important to discover outstanding talent at an early age and cultivate it through an appropriate form of education. From this

[3] The Teacher Evaluation System was introduced in 1957; the Ministry's objective was to control teachers by using a rating system that evaluated their "loyalty and love of education" as judged by the school principal. The most problematic feature of this system was the fact that the teacher's rating remained a secret and was generally used to promote only teachers who supported the government's educational goals.

point of view it is necessary at the end of the period of compulsory education[4] to measure the child's competencies and aptitudes, and on the basis thereof to provide guidance regarding the path that will lead in the future to both individual success and usefulness to the nation as a whole. With this in mind the Ministry has been giving a great deal of thought to the best way to carry out a scholastic achievement test on a nationwide scale. [*Monbu Jihō*, November 1960]

The following year, the Ministry put out an educational white paper titled *Japanese Growth and Education*. "Growth" here did not mean the child's growth, but economic growth. This report was a landmark in the sense that it signaled the direct subordination of educational policy to economic policy.

III. Enforcement of the Test
and the Destruction of Education

What changes in the school environment were actually brought about by the institution of the Scholastic Achievement Test?

Munakata Seiya and Umene Satoru et al., in "The Ad Hoc Report of the Academic Investigation Group on the Ministry of Education's Scholastic Achievement Test in Kagawa and Ehime Prefectures," have conveyed the changes in sharp detail. As the schools in Ehime and Kagawa became absorbed in the upcoming Scholastic Achievement Test, preparation for the exam became part of the everyday school regimen. Students who generally did not do well at school were advised to stay home on the day of the testing so that the school's overall showing would improve. No matter how one looks at it, this was taking a corrupt and cynical view of education.

In its editorial column "Kyōiku no Mori" ("Educational Forest") the *Mainichi Shimbun* put the surgeon's scalpel to this corruption of education and aroused both the interest and suspicion of the public. Subsequently public opposition to this testing program increased dramatically. As a result, the Ministry of Education was forced to abandon its plan to administer the test on an all-inclusive nationwide scale, and from 1964 it was conducted as a 20-percent sampling examination.

Nonetheless, this did not diminish the fundamentally economic concerns at the base of the Scholastic Achievement Test. Overall good per-

---

[4] In Japan, nine years—six in elementary school and three in lower secondary (or junior high) school.

formance in the testing competition was viewed as a step towards the economic well-being of each region and prefecture in an age of rapid development. An episode reported from Ehime Prefecture discloses the true state of affairs at the time. In response to charges that the Scholastic Achievement Test was improper, the Secretary-General of the Ehime Prefecture Liberal Democratic Party was quoted as follows:

> Prefectural Governor Hisamatsu told Matsushita Kōnosuke [chairman of one of the nation's largest electronics manufacturing companies]: "Ehime's education has been normalized,[5] and it is in second place among all the prefectures in the Scholastic Achievement Test results." Mr. Matsushita was greatly impressed, and said, "If there is a place with so many good young people, I want to locate some of my business there," and made provisional arrangements for putting one of his subsidiary companies in the prefecture. The enticement of a factory to Ehime was most strongly influenced by the Scholastic Achievement Test. "If any fault is found with the results of the Scholastic Achievement Test, . . . if there is anything bogus about Ehime's being number two in the nationwide test results, that may mean the end of the talk about a new factory." [*Asahi Journal*, July 19, 1964]

The plans for a new industrial city and the luring of factories to the Setouchi region of Shikoku and to other less developed areas were a manifestation at the regional level of the policy promoting rapid economic growth. Within the context of these developments the Scholastic Achievement Test took on its real meaning.

IV. Foundations for Opposition

It will be unconscionable if the upcoming court decision is formulated without consideration of the changes brought about in education by its repositioning as one link in the policy of rapid economic growth unleashed in the 1960s—in other words, without consideration of the process by means of which education lost its autonomous value as education. The evidence for this point of view is more than amply provided by the transformations in education over the past fifteen years.

---

[5] "Normalization" was, and continues to be, a code word for the establishment of administrative control over education and the undermining of the influence of the Japan Teachers' Union (Nikkyōso).

The policy which equated rapid economic growth with the development of human abilities—manpower policy—advanced the trend towards unifying economics and education. The Ministry of Education's 1961 white paper made this connection in a straightforward fashion. The Economic Deliberation Council, too, stressed the link with education through slogans such as "Collaboration of Industry and Schooling" and "Triumph of Ability-First." The labor economist Sumiya Mikio has characterized this period as the time in which "in education, as in other areas of social life, economic demands were given priority."

What changes were actually imposed upon education during this period? The economic powers in Japanese society were criticizing postwar education for its uniformity and demanding the diversification of education in accordance with ability and aptitude. In particular, the very act of strategically discovering highly talented individuals at an early age for the purposes of economic growth bespoke a deep desire to control the destiny of Japanese youth. This was closely tied to a demand for cultivation of respect for highly talented people within school education in particular, and throughout society as a whole, "in a manner befitting an age of dynamic technical innovation."

Under the ideology of ability-first in education (see Chapter 13), which attempts to legitimate the rationalization of a capitalist form of economic "life," the school system was diversified in response to demands for the desired work force. Thereafter, there was no longer even the pretense of viewing the school as a place in which to discover and develop the possibilities in all children. The schools would thereafter be obliged to function as places for the discovery and selection of a range of abilities strictly dictated by, and focused around the logic of, the promotion of economically useful talent.

The turning of tests into ordinary educational activities, coupled with the ideology of "throw-away education" produced the conditions in which education would itself be denigrated. This was explained of course as a manifestation of basic economic rationalism. In turn we find the desire that "not a single child be left behind in his studies" being denigrated as the futile wishes of sentimental teachers.

Why has this come about? The policy of diversification desired by the economic world in Japan, in line with the ideology of ability-first, did not require teaching that could be understood by all children. This cynical policy was rather intended to produce a number of stragglers who, when they sought employment after graduation from lower secondary schools, would be valuable as inexpensive labor. On the other side of the equation were the 3 percent to 5 percent of highly talented students who would be singled out at a young age and guaranteed an outstanding education that would equip them to become Japan's managerial class or to provide the foundations for the development and implementation of scientific technology in industry. Based on theories of inherent differences in ability and IQ, this policy provided the justification for wide discrepancies in educational expenditures that gave the lie to the Ministry of Education's repeated claims that educational opportunities had been equalized. The 3–7 system in Toyama is a classic example of this way of thinking (see Chapter 13).

Restructuring of education to bring it in line with the principle of ability-first has led to the implementation of a five-stage scale for evaluating students relative to one another. This method, which is discussed in detail in Chapter 11, is particularly well suited to the policies of selection and diversification that have been desired in economic circles and put into effect through the administrative guidance imposed by the Ministry of Education.

The lower secondary school students who are being ranked through the almost daily barrage of school tests are thereafter distributed among a wide variety of upper secondary schools which are themselves marked by considerable differences in quality. Moreover, high school students are increasingly losing the desire to learn because they are going to schools not of their own choice but chosen for them strictly on the basis of these test scores. In such an environment even conscientious teachers find it virtually impossible to do their work, and meaningful interactions between students and teachers cannot even begin to take place. Is it any wonder that we hear about dramatic rises in the number of cases of delinquent adolescents bullying their fellow students? And can anyone really be surprised when reading about the scourge of teenage suicide in present-day Japan?

In the face of these bitter realities, the Ministry of Education has finally begun to recognize the failure of its policies for school diversification and has been obliged to take steps to correct these conditions. Ministry spokesmen now have to respond to the demands of parents for upper secondary schools that accommodate all kinds of students and educate them equally. At the same time the Ministry has to respond to society's need for more and more high schools as ever-increasing numbers of students seek to go beyond the level of compulsory education. The combined effect of these conditions has brought the crisis of upper secondary education under closer scrutiny as one of the most pressing problems confronting contemporary Japanese society.

Amazingly enough, there are still people who want to think that these horrendous conditions are fundamentally unrelated to the problems posed by the institution of the Scholastic Achievement Test. While it is certainly true that the decision to implement the test on an all-inclusive basis was rescinded in response to the criticisms of parents and teachers, and that the Fukuoka District Court branch in Kokura ruled in 1964 that enforcement of this testing violated Article X of the Fundamental Law of Education with its injunction against all forms of improper educational control, nonetheless the underlying reality of the testing remains unaffected. Thus, regardless of whether or not the test is repeated every year, or whether it is directly imposed on every lower secondary school student in the nation, its symbolic importance as an expression of the values dominating education in Japan today remains largely intact. These values underscored the Ministry of Education's use of the Scholastic Achievement Test as a way to normalize its policies designed to subordinate the diversification of upper secondary schools to the plans for industrial expansion that were being forged by the nation's economic leaders. Once the continuous testing and ranking of students was routinized and made a key component of the educational culture of our country, then a simultaneously conducted, all-inclusive nationwide achievement test would become unnecessary. In this sense the Scholastic Achievement Test had become expendable because the values of that testing system had already become an accepted part of educational life and its underlying reality.

As a consequence of this new state of affairs, education has largely ceased to function as an enterprise designed to guarantee the rights of all Japanese children and youth to a democratically oriented character development. Nor can our schools contribute to the creation of a national culture based upon the value of respect for individuals; they are now little more than a part of the social machinery for developing and distributing manpower in line with official economic policy. The Scholastic Achievement Test played a strategic role in laying the foundations for the diversification of upper secondary education demanded by our current industrial structure. In short, economic values have been used to deny the validity of all pedagogic objectives which are vital for preserving the autonomy of education.

The Scholastic Achievement Test was planned and executed to grease the wheels for the policies of manpower development that were an essential part of the comprehensive program for high-speed economic growth. The Supreme Court should, in its upcoming decision, acknowledge that the policy of upper secondary school diversification and the testing system through which it was advanced have wreaked havoc upon the central values underlying postwar education.

Criticism of the Scholastic Achievement Test has provided a valuable tool for diagnosing the pathology and corruption visited upon Japanese education since the 1960s. Thus recent efferts to legally challenge the legitimacy of the State's use of its administrative authority have also played an important role in the development of a democratic education movement by providing an opportunity to more fully work out in concrete terms the basis for an independent educational logic.

9 The Structure of Educational Authority: A Critique of the Supreme Court's Ruling in the Scholastic Achievement Test Cases

In this essay I will analyze the decision handed down by the Supreme Court with regard to the Scholastic Achievement Test in order to clarify the three major issues it raises: (1) the locus of educational authority; (2) the meaning of educational freedom, i.e., how to interpret Articles 23 and 26 of the Constitution; (3) the problems of who should determine the contents of education and how this should be done in a way that wins the assent and support of the People.[1]

I. The Locus of Educational Authority

Immediately after the Supreme Court's decision was handed down, one newspaper commented that it "finally brought to a conclusion" the struggle over educational authority (*Asahi Shimbun*, May 21, 1976, evening edition); however, another declared that the decision "did not touch on the issue of educational authority at all" (*Tokyo Shimbun*'s evening edition of the same day). How can a single ruling be interpreted in such widely divergent fashions? To resolve this problem, let me begin by examining the way the court dealt with the historical background to these problems:

> The State's general interest in education has steadily grown as the system of public schooling has expanded; its efforts to intervene in and control the internal mechanisms of educational administration have grown in direct proportion thereto. However, this has also given rise to an ongoing reconsideration of the true nature of education and the proper manner in which it should be conducted. As a result of these reflections, the problems of who is in the best position to decide the most important questions regarding the education of our children, and who should be in charge of it, have been widely investigated in recent years. Moreover, new concerns have been voiced in relation to the extremely important problem of the propriety of State control and the limits which should be imposed upon its interventions.

[1] The background to this case is discussed on pp. 180–187 and in Chapter 8.

222

The judgment goes on to boil the controversy down to the problem of where the "authority to make decisions about the actual contents of education" should properly reside:

> There are two diametrically opposed viewpoints with regard to the question of to whom, within the legal system in effect in our country, the authority and competence to determine the contents of children's education properly belongs. One of these has provided the foundation of the government prosecutor's case; the other has underwritten the arguments of the defendants' lawyers. However, because each of these positions is too extreme in its basic orientation, this court is unable to find either one of them suitable for complete adoption.

A. Rejection of the State's All-Inclusive Intervention

What are the "two extreme ways of thinking" that the court rejected in its decision? The judgment summarizes the first of them like this:

> One of these interpretations sees the education of children as a shared concern of all the People—in other words, not just a concern of their parents. From this standpoint the public education system is viewed as having come into existence in response to all of the People's expectations and requirements, and therefore, it is argued that it should be managed from the perspective of the nation as a whole. According to this theory, control should be both exercised and realized to meet all of the People's educational needs, and under the system of parliamentary democracy adopted by our Constitution, it is argued, this can only be concretely achieved through legislation enacted by the Diet. Here, and only here, the argument goes, can the national educational will be determined. Thus, the proponents of this theory insist, the methods and content of public education should be determined by Diet legislation. The organs of the State's educational administration, inasmuch as they are founded on the powers afforded them by the national legislature, therefore possess, according to this doctrine, a wide-ranging authority to make definitive determinations of public policy with regard to these educational matters.

This way of thinking employs the notion of parliamentary democracy to legitimate the all-inclusive intervention of the State into education; it was at the heart of the prosecutors' final summation on behalf of the Ministry of Education. Moreover, it also appeared in the "notification" (*tsūtatsu*) sent out by the Ministry of Education immediately after the Sugimoto decision on textbook screening (see Chapter 6) was handed down:

> Public education must be carried out by the State for the benefit of the People on the basis of the national will. In order to realize the national will in the realm of education, it is necessary for the State to act as the recipient of the People's educational authority as it is democratically formulated in the Diet. Thus the State and only the State must act as the agent of the People's educational authority. Accordingly, in cases where there are sharp disagreements amongst the People regarding the ideals and objectives of public education, it is critically important to rely upon the procedures of parliamentary democracy to determine precisely what the national will shall be. Moreover, the only way to realize the general will of the People with regard to education as it is expressed in legislation ratified by the Diet is to entrust it to the organs of national educational administration which are legally empowered to act upon that will. As for teachers and others whose job is to conduct education on a day-to-day basis, the only way they can discharge their responsibilities to the nation is by submitting to the control of the agents of the State's educational administration. [Ministry of Education Directive, "Concerning the Decision on the First Suit on the Textbook Screening System," August 7, 1971]

It is extremely significant that the recent Supreme Court decision on the Scholastic Achievement Test rejected the Sendai Higher Court's earlier acceptance of the Ministry of Education's argument that it has the right and responsibility to intervene in any and all educational matters on the grounds that within the framework of a system of representative democracy, it is the only legitimate representative of all the People. While it is true that in the end the Supreme Court recognized the State's responsibility towards education and the propriety of its interventions, and that in the last analysis the results may very well be the same, it is imporant to note that because it did so on the basis of a very different logic its decision has a strikingly different theoretical structure. Thus we should view with much suspicion the statement by the Minister of Education, at a briefing immediately after the ruling was handed down, that this decision once again affirms the correctness of the legal interpretation that the Ministry of Education has for a long time taken with regard to the Constitution and the Fundamental Law of Education.

B. The Consciousness of the Sugimoto Decision

On the other hand, there are a number of serious problems in the way the Supreme Court grasped and subsequently rejected the claims of the lawyers for the defendants in the case, the prefectural teachers' unions:

> The other view [that advocated by the defendants' side in these cases] is premised on the idea that Article 26 of the Constitution, guaranteeing the child's right to an education, means that education must be organized and conducted as an obligation to the child. According to this way of thinking, the bearers of this obligation are parents in particular and the nation as a whole, and the public character of education results from the collectivization of the parental duty to ensure that their children are properly educated. From this standpoint the supporters of the defendants' view argue that Article X of the Fundamental Law of Education was instituted to make sure that public education would be conducted as a direct responsibility to the People as a whole and not as a responsibility to the State (as was the case before the war). Thus, they argue, the involvement of the State, as the main agency of public authority, should be limited to those activities necessary to consolidate the various conditions under which the citizenry's educational obligation can be carried out. As a matter of principle, they maintain, the State should not be understood as having the authority to intervene in the contents and methods of children's education. In this vision of education, teachers, as the actual agents of the teaching process, and as professionally trained specialists, should determine the contents and execution of education as part of their educational and cultural responsibility to the People as a whole. The guarantee of academic freedom in Article 23 of the Constitution is thus taken as meaning that the freedom of scholarly research should be extended to include the freedom to teach as well. This freedom of teaching, it is insisted, does not apply only to higher education, but, from the very nature of education itself, to ordinary education as well.

It is clear that the Supreme Court was thinking here of the Sugimoto decision, which definitely rejected the theory of the State's authority over education, arguing:

> The bearers of the obligation to educate the child, in a manner befitting the notion that in a democratic society the child has a right to receive an education, are the citizens of the nation as a whole and the child's parents in particular. In clear opposition to the ideology which mandated that the State held all educational rights and authorities, the new idea of the People's educational responsibilities can well be called the theory of the People's educational freedom. The only educational responsibility that the State bears [in postwar Japan] is to help the citizens of the nation carry out their educational obligations to the younger generation. Therefore the powers conferred upon the State are intended to help it to discharge its educational responsibilities and by no means require the State's interference with the contents and inner workings of the educational process, nor do they provide any justification for those who would use these powers for such ends. Quite to the contrary, these powers should be thought of as merely enabling the State to consolidate the conditions necessary for cultivating education itself. It must be firmly repeated that by no stretch of the imagination do they permit the interference of the State in the inner workings of the educational enterprise.

C. Is a Compromise between These Conflicting Views Really Possible?

These two viewpoints have been summarily termed the theories of the State's educational authority (*kokka no kyōikuken ron*) and the People's educational authority (*kokumin no kyōikuken ron*). There has been a widespread tendency to interpret this decision of the Supreme Court as a repudiation of both theories. For example, the journal *Gendai Kyōiku Kagaku* (*Modern Educational Science*) criticized the ruling like this:

> The first problem is where the authority to control children's education resides: with the State or with the People. This is also one of the central issues in the dispute underlying the Ienaga textbook trials. The Supreme Court, by ruling that "both are too extreme and one-sided, and neither can be adopted," rejected the notion that one must choose between these two alternatives.

["Commentary on Educational News"; *Gendai Kyōiku Kagaku,* Meiji Tosho 230]

However, will this decision actually lead to a state of affairs in which both can or will be rejected? Indeed, the arguments of the prosecutor and those of the defense were turned down, but can this in fact be seen as a compromise? Is it possible for there genuinely to exist a theory of educational authority within which educational power resides neither with the State nor with the People?

D. The Meaning of This Evasiveness

While it is possible for sovereignty to reside either in the State (or in some cases a monarch) or in the People, it is quite impossible for it to reside halfway between the two. Moreover, in a state established on the basis of the principles of democracy or popular sovereignty, it is quite simply impossible for the locus of educational authority to be conceived apart from the People.

Thus, under Japan's Constitution and Fundamental Law of Education, which are premised on popular sovereignty, there should be no question at all of whether the People or the State have the right to control education. It must be understood as self-evident that educational authority resides with the People.

Accordingly, the Supreme Court's attempt to formulate a third theory regarding the locus of educational power can hardly be thought of as constituting a correct understanding of the nature of educational life in a democratically organized society. A careful examination of the court's decision reveals in fact that the judges worked very hard to avoid rendering a clear statement on the true "locus of educational authority." And when we consider that the major premise of the postwar judicial system is that the courts should always remain faithful to the principles embodied in the Constitution, then it should also follow that in a system based on popular sovereignty, the only ruling that the Supreme Court could have arrived at was that the People are the proper masters of the nation's educational system.

Interestingly enough, even the Ministry of Education has been obliged to formally acknowledge what I am calling the theory of the People's educational sovereignty when attempting to formulate its new version of the State's educational supremacy. In the previously cited directive which was sent out after the Ministry's practices were castigated in the Sugimoto decision, there was a formal acknowledgment of "the People's inherent educational authority." But in reality the logic of representative democracy was merely being used to support the claim that the government had to actualize these rights for the People because the latter are unable to directly do so for themselves. In other words, while the Ministry of Education's theory formally rests upon a recognition of the People's rights to and authority over education, in actuality this is merely a form of logical manipulation designed to legitimate the State's all-inclusive power over education.

This leads me to point out that while within the existing Japanese State there is no room whatsoever in a formal sense for a doctrine of State control over education, in actuality the battle lines are drawn over whether the State or the People have the power to control education. The Ministry of Education and the State's prosecutors have been obliged to recognize this. At the very least, this can be regarded as the historical legacy of Imperial Japan's defeat in the Pacific War, and the creation of a democratic Constitution.

The current decision, because it avoids a clarification of this issue, can be thought of as a highly political decision. While it should be evident to everyone that under a system of popular sovereignty educational power must reside with the People and not with the State, we must still overcome the problem of how to fully realize the People's educational powers, and of how to assign a position to the State and its authority within those new arrangements.

II. Concerning Educational Liberty

A. The Interpretation of Article 26

How then did the Supreme Court's decision in the Scholastic Achievement Test case construe the structure of the People's educational rights and authority? To clarify this issue, let us begin by looking at the way the decision interpreted Article 26 of the Constitution, which stipulates: "All people shall have the right to receive an equal education correspondent to their ability" and "All people shall be obligated to have all boys and girls under their protection receive ordinary educations as provided by law. Such compulsory education shall be free."

> According to the provisions of this article, it is clear that the State, based on the ideal of a modern welfare state, has a responsibility to positively establish the organs of public education and make them available for the use of the People.
>
> Furthermore, in light of the absolute necessity of the child's receiving a basic education, this article also makes it clear that

parents have an obligation to ensure that their children receive such an education and that the State has an obligation to shoulder the expenses required to make this possible.

As can be seen from this passage, the court grasped the general significance of these provisions of the Constitution. It then went on to discuss the basic educational thinking that underlies these stipulations, as follows:

Behind this provision is the idea that each and every member of the nation has the inherent right, both as a human being and as a citizen, to undertake the study and learning necessary for the completion of his or her character formation, growth, and intellectual development. In particular, children, who cannot prosecute their studies without the help of adults, have the right to expect such help. Article 26 of the Constitution imparts to this expectation an inviolable legal foundation. The education of children is not, in other words, the prerogative of those who administer and conduct education, but an obligation imposed upon those who, by virtue of the nature of the work they do, are in the best position to most effectively help realize the child's right to learn.

The interpretation of Article 26 expressed here clearly has in its background notions of the citizenry's rights to learn, particularly the child's right to learn. This point of view has been theoretically developed in the fields of educational science and educational law since the 1960s, and, as we saw in Part I, has a bona fide genealogy in modern intellectual history as well. The theories that support this way of thinking have been energetically expounded upon so that they are now commonly accepted outside of Japan. And even in Japan constitutional scholars who are normally conservative on educational issues have come to accept these doctrines after they were first reflected in the Sugimoto decision (see Chapter 6).

According to the bureaucrats in our Ministry of Education, however, this educationally oriented logic is an utterly fanciful creation of sedition-minded scholars, and it has absolutely no grounding whatsoever in existing law. Thus the fact that these ideas have been confirmed in principle by the justices of the Supreme Court is perhaps the greatest merit in what is otherwise a basically reactionary judgment.

B. The Intellectual Lineage of "the Child's Rights"

The idea that people inherently possess the right to learn both as human beings and as the citizens of a democratic nation developed as an intrinsic part of the modern discourse on the meaning of human rights as its manifestation on the plane of spiritual freedom. These ideas have also been introduced into contemporary discourse as a consequence of the "discovery of the child" (Philippe Aries) and the recognition of children's special rights, in particular the right to learn.

Thus it is exceedingly important to understand that these concepts did not emerge together with the idea of the welfare state. In truth these ideals are much older: their roots extend back to the very beginnings of human thought about the meaning of freedom and liberty and the rights which must be guaranteed to protect them. The modern state should be viewed not as the creator of these rights but only as their guarantor. Likewise the State as it now exists must be thought of as bearing a specific responsibility to ensure these rights and liberties for each and every member of society. With regard to education in particular, the State must therefore be understood as being under an obligation to establish educational institutions and absorb the financial burden of running them in order to guarantee the realization of these rights in a concrete form. Parents, for their part, should be held accountable for making sure that their children are sent to school and receive an education.[2]

While the term "welfare state" is frequently used in this decision, it is rarely used in a precise fashion, nor does its usage show any deep awareness of the intellectual relations and lineage outlined above. Nonetheless, the court has declared that the State's participation in the organization of education should take the form of "an obligation to set up the various institutions for education and make them available to the People for their use." This decision also affirms both the compulsory and the free character of public education by stating that parents have an obligation to send their children to school and that the State has a responsibility to pay for this schooling.

By acknowledging the special character of the child's right to learn, the Supreme Court has recognized that this right is not one that its nominal bearers can sufficiently realize by their own individual efforts. Education must be organized to fulfill the child's rights to learn, and this imposes a particular set of obligations upon those whose work is to educate. However, as the court has wisely pointed out, "this does not constitute a prerogative of control on the part of those who are directly responsible for conducting and administering education." I

---

[2] This notion has an additional significance in Japan, where parents are often reluctant to send to school children who are physically or mentally incapacitated.

want to call attention to the fact that at the root of this interpretation of the general significance of Article 26 of the Constitution is a basic recognition of the People's educational rights, in particular the child's right to learn.

C. On the Authority to Determine the Contents of Education

What kind of thinking is revealed in this decision regarding the people who are in a position to work to concretely realize the child's right to learn?

> Even if we postulate that the education of children must be conducted primarily for the good of the child and that this is an obligation imposed upon those who provide the child with his or her education, this does not in itself lead to a clear and unambiguous resolution of the problem of who should determine the appropriate contents and methods of instruction. In fact, on the basis of this principle it is quite impossible to determine who could even make such decisions.

While keeping in mind the arguments of both the prosecutors and the defense lawyers in this case, the text of the court's judgment continues as follows:

> In other words, there is nowhere in the relevant clauses of the Constitution any basis whatsoever for declaring in a straightforward and unequivocal manner whether the contents of the child's education should be decided through the procedures generally used for determining the political will of the country, or whether this should be undertaken in a manner completely free from the control and interference of politics—in short, as a problem that should be dealt with strictly within the social and cultural arenas of national life.

The justices of the Supreme Court are indeed correct in concluding that Article 26 of the Constitution does not directly provide the basis for resolving this problem. The question which we must address therefore is how this troublesome issue can best be clarified.

D. Rereading the Constitution
   from an Educational Perspective

At this point the argument presented in the court's decision turns to an examination of Article 23 of the Constitution and the way it entered into this case:

> We have also heard the opinion expressed that teachers should be recognized as the possessors of an inviolable freedom to give instruction as they themselves best see fit to do so. On this basis it is claimed that teachers should not therefore be forced to submit to any interventions or forms of control imposed by publicly constituted bodies. Moreover, the advocates of this viewpoint declare, teachers should be free to determine the contents of the education the children in their charge should receive. The court cannot, however, accept or endorse such an opinion.

Observing that neither Article 23 nor 26 declares who should be the subject (*shutai*) charged with the responsibility of determining the contents of education, the court then went on to adopt the position that to answer such questions it is first necessary to go back to the nature of education and rethink these problems from that perspective.

It is generally thought that because children have an inherent plasticity, they are very much open to the influences of the environment in which they grow up. Thus it is also widely believed that the kind of education which is bestowed upon them plays a major role in determining the kind of adults they will become in the future. Therefore it is completely natural that all those who have an interest in or concern with the outcome of the child's education should want to exert control over the actual processes of structuring and carrying out that education from their respective standpoints. The child's education should be conducted primarily for the benefit of the child, and although this suggests that it is necessary for all of the parties who have an interest in education to cooperate for the good of the child, in reality it is unavoidable that, as a result of widely divergent ideas about what is best for the child, many conflicts and contradictions should arise when it comes to actually determining the appropriate contents of education. It is for the reasons cited above that the Constitution does not provide any clear or fixed standards for resolving these conflicts and contradictions.

However, is there some way to minimize the negative effects of these conflicts and limit their destructive effects upon the educational process as a whole? The court's decision proposes the following solution:

> The most rational solution to these problems is one based on an attitude of mutual respect in which each of the directly concerned

parties recognizes the constitutional rights of the others and seeks to establish a framework for compromise and accommodation.

However, it is not at all clear what the court has in mind when speaking about the "constitutional foundations" of the rights of the various parties in these conflicts. It is indeed true that the Constitution does not express any definitive conclusions about who should decide upon the contents of education and the framework within which that authority should be exercised; however, if the Constitution is viewed as a whole and considered with regard to its inherently democratic values, then I believe it is indeed possible to read it as providing positive direction about how the locus and limits of this authority should be construed. In other words, instead of isolating phrases from different places in the text of the Constitution, the court, by taking a broad view of the essence of education and the logic of intellectual freedom that is required to support its activities, could have arrived at a significantly different interpretation.

E. The Fundamental Irreconcilability of Politics and Education

The court's decision approaches the problem of the appropriate limits upon the authority of parents, teachers, and the State regarding determination of the contents of education as follows:

> In the first instance the parents, based on their natural relations with the child, have the most profound interest in his or her future; therefore they are recognized by this court as having the right to exercise control over their child's education within circumscribed bounds. This parental authority with regard to education should be exercised mainly regarding instruction within the home, outside of school, or in relation to the choice of schools.

As for the "freedom of private education" and the "intellectual freedom of teachers," the Court also upheld this "within certain fixed limits and spheres of activity."
As for the role of the State:

> In those domains outside the purview of parents and teachers, the State, as one phase of its administration of the affairs of the nation, should formulate and implement appropriate policies which will systematically realize the general will of the People with regard to their commonly shared educational problems. Thus as

long as it operates within necessary and reasonable limits, the State has the authority to make decisions regarding the contents of education in order to protect the interests of the child and to serve those of society in general. Nowhere in the Constitution is there any stipulation which mitigates the validity of this interpretation. Indeed it is only the State which is in a position to act in the best interests of the nation as a whole.

Concerning the meaning of these "necessary and reasonable" limits, the court argued that, given the nature of today's party politics, "it is desirable that these forces be restrained to as great an extent as is possible."

Determination of the affairs of state in accord with the principle of governance by the majority party is not the same thing as a unified expression of the national will but merely an expression of ongoing attempts to resolve conflicts between competing interests. For this reason the intervention of majoritarian politics into education must be constrained.

It is important to take note of the logic employed here because it supports our claim that the educational import of the Constitution should be derived from a consideration of its overall structure rather than on the basis of its separate provisions. In other words, when thinking about the "constitutional foundations" of our educational system, it is critical to focus upon the relations between the modern state and human rights which uphold the very being of the Constitution. This way of thinking, moreover, underscores the idea that education, which is essentially "a cultural undertaking closely related to the interiority of human values," should be conducted apart from the strains and tensions generated by partisan politics.

Thus, when one sets out to interpret the meaning of the basic laws governing the establishment and operation of education, it is indispensable to keep in mind the fundamental tensions and incongruities between party politics and the logic underwriting the nature of education. The problem we confront when reading the Supreme Court's ruling in the Scholastic Achievement Test cases arises from the extent to which the court has correctly understood the nature and logic of education.

F. The Sphere of Authority of Parent and Teacher

While the words employed in the court's decision suggested an understanding of the essence of education, their usage belies a fatal flaw inasmuch as the judgment they give expression to totally overlooks the abuses caused by the enforcement of the Scholastic Achievement Test. Likewise the State's authority over education is indirectly affirmed by a process of linguistic elimination that closely resembles this rhetorical chicanery. This is accomplished when the court's decision argues that "outside the areas freely entrusted to the authority of parents and teachers, the State, within necessary and reasonable limits, shoulders the responsibility to determine the contents of education."

How did the court see the scope of the freedom and authority of parents and teachers? Let us first examine the decision's declaration with regard to parents.

> The parent's education of his or her child is, in its most basic and fundamental aspects, one part of the custodial role entrusted to them by virtue of the natural relations that bind parents and children together. . . . Therefore parents should be recognized as possessing definite rights of control over the education of their children, particularly given the fact that they have the most direct concern for the child's future well-being and are in the best position to exercise good judgment when and where that is called for. In short, the parent has the freedom to educate his or her child.

But when it came to specifying the contents of these parental liberties with regard to education, the Supreme Court adopted an extremely restricted interpretation of the scope of these freedoms:

> The educational liberties of the parent are hereby recognized as pertaining in the main to the education given at home and outside of the school or to the parents' freedom to select the school which the child shall attend.

G. Lack of Understanding of the Relation between School and Parent

Restricting the parent's educational liberty to the freedom of school selection while proclaiming the parent to be the "party most concerned with the child's future" and "the person in the best position to exercise [educational] discretion" reveals a shocking lack of understanding with regard to the real import of the ties between parents and schools. This lack of understanding is testified to by the court's declaration regarding the meaning of Parent-Teacher Associations (PTAs) and their activities.

Established during the period when the postwar reforms of education were first enacted, these organizations were created to provide the forums in which parents and teachers could meet and discuss the education being provided in the schools and work out measures for its improvement. In other words, the PTA was intended to make it possible for parents and teachers to form a partnership in which they could collectively work to guarantee the educational rights of the child. But these activities become quite impossible when education is viewed from the perspective offered by the Supreme Court, in which school education and home education are compartmentalized and effectively shut off from one another. When this isolation is made the foundation for educational thought and organization, how in the world can parents and teachers cooperate to guarantee the educational and developmental rights of the child? Indeed, it is only through groups like the PTA that parents can organize and collectively present their educational desires to those working in the schools to educate their children. When we view the school as the agency within society entrusted with the task of realizing parental educational authority, it is clear that these interactions and the process by means of which they are achieved are completely natural and desirable. In spite of the Japanese State's continuing efforts to usurp this authority for itself, there are still dedicated parents and teachers who have not forsaken their commitment to the realization of these ideals.

Furthermore, to the extent that the school districting system in effect in Japan is one in which parents have no choice about which school to send their children to, apart from the choice of a private school, the parental liberty valorized in the Supreme Court decision is a nonexistent one. For this reason too it is important for parents and teachers to jointly shoulder the responsibility for determining the contents of the learning that underwrites the child's education and development.

The Supreme Court's decision gives further evidence of its inherently self-contradictory nature by declaring on the one hand that the parent has a "definite power of control" in regard to his or her child's education while at the same time insisting that this does not extend "to control over education itself." Here we find another telling example of the Supreme Court's lack of educational understanding.

H. Regional Autonomy and Residents' Educational Authority

Because the education of individual children is also the process by means of which the next generation is cultivated, it is a matter of deep concern not only to the parents of those children but also to the older members of society in general and the inhabitants of the region in which they live in particular. The postwar reformers of Japanese education had this in mind when they asserted the principle of regional autonomy as the new foundation for educational control, and the recent Supreme Court decision acknowledged this as well when it called this principle "one of the cardinal rules of educational administration." In other words, the importance of the principle of regional educational autonomy is not simply that it formally recognizes the responsibilities of locally constituted governing bodies: it was designed to make sure that the educational demands of the inhabitants of an area would be actively reflected in the administration of local education. Thus this principle should never be lost sight of in all discussions and debates on the nature of educational authority.

When farmers, for example, whether or not they have children, are concerned about the reality and future of agriculture, it is quite natural for them to worry about how agricultural issues are presented in textbooks and discussed in schools. It is entirely appropriate, therefore, that their demands and criticisms be taken into consideration when textbooks are selected and teachers formulate their instructional objectives.

The problem, of course, is what should be done in those cases where contradictions and conflicts arise between the authority of parents and local inhabitants on the one hand and the school and teachers on the other. In such cases, after all sides have aired their views, the responsibility and authority for judgment should be entrusted to the school, teachers' groups, and, in the last analysis, the individual teacher. The autonomy of educational authority has to be recognized as ultimately based on the teacher's professionalism.

I. The Freedom of Instruction

Let me now turn to an analysis of what the court said about the scope of the teacher's educational authority. "Within clearly defined limits," the court declared, "the instructional freedom of teachers is affirmed." It expressed its understanding of the extent of these liberties in terms of an interpretation of Article 23 of the Constitution's stipulations regarding academic freedom.

> This court cannot accept the construction of academic freedom according to which teachers' possession of instructional freedom is taken to mean that they are exempt from the control and inter-

ventions of the State, and according to which they are viewed as totally free to determine the contents of the education given to the children entrusted to their care as they themselves see fit.

Nonetheless this decision does represent a marked improvement over previous interpretations of the meaning of academic freedom which limited it to those teaching and doing research in universities.[3] Thus we can take some satisfaction from the fact that we have been able to induce the justices of the Supreme Court to declare in principle that even in the world of ordinary education, "instructional freedom must be guaranteed within fixed limits." On the meaning of this freedom, the decision reasons as follows:

> The court believes that the freedom of instruction should be guaranteed within certain fixed limits. This is no more desirable in principle in the case of university professors whose work is to conduct scholarly inquiries and to provide instruction in difficult subject matters than it is in the case of teachers in lower-level educational organs whose main responsibility is to transmit basic knowledge to and develop the fundamental abilities of their students. Moreover, as teachers are no longer required by the State to present only specifically approved ideas, and because the child's education demands direct human contact between teacher and pupil, the former must be free to use his or her discretion in choosing the best instructional materials and the most appropriate methods for teaching them.

In this passage we can see in a highly concentrated form both the strengths and weaknesses in the educational consciousness of the Supreme Court. We must first acknowledge the importance of the court's recognition that it is inappropriate for the State to compel teachers to give instruction only in specifically approved ideas. In this spirit the court reiterated the fundamental ideas running throughout the postwar reform of education, the notion that "the agents of the State should neither decide where truth resides nor what constitutes reality." Here we can detect the distant echoes of Condorcet's claim that public education should be made independent of the authority of the State and the French constitutional scholar Duguit's opinion that "the State must not possess its own doctrines." These ideas reflect the characteristically modern recognition that the bearers of public authority must

[3] This point is more fully discussed in Chapter 3.

be restrained from using their authority to venture into the realms of culture and belief.

From this perspective it is both exceedingly important and entirely appropriate to reexamine the legally binding powers claimed by the Ministry of Education for its Course of Study, its textbook "screening" system, and the in-service training programs it administers (see Chapter 10) because the officially enforced observance of each clearly violates the injunction which prohibits the State from establishing its own doctrines and forcibly compelling their systematic observance. Accordingly, the text of the Supreme Court decision in the Scholastic Achievement Test cases will undoubtedly become an important point of departure for educational debate in the future.

The second aspect of the court's ruling that deserves our praise is its recognition that, owing to the nature of education itself, it is necessary for teachers to have the freedom to exercise discretion on the basis of "direct personal contacts" with the children in their care. When this is compared with previous interpretations of academic freedom in Japan that limited it to those working in universities and in the same spirit declared "lower-level educational organs" to be intrinsically and substantively different from institutions of higher learning, it becomes abundantly clear that this judgment represents an important theoretical advance in the educational understanding of our judiciary. By openly declaring that the teacher's pedagogic freedom is a fundamental requirement for the successful prosecution of education, the justices of the Supreme Court have shown just how much they learned from adjudicating the controversies that grew out of the Ministry of Education's attempts to impose its Scholastic Achievement Tests on the youth of this nation.

J. Glaring Inadequacies in the Court's Educational Consciousness

Notwithstanding these obviously laudable aspects of the logic displayed in the court's decision, its understanding of education is by no means flawless. This is particularly evident in the way the court has understood the idea that education should be conducted in relation to the individuality of the child. Education, we have learned, opens up the child's humanity and individuality by imparting knowledge of truth and reality, thereby leading to the cultivation of adolescents who possess free personalities. Most regrettably, however, the recent decision of the court does not contain a single word about the significance of culture and scholarship for human beings, nor does it touch upon the fact that truth makes people free and helps us to develop our individuality. Moreover, we can detect clear residues of the prewar ideology (see Chapter 3) that legitimated the isolation of education from scholarship in the statement that university work is primarily concerned with "free scholarly inquiry and study" while the sole objectives of lower-level education are merely to "transmit knowledge and develop ability." Had the judges reflected more carefully on the true nature of education, they would have shown more appreciation for the fact that even the "transmission of knowledge and the development of ability" are possible in a meaningful sense only when schoolteachers are able to freely inquire into the contents of the education they are called upon to provide, and when they supplement their personal contacts with the child with a scientifically grounded understanding of childhood development.

Consequently, the "flowering of the child's inherent possibilities as a human being" cannot be simplistically understood as the result of merely living and growing up within a particular cultural environment. Likewise the social values at the heart of a culture are not automatically reproduced in its young without a great deal of effort on the part of all involved. This requires that teachers' understanding both of their own cultural values and of teaching techniques be backed by an intelligent understanding of the child's intellectual and moral development. In order to make cultural values into spiritual forces capable of stimulating these forms of human development, teachers' professional abilities must be such that they can convert these underlying values into concrete educational values.

Thus, because the teacher, to be a good teacher, must relentlessly inquire into the nature of these educational values, he or she must be guaranteed the freedoms of inquiry and scholarship. In other words, this claim is made not with reference to the teacher but rather in conformity with the very nature of the educational enterprise itself. To guarantee that children have the opportunity to become the masters of the spiritual liberties required to substantiate a democratic form of social life, they must be nourished through a creative form of educational practice itself supported by free inquiries that will directly lead to meaningful encounters with truth and reality.

If the justices on the bench of the Supreme Court had spent more time pondering the nature and meaning of education, they would not have been able to employ weak and vacillating expressions like those criticized above, while vaguely and imprecisely affirming the freedom of instruction. That our judiciary is capable of acting in such a responsible manner is testified to by the decision handed down by

Judge Sugimoto, which astutely declared that the primary objective of education should be the "cultivation of truth":

Since children at the stage of compulsory education have yet to achieve the high levels of conceptual understanding found among university students, it is not appropriate to provide them with the results of scholarly research in an unreconstituted form as they clearly do not have the capacity to digest such learning. Nevertheless, because they do have the right to be educated in the truths ascertained by such scholarship, those responsible for the education of children should endeavor to shape these findings and present them in conformity with the child's mental and physical development to ensure that these truths can be understood. Furthermore, the teaching methods which should be employed to realize these ends must help the child to develop the capacity to think critically about the world and to perceive it as a totality. This should form the underlying reality of "educational considerations." It is indispensable for the proper prosecution of these educational considerations that teachers achieve an understanding of the relations between the physical and mental, psychological and social, environments in which children develop; for this they must rely upon the efforts and results of the science of pedagogy. In other words, the very exercising of these educational considerations must be conceived as itself one type of scholarly practice, and its freedom must be preserved accordingly. Thus the indivisible unity of scholarship and education must be clearly recognized.

K. The Foundations and Substance of the Teacher's Freedoms

Even though the Supreme Court's decision had already acknowledged the teacher's "instructional freedoms within definite limits," because teachers "exert a strong, even dominant influence on children" and because "it is necessary to maintain educational standards on a nationwide basis," the court ultimately declared that "it is impermissible to grant teachers working in the organs of lower-level education complete educational liberty." In this light, the justices strongly concluded, these freedoms must be "repressed."

What in the world could the court have had in mind when it declared that "complete educational liberty" must not be permitted? If this was interpreted as meaning that "teachers may teach anything they want in any manner they deem appropriate," then the court really has no understanding at all of what instructional freedom is all about. After all, it should be evident even to those justices that calls for educational freedom are not based on the notion that such freedoms are unrelated to the teacher's responsibilities.

When we speak of the instructional liberties of the teacher, we are referring to the freedoms they require to facilitate the development of the child's possibilities as a human being. These possibilities can only be realized in an orderly fashion, we have learned, when teachers organize their instruction in conformity with the logical development of the child's mind and his or her capacity to absorb truth and reality. Therefore, education should be conducted, and its concrete objectives defined, from a standpoint rooted in an awareness of the close relation between learning and human development. Moreover, once this is taken into consideration, it should be manifestly clear that the idea of allowing the teacher to do whatever he or she wants to do in the classroom is the antithesis of *education*.

In order for teachers to satisfy the inherent requirements of a humanly meaningful form of education, it is absolutely imperative that they possess a free and magnanimous spirit. Accordingly, the desirability of the teacher's instructional freedoms must be understood as originating in the nature of the educational process itself. It does not serve any useful educational objective to reduce these liberties to mere formalities by means of narrowly drawn legal interpretations of Article 23 of the Constitution. In this regard we must indeed praise the Supreme Court's decision in this case for its willingness to recognize the inherent relation between Article 23 (academic freedom) and Article 26 (the child's right to an education). These rights, as they pertain to the People in general and to children in particular, only become substantively meaningful when considered from the standpoint of the need for human beings to continue learning and developing over the whole course of their lives. This means that education must be organized so as to make the insights it imparts a vital contribution to the development of human individuality. As the court's decision rightly recognized, this means that teachers must understand that they have a duty "to plan their pedagogic activities so that they directly supplement the child's right to learn." But, it must be added, in order for teachers to fulfill these responsibilities, they must also commit themselves to unceasingly undertaking research into educational contents, teaching materials, childhood development, and instructional practices. *The freedoms which should be guaranteed to teachers are the liberties required to make the realization of this spirit possible.*

L. Administration of Educational Content and Interpretation of Article X of the Fundamental Law of Education

Let me now conclude by examining the logic underlying the court's ruling in this case on the foundations and scope of the State's educational authority and competence. Having already acknowledged that parents and teachers possess "educational liberty within fixed limits," the decision now went on to state:

> With regard to the problem of organizing the general will of the nation as a whole in relation to education apart from these particular realms of discretionary authority, it is the court's judgment that the State is in the best position to make such determinations and execute them as part of its administration of national policy. Therefore the State should take whatever measures are necessary, within the framework of the Constitution, to realize the interests of society in general, and to protect the interests of the child in the field of education. Within this context the State is therefore recognized as legitimately possessing the authority, when and where it is necessary, to determine the contents of education.

However, this argument is trapped within an internal contradiction that vitiates its reliability. In brief, how is it possible to talk about the State's "determining and executing the educational will of the nation as a whole" in a society that is supposed to be organized on the principle of representative democracy? In other words, is it even appropriate for the State to be engaged in the business of fixing the interests of society and its members, parents, teachers, and children in the realm of education? Let us look once again at the language used in the court's judgment:

> It is clear that within a system of government based on the principle of majority party rule there is an inherent danger that in determining the national will with regard to those inner dimensions of life concerned with culture, and values, the majority party will attempt to use the machinery of government to make its values the country's values. Because this danger is particularly great in the world of public education, it has been thought that restraints must be imposed on the State's capacity to interfere with the determination of educational contents so as to protect the People from the undesirable influences of sectarian political ideologies and

narrowly construed private interests. With this in mind our Constitution was written to give public recognition of the fundamental freedoms of individuals and to declare that national administration should respect the personality and character of individuals. Moreover, Articles 13 and 26 of the Constitution expressly forbid the State from advancing false knowledge or one-sided ideologies and insist that the child's rights to develop as a free and independent human being must be scrupulously respected.

How does this passage square with the previous one in which the court declared that "the State is in the best position" to organize and execute the People's educational will? This is a very important question because it is not at all obvious, given the interpretation of the Constitution quoted above, why the State should be viewed as being the appropriate arbiter of the contents of public education. An answer to this question can be found in the court's reading of Article X of the Fundamental Law of Education.

The decision first examines the legislative process by means of which the Fundamental Law of Education was enacted, and in doing so fully acknowledges that this law was established as the final stage in a critical reconsideration of the appropriateness of the State's control over education in the prewar period. The court's decision also declared that the legal character of the Fundamental Law is such that it occupies the central position in our system of educational laws and that all educational aims and objectives should be formulated in accord with its basic provisions. It is also extremely significant that the court went so far as to include the administrative organs of the State among those bodies that may attempt to "impose improper influence" over education, and therefore declared that the Ministry of Education lacks the authority to institute a nationwide Scholastic Achievement Test.

In the last analysis, however, the court found that administration of the Scholastic Achievement Test fell within the scope of what is legally permissible. But this was only because the court chose to overlook the decisive role played by the Ministry of Education in both the organization and implementation of the testing, focusing rather on the fact that, technically speaking, the decisions to conduct these exams were made by the various prefectural boards of education. Of course this conveniently ignores the fact that since the repeal of the 1948 Board of Education Law in 1956, all the members of those prefectural boards have served at the pleasure of the Ministry of Education.[4]

---

[4] Since this ruling was handed down it has been precisely along these lines that

The court declared in the end that the Ministry of Education's Course of Study is therefore legally valid because it conforms with the basic principle of a democratic form of education, which it saw as based on the guarantee of equal opportunity and the uniform maintenance of clear, nationwide standards. However, when the court offered a concrete judgment on the extent to which those standards should be established, it also stated that in certain respects the provisions included in the Course of Study are too detailed and thus inappropriate because they give too much legal authority to this official curriculum. Nevertheless, the court concluded: "It cannot be said that in all cases the Course of Study is unreasonable." On this basis the Ministry of Education has claimed that the Supreme Court indeed recognized the validity of its Course of Study, and it has subsequently attempted to ignore the aspects of the ruling which were critical of the Ministry's activities.

Therefore, while on the one hand it avoided upholding the appropriateness of the Scholastic Achievement Test as a matter of educational policy, at the same time the court declared that the testing did not constitute an improper form of control. It used this distressing logic to at one and the same time criticize the Ministry of Education and acknowledge its authoritative position with regard to the control of Japanese education.

It thus seems we cannot look to the courts for authoritative rulings about the propriety of the government's educational policies; rather, we must appeal directly to teachers, parents, and the People at large for a true judgment of the validity of the Scholastic Achievement Test and everything it represents in Japan's educational life. Nonetheless, the implications of the Supreme Court's judgment clearly show the inappropriateness of that policy.

---

the Ministry of Education has enforced its will upon educational administration: the Ministry itself does not act, but it directs the activities of prefectural boards of education, which it has the power to control through its veto power over board appointments.

10 The Struggle to Control Teachers' In-Service Training

I. Conditions of In-Service Training

A. Countermeasures against the Teachers' Union

Minister of Education Takami Saburō recently discussed the government's current plans for educational reform in a televised symposium. He identified the aim of the reforms recommended by the Central Council on Education as improving the quality of teaching by enhancing teachers' working conditions and training. The tone of Minister Takami's remarks left the viewer with the clear impression that he would be working to make it easier for high-spirited youths burning with a mission to serve the nation as teachers to enter the educational world.

One wonders, however, whether the conceptual framework presented by the Central Council is really adequate for attracting such outstanding young people to the teaching profession. It most definitely does not appear so to the majority of those working in our schools as teachers, for even more than improvement in their financial conditions these teachers want more substantive freedom in their work environment and guarantees that they have the freedom to develop more creative forms of educational praxis.

In another forum televised shortly after publication of the Central Council's report, a number of teachers publicly challenged Council Chairman Morito Tatsuo, insisting: "More than increased pay, what we want is greater freedom!" Neither the chairman nor Minister Takami offered a single word of response. This challenge and the official refusal to acknowledge the teachers' complaints symbolically captured the crux of today's educational problems.

At the core of the council's report are a number of measures intended to strengthen the State's administrative control over education. Among these strategies we find the introduction of a job-ranking system that completed the framework of administrative control established in the 1950s and 1960s, the enforcement of a sliding wage system based on a bureaucratically dominated evaluation of teachers' competency, and the implementation of a number of measures designed to complete the system of State-organized in-service training programs. The combined effect of these measures has two major implications. First, it threatens to make our teachers' desires for personal advancement directly dependent upon the power of a centralized system of administrative control. Thus, to realize their desire for higher positions within the organization of the school, teachers will increasingly have to perform successfully within government-sponsored programs of in-service training (*kenshū*). Moreover, as only those teachers who have already been deemed ideologically deserving of such training will be given the opportunity to participate in the necessary in-service programs, the organization of elites within the school system will increasingly come under the direct control of the Ministry of Education.

Second, the power of the teacher's educational evaluation system will be further intensified. Designed to stifle the teacher's freedom to experiment with creative educational practices, it has functioned as one of the tools used by the Ministry of Education in its efforts to break up the Japan Teachers' Union (Nikkyōso). This system, however, is caught in its own contradictions: while on the one hand the Ministry of Education has adopted the attitude that teachers are professionals and not laborers, at the same time it has refused to recognize any legitimate interests for the union apart from economic ones. By enforcing the measures in the Central Council's report, the Ministry can be expected to continue applying pressure on teachers' autonomous research activities in order to stifle educational freedom.

The government's attitude towards teachers' attempts to organize their own forums for research and further study was well represented some years ago by then Minister of Education Araki Masuo. Using violent language, he denounced the Teachers' Union-sponsored research assemblies as illegal activities:

> By criticizing the officially proclaimed Course of Study, which has the force of law, they constitute themselves as members of an illegal assembly. They are educational thieves!

As an official pronouncement by the possessor of the State's highest administrative authority over education, this statement directly reveals the thinking of those who control the educational life of the Japanese people. Participants in independent educational research assemblies are looked upon by their official superiors with suspicious eyes, so much so that in various parts of the nation such research must be conducted in secret. There have even been cases in which principals would not allow the classrooms in their schools to be used by teachers for educational research meetings. Boards of education have been known to refuse teachers permission to officially participate in independently (non-governmentally) organized meetings. Documents have also surfaced which forbid the use of public funds for the purchase of books written by known advocates of the Teachers' Union research program. With the exception of a few areas having reformist governments, these efforts to stifle independent educational research may be described as a nationwide phenomenon. In Hokkaidō teachers have received disciplinary dismissals for participating in nationally organized research assemblies without having secured the permission of their principals. In Kyūshū, upper secondary school teachers have been removed from their jobs on the grounds that they did not follow the Ministry of Education's official Course of Study.

In summary, it can be said that within the framework of the Education Ministry's administrative guidance, the freedoms of Japanese teachers to independently pursue work-related research and to develop creative forms of educational praxis are being systematically usurped.

B. The Ministry of Education's Interpretation of Administrative In-service Training

The Ministry of Education has gone to great lengths to restrain teachers' freedom to engage in independently organized research activities. In order to back up these attempts to strengthen the State's administrative control over in-service training, Ministry ideologues have produced a number of legal theories designed to validate their repressive positions. It is not surprising, moreover, to find that their administratively controlled in-service training is itself largely given over to discussions of how to apply this legal ideology as a tool of educational control. Let us examine some examples of the way the Ministry interprets the place of law in Japanese educational life.

Imamura Taketoshi of the Ministry of Education has provided the following argument about the meaning of rights and authority in the world of education:

> Rights are legally stipulated powers—in other words, powers that only come into being through legal enactment. To call a *right* that which is not specifically mentioned as such in a law is the work of a fool or scoundrel. For example, "educational rights or the right to resist" are mentioned, but not in the way spoken of in the Constitution. Thus educational rights are explained not in the

constitutionally stipulated sense of the right to receive an education, but rather, fantastically, as the teacher's rights of expression or the teacher's right to independently decide upon the curriculum he or she will teach. However, this is a misbegotten understanding of "rights." ... The authority to determine the contents of the academic curricula from primary through upper secondary school rests firmly with the Minister of Education. Accordingly, not only is this not the right of teachers, it is none of their business. [*Kyōiku Gyōsei no Kiso Chishiki to Hōritsu Mondai (Fundamental Understanding of Educational Administration and Its Legal Problems)* rev. ed., Dai Ichi Hōki Shuppan, p. 52]

Imamura goes on to dismiss Tanaka Kōtarō's long-established theory of educational rights (see Chapter 4) by trivializing it as a merely philosophical understanding[1]:

While Professor Tanaka's theories are worthy of the highest respect, there is nothing written in existing law that ensures what he calls "educational rights." Nowhere have I seen it written that the professional activities of educators originate in the cultural and scholarly character of the educative function. Nor do I know where it is stated that these activities should be free from bureaucratic supervision.

Takahashi Tsunezō of the Ministry of Education has written in *Kyōshi no Kenri to Gimu (The Rights and Responsibilities of Teachers)*:

According to the Provisions of the Special Law Concerning Public Servants in Education (in particular Article 19, Clause 2, and Article 20, Clause 1), there is a basis for talking about in-service training as a teacher's right and there are grounds for recognizing a request for it. However the right to award teachers the opportunity to receive in-service training experience is firmly vested in the authority of their superiors. There is no recognition of teachers' authority to administer in-service training.

There is no need to tediously explain that notions such as the teachers' authority over in-service training or their power to or-

---

[1] The reader will recall that Tanaka's philosophy was the informing spirit behind the promulgation of the Fundamental Law of Education. Tanaka argued that the guarantee of freedom from improper control over education also meant that legislators and bureaucrats were obliged to let educational matters basically be decided by the People at the local level.

ganize and control the school have absolutely no legal meaning whatsoever.

Sagara I'ichi, professor of educational administration at Kyoto University, testifying as a Ministry of Education witness at the second textbook screening trial (see Chapter 7), presented a line of thought which sought to deny the teacher's freedom to conduct research. Professor Sagara took issue with testimony previously presented before the court on Clause 61 of the I.L.O.-UNESCO *Recommendations on the Status of Teachers*, which declared, "Teachers shall have academic freedom in matters pertaining to the fulfillment of their duties." In his remarks Sagara followed a typical Ministry of Education line of reasoning, reminiscent of the prewar ideological distinction between scholarship and education, when he declared:

> There is no mention here of the freedom to conduct research. . . . While teachers in universities carry out research and convey the findings to their students, the principal calling of primary, lower secondary, and upper secondary school teachers is simply to teach. Research may well be necessary and good for these ends, but there exist no legal guarantees of the freedom to do so.

Academic freedom which does not include the freedom to carry out research is, however, literally nonsense.

The "Guiding Principles" (Clause 6) of the I.L.O.-UNESCO *Recommendations* presents an understanding of the teaching profession that those in charge of Japan's educational administration show great reluctance to recognize. This becomes particularly clear in Professor Sagara's rejection of the following passage from the *Recommendations*:

> We recognize the job of teaching as having the status of a professional occupation. It is rigorous and unyielding research that makes the teaching profession possible. Moreover, the demand that teachers acquire the specialized knowledge and techniques that careful research makes possible is one manifestation of their being expected to work for the public good.

To this Sagara responded:

> At the very most this meant "training" or "further education." "Research" is a rather poor translation. [Sagara actually used the English words used here.]

When it was pointed out to him that the original word in the *Recommendations* was "study," he answered:

> Oh, it's "study," is it? That's what you're translating as "research" [*kenkyū*]? . . . "Study" is quite different from the research we do in universities.

In this fashion he twisted the original meaning of the words in question. His eagerness to deny the necessity of teachers' research as well as their freedom to do so is typical of our educational officials and their prominent ideologues such as Professor Sagara.

When asked to present his understanding of the words "research" and "in-service training" as stipulated in Article 19 of the Special Law on Educational Public Servants (Kyōiku Kōmuin Tokureihō), Sagara offered the following:

> Well, as for the word "research," ah, yes, well, while it might etymologically have the meaning being suggested in this court, within the text of the Special Law I don't think it has much weight . . . . And even if the word "research" does appear, I am convinced that there is no sense of necessity associated with it.

Upon then being asked, "Is it your understanding, then, that 'in-service training' as stipulated in the Special Law does not imply 'research'?" Sagara replied: "Yes, that's what I think. I believe that this is what was intended at the time the law was enacted. Even now I still believe this to be so."

We see here the extraordinary efforts that those who control Japan's educational system are willing to make in order to deny to teachers the freedom to carry out independent research.

C. Administratively Controlled In-Service Training

It is extremely important to note that at the same time the Ministry of Education is attempting to suppress independent educational research through its high-handed legal interpretations, it is also trying to strengthen its own control over bureaucratically administered in-service training. Since the 1958 revision of the official Course of Study, in-service training has primarily focused on ministerially mandated changes in the curricula designed for use in Japan's schools. It has been administered at government-run institutions. The training offered in such places takes the form of lectures at which official communications from the Ministry of Education are presented (*dentatsu kōshū*).

Under the auspices of boards of education—and thus of the Ministry of Education, which controls the boards through its veto power over appointments to membership—the training provided varies with the administrative positions of the recipients. There are accordingly communications pertinent to principals, head teachers, educational consultants (*shidō shuji*), etc.

Paralleling these activities, money has been made available through the Ministry of Education for the establishment of regional educational centers, where efforts are made to organize a hierarchy of central and local educational research groups. The Association of Japanese Teachers (Nihon Kyōshi no Kai) was established in 1963 as an officially sponsored opponent of the Japan Teachers' Union (Nikkyōso).

Government-controlled in-service training is in full bloom. Teachers in their forties who desire to advance to positions as head teachers and principals enroll in the programs at officially sponsored institutes so that they can receive the training necessary for success on the exams that aspirants to these positions must pass. Recently hired teachers, who work contractually for a probationary period, are required to participate in government-organized in-service training by order of their school principals. Great stress is placed in the training of new teachers upon their obligation to yield to, and obey the dictates of, their superiors in the administrative hierarchy of the school system in which they are employed. This particular brand of training is closely tied to the government's efforts to dissuade young teachers from entering the Japan Teachers' Union.

Prior to their appointment as teachers, those aspiring to do such work are subjected to a barrage of examinations and rigorous political interviews. Those who are finally selected find themselves in a highly unstable position as their continued employment is contingent upon the ratings they are given by principals who order them to attend in-service training sessions. At these compulsory sessions, they are subjected to clear messages about what kind of mold they are expected to fit into.

What actually occurs in the Ministry of Education-sponsored in-service training sessions on which large sums of our tax money are being spent? Let's look at one example. In the summer of 1971 a session was held at the foot of Mt. Fuji for "loyal" teachers. In addition to criticizing communism, great importance was given to drilling and cramming into the participants' heads the legal interpretations intended to legitimate the expansion of the administrative apparatus that already officially controls Japanese educational life.

During a party held on the final night of the gathering, the following Oath to Friendship (*yūjō*) was jointly proclaimed:

To honor the deep feelings of friendship awakened through lodging here together as members of the Alumni Association of the 10th Central In-service Training Group, we shall in the future as a matter of course aid each other by providing accommodations and whatever tourist guidance might be required during travel within the country. And should one of us commit some indiscretion, we pledge to most vigorously keep his secret. [*Asahi Shimbun*, October 26, 1971]

We should not dismiss this as mere party games: it shows one of the basic characteristics of government-organized in-service training. The fact that the Ministry of Education sponsors in-service training in cooperation with boards of education is not in itself inherently objectionable. Nor is the encouragement given it by principals. However, inasmuch as in-service training is used as a means of stifling the teacher's spontaneity, as a means of forcibly counteracting independent research, and as a vital link in the system for controlling teachers' advancement through Ministry-administered teacher evaluations, it is deeply flawed and highly problematic. If permitted to continue as it has until now, it will in the end inevitably corrupt in-service training as a means of educational improvement.

What then is the image of the "desired, average teacher" generated by this policy of strict control? An answer can be found in a book compiled by the Study Group on the Problems of Teacher Training (Kyōshi Yōsei Mondai Kenkyūkai) entitled *Primer for Taking the Qualifying Examination*:

Taking a long-range view, even if one's income as a teacher is low, it is stable and there is a guaranteed pension. To a certain extent one is the beneficiary of social esteem, and there is not the intense struggle for existence that is found in the private sector. For people who are planning to pass a modest, calm, ordinary life, other than being the chief priest of a [Buddhist] temple, there aren't many occupations so suited to this type of life. The teaching profession is not cut out for hot-blooded, active people. They would be better off joining a labor union or the nation's Self-Defense Forces.

Education critic Muramatsu Takashi pointedly suggested that "no special talents are required to become a teacher." He stipulated that the potential teacher should "like children," have a "peaceful character," and "not be narrow-minded or predisposed towards any ideology" (Mainichi Shinbunsha, *Kyōiku no Mori*, vol. 10, p. 112).

The recently popular expression "*demo shika kyōshi*" (only a teacher) captured the widespread idea that the work of the teacher is "an easy way to make a living." In fact, a desire for large numbers of these average teachers inspired the policy that has led to tightly controlled teacher training. Within the in-service training system a small number of loyal teachers were also being selected and prepared for special service as the administrators and guardians of these new recruits for the well-balanced educational world envisioned by the Ministry of Education.

II. The Fundamental Law of Education and In-Service Training

A. The Prewar Situation

In prewar Japan teachers were expected to function in their dealings with children and their parents as the Emperor's servants (*Tennō no kanri*). At the same time teachers were expected to be servile and submissive towards superior authorities and towards the possessors of local administrative power. Whatever discontent they might have felt as members of the lowest stratum of civil servants was later dissolved within their heightened consciousness as the front line of Japanese fascism in the 1930s and 1940s.

The servility of teachers was the outcome of a well-articulated policy that can be clearly traced back to the Regulations for Primary School Instructors (Shōgakkō Kyōin Kokoroe) issued in 1882. Natsume Sōseki sarcastically portrayed the groveling, servile teacher in his caricatures in the novel *Botchan*. Under the System for the Mass Mobilization of the National Spirit (Kokumin Seishin Sōdōin Taisei) formulated during the 1930s, even the teachers' everyday liberties, not to mention their freedom to conduct research, were tightly controlled and regulated.

The paradigm for the relationship between government officials and schoolteachers can be observed in the Regulations given to all graduates of the First Normal School in Aichi Prefecture in 1883. Regarding research activities, the Aichi document declared:

> Participate in proper societies for the study of the arts and sciences, but never join groups whose meetings breed doubts. If you come

into contact with seditious or dangerous writings, report this immediately to and discuss them with your school's principal.

The Regulations also prescribed appropriate behavior for teachers with regard to dress, housing, and the disposition of salaries:

> In finding a lodging house you must not decide on your own, but rather right from the beginning rely upon your principal to choose for you. . . . You must not lodge in a house having a daughter of marriageable age and you must avoid a place where there is a jealous young husband.
>
> You must not lend money. Deposit your wages every month. Invest in national bonds or, if it be appropriate, contribute your salary to your parents. By all means present photographs of your parents to the master of your lodging house. Think of yourself every day as working for your Emperor and family.
>
> Avoid passing by private dwellings in which female teachers reside.
>
> Keep your attire simple and maintain an orderly appearance. Keep your hair closely cropped and do not put your hands in your pockets.

Even this brief selection from the official policies in Aichi suggests the detailed scope of the regulations imposed upon schoolteachers.

The basic principle running throughout the Imperial education system was the complete separation of scholarship (*gakumon*) and education (*kyōiku*). (See the more detailed discussion of this problem in Chapter 2.)

B. The Fundamental Law of Education and Unrestrained In-Service Training

As discussed in Chapter 4, the establishment of Japan's postwar educational system, rooted in the values of the Fundamental Law of Education, was accompanied by a radical transformation of our basic educational *Weltanschauung* and our image of what a good teacher should be. This bold quest for change gave voice to the desire of the Japanese citizenry for a reconstitution of the very foundations of educational life. No longer would education be thought of as an Imperial prerogative; henceforth it had to be recognized as a constitutionally guaranteed right of the People. Because the teacher's work was reconceived as helping the young to become the upholders of a peaceful and democratic society, it was recognized that both academic freedom and the liberty to create new educational practices had to be vigorously supported in order to guarantee the conditions necessary for the new role of teachers.

The preface to the Summary of the Draft for a Fundamental Law of Education, submitted to the Thirteenth General Session of the Educational Reform Council on November 29, 1946, states:

> Educators in our country have in the past been deficient in self-awareness and critical reflection. Education has shown little if any respect for the modern scientific spirit or traditional religious sentiments. Moral education became completely formalized, and our educational life lost all forms of spontaneity. Eventually all arenas of learning and teaching fell under the sway of militarism and ultranationalism. To correct this most troubling situation, education must be reformed right down to its roots.

Concerning the problem of educational administration, the draft summary forthrightly declared:

> Educational administrators have to respect academic freedom and educational independence. Their efforts must be limited to securing and regulating those conditions necessary for the fullest possible realization of educationally conceived objectives.

Even in the Ministry of Education's Draft of the Fundamental Law of Education, presented to the Diet on January 15, 1947, the same spirit of respect for educational autonomy is amply apparent:

> Education shall not be subjected to improper political or bureaucratic control. It shall bear an independent responsibility towards the Japanese people. With this consciousness firmly implanted in their thinking, our educational administrators shall respect academic freedom, and we must endeavor to bring about the various conditions necessary for the realization of fundamentally new educational objectives. [quoted from Suzuki Ei'ichi, *Kyōiku Gyōsei*, University of Tokyo Press, pp. 291–94]

In the completed text of the law provisions were made regarding "respect for academic freedom" (Article 2), "guarantees of the teacher's status" (Article 6), and "the independence of educational authority in conjunction with limits on the responsibilities of educational administration" (Article 10).

The early postwar Courses of Study were also compiled in accord with the spirit outlined above. However, since the revisions of 1958 the Course of Study has come to play the central role of controlling educational content through the legally binding power given it by the Ministry of Education.

The first Courses of Study were intended to replace the prewar Rules for Teaching (Kyōsoku). In fact, in the earliest edition (1947) there was an unambiguous condemnation of the prewar educational formulas for imposing unified control from above:

> From this time forward, however, we will proceed from the bottom up, drawing upon the collective efforts of all involved.

There was little room for confusion about the nature of this new type of "official" document.

> This work was written as a handbook to help teachers as they conduct their own research and struggle to give birth to a curriculum that will both respond to and help shape the demand for a new way to raise children in our society.

It was seen as necessary for teachers to inquire freely into the content of teaching materials and the composition of a well-integrated program of studies, in order to respond to the interests and abilities of children as well as to the particular educational needs in the various regions of the country. Concerning the compilation of curricular materials, the Course of Study contained the following comments:

> The curriculum should be decided upon at each school, after careful determination of those educational objectives appropriate to the work of the school in question. This requires consideration of the realities of social life in the community in which the school is located. Teachers should attempt to formulate the curriculum that they will teach only after engaging in this kind of critical self-reflection.

When we view these passages as expressions of a fundamentally new form of undertaking, it becomes clear that they led to a new vision of the relation between the construction of curricula and the activities of teachers, a vision premised on the idea that teachers must be free to conduct educational research and verify their findings through their everyday activities. Therefore, it was thought that the central role in curriculum organization could best be performed by groups of teachers acting in a democratic fashion.

The revised edition of the Course of Study issued in 1951 expanded on the nature of curriculum:

> Since the construction of curricula is best accomplished when there is mutual interaction between students and teachers, the Course of Study is best understood as an aid to teachers, a set of suggestions to be used as a point of reference.

To underline the non-coercive nature of these early Courses of Study, the phrase "Suggested Plan" (*shian*) was written clearly on its cover. This shows that at this time there still were assurances that teachers' freedoms would be respected. The freedoms extended to teachers included the liberty to do teaching material research as part of their efforts to organize the curriculum they would then freely teach.

One of the major influences on this educational reform aimed at guaranteeing "educational freedom" came from the report of the First American Education Mission, a group of twenty-seven American educators who arrived in Japan in March of 1946, and whose report provided the framework for reordering educational discourse in postwar Japan. (See Chapter 4 for a detailed discussion.)

The mission's report declared that "an education that is administered from the top down must give way to education conceived as a responsibility and a privilege at every level of society." Concerning the duties of teachers and administrators, it stated:

> The best capacities of teachers flourish only in an atmosphere of freedom. It is the business of the administrator to furnish this, not its opposite.
>
> As soon as they have been suitably prepared for their professional work, teachers should be left free to adapt content and methods of instruction to the needs and abilities of their pupils in various environments and to the society in which they are to play a part.
>
> The essence of this discussion of the aims of education is that freedom of teaching and of inquiry must be encouraged not only for the preservation but for the enrichment of the national culture of Japan. The ability to distinguish between fact and mythology, between the real and the fanciful, flourishes in a scientific spirit of critical analysis.

Thus we can see that by imposing limitations on the scope of the State's administrative responsibility for education, and by encouraging the creative educational practices of our teachers, the American architects of Japanese educational reform sought to give concrete expression to the ideals of a democratized educational administration. These measures acknowledged the educational liberty of teachers and attempted to provide guarantees which would facilitate the development and expansion of autonomous research activities and eventually substantiate the vision and ideals of a new educational order.

III. The Educational Research Movement

A. The Union Movement and In-Service Training

The postwar teachers' movement grew out of a firm resolution that the transgressions of the prewar era must never be repeated. Teachers felt a deep responsibility to see that such tragedies would not be revisited upon the citizens of the Japanese nation, and struggled in this spirit to concretely realize the principle of "educational freedom."

In June of 1947 a congress was held to consolidate the two factions of the early postwar teachers' union movement. The outcome of this gathering was the formation of the Japan Teachers' Union (Nikkyōso). The general principles adopted by the congress were the following:

(1) In order to discharge our important professional responsibilities, we will work to build up our economic, social, and political position and status.
(2) We shall work to democratize education and secure the freedom to conduct research.
(3) We join together to establish a democratic state whose citizens love and cherish peace and liberty.

We find here a concise statement of the tasks confronting the teachers' union movement at the time of its inception. Teachers in the postwar environment had joined together to fight for their own economic welfare while at the same time they struggled to bring about the dissolution of the Japan Educational Association (Nihon Kyōiku Kai), an organization that had inherited the mantle of the prewar Imperial Education Association (Teikoku Kyōiku Kai). While organizing to resist the Ministry of Education's officially sponsored training courses, teachers pressed their demands for the democratization of education and the freedom to autonomously undertake their own educational research. These demands were understood as crucial components in the long march towards the establishment of a democratized form of political, cultural, and educational life for a new Japan.

However, early on, the movement was polarized between educationalists and those who emphasized the economic and political dimensions of the teachers' struggle, and it cannot be denied that there was a tendency to downplay the importance of the campaign for the institution of creative educational practices. At a nationwide meeting of leading union officials held in December 1949, this weakness was openly discussed, and the proposals drawn up at this conference proclaimed:

> In order to realize the ideals of educational recovery, greater efforts must be made both to strengthen the social and economic foundations upon which education rests and to further our understanding of those goals which are uniquely educational. With regard to the first of these agendas, our organization has made great strides towards fulfilling its historical role, but with regard to the second we must admit the poverty of our enthusiasm and the meagerness of our research and accomplishments. . . . At this critical juncture we must dedicate ourselves anew and more adequately organize research activities in accord with our basic goals. If we fail to establish the J.T.U.'s leadership through research in the areas of cultural life, the desired renaissance in education will be aborted in midstream and the union will invite its own destruction.

Proceeding from this frank admission of weakness, the union vigorously defined as its immediate objective the organization of research activities oriented towards the development of creative educational practices. The union held its first nationwide Educational Research Congress in 1950, following the outbreak of the Korean War and amid heightened domestic tension over the peace and defense treaty concluded with the U.S. government. In preparation for that first congress the union's leadership issued an announcement that set forth the tasks of the Research Movement and the meaning it was intended to have for teachers:

> (1) Our Educational Research Movement must grasp the problems of education and culture in connection with political, economic, and other social problems. It should democratically evolve to the level within which the "struggle to preserve our livelihood" and

the "struggle to defend our rights" are seen as essentially one in nature. This unity results from our underlying objective of constructing an educational culture that seeks to emancipate working people.

(2) In our educational activities we must not be permitted to become isolated or to suggest an attitude of complacent self-righteousness. Each teacher's research problems and experiences must be opened to criticism and evaluation. Herein lies the path that will make it possible for the methods of scientific research to produce important social results. For these ends we must work to secure the development of an educational research movement that will be known by its cooperation, organization, and independence.

(3) The educational and cultural spheres of present-day Japanese life are beset by confusion, corruption, and every imaginable type of bias and prejudice. To rescue our young from these destructive conditions and establish the foundations for democratic educational planning, a new form of educational praxis must be autonomously developed. It is our historical role as educators to bring about this most vital transformation.

The union proposes to sponsor Educational Research Congresses to respond to these needs of our times.

One of the most important issues that has been subsequently addressed by these congresses is how to make education a valuable tool for promoting peace. However, the research movement organized on the basis of this shared spirit did not automatically realize its goals from the beginning. At a meeting of the Teachers' Union Central Committee held in March of 1953 there was heated discussion on the proper place of the Educational Research Movement within the larger structure of the union movement. The following conclusions were reported:

Today it has become clear that the principles of our economic, political, educational, and cultural struggles are intrinsically related to one another. This means that we must clearly require the union's leadership to show a deeper and wider enthusiasm for the areas of scholarship and national cultivation.

In this sense the work of the Educational Research Congresses must not be construed as the amalgamation of essentially disparate projects and objectives, but should be organized rather with the fullest possible consciousness of our historical task. This approach and this approach alone will make it possible for us to mobilize the collective energies of our membership.

These reflections have been repeatedly reiterated in subsequent years, and research congresses have proved to be valuable forums for sharing and raising the quality of educational research. These efforts have also proven themselves worthwhile by helping to define the "individuality" of the teachers' union movement in our country. Teachers' awareness of the significance of research-oriented practices has also been deepened through the activities of the congresses organized by the union. In particular this has been true with regard to the importance of educational autonomy and pedagogic independence.

Many observers have noted the difference between union-assisted research assemblies and the in-service training sponsored by the State. University of Tokyo sociologist Hidaka Rokurō, for example, has written:

From the first J.T.U. Research Congress I was struck by the excitement of the exchange of ideas and the collision between different opinions. These meetings were much more interesting than standardized government ones in which there were lectures on how to use the Ministry of Education's Course of Study. Our discussions were so fascinating precisely because we had the freedom to discuss the actual conditions found in our schools and how we could jointly develop the abilities required to deal with the problems found in those conditions. Can anyone even imagine such enthusiastic discussions at a Ministry of Education-organized session where official communications are transmitted? When somebody is judged as being in official error at one of these meetings, he is immediately subjected to a litany of the ministry standardized version of educational truth. In our union assemblies it is diversity itself which is respected. [*Shisō*, March 1959]

The Educational Research Movement was premised right from its inception on the principle of respect for the spontaneity and autonomy of each and every teacher. There are cases, however, in which independence within the research movement has produced strains within the union. Katsuta Shuichi, professor of educational philosophy at the University of Tokyo, frequently addressed the meaning of teachers' independent research and the question of teachers' responsibilities as intellectuals; he discussed the relation between research and the union in an essay written in 1958 for *Kyōiku Hyōron*, a journal published by the Japan Teachers' Union:

Educational research should not be aimed directly at strengthening the organization of the teachers' union but should be dedicated rather to producing independent-minded teachers who possess a strong sense of professional responsibility. Through the shared learning these meetings make possible, the teacher, in his capacity as an educational laborer, should enrich his practice as a servant of the People. It cannot be doubted that in the long term this will cultivate all the energies available to our union. If, however, educational research is only considered in a short-term perspective, as a mere means for strengthening the organization of the union, then educational research will have most unfortunate consequences. What is most important in the last analysis is the nurturing and cultivation of a democratic form of education. It is to these ends that the union's research activities must be directed. . . . Therefore we must look to the union's organization to fulfill the responsibility of guaranteeing the teacher's freedom to pursue research. [*Kyōiku Hyōron*, October 1958]

On another occasion Professor Katsuta argued:

What is most objectionable in government-manufactured research assemblies is the anti-independent spirit that will not recognize the value of freedom. Regardless of their contents, these meetings exert counter-educational influences. Even if this is not immediately visible, government intervention imposes constraints on the freedom of union members to openly express their thoughts, which is tantamount to forfeiting the freedom to do research. ["Kyōiku Kenkyū ni okeru Kyōryoku ni tsuite" ("On Cooperation in Educational Research"), *Kyōiku*, July 1959]

Katsuta has here candidly pointed out the problematic points in the relationship between the union movement and educational research on the one hand and between educational research and the teacher's independent inquiries on the other. Educational research, centering on the everyday questioning and practice of the teacher as an independent intellectual, can only develop through group investigations and the exchange of the results of research. It is of the utmost importance for the success of our educational research movement that freedom be guaranteed. It is on this point that we are so radically at odds with the government's bureaucratically imposed in-service training.

B. The Nongovernmental Educational Research Movement

The Minkan Kyōiku Undō (Nongovernmental Education Movement), which may be thought of as the underground current of the Educational Research Movement, is the successor to the prewar alliance in resistance to governmental control over education. The members of this alliance of teachers have probed deeply into the basic problems of education and the responsibilities of teachers in ways that are unheard of in the Ministry of Education's in-service training assemblies.

One of the shared tenets of this movement has been the conviction that educational practice should be based on genuine scholarly research. As teachers learn to objectively evaluate their own educational experience, this argument goes, they can begin to produce a higher quality of teaching. By deepening their self-awareness as researchers, teachers are able to develop more inquisitive and creative forms of educational activity. This is the process by means of which teachers begin to understand the indispensability of pedagogic freedom.

One of the first efforts made in this direction during the early postwar years was the work of concerned historians who in 1949 organized the Rekishi Kyōiku Kyōgikai (History Education Council). The statement of purpose issued by the members of this body set forth their attitude towards historical education:

> Historical education seeks to cultivate the People's self-consciousness as the proper subjects of historical creation and as the bearers of an international spirit. To this end historical education must be strictly founded on the achievements of historical scholarship, and should rely only on correct educational theory. It must be independent from all influences that are not grounded in scholarly and educational truths.

When the Kyōiku Kagaku Kenkyūkai (Society for the Scientific Study of Education) was reestablished in 1952, its members declared:

> We shall endeavor to promote a Japanese education that aims at peace and democracy, and we declare our intention to work for the establishment of our country's independence.

One of the main aims of this society is to help reformulate education so as to make it more fully responsive to the welfare of the masses.

The members of this organization of university professors and school-teachers believe that reform of education must be based on a "scientific comprehension of nature and society." Accordingly they argue that both the educational liberty of teachers and the child's right to learn must be firmly protected.

The Sūgaku Kyōiku Kyōgikai (Council on Mathematics Education) was formed in 1951 in reaction to spreading criticisms that the so-called "new education" was anti-scientific and unsystematically composed of discrete units of what the government was labeling "life-centered learning." The efforts of this group to "unify science and education" set the tone for much of what would later be attempted in the Minkan Kyōiku movement. Its members have continuously made important contributions to the investigatory practices of classroom teachers. They have been particularly helpful in clarifying the methodologies of educational research:

> The actual work of research can properly develop only when there is an organic unity between theory and practice. Theorizing is the search for the laws hidden behind the complex and diverse phenomena encountered in the living world. Practice is the discovery of the unexpected facts in the actual world; while connecting old theories, it also leads to their transformation. It is the goal of our work to successfully bring about the unification of these two dimensions.

The unity between theory and practice has been advanced by outstanding theoreticians and practitioners alike, and it has come to be more widely accepted that the teacher must also be an educational researcher. An inquisitive spirit helps the teacher develop the consciousness necessary for becoming a creative practitioner. Only then can the promise of educational professionalism be truly realized in practice.

This professionalism should not, however, be limited to research into the content of the educational process. Scientific truths and realities must be related to the living actualities of each and every child's life. The importance of this agenda provided the impetus for the creation in 1951 of the Nihon Sakubun no Kai (Japanese Composition Association), a body of teachers who have made progressive, practical strides in the field of creative written self-expression. In the association's general plan (1958) we read:

> As inheritors of the prewar accomplishments in the field of com-

positional education, it is our task to create and make popular a
new body of educational practice centered in students' efforts to
express their ideas and feelings in writing. Simply stated, we think
of our students as people who are living and learning. Our goal
is to help them become skilled in presenting in their own words,
so that they can make others understand just what it is that they
feel in their hearts and think with their budding intellects about
nature and society as they encounter and learn about these realms
of reality in their schooling. By encouraging students to translate
their thoughts and feelings into prose, we seek to cultivate their
powers of observation and expression both as individuals and as
members of the classroom groups they belong to. [Minkyōren,
ed., *Nihon no Minkan Kyōiku,* vol. 1, Yūri Shuppan]

The work of a teacher in helping students reapprehend the truths
they have learned about nature and society within the context of their
individualized thoughts and feelings is of primary importance. Yet the
ability to express such truths as individual human beings is by no means
an easy one to develop. These goals cannot be accomplished unless our
teachers themselves possess the intelligence and sensitivity necessary
for entering the inner lives of each and every one of their students
with insight and discretion. Furthermore, it is necessary for them to
be honest to a fault in their everyday educational practice.

The work of educating children and adolescents to become the upholders of a broadly based culture resting on firm foundations is possible only when they are respected as individuals who possess creative
and inquisitive spirits. The prewar method of life-centered composition
was, within what the literary giant Sōseki described as Japan's vulgar
and superficial modernization, of a completely different nature. Yet
it can still be evaluated as work designed to deepen the roots of cultural
creation. As inheritors of this prewar legacy, those teachers committed
to education through composition writing are nurturing the soil for
a more firmly rooted cultural life in Japan. Thus the Course of Study's
enforced educational agenda that attempts to suppress the creativity
of the human spirit of such teachers is truly hard to endure.

One of the most prominent names in the postwar nongovernmental
educational movement is that of Saitō Kihaku. His life itself presents
us with a striking image of what a teacher can truly be. In the 1960s
one of the major challenges to the educational research movement
centered around the attempts to bring scientific discipline and order
to the inner workings of the educational process. In response to calls
for teachers to conduct their work in the spirit of scientists and re-

searchers, Saitō sought to open up the meaning of science itself as a cultural form. Likening education to an artistic practice, Saitō worked to replace the image of teachers as transmitters of scientific truths with a new one in which they appeared as directors on a stage—artisans whose work is drawing out the creative possibilities inherent in youth:

No matter how precisely and scientifically research into teaching materials is carried out, in and of itself this will not further the aims of instruction; only when the teacher as an individual invests the richness of his individuality, his knowledge and sensitivity as a total human being, and brings these qualities to his encounters with youth, only then will it be possible to more fully develop the ability to give instruction.

Regardless of the extent to which one's instruction is scientifically correct, this does not ensure that one's teaching will unfold successfully. It is only through the richness of the individual teacher as a human being that significant strides can be made towards realizing his deepest pedagogical potentialities. [*Jugyō no Tenkai, Saitō Kihaku Zenshū*, vol. 6, Kokudosha, p. 20]

For Saitō, teachers should first and foremost think of themselves as practitioners of the art of instruction. To pursue his art, the teacher must employ the full scope of his capacities as a human being. The educational process in this approach is made up of the tasks required to creatively challenge that manifold of possibilities known as the child. In short, it is a process of risk and adventure.

Education is a creative enterprise, in the same way that art is. When the child's creative capacities are raised, his basic academic and artistic powers of expression are also heightened. Accordingly, when the creative attitude of artistic endeavors is brought to bear on education, the teacher becomes an artist. To the extent that the teacher does not approach his work with the creative touch of an artist, the child is not extended his proper due as a student. This being the path of creation, it is one always filled with difficulties and hardships.

It is work not unlike clearing a path through a jungle. However, when a teacher approaches his tasks in this manner, when he approaches his life this way, the teacher can truly become an artist. Therefore the claim that "freedom is the sine qua non of the teacher" can be proudly and openly enunciated by the teacher himself. [*Jugyō Nyūmon, Saitō Kihaku Zenshū*, vol. 4, p. 117]

Katsuta Shuichi, who as chairman of the Society for the Scientific Study of Education played a leading role in directing the nongovernmental educational research movement, has worked to further the teacher's self-awareness as upholder of educational research. The encounters Katsuta arranged between teachers and professional researchers at autonomously organized research assemblies did much to hasten the realization of the movement's aims. In an article for the August 1967 issue of *Kyōiku* (the society's journal) entitled "Research Assemblies," Katsuta wrote:

The most practical pedagogical research is not simply psychological or sociological inquiry that leads to immediate practical applications, but inquiry that discovers pedagogical laws and principles. To the extent that research veers away from this pattern, it loses its creative edge. This work stands exactly midway between artistic creation and scientific inquiry. Furthermore, it is only to the extent that it partakes of both qualities that truly outstanding practices and correct theoretical research become possible.

Regarding the foundations of academic freedom, Professor Katsuta has written:

Because the work of creative teachers is supported by research into instructional methods, teaching materials, and childhood development, it is absolutely legitimate for teachers to press their demands for academic freedom.

To the extent that educational professionalism is bolstered by science, the work of the educational professional can contribute to the continued growth of the child. And to the extent that a refined spirit and techniques resembling artistic creation are necessary, it is only natural to insist upon academic freedom. If, however, educational research is administratively controlled in the form of authoritative orders from above, and if there is no freedom left for autonomous decision-making about work-related duties, far from being professional in character, this "research" becomes nothing more than bureaucratic subcontracting. ["Chishikijin toshite no Kyōshi no Sekinin" ("The Responsibilities of Teachers as Intellectuals"), *Kyōiku*, May 1968, p. 12]

The cardinal principles of the inquisitive and creative teacher, Katsuta has taught us, must be stubbornness, flexibility, and an active spirit. "The teacher must be flexible enough to feel anguish and distress and, through the workings of a sympathetic heart and scholarly inquisitiveness, develop a creative educational practice to help relieve them. The teacher must also stubbornly resist when threatened by our educational authorities. If teachers do not possess this three-sided liveliness of spirit, they will not be able to overcome the obstacles littering our current educational environment." Here is a most invigorating image of the teacher as an intellectual in present-day Japan.

IV. What Is In-Service Training for the Teacher?

A. The Significance of Autonomous Training

As can be understood from the above sketch, the postwar educational research movement has developed into an independent force through the cooperation of diverse individuals. Of course there have been many theories concerning the social functions of education and the responsibilities of teachers, and as a result of the give and take of mutual criticism there were also numerous occasions when emotional antagonisms burst forth. In the last analysis, however, these differences proved to be highly beneficial by providing the participants excellent opportunities for deepening their understanding of education and improving their capacities to work as teachers. Each teacher was afforded greater opportunities to intelligently decide what type of teacher he or she wished to be, and all were better able to learn from one another. In short, when these differences were expressed in a spirit of tolerance and broad-mindedness, they proved to be enormously fruitful for the growth of our movement.

At this point in time it is important to reconfirm the values embedded in the new image of the teacher generated by our educational movement. The most significant contribution has been the increasingly shared conviction that educators bear a responsibility to nurture the young as they develop into the citizens who will in the future be the sovereign rulers of a democratized Japan. Thus our movement has worked to raise teachers' consciousness to the importance of the fact that education brings about the flowering of each and every person's inherent capabilities as an autonomous human being by opening the pathways to scientific and cultural understanding.

Second, teaching has come to be understood by the members of this movement as an essentially creative undertaking, one which requires both the investigative spirit of the scientist and the patient discipline of the artist. Thus the teacher our movement seeks to develop is one who possesses the human qualities required for entering into the world of the child and sharing his or her joys and sorrows. In other words, we have sought to encourage the appearance of teachers who as individuals can intuitively feel their way into the recesses of the human heart.

In a word, the teaching profession can be defined as a form of "creative, human research" that must be undertaken by the possessors of a liberal spirit operating in a free atmosphere. Thus, when the Ministry of Education denies the teacher the freedoms to inquire and develop a creative and continually inquisitive praxis, that is tantamount to forcing the teacher to stop being a teacher. These unacceptable interventions also rob the teacher of his or her very humanity.

Kenshū (in-service training) as a legally constituted term is a contraction of *kenkyū* (research) and *shūyō* (training or cultivation). Thus the Ministry of Education's interpretation of in-service training as being fundamentally different from research is misconceived. If we define just what it is that results from adding research and training together in relation to the work of our teachers, it should be clear that much more is involved than the simplistic "scientization" of education. There should also be the rigorousness and richness of a creative process of inquiry. Therefore it is indispensable that the teacher have the temperament of a scientist, the individuality of an artist, and a personality revealing the richness of a fully developed human being. The unity of these three attributes should be the outcome of an ongoing commitment to educational research and study.

Education is a most troublesome and complicated process. It requires direction only teachers can provide by mediating between the teaching materials chosen for instruction and the children or adolescents these materials are presented to. It is a process of overcoming the limits by which young people always find themselves surrounded. At the same time it is an unending process in which the teacher overcomes his or her own limitations and is regenerated as a human being. This dimension of education, which we should rightly call "cultivation" (and which is discussed in Chapter 12 of this volume), when pursued in tandem with scientifically structured research, can well be understood as the best explanation of the concept of *kenshū*. If we think about in-service training in this way, then it cannot possibly be thought of as a denial of the teacher's freedom to conduct research. In fact, it should be nothing other than the process by means of which teachers autonomously give form—free from governmental control, but under the strict discipline they themselves erect—to their own pedagogic activities.

For teachers to truly fulfill their duties as teachers, they must rigorously examine themselves and unceasingly attempt to improve themselves. Those teachers who meekly submit to governmental control, and who are content to offer themselves to the State as subcontract laborers, thereby contribute to the threatened destruction of the very foundations of academic freedom. This is really equivalent to their renouncing the right to call themselves teachers. Thus the process to which I am trying to call attention can only take place when teachers support one another, share the results of their research, and constructively criticize one another.

It does not follow from this, however, that independence and autonomy can only be established in the absence of all restraints. Independence is not measured simply by the strength with which one presses one's claims. It emerges as one undertakes the task of coolly objectifying one's own practices of inquiry. By comparing one's own practices with those of one's colleagues and incorporating what one can learn from their achievements, one can enrich the quality of one's own activities. Here the freedom to pursue one's profession begins to yield socially constructive results. This kind of independence must be grasped as underwriting the methodological self-consciousness necessary for realizing the kind of educational praxis I have been discussing as truly desirable.

Autonomy can only be established within the framework of professional solidarity. The only restraints that should be imposed on the teacher's freedom of research and educational practice are those imposed by truth and reality. By following this path, teachers can contribute to the strengthening of professional solidarity, for solidarity, like justice, is made strong and viable in proportion to the extent that it rests on the pursuit of truth.

The willingness to observe and learn from one another is crucial for cultivating the consciousness of solidarity amongst those shouldering the burdens of creating a new system of national education. It is our task to see that in time it grows strong enough to secure the independence of educational authority and the freedom of educational praxis.

B. The People's Rights to Learn and the Power to Organize In-Service Training

Article X of the Fundamental Law of Education helps us to define the responsibilities of teachers by declaring that education is "directly responsible to the whole People." In other words, teachers have a responsibility to impart vitality and substance to the People's right to learn. This helps us to define both the extent of the teacher's professional obligations and the directions in which they should be carried out. Proceeding in this fashion, let us consider what is involved in the claim that the People are the true subjects of the right to learn, and that they must be respected as the ultimate possessors of the freedoms that make intellectual inquiry both necessary and possible.

There may well be readers for whom the expression "the People's right to learn" is strange and unfamiliar. But if they reflect carefully upon the arguments presented in this book, they will understand why I want to claim that these rights should be thought of as natural and their appropriateness self-evident. Modern constitutions guarantee the rights of all people to free thought and self-expression in the pursuit of happiness. The meaning of these guarantees is premised on the notion that all people possess the right to know the truth and freely pursue it. Thus what we are calling the People's right to learn is a synthesis of the right to know the truth and to freely inquire into it, for in the last analysis this is what makes the pursuit of happiness and the freedom of expression truly possible.

I believe it can be said that the idea of the People's right to learn is both a necessary concomitant of the notion of popular sovereignty and a focus for thinking about how to deepen the consciousness of those whose duty is to fulfill the responsibilities of this sovereignty. Political participation without the right to know is just what those in power today wish to perpetuate as a purely formalistic system of democracy. The alienation of this age—what C. Wright Mills calls alienation from the truth—is an identifying mark of this particular brand of political culture. If we accept Sigmund Neumann's idea that today's mass "political illiteracy" is a product of propagandization sponsored by those who wield the levers of political control, then it follows that only by actually realizing the People's right to learn can this situation be reversed and the ideals of popular sovereignty and human rights be given real substance.

It is of paramount importance therefore that the ideals embodied in the notion of the right to learn be allowed to take root and grow within the consciousness of each and every citizen. All must come to see these rights as personally meaningful and vitally necessary for their well-being. This consciousness must in turn express itself in relentless demands for the right to freely learn and inquire. The reader should note that the basic orientation being described here is diametrically opposed to the one revealed in the government-propagated discourse on lifelong education (*shōgai kyōiku*).[2]

Thus when we insist upon the need to guarantee the autonomy of

[2] "Lifelong education" is what the government calls its policy of unifying all levels of educational activity under Ministry of Education control. This includes the regular school system as well as what has come to be known in Japan as social education

learning, what we really mean is the independence of education from governmental control.

While this right to learn is most markedly manifest as the freedom to conduct one's own inquiries, it should also be considered an imperative imposed upon the work of the professional researcher. Notwithstanding the arguments of government ideologues like Professor Sagara, study is *both* learning and inquiring. The argument that there is a fundamental incompatibility between them has been a major element in Japan's distorted modernization in which the natural connection between scholarship and education has been forcibly severed. (This matter is more extensively discussed in Chapter 3.) This argument is also responsible for the impoverishment of our nation's cultural consciousness.

It is our task today as teachers to bring about fundamental changes in the Japanese people's thinking about the social responsibility of scholarship and learning. We must work to convince our fellow countrymen that the freedoms bestowed upon our organs of research as well as the freedoms to learn and inquire guaranteed to the citizenry at large are based on a "national trust" of which we are all equally the beneficiaries. Only when we have been successful in these efforts will there emerge the consciousness required to recognize that academic freedom is not a form of wanton liberty but is rather a fundamental social responsibility.

The most concrete manifestation of the People's right to learn is the right of our young people to develop their potentialities and, as members of a new generation, to surpass their elders. The duty to preserve and defend these rights of the young primarily belongs to parents, not to the Ministry of Education or the State. But since parents are not able to fulfill this obligation individually, public schools have been established to make possible the collective realization of this solemn responsibility. And it is to the teachers who work in these institutions as educational specialists that parents entrust the responsibility for their childrens' schooling. As parents entrust these rights to teachers because of the latter's professionalism, then in cases where the parents' trust is not repaid, parents should be able to criticize teachers and reiterate their basic educational desires. Public education therefore is essentially a joint undertaking of parents and teachers designed to guarantee fulfillment of the child's rights to grow and learn. In the final reckoning it requires their mutual support and cooperation.

There are of course people who refute this interpretation of public

(*shakai kyōiku*), which contains a wide range of educational pursuits aimed at those no longer in school.

education as irrelevant on the grounds that it is nowhere stated in the law that parents have the freedom to choose their children's teachers. However, as I see it, even within the Japanese system with its rigidities, parents retain a latent and inalienable right to choose both the schools and teachers they believe will best serve the needs of their children. Once this is accepted as a basic and commonsensical premise, then it follows that greater efforts must be made to eliminate disparities between teachers as well as schools. This means enhancing the abilities of all teachers in all schools as the most effective way to guarantee the parental right to select teachers and schools. Since it is impossible for parents to directly exercise the right to select teachers and schools on behalf of their children, it is *necessary* for teachers to collectively improve their skills through autonomous in-service training. Once public schooling is viewed from the perspective of the People's rights to learn and be educated, then it becomes very clear why a high degree of professionalism and independently organized group efforts are so important to the success of the educational work done by teachers.

With regard to the independence of teachers' research, the idea of group effort has two meanings. The first pertains to the effectiveness of the research results that are exchanged and mutually criticized. Teachers' study circles, no less than local and national educational research assemblies, are a way of organizing research for precisely these ends.

Second, as can be readily be understood from what I have already argued, it is impossible for teachers to fulfill the tasks parents entrust to them if they fail to organize groups in the schools they work in with the aim of enhancing the quality of the activities they collectively generate. With regard to matters such as organizing the school year into a coherent educational experience, the importance of educational research, in the actual school environment, cannot be overstated. The teacher must resolve to act as an independent intellectual, even if alone—as an inquisitive and creative educational practitioner. While working to improve their abilities through participation in a wide range of research groups, teachers should also seek to form study groups within the schools they teach in. The fruits of one teacher's efforts can be reflected in the total effectiveness of the school through research exchanges among colleagues that contribute to the creation of a unified community for students to grow and learn in.

The teacher's *right* to autonomous in-service training is premised on both the teacher's and the ordinary citizen's freedoms to inquire; it is also closely related to the basic nature of education and the professionalism required of all educators. In the last analysis this right must be defended by the individual teacher him- or herself, but ideally, and in practice as well, it must be protected by all teachers' groups active in the sphere of public education.

C. In-Service Training—To What End?

If we think of our teachers' educational autonomy as something entrusted to them by parents on account of the former's professionalism, then it is all the more clear that teachers must conduct their research into the complexities of educational practice for the sake of the public good. Proceeding on this basis, teachers should conduct their inquiries in order to better organize teaching materials so that they can be presented in a manner which conforms with the logic of the child's developmental stages. Through educationally motivated investigations centered on the problems of classroom instruction, the teacher should attempt to accurately follow the steps in the child's learning process so as to make them yield further opportunities for understanding and responsiveness to pedagogic guidance. After all, this is what it means to be a professional educator, and this is precisely what we should expect from such professionals. Moreover, such training should enable teachers to successfully organize creative educational encounters in which their students experience the joys of learning through personally meaningful forms of discovery. This process, the essence of well-organized teaching, can be likened to the creative process of artistic achievement inasmuch as it freely makes use of all available materials and the skills or techniques needed to transform them into something new and exciting.

The ultimate beneficiaries of these educational researches must of course be the youth of present-day Japanese society, for whom the process of learning should be both meaningful and personally satisfying. Thus the educational process should be engaging for both the child and the teacher. To elevate this process into one rooted in deeply shared forms of understanding and sentiment, teachers must open themselves up to critical reflections about their own lives and activities so that they can learn from the educational work they are involved in. Only then will our goals be realizable.

It only becomes possible for teachers to meaningfully discharge their duties to guarantee young people's rights to learn when they consciously address themselves to the problem of how to live in the present age. This does not mean, of course, that teachers should impose their own life-style upon their students. Sharing the same social and historical conditions that children live in, the teacher should be sympathetic to students as they pursue their various inquiries. If this sympathy is not, however, mediated by a respect for "the rights of the new generation," then an education that cultivates true independence cannot emerge.

The focus of the teacher's research should be the educational materials, children, and pedagogic practices that are the objects of his or her daily work. But in order for these inquiries to have more than merely academic interest, the teacher must live as one who continuously inquires into the nature and problems of the modern world and his place in it. Only in this way can the teacher's professionalism truly become a vital social force and win the trust and confidence of young students. This is also the way to put parents at ease so that they can entrust the child's education to the teacher.

In order for teachers to successfully perform their duties as teachers, they must continuously be engaged in autonomously organized research. This is nothing less than a matter of professional ethics. It is also closely linked to the role of educators as important contributors to the democratization of present-day Japanese life. By making themselves the subjects of what Uehara Senroku has called "a problematized perceptual awareness," teachers must struggle to develop the ability to make the world meaningfully problematic for the child through their pedagogy. This is the true road that leads teachers to the pride and self-confidence they require to do their work well. The underlying reality of ideas such as the "teacher's responsibility as an intellectual" or the "ethics of educational labor" can only materialize as a fully developed educational autonomy amid the flowering of new forms of meaningful intellectual praxis.[3]

The arguments I have been presenting on the importance of the right to learn and be educated are based on the idea that educational authority belongs to the People, not the State. Making this the focal point of educational practice helps us clarify the substance of the teacher's professionalism as it directs our attention to the fact that education should serve the People rather than the State. Accordingly it is teachers' independent in-service training[4] that gives vitality and meaning to

---

[3] In a memorial address to the Fukui Prefecture Research Assembly in 1961, Mutai Risaku raised the issues of the unity and opposition of individual and group and of educational and political activities: "The important thing today is not an excess of teachers' moral consciousness but rather its poverty. I think teachers must work assiduously on the problem of morality as it impinges upon educational praxis. Thus teachers must struggle against their own egoism and, without buckling under to the power of state authority, fight against those who show contempt for human nature. This is how they can discharge their primary duty to the People they serve and defend the rights of the younger generation. . . . Teachers! Band together to proudly hoist the banner of educational ethics!"

[4] I maintain that in fact "in-service training" that is not autonomously organized should not be called in-service training.

educational professionalism. The vitality of educational profession-alism comes of course with the creative and inquisitive practices that research assemblies should be primarily dedicated to improving. These gatherings are therefore very important moments in the struggle to give efficacy to the idea of the teacher's educational rights.

We in the education movement have a very different understanding of existing law from that displayed by the Ministry of Education and its various ideologues. This is because we take the keystones of edu-cational law more seriously than those who see laws merely as devices to legitimate bureaucratic encroachments upon educational liberty. For example, Article X of the Fundamental Law of Education stipu-lates the independence of educational authority and the autonomy of education; Article XXVIII of the School Education Law provides that it is "teachers who shall rule and administer education." If the stipula-tions on research and in-service training in Article 19 of the Special Law on Educational Public Servants were actually respected by the State's administrators, then we wouldn't have a fraction of the prob-lems we face every day. The previously cited I LO-UNESCO Re-commendations on the Status of the Teacher that proclaimed the teacher's job-related academic freedom and the necessity of ceaseless research in pursuit of professionalism fully corroborates the positions that we have advocated in the Educational Research Movement:

> There must be assurances that teachers can freely organize their own in-service training not on the basis of work orders but simply as a point of principle.

If the teacher's freedom to conduct independent in-service training is usurped, he or she loses the capacity to truly function *as a teacher*, and it becomes impossible to fulfill the duties of *an educator*. Thus in-service training is indispensable to the very essence of the teaching profession.

Our understanding of teachers' rights with regard to their in-service training can only be deepened through further research and inquiries into the basic nature of educational professionalism. We must never lose sight of the fact that the most important thing is the ongoing de-velopment of an independent educational research movement. We must therefore work to continue enriching the basic awareness that the right to engage in autonomously organized in-service training is a vital right for teachers in particular and for education in general.

Postscript—1987

This essay was written some years ago, but the conditions under which teachers work today are, if anything, even more depressing from the point of view of free and independent inquiry.

Participation in research assemblies and other such activities sponsored by teachers themselves under the auspices of the Japan Federation of Teachers or other organizations is discouraged or penalized. A new teacher licensing system, which would require re-accreditation in mid-career, has been proposed by the Extraordinary Council on Education (a blue-ribbon advisory commission appointed by the Prime Minister in 1985). The Ministry of Education has set up its own training and research program, including a newly inaugurated one-year training course for new teachers. Opposition among teachers to the Ministry's program has begun to appear, beginning in Kyoto. While many of these programs are still in the inaugural stages, they seem to emphasize administrative duties rather than teaching techniques and instructional content; open discussion and questioning is not a part of the training courses; and participation is mandatory. The danger is real that these programs will be used to tighten control over teachers and penalize those who do not conform with the bureaucracy's idea of "the good teacher."

11 Student Evaluation and Personal Control: The *Naishinsho* Decision

I. Introduction

We have already seen how the values and priorities dominating Japanese educational life are routinely built into the work of the schools through the Ministry of Education's Course of Study and its regulation of textbook certification (see Chapters 6 and 7) and how this system of ideological control is officially supplemented through the State's attempts to manage the operation of teachers' in-service training programs (see Chapter 10). In Chapter 8, I examined the role testing has come to play in the general perversion of Japanese education, and in Chapter 13, I will discuss the ways this has led to the normalization of a system by means of which our youth are ranked and classified for incorporation within the world of work in response to the demands of industry. I would now like to analyze the ways these values and priorities also manifest themselves in the system of personal evaluation in which lower secondary school teachers are obliged to judge the behavior of the students under their control.

One of the most prominent features of this system is the way it has obliged teachers to function as agents of the managerial control apparatus regulated by the Ministry of Education. Thus, as these forms of domination are increasingly tightened, teachers are continually being made to function as the State's deputies in framing, regulating, and setting the directions for the future activities of our youth.

In addition to the more obvious forms of control exercised by teachers, such as enforcing school and classroom regulations and punishing those who violate these rules, there is also the hidden form of control resulting from educational evaluation in the form of report cards and *naishinsho* documents.[1] On the basis of these systems, it can rightly be

---

[1] The *naishinsho* is a confidential report used as a means of evaluation by upper secondary schools when deciding whom they will admit. These reports are issued with the signature of the student's lower secondary school principal based upon information provided by the student's classroom teachers regarding character, behavior, and course grades. Although the student of course knows his grades, he is not provided access to the crucial information regarding his ranking on the predetermined five-stage scale which is used to classify students' behavior relative to one another. Moreover, because neither students nor their parents are allowed to see

argued, the ideologies of managerial efficiency and strict discipline have hastened the deterioration of the teacher's educational prestige and pedagogic authority. Thus, as the tendency towards intensification of educational control becomes more and more conspicuous, we are increasingly hearing of cases in which the personal rights of children are being shamelessly violated.

Although physical punishment is forbidden by our School Education Law, physical brutality on the part of both teachers and students has been steadily growing, so much so that the situation today is indeed very serious. But while the significance of physical violence against students is relatively easy to grasp, the meaning of the psychological violence exercised through everyday behavioral evaluation is much more elusive. The seriousness of this problem is compounded by the fact that in altogether too many cases teachers are themselves totally unaware of the ways in which they have been transformed into agents of the State's encroaching administration of our inner, private lives. Moreover, the challenge of exposing this situation is made more difficult by the disguises in which these forms of ideological regimentation are cloaked. In this essay I will therefore examine the vexing problems of student evaluation and personal control in order to exhume the most troubling issues raised by the practices that constitute the current *naishinsho* system.

II. The *Naishinsho* Trials and the Problem of Educational Evaluation

In order to grasp the seriousness of these problems it is absolutely essential not to lose sight of the fact that the secretive system of student evaluation known as *naishinsho* has proven its usefulness as a tool for controlling Japanese students largely because it has been skillfully manipulated to control the activities of teachers as well.

The potency of this system of student evaluation results in large measure from its having been effectively routinized within the full complement of everyday educational practices. Although its power becomes particularly evident at the time when lower secondary (junior high) school students attempt to gain entrance to upper secondary (senior high) schools, it must be understood that this reporting system exerts its influence throughout the educational apparatus as a whole. In other words, while the importance of the *naishinsho* report becomes

---

these reports, challenge their validity, or make appeals to have them altered, the system of *naishinsho* reporting has come to function as the "invisible whip" used to keep Japanese students in line.

particularly evident when it plays a critical mediating role as a determinant of the student's move from lower to upper secondary school, and thus its long-range importance rests with its influence in determining the student's future status as a worker and as a member of society, it is no less important for the chilling effects it exerts upon the spontaneity and vitality of the adolescents it is imposed upon.

The fact that both students and teachers concentrate a great deal of their attention upon this system for evaluating the everyday activities of the student reflects the strengthening of the framework within which educational evaluation has been routinized. The commonly voiced threat "If you do thus-and-so it will affect your *naishinsho!*" shows the extent to which the everyday activities of students have become locked within fixed forms of expression and the degree to which the autonomy of their developmental strivings has been arrested. As children impose restrictions upon their own activities out of fear of the *naishinsho* report, their vital energies begin to atrophy.

As we already observed in the case of the textbook screening and Scholastic Achievement Test trials, these attempts by the State to strengthen its control over Japanese education have not gone unchallenged. In the "*naishinsho* trials" we have recently seen the propriety of this system called into question, and the behavioral categories mandated for reporting therein have been subjected to severe criticisms. Through the course of these judicial challenges ample evidence has been presented revealing the extent to which Japanese education is being distorted by the power of State and prefectural administrative authorities to regulate educational rating and evaluation. These cases have also been exceedingly useful in helping to raise the level of awareness of the members of Japanese society regarding the dangers to their freedom of expression resulting from the ways educational evaluation has been organized.

Let us briefly review the incident which gave rise to this case and discuss the problematic points in both the first and second rulings handed down in response to it by our courts.

Hosaka Nobuto, a third-year student at Kōjimachi Lower Secondary School in Tokyo's Chiyoda Ward, was refused entrance to a Tokyo Metropolitan upper secondary school as well as three private schools in spite of the fact that he had sufficiently demonstrated his ability to meet all of their strictly academic standards. He was denied entrance to these schools because of unfavorable *naishinsho* reports. In fact, he was viewed so negatively that even on the day of his graduation from Kōjimachi Lower Secondary School he was barred from the graduation ceremony and prohibited from participating in it.

Charging that he had been deprived of his right to learn as a student, Hosaka brought suit against the city of Tokyo and its Chiyoda Ward, demanding compensation on the grounds that they both have a responsibility to supervise lower and upper secondary schools within their respective jurisdictions. As Hosaka's suit progressed, public attention was drawn anew to the ways in which secret reporting on children was still being carried out. This has sparked lively discussion concerning the limits of teachers' discretionary authority and has brought into clear focus some of the most serious problems plaguing education in Japan today.

The *naishinsho* used in Hosaka's school required information on the student's scholastic achievement, health, and absences from school, as well as a column entitled "Record of Behavior and Character." Within the thirteen categories under this heading, Hosaka was given the lowest ranking, "C," on "spirit of self-examination," "public-spiritedness," and "fundamental life habits," and "B" on all the others. In the light of accepted practices this constitutes a very low evaluation for one aspiring to enter an upper secondary school.

According to the teachers' remarks in the column provided for making "special comments":

> When this student was in his second year he attempted to organize a chapter of Zenkyōtō[2] for the lower secondary school students of Kōjimachi and distributed inflammatory materials. On the occasion of the school's culture festival (*bunkasai*) he shouted inflammatory slogans and caused disturbances with students from other schools on the Kōjimachi campus by scattering leaflets from the roof. He participated in meetings of the university student ML Faction.[3] Failing to heed the warnings of the responsible school authorities, he continued to distribute leaflets and even wrote graffiti on the walls of the school.

In the column provided for recording absences under the category of "Principal Reasons for Absence" is recorded: "Due to colds, fever, and fatigue resulting from participation in political meetings and demonstrations."

The motives of the upper secondary schools that received this student's *naishinsho* and then decided not to admit him are not completely

[2] An offshoot of the student organization formed by university students in the late 1960s.

[3] One of the Maoist factions of Japan's student left. "M" is Mao Tse-tung; "L", Lin Piao.

clear. Let it suffice to say, however, that not a single one of them, from the depths of their democratic "educational considerations and concern," was capable of admitting the political activist Hosaka.

Let me turn now to the two principal issues considered in the courtroom. The first is whether or not the materials entered in Hosaka's *naishinsho* were based on the precise reporting of facts. The second is to what extent materials disadvantageous to the student, even if factual, should be included in the *naishinsho*, a document necessary for entrance to upper secondary schools. Discussion of these issues revolved around the problem of whether or not such judgments properly belong within the sphere of activities left to the teacher's discretion.

Hosaka's suit was assigned to the Tokyo District Court, which handed down a first ruling on March 28, 1979. This decision recognized the plaintiff's claims and ordered the defendants to provide compensation for the damages suffered by Hosaka. We can detect in this decision the influence of the thought articulated in the first textbook trial (the Sugimoto decision discussed in Chapter 6) that recognized the child's right to learn as "given by nature":

Education should be undertaken from the standpoint of the child's right to learn. Therefore it should be organized to help realize the complete formation of the child's character; in other words, it should be conducted primarily in the interest of the child, and educators should be imbued with this sense of responsibility.

From this standpoint the court argued as follows about documents such as *naishinsho*:

These documents must be drawn up with impartiality and fairness, in as objective a fashion as possible, in order not to improperly infringe upon the student's right to learn.

Based on this outlook, the court examined the concrete facts relating to the materials entered on Hosaka's *naishinsho*. Concerning this student's way of thinking and his expressive behavior, the court opined that they represented the "unstable self-assertion" and "defiance of the established order" characteristic of young people who, developmentally speaking, are in the second phase of rebelliousness[4]:

[4] Popular Japanese psychology recognizes two phases of normal rebelliousness: the first is seen in young children and is generally tolerated if not indulged by parents. The second phase comes during the period of early adolescence, the lower secondary school years that Hosaka's *naishinsho* reported on. This rebelliousness is less generously tolerated by adults in positions of authority.

Even behavior that is judged to be inappropriate, when it is thought of as part of the period of self-formation, should be met with prudent care and consideration.

We find here that the court recognized the importance of adopting a strictly educational viewpoint in dealing with cases such as Hosaka's. Moreover, concerning the freedoms of thought and expression the ruling declared:

Even in public lower secondary schools the student's freedoms of thought and belief must be guaranteed to the utmost extent. The court finds it unlawful to classify and evaluate students on the basis of their thoughts and beliefs.

In conclusion, the court found the evaluation of the student in this case to be "unfair and unreasonable." The activities of the Kōjimachi Lower Secondary School that were directed against Hosaka, it ruled, "overstep the scope of the discretionary authority to produce educational evaluations and therefore constitute a violation of the law."

The defendants immediately responded to this first judgment by instituting an appeal in the Tokyo Higher Court, which handed down its ruling in the case on May 19, 1982. This decision reversed the findings of the Tokyo District Court, arguing that the evaluation transmitted in the *naishinsho* in this case fell well within the scope of the teacher's discretionary authority. The higher court declared that when a student's behavior

violates the regulations of the student assembly and reaches the point that it transgresses the order and discipline of the school, the principal of the school in question can give instructions to the teachers under his control to notify upper secondary schools concerning the student's misbehavior so as to aid the latter in their selection of students for entrance. This constitutes neither a violation of the student's freedoms of thought and belief nor educational discrimination on the basis of the student's thinking and convictions.

Ruling in this vein, the court found that the claims put forth in Hosaka's original suit were totally devoid of reasonableness. The higher court judgment went on to argue:

Notwithstanding the original plaintiff's claim that all people are guaranteed the rights to learn and advance to higher-level schools in response to individual abilities, following from the inevitable limitation of places in these schools, it is only natural that at the time of academic advancement selection be made on the basis of ability.

There are cases in which documentary materials are advantageous to the student as well as those in which the matters reported on are detrimental to the student. (If we look at this from the broad perspective, reporting which is advantageous to the student being reported on can be seen as disadvantageous to his rival and vice versa.) It is in the nature of the case that things should be this way. In fact, it is impossible to imagine a reporting system that is only advantageous to those being reported on. For this reason the opinion expressed by the original plaintiff that the school principal should not order the recording of material detrimental to his academic advancement is lacking a rational foundation and must be seen merely as his personal view.

Thus the higher court declared Hosaka's claim to be "thoroughly unacceptable."

This interpretation leaves no room for doubts regarding the circumstances in which today's education transpires and affirms the validity of present-day forms of control.

Moreover, the Tokyo Higher Court rejected Hosaka's claim that being denied access to his graduation ceremony (he was awarded his diploma in a separate ceremony held for him alone) constituted a violation of his right as a student to learn.

This second decision was based on the following arguments concerning the meaning of the right to learn:

Because school education cannot even get off the ground without cooperation between those conducting education and those who receive it, the right to learn in school of lower secondary students is essentially a passive right. Thus the right to receive an education is predicated upon cooperation with the school and teachers. This should not be thought of as constituting the right to struggle against the school and teacher. From the already recognized facts in the case it is clear that there is no basis for Hosaka's claim that participation in the official graduation ceremony was essential to the exercise of his right to learn. Furthermore, it absolutely cannot be said that Principal Nozawa's previously stated measures were a violation of the plaintiff's right to learn.

While they use the terminology of "right to learn," the justices of the Tokyo Higher Court seem to have learned nothing from the discourse on this right developed within the academic world of educational law. When this right is viewed as no more than the right to passively receive the education that is given, its true import has already been vitiated. I would like to call the reader's attention to the ways in which this has led to a substantive denial of the discourse on the right to learn.

There is also a danger in the perception of the higher court regarding the meaning of the freedoms of thought and belief. According to this court's ruling, the lower secondary school is in fact obliged to present documentary material containing data designed to help the upper secondary school make the requisite judgments concerning the students they will admit. As previously mentioned, the court declared that this should not be taken as a violation of the freedoms of thought and belief or as constituting educational discrimination.

At first glance this appears quite reasonable. In fact, when such documents are constructed as diagnostic charts that help pinpoint a particular student's developmental problems and are forwarded to those who will have subsequent responsibility for his or her education, then rather than being an exercise in discrimination they become a truly vital part of the educational process. The existing reality, however, is that this system provides a method for effectively discriminating against those who are critical of the school and the social order that it seeks to reproduce. In the final analysis the mere act of recording information (as in the case of Hosaka) on the student's thought and political activities cannot but be tied to "educational discrimination on the basis of thought and beliefs." In such a case it is only by *not* recording such information that the student's freedoms can be protected.

In the best of circumstances the freedoms of thought and belief mean that even if the student expresses his convictions, he should remain free from all forms of discrimination. In an environment such as ours, where social discrimination on the basis of intellectual convictions is already all too apparent, these freedoms should also be seen as freedom from having to express one's beliefs or from having them represented by others in documents like the *naishinsho*.

Accordingly, the report on Hosaka's behavior in which he was given the lowest possible evaluation, even though its contents were represented as being educationally oriented, was, in reality, totally different from genuinely educational forms of consideration. Such reporting must be identified as a wanton disregard of those freedoms of thought and belief which are really essential from an educational point of view. These forms of reporting must also be labeled as deviating from the proper scope of the teacher's discretionary authority.

Concerning this latter point the first decision in the case, handed down by the Tokyo District Court, deserves our respect for its enthusiastic defense of the freedoms of thought, belief, and expression of young people who are still in the process of developing.

III. Methods and Procedures for Resolving Educational Disputes

This case has brought to a head a number of problems concerning the methods and procedures available for resolving matters of educational contention—namely, how should we think about the relations between education and justice and the ways in which educational trials are conducted?

While I was one of those who enthusiastically welcomed the ruling handed down by the first court, on logical grounds I sense a number of problematic points to which I find it difficult to give my complete assent.

First of all there is the problem of whether it is appropriate for the courts and judiciary to pass judgments on whether or not the methods of educational evaluation used in the school's compilation of *naishinsho* reports exceed the proper scope of the teacher's educational discretion.

With regard to this point alone, the ruling of the Tokyo Higher Court that these activities fall within the limits of the teacher's discretionary authority seems unobjectionable at first glance, but it must be pointed out on further consideration that this turns the problem addressed by the ruling in the first trial upside down.

I take the following position on the problem of the courts' jurisdiction in these matters. Judgments on whether or not problems arising from transmission of *naishinsho* documentation fall within the scope of the teacher's educational discretion should be primarily based on educators' professional judgment. Furthermore, in cases where it is determined that these activities go beyond the scope of the teacher's discretionary authority, methods and procedures for seeking legal redress must be made available. If such procedures are lacking, I do not think it is appropriate for the courts to be put in the position of being able to pass judgment on whether or not the educational evaluations being challenged belong within the sphere of educational discretion.

Both the first and second rulings in this case, because they fail to adopt a strictly conceived procedural outlook, must be seen as themselves rendering judgments that transcend the scope of the judiciary's discretionary authority. However, since there are no provisions in effect to systematically guarantee recourse to such procedures, there is nothing left for us to do but increase our efforts to create such procedures and continue inquiring into the pros and cons of the educational understanding revealed in these two rulings.

If we carefully examine the present case from this viewpoint, I believe the materials recorded in Hosaka's *naishinsho* can be shown to reveal official malfeasance that transgresses the proper limits of the teacher's discretionary authority.

However, this interpretation requires a totally different approach from that of the court which endorsed *naishinsho* reporting as falling within the proper scope of lower secondary schools' discretional authority. Of course we cannot avoid observing that the educational judgment of the school involved in this case was pathetically weak and marked by a highly pronounced crudeness. It is certain that such practices cannot stand up to serious pedagogic criticism.

The first court judgment found the actions of the Kōjimachi Lower Secondary School illegally going beyond the scope of the teacher's discretionary authority. In direct contrast, the second judgment ruled that such actions were legal because they did properly fall within the scope of the school's discretionary powers.

To speak, however, of these discretionary powers as falling within the scope of the teacher's legal authority is to go against the very principles of educational logic, and it is here that the heart of the problem lies. Furthermore, these judgments should be reached not in the courtroom but in an appropriate, educationally related organ wherein professionalism defines the standards of decision-making. This argument highlights the need for mechanisms seeking legal redress concerning the pros and cons of such judgments.

Speaking more precisely about the data recorded in the *naishinsho* prepared by the school in question, we can distinguish between matters falling under the teacher's discretion and those that illegally exceed those boundaries. Concerning the "A," "B," and "C" ratings that can be given for the items in the column on "character and behavior," I suppose the decision on which to assign falls within the limits of the teacher's discretion. However, when it comes to supplementary notes that are clearly related to the student's freedom of thought, belief, and expression, there most definitely is a problem of providing avenues for seeking legal redress. When it is recorded under the heading of school attendance that the student "was absent due to fatigue caused by participation in political demonstrations," then clearly the student has a problem challenging the illegality of this supersession of the teacher's discretionary authority. These problems, particularly as they pertain to the human rights of minors who are still growing and developing, must be clarified from a standpoint that addresses the question of how to guarantee procedures for seeking legal redress. Concerning this point, I believe the ruling of the Tokyo District Court has raised serious and proper issues that demand further examination.

However, directing attention to the impropriety of assigning a "C" in the column provided for evaluating "character and behavior" is different from insisting that such methods of educational evaluation are simply illegal. Thus for the time being we must direct our efforts to the problem of more rigorously defining just what it means to "fall within the scope of the teacher's discretionary powers."

The first ruling in this case was based on an examination of the factual question of whether or not the plaintiff participated in the meetings of the ML Faction. It concluded, "It is not confirmed as a matter of fact that the plaintiff participated in such meetings." The second ruling, in contrast, assumed Hosaka's participation to be a matter of fact. However, the real problem is not whether the charge that he participated in such activities is based on fact or not, but whether the courts should even be inquiring into such matters. It is my conviction that entering such matters on a *naishinsho* document constitutes an illegal deviation from the legitimate scope of the teacher's discretionary authority. In short, the recording of such information goes against the principle of *educational* evaluation. This is the only judgment that I believe the courts could have rightly handed down.

IV. Procedures for Dealing with These Problems

This leads us then to the problem of what kinds of procedures and methods can and should be made available for appeal when there are doubts regarding the exercise of educational discretion.

Of course, in the absence of a democratic reordering of the entire apparatus of educational administration, thinking about this problem by itself ultimately leads nowhere. The resolution of such procedural questions should be the work of committees of professional educators whose members possess a high degree of professional expertise and the authority that derives therefrom. These committees belong within boards of education but should be given the authority and responsibility to act independently from the established channels of educational administration. The function of such committees should be mainly to provide advice about the teacher's educational praxis. The work of these committees should be close to that of today's educational consultant (*shidō shuji*), but it would be desirable if these committees were made up of individuals truly possessing educational powers of discernment.[5]

The educational evaluations produced by these consultative bodies should come in response to specific requests; while giving advice, these committees should also suggest appropriate directions to follow. Concerning the scope of the teacher's educational discretion as well, these committees should be free to make appropriate judgments and recommendations.

Remedies should only be sought through the courts in cases found by these groups to constitute transgressions of the proper boundaries of the teacher's discretionary authority, and with regard to problems pertaining to the legitimate scope of administrative guidance.

Today, because intermediate forums for resolving such problems are unavailable, there is confusion surrounding the relation between education and the courtroom. For example, questions of whether or not the content of textbooks is *academically* correct are inappropriate for judgment in a court of law. The same is true of questions about the propriety of the means used when the teacher invokes his discretion as a teacher in areas such as educational evaluation. Only questions involving the problem of how to guarantee the child's rights to learn should be made problems for consideration by our courts. However, cases such as those some parents are now bringing into the courts, which result in decisions about whether or not the use of certain supplementary textbook materials violates the child's rights to learn, are in the last analysis inappropriate for decision in courts of law.

V. Educational Evaluation and Its Ethos

Of course even if intermediary organs based on what I am calling *edu-*

---

[5] The work of today's educational consultants is located within the school education section of board of education secretariats. With the transformation of boards of education from elected to appointed bodies, the work of educational consultants was altered in ways that had important ramifications for the organization of educational practice. What began as supervision of the teacher's educational activities gradually came to function as a means of exercising control in conformity with the aims of the Ministry of Education. These realities have led us to seek fundamental reforms in the work of educational consulting so as to promote a high degree of professionalism and guidance responsive to the demands of educational praxis.

cational authority are established and appropriate procedures adopted, unless the foundations of our ways of thinking about education and educational evaluation become more widely accepted, then these procedures will still lack the real meaning they should come to possess.

In conclusion, then, I would like to make some observations on the ethos of educational evaluation.

(1) In recent years, the scores given in *naishinsho* ratings in places like Hyōgo and Kanagawa prefectures have come to have greater weight than entrance examinations in high school admissions. Owing to the enhanced status of the *naishinsho*, students have on an everyday basis been placed under severe psychological duress. We find increasing numbers of cases in which rules are violated in undercover ways, and there has also been an acceleration of violent outbursts. The change from admission to public high schools solely on the basis of examinations on academic subjects to a system that gives heavy weight to *naishinsho* reports came in 1966 in response to a Ministry of Education "notification" to the prefectural boards of education that stated: "Greater importance will be given to questionnaires" (meaning the *naishinsho* forms). Recently, under the pretext of criticizing education that overvalues "intellectual training,"[6] arguments have been made in favor of including (in addition to the student's academic achievements) *naishinsho* information on personal character, club participation, and social service activities within the category of "behavior." There has been a nationwide increase in the tendency to move in this direction. It has been widely reported that in Aichi Prefecture a system of relative evaluations has been introduced in the *naishinsho* used there. Under the heading "general evaluation of character," teachers have been instructed to give a low "C" ranking to 10 percent of their students.

There are also many serious problems with the idea of using a five-stage system of relative evaluation to judge the academic achievements of our students. As is true with regard to the system of evaluation imposed upon the student in the form of the *naishinsho*, the values at the heart of this system are essentially anti-educational. Under these arrangements, in a class of forty-five students grades are made to fit a "normal distribution" curve. Grades "5" and "1," the highest and

---

[6] Criticism of "intellectually oriented education" (*chiiku henchō kyōiku*) is in reality an attack on the postwar reforms aimed at democratizing education. Use of the phrase dates back to the publication in 1955 of a Liberal Democratic Party-authored pamphlet entitled "Deplorable Textbooks."

lowest, are each given to 7 percent of the students; "4" and "2" are each given to 24 percent; and "3" is given to the remaining 38 percent. This distribution has worked to create a ranked ordering of all students. While this may well be seen as an efficient form of rating, it is impossible to view it as legitimately constituting a proper form of educational evaluation.

In response to such criticisms, a few adjustments were made in the procedures for entering remarks on report cards that permitted the individual teacher to exercise some ingenuity, but for official reporting of academic progress the five-stage system has been vigorously defended. This has been particularly true in the case of materials like the *naishinsho* which have been officially endorsed as containing information that must be considered when upper secondary school admissions decisions are made.

However, the laws upon which the normal distribution (Gauss curve) of the five-stage relative evaluation system is based are for the most part used for determining probability in the world of natural phenomena. It is only possible to view this as corresponding to the distribution of human talents and competencies if these are grasped as genetically determined; and of course this way of thinking is incompatible with the approach to human competencies that sees them as the outcome of development through education and learning. An education that aims at the full flowering of the possibilities of all persons for this very reason implies a challenge to such normal distribution curves. Teachers who in their everyday educational practices work to create this type of education, when forced in the final stage of evaluating their students to employ an evaluation system that is completely opposed to the aims of their efforts up to that point, cannot help but feel like the victims of spiritual torture.

(2) As disagreement concerning educational evaluation continues to increase, criticisms of the concept of educational evaluation itself have been voiced, and there are those who think that the present system should be thoroughly repudiated. There are even cases in music classes where teachers have used the argument that evaluation is impossible and have uniformly entered the rating "3."

However, such decisions by teachers, while they may very well have a great deal of symbolic significance as expressions of a basic resistance to today's patently anti-educational types of student evaluation and the ideology that underwrites the dehumanizing ranking of students by tests that this system is based upon, in the end only constitute symbolic forms of protest.

Evaluation is an indispensable part of educational praxis. It helps the child certify how far he or she has come and helps the teacher examine his or her success in furthering the child's growth. In the absence of such reflection, education cannot move forward. Running throughout teachers' research on instructional materials and practices is a demand that attention be paid to the needs of the child. It is this concern in fact which should define the perspectives employed in educational evaluation.

If the importance of evaluation is denied, instruction is allowed to become an irresponsible exercise that passes over the heads of children, and degenerates into a one-sided affair in which knowledge is merely poured into the heads of students.

(3) For these reasons alone it is absolutely necessary that teachers approach educational evaluation mindful of the opportunities it affords for encouraging children and giving them a greater sense of self-confidence. In adopting this approach there must be clear rejection of techniques of evaluation that have produced feelings of inferiority and an atrophying of children's interest in their own development.

The "report card" has served to intensify the destructive tendencies of educational evaluation in Japan. It should be redesigned to function as a communication from the school to the home with the aim of furthering cooperation between teachers and parents so as to support and assist the child in his development. Accordingly, a wide variety of techniques should be utilized in recording information on the student's academic maturation. In this context, no matter who the child is, without fail he possesses at least one or two excellent qualities in which he should rightly take pride. It is desirable for teachers to discover and encourage these strong points, and for report cards to report on them. However, it is most undesirable to affix the rank of "A," "B," or "C," as is presently done, for example, when information is recorded on behavior or special characteristics of personality. In a class of forty-five students, if there are students who are uneven-tempered yet rich in creative drive, there are also students who present themselves as unrewarding drudges.

Children who hold their own opinions but do not easily cooperate may at first glance seem to be deficient in sociability; upon further examination, however, their behavior may well bear witness to a valuable sense of independence. Ranking these most individual of attributes as "A," "B," or "C" is not only impossible but meaningless. If such methods of evaluation continue to be employed, they will go on inviting injurious results.

(4) Evaluation should be utilized only for educational purposes and should never be made to serve any other objectives, just as the school register should not be used to provide data for those conducting investigations related to marriage.[7] From the standpoint of educational logic it is equally inappropriate to use the "A" s, "B" s, and "C" s recorded under the *naishinsho* heading of "character and behavior" for determining the child's academic advance. Both this method of evaluation and the ways it is used are seriously in error as far as *education* is concerned.

If, however, evaluations of students are put into writing as diagnostic reports on development and education, and sent on to the teachers who will be responsible for these students in the following academic year, they can be used educationally to help the new teacher carry on the work of helping the students grow. As a matter of principle these reports should not be secret but should also be made available to students and their parents. This is similar to the idea of making the diagnostic charts used in medical treatment available to the patient as a matter of principle.

Educational evaluation must constantly affirm the principles required to guarantee children's growth and learning, and should not be used to fit children into a fixed framework intended to control them.

---

[7] In Japan it is not uncommon for parents to hire private investigators to find out as much as possible about prospective marriage partners for their children. —Trans.

Part III

Individualism and Egalitarianism in Japanese Education:
Myths and Realities

Introduction to Part III

The final section of the present volume analyzes the major attempts to reform Japanese education made in the 1960s and 1970s, and concludes by criticizing the official efforts being exerted in the 1980s to "prepare Japanese education for the challenges of the 21st century." What emerges with particular clarity is the historically evolving relation between the manpower requirements of the Japanese industrial world and the policies of educational "diversification" and "individualization" adopted by politicians in the ruling Liberal Democratic Party and implemented by bureaucrats in the Ministry of Education.

Each of the three essays selected for this section presents data showing that Japan's officially proclaimed policies for educational reform have systematically usurped the rights, constitutionally guaranteed to all citizens in a democratic society, to freely grow and develop into self-governing human beings. At the same time, they build upon these criticisms to theorize about the best way to guarantee these inalienable educational rights at all of the various stages in a citizen's life. Within the context of the tensions these texts generate between a critique of the "violation of basic human rights" and the transformation of educational authority required for their realization, the author begins to set forth the outlines of his philosophy of education and its relation to a theory of political practice designed to democratize society.

The challenges implicit in the re-democratization of Japanese educational life are examined in relation to several important questions: How should the relations between the systems of public education and social selection be structured so as to promote genuine equality of opportunity? How should a national system of public education be structured so as to balance the requirements of individual, personal development with those of national economic growth? Exploring these issues allows the author to unpack a number of the most perplexing political problems and paradoxes that contemporary Japanese

297

society faces while moving forward as an economic superpower.

Discussing these problems, the author explores the important transformations which have taken place in the interpretation of modern concepts such as meritocracy and egalitarianism, and analyzes the appearance in Japan of the phenomenon
called "academic pedigreeism." But unlike the educational
sociologists, psychologists, and economists in Japanese society
who uncritically accept and premise their work on the subordination of educational values to economic ones, he attempts
to lay bare the ideological agenda embedded within Japan's
leaders' ideas about the proper relation between education
and national development. Thus, in addition to showing how
the Japanese educational system has been repeatedly mobilized since the early 1960s to support the nation's industrial
policies, the analyses presented in these essays reveal the highly
destructive human costs which Japanese young people have
been forced to pay to make this possible. The thoughtful reader
will recognize the urgent warning implicit in these texts about
the dangers involved in imitating the Japanese model—dangers
to which those in the West who speak about the Japanese "educational challenge" and "commitment to education" unfortunately appear oblivious.

12 Equality and Individuality in Education: Towards a Reformation of Pedagogic Values

Very few people, when seriously discussing the deplorable conditions of education in Japan today, would not mention the furious intensification of examination competition and the pathological phenomena it has spawned.

Inasmuch as the schools have been forced to function with cold efficiency as the agency of social selection and competition, they have given birth to two types of young people. On the one hand they have given us lethargic youth who feel themselves to have been cast aside by society, while on the other they promote the emergence of unfeeling, imperturbable elitists for whom studying is equated with kicking any and all potential rivals down into the mud. Our youth are being selected on the "objective" basis of standard deviation (*hensachi*) and sent along to our "diversified" and hierarchically ranked upper secondary schools. The result is that differences in quality among secondary schools have widened sharply. As secondary schools are polarized into those designed to prepare students for entrance to elite universities and those organized to educate those classified as non-achievers, the democratic ideal of a unified secondary school education has disappeared, and secondary education itself sinks deeper and deeper into a dangerous and destructive morass.

What meaning does the recently announced Revised Course of Study for Upper Secondary Schools[1] actually have as a response to these conditions? The number of required subjects has been dramatically reduced, electives increased, and a certain leeway recognized for the school's own arranging of the curriculum its teachers give instruction in. There are also recommendations for "class composition on the basis of proficiency." This plan has been greeted by the media as a "boldly diverse and flexible response to the realities of a 93 percent rate of advancement to high school, and to the striking growth in students' academic abilities and aptitudes" (*Asahi Shimbun*, June 23, 1978).

We can see in the condensation of the contents of the Course of

---

[1] See the Introduction to Part II for a description of the Course of Study. Since the time this essay was written, new revisions have followed the trajectory outlined here.

Study, to a level half that found in the previous one, a definite reaction to the "meddlesome interference" in the administration of educational content that has characterized Japanese education in recent
years. It is certain that the result of educational litigation, from the
Sugimoto decision on textbook control to the Supreme Court's ruling
on the Scholastic Achievement Test problem, has been the curtailing
of the Ministry of Education's attempts to dominate the organization
of the contents of education.[2] Yet, on the opposite side of the ledger,
to the extent that the Course of Study has been "more carefully selected" and its standardizing and legally binding powers increased,
the degree of influence exerted by administrative discretion has in
reality been markedly intensified. In the wake of these developments,
there are increased dangers of even greater governmental control.
"Because it is not written in the Course of Study" has become a justification for ignoring certain areas of learning,[3] and this only multiplies
the danger.

One other major problem with the current revisions is the stated
emphasis on "thoroughgoing diversification and flexibility." This
should not be seen as a change in the policy of diversification that the
Ministry of Education initiated in the 1960s, but rather as its culmina-
tion. Within the framework of this policy, the ideals of equality and
diversity stand in basic opposition. To the extent that we can grasp
the fact that this notion of diversification does not mean individualization, we can achieve a critical position from which it becomes possible
to analyze the most troublesome problems plaguing current-day education.

According to the Ministry of Education's commentary accompanying the text of the revisions, "These revisions have been undertaken
so as to provide an education in response to the student's individuality
and abilities." The number of required credits has been reduced "so
as to provide an education in response to the needs of a diversified
student body," and the curriculum has been redesigned with the focus
on elective subjects so as to "meet the individual's ability, aptitude,
interests, and concerns."

However, according to Sasaki Susumu, who has for many years
carefully followed the changes in the upper secondary school curriculum:

[2] Chapter 6 discusses the Sugimoto ruling on textbook control, and Chapter 8
treats the controversy surrounding the Scholastic Achievement Test.

[3] For example, the history curriculum for public high schools (upper secondary
schools) has been trimmed, with European history de-emphasized, and junior high
(lower secondary level) English instruction has been cut back.

The last time the student's "individuality" was seriously recognized in the Course of Study was in the 1955 edition. "Individuality" has long since become a dead word in the Course of Study. This time it only appears in the chapter headings of ministerial explanations, and even there it is nothing but a mockery. We must take notice of the fact that it never appears in the real body of the text, and that its use in chapter headings is merely to disguise the real purposes expounded upon in the text. [*Kyōiku*, September 1978, special edition]

I believe that this criticism penetrates right to the heart of what the current revision is all about.

At the crux of today's crisis-plagued educational conditions stand the ideologies of control and standardization that inspire our educational administration authorities and provide them with their justification for the misbegotten policies of "diversifying" the educational system on the basis of the principle of "ability-first." The focal point of this problem is the way the seemingly contradictory policies of standardization and diversification have been made into a set and pushed forward in tandem. The Ministry of Education has characterized postwar education as "standardized egalitarianism" and has proposed "diversification on the basis of ability" as an alternative. In actuality, however, diversification on the basis of ability is premised on a one-dimensional value system; it is an attempt to make the scale which underlies *this* value orientation the *one* and *only* valid measure of our citizens' social worth.

In this essay I shall therefore analyze the problematic nature of this educational diversification on the basis of ability, and suggest a way in which equality and individuality can in truth be made compatible.

I. The Ideologies of Ability-First and Academic Pedigreeism

The causes of Japan's ridiculously over-heated examination competition have been found to lie in our society's predisposition to academic pedigreeism, and there has begun of late a discourse in search of a way to escape from this examination madness. Both those in charge of formulating educational policy and their critics are in agreement, if on nothing else, on the need to overcome this insanity.

It is beyond doubt that the problem of how to reform examination competition is inseparable from the problem of how to transform a society that measures the worth of individuals almost solely on the basis of their academic pedigrees. The question we must thus address is how we can grasp the relationship between the notion of "ability-first" and the ideology of "academic pedigreeism." It is generally thought that societies organized in terms of the principles of efficiency and meritocracy are directly opposed to those founded on the principles of pedigreeism and the rewarding of those who possess such badges of honor. As a variant of the latter, an "academic pedigree" society is one in which those who possess good academic credentials, even without real ability, are given the most socially advantageous positions and the greatest social respect. "Academic pedigreeism" is therefore a term designed to express the estrangement between schooling and ability and the pathological conditions that result as a necessary consequence thereof. In other words, in an age and society where money or connections can ensure matriculation, even in the absence of true abilities the resulting academic pedigree gives the credentials necessary for becoming successful. The scandals surrounding the contributions to private schools at the time of matriculation, particularly medical programs, are a straightforward example of the subterranean forces that emerge as a result.[4]

One more expression of the antagonism between the concepts of meritocracy and degree-ocracy is found at the time students graduate and find employment. Here academic pedigree has come to serve as a tentative index of ability. Even after beginning employment, it often seems that one's chances for success and promotion are settled in advance, on the basis of the school one graduates from (or, more precisely, the department thereof) and the year of one's graduation. An academic pedigree society is thus one in which there is no need for competition to demonstrate one's abilities and merits to society, and in which the degree is the actual passport to success.

Let us consider, for example, a major governmental enterprise such as the National Railways, which is a classic case of Japanese officialism. The "elite course" of advancement within the company is tightly closed to all except those who, having graduated from a fixed number of prestigious universities, form a special manpower pool of individuals who while they are young serve as stationmasters in the provinces,

[4] In recent years there have been a number of scandals in which students were able to buy their way into medical schools in spite of not having been successful on the schools' entrance examinations. There have also been cases in which criminal charges were brought against individuals connected with universities who sold information about their schools' entrance examinations to students in advance. The fact that there are parents who are willing to pay exorbitant sums to illegally obtain examination questions and answers for their children underlines the seriousness of the situation.

then return to the home office assured of success even if they have not done anything of distinction. The principles that run throughout this organization are academic pedigreeism and ranking by seniority. The system of personnel employment from a number of specially designated schools serves to supplement and complete these arrangements.

Today's academic pedigree disease might better be designated a social pathology which has its etiology in the frantic desire to enter a famous university, for what is socially serviceable is the status of the university's diploma, rather than anything one might learn there. It is in the thronging of examinees to the small number of socially valued, high-ranking universities that the viciously intense examination competition plaguing Japanese education begins.

In the postwar era, particularly as a result of the "popularization" of universities in the 1960s,[5] the structure of job-seeking among college graduates changed drastically, and the concentrated convergence on the most prestigious universities was accelerated (Ogata Ken, *Gakureki Shinkō Shakai*, Jiji Tsūshinsha, 1976). Furthermore, due to the ethos of the Japanese university, in which entrance is difficult while graduation is comparatively simple, the struggle has become centered on high school selection at age 15 and university entrance at age 18; competition at these stages has become all the more extreme.

The OECD Investigation Commission which came to Japan in 1970 commented on the academic pedigree society in its 1972 report:

> From the point of view of the average person, social evaluation in the universities creates rigid rankings of superior and inferior, better and worse. The high school's value is predicated solely on the extent to which it sends its students to esteemed universities, and they are ranked comparatively on the basis thereof. Furthermore, the majority of employers do not ask what knowledge or abilities the graduates possess, but make their decisions with regard to the results of the individual's college entrance examination; in particular which department of which university did these tests enfranchise the student for. On one day at the age of 18 on the basis of the score obtained, the rest of his or her life is determined. In other words, the college entrance exam in Japanese society has been created as a mechanism of selection which has a major influence on the student's future career. As a result there

---

[5] The number of high-school graduates advancing to various forms of higher education jumped from 10 percent in 1960 to 24 percent in 1970, and again to 38 percent in 1980 (Ministry of Education statistics).

is no longer selection on the basis of aristocracy, but in its place a kind of degree-ocracy has come into being. This is more certainly egalitarian in comparison to a hereditary class system, and possesses greater elasticity. But in comparison to systems initiated by societies in which the long-term accomplishments of the individual are made the measure for distributing people to appropriate professions and positions, or to those where people receive an education in response to their desires and the needs incumbent upon them, and can have their positions raised in accord with the development of their abilities, the system of academic pedigreeism is one lacking in flexibility and resilience, and is actually quite despotic. [*Japanese Educational Policy*, OECD Educational Research Investigation Commission, 1972]

The conditions of examination competition in Japan certainly appear abnormal in the eyes of Europeans. Joseph Pittau, the president of Sophia University in Tokyo, in an article on Japanese education (*Asahi Shimbun*, September 2, 1978), remarked:

It is often joked about, but the passage in the Bible which says "Seek ye first the Kingdom of God and all other things shall be given you besides" becomes, in the thinking of the Japanese people, "Seek ye first the Kingdom of the schools, especially famous schools, and you will be given everything else." Most families think this way. What one should do after entering one of these famous schools, or what one wants to do with one's life, are questions the Japanese do not think about very much.

These criticisms provide a penetrating look at the academic pedigree society of Japan. They highlight the reality: first-rank schools are linked to first-rank corporations through the job-placement system, and Japan's industrial society places major emphasis on major corporations. When we add to this the reality of the worker's strong consciousness of belonging to a corporation, the truth of Father Pittau's comment becomes that much more striking.

The OECD report quoted above assigned academic pedigreeism to a position halfway between social systems based on inherited status and those based on merit and ability. The report in fact constitutes a criticism of academic pedigreeism from the perspective of meritocracy. However, the principle of meritocracy itself is a fundamental problem in Japanese society today. (See Chapter 13 for a fuller discussion of this point.)

We should not view meritocracy and academic pedigreeism only as antagonists. The problem is that, as a historical tendency, schooling has gradually become an index of ability. If the universities were not so influenced by money and were not viewed as places for acquiring a kind of social lineage, but were run rather with regard to real abilities and capacities, then the university entrance exam would indeed have meaning as a certification of ability.

The problems for both today and the future lie herein. First there is the problem of the nature of those abilities necessary for acquiring the pedigree of education and the qualifications that appear to support it. In the simplest of terms, these are the abilities that can be measured on a test, and the capacity to respond quickly on a test is one type of intellectual excellence. However, the abilities that center on strength of memorization and speed of response constitute merely one part of the wider spectrum of human capacities. When these abilities are given too much importance, the result is people who lack both creativity and curiosity. When these skills are seen as subsuming the whole of human ability or as the most representative of human capacities, the other abilities young people might develop are worn down and eventually disappear in the mist generated by the competition for marks.

The sad reality is that today's conditions seem to be encouraging just such a chain of events. The adoption of the Unified Screening Test[6] is a case in point. In a bizarrely objective sense, it offers a way to attach an order to the academic powers and abilities of all 300,000 students who sit for this exam, and rank them from number 1 to number 300,000. Based on this "precise" numerical evaluation of academic prowess, universities that accept these students can also be ranked. Thus the concept of standard deviation has been made into a tool for controlling what goes on in schools, as it comes to be thought of as an accurate indicator of real ability.

In this way an equation has emerged in which *academic pedigree = academic ability = ability*. As this pedigree becomes an index of ability, the ideology of pedigreeism becomes inevitably linked to the ideology of ability-first, and the examination competition becomes more and more overheated.

[6] The Unified Screening Test (*Kyōtsū Ichiji Shiken*) was instituted by the Ministry of Education in 1979; the stated aim was simplifying entrance to national universities by replacing the entrance examinations held by each individual university with a single test to be used by all of them. However, the universities' reluctance to give up their own examinations has resulted in a situation in which the Unified Screening Test is just one more test, which students must pass in order to qualify for taking the examinations of the individual national universities.

II. Standardized "Diversification"

Behind the equation of academic pedigree with ability and the intensification of examination competition is the emergence of a one-dimensional value system in which economic priorities supersede all others.
Former Minister of Education Nagai Michio has observed that Japan
became a recognizably competitive society during the Meiji era, but
that around 1960 this became a particularly pronounced feature of the
social landscape. The reason he cites is the increased rates of advancement to upper secondary school and to college. In answer to the question of why it has come about that practically everyone is going to high
school and—if possible—college, Nagai has argued:

> It was already clear by 1960 that people who were in possession
> of high levels of education were attaining advantageous positions
> in society. This had become strikingly apparent to those who were
> not possessors of these academic qualifications. Thus parents who
> themselves had not had an advantageous education were naturally
> willing to invest substantial energy and expense in their children's
> schooling. The consequence has been that in less than twenty years
> Japan has become a viciously competitive society. Yet if we look
> carefully at all of this it can no longer be said that a college grad-
> uate is at a marked advantage. We have now reached a point that
> was absolutely unthinkable in 1960; however, the consciousness
> of most people is the same as that found in 1960. [*Jurisuto* (*Jurist*),
> special issue on education, 1978]

It is certainly true, as Nagai has argued, that education in the 1960s
was moved by economic forces that have since come to dominate it.
In the realms of social values and belief systems as well, a hierarchy
has taken shape along the axis of economic values. Educational policy
was assigned a position as one link in the policy of promoting high
economic growth. The idea of recomposing education as an activity
that must respond to economic demands and requirements was soon
seized upon as an important factor that would determine the success
or failure of the government's high-growth policy. This was also used
to substantiate essentially anti-democratic criticisms of the postwar
reforms of education based on the Fundamental Law of Education
and the 6–3–3–4 system,[7] criticisms that called the fruits of these

---

[7] The 6–3–3–4 system—six years of primary school, three years each of lower and
upper secondary school, and four years of college—was adopted after the war to

profound changes "standardized egalitarianism." This criticism in turn provided the basis for a "reform of the reforms." As was suggested in the 1963 Report of the Economic Deliberation Council, this meant a rejection of the aspirations towards equality and a restructuring of both our social and educational systems on the basis of an ideology which values ability over all else. This led to a reconceptualization of the school in which it was made to function as a mechanism for manpower selection in accordance with the State's and the economy's require-ments for labor power. In other words, the school was reconceived as an ideological State apparatus, the apparatus for creating "the desired Japanese."

The statements of the educational sociologist Shimizu Yoshihiro (who participated in the long-term planning of the Economic Delibera-tion Council) reveal the shared conception of the formulators of edu-cational policy at this time. Shimizu criticized postwar education:

> ... particularly upper secondary education, because it has over-looked the opportunities to diversify education in response to differences in ability and aptitude. Too much emphasis has been placed on the word "equally" in Article III of the Fundamental Law of Education, and too little on the idea of "in accordance with ability." [20 Nengo no Kyōiku to Keizai, Tōyōkan Shuppansha]

This diversification in response to ability meant subordinating edu-cation to economic demands; in other words, it meant a substantial conversion in response to the labor requirements of Japan's industrial world. According to Shimizu, "education in itself does not have any objectives; what Japanese economic growth requires from educational policy is the cultivation and supply of a good-quality labor force." The argument, then, is that educational planning should be devised so as to respond to these demands.

At the same time the Ministry of Education issued a white paper called Japanese Growth and Education. "Growth" here did not refer to the human development of children or adolescents, but to the growth of the Japanese economy. This symbolized the educational ethos of the day.

Thus, in response to a policy of high economic growth, a new value hierarchy was being instituted with economic values at the apex. At the minimum it can be said that through these efforts the system of

---

replace the prewar dual-track system; it was intended to produce a more egalitarian education on the American model.

values embodied in the postwar reforms was being seriously eroded. Ironically, this policy was called a "policy for diversification." In what sense of the word, however, can this be true?

It is certainly true that during this period our secondary schools were "diversified" and our colleges further differentiated. However, as a consequence of this process it has become all too clear that the ordering of institutions and individuals on the basis of unified standards ultimately rests on measures of academic achievement rooted only in equations of "standard deviation." Both colleges and upper secondary schools lost their previously cherished individual character as students devoted all their efforts to preparing for the severe entrance examination competition. When these students finally enter university, they are placed in a situation where they can enjoy a four-year moratorium on living and thinking, by virtue of their special status as candidates being groomed for positions as ordinary salaried workers within the Japanese industrial Leviathan.

Since these changes have been effected in educational policy, the social consciousness of upper secondary school students has also undergone a rapid transformation. This can be seen in the data from an ongoing attitude survey undertaken at a school in Nagoya that has collected information on the same set of items since 1960. In response to a question about one's own future, the percentage of respondents answering that they have "high hopes" declined from 61 percent in 1960 to 11.6 percent in 1976.

In response to the question "What are your goals for the future?" the percentage answering "To make money" steadily increased, from 5 percent in 1960 to 24.2 percent in 1976. The percentage responding "To become a person useful to society" declined from 24 percent in 1960 to 9 percent in 1976.

In the area of support for political parties and positions on political issues, there has been a decline among young people in support for reformist policies and a trend towards conservatism. Those showing support for the socialist or communist parties dropped from 43 percent in 1960 to 22 percent in 1970, and down to 20 percent in 1978. It is frightening to what extent and in what directions the changes in social policy are reflected in attitudes among youth.

In society at large, the uni-dimensionalization of values under the rubric of economic values has gone forward, and in the schools the criteria for evaluating human beings have been unified and reduced to a standardized set corresponding to the main examination subjects: Japanese language, English language, mathematics, social studies, and science. The ranking of human beings has proceeded on the basis of test grades, has been tied together through the equation *graduation* = *employment*, and resulted in today's *academic pedigree* = *ability-first* ideology.

All of this represents a systemic restructuring of education on the basis of the emphasis placed in the 1960s on ability-first and manpower development.

The policy of diversification has been presented as an antidote to standardization; yet in reality it is the exact opposite of individualization. If we look at the standardized control that has been applied to the contents of education along with the policy of "diversification," it becomes clear that this diversification has certainly not been aimed at producing a more individualized form of education. The Scholastic Achievement Test, which played a leading role in carrying out the policy of diversification, shows this reality all too clearly. While purporting to measure the extent to which the 1958 revisions in the Course of Study had been faithfully brought into the classroom, it also provided a procedure for the systematic ranking and numbering of the academic prowess of each and every lower secondary school student. The ranking of individual students on a nationwide scale through the standardized criteria of grades has also stimulated the ranking of high schools based on the performance of their students.

III. Equalization and Individualization

As the policy of diversification initiated in the 1960s undercut the drive towards a more substantive form of egalitarianism in educational life, it gave rise to a new set of highly troublesome problems. First, as a result of the decision to recognize economic disparities as a natural given, all values were ranked in a hierarchy with economic values at the top. This is a clear departure from the pluralistic value-oriented ideals of the early postwar educational reforms, instituted in reaction to prewar education's standardization and overcontrol. Thus, in addition to opening educational opportunities to all, the new educational ideals were grounded in a deep respect for the sanctity of the individual and an abiding esteem for the qualities and differences of individual character. The major objective of these reforms was to provide an education that would give the fullest possible scope for developing the potential of every individual. This was clearly laid out in the Preface and Article I of the Fundamental Law of Education and was even visible in the Ministry of Education's *Plans for a New Education*. This pamphlet, which was widely read as a signpost on the road leading to the creation of a new education for Japan, along with describing the ideals for education as "respect for humanity, character, and individuality," attached concise explanations of what was meant by each of these terms. Humanity was defined as "the qualities, dispositions, abilities, and needs the human being is originally endowed with." Character, "those attributes that people must possess so as to be human, comes into being as the various capacities that the human being is naturally endowed with and which are realized by a unified and free mind that has, and can act upon, its own opinions." As for individuality, "it means the unique temperament of each and every human being. All people are endowed with a common humanity, and although everyone has a character which should be equally respected, since human nature appears in different ways due to differences in character, everyone possesses peculiar features which should be recognized on their own merit apart from those of all other people. This is individuality. . . . People should follow their own individuality and develop their humanity, and through the workings of their character act so as to serve the good of human culture."

It is just as important for us to take note of the fact that Article 26 of the Constitution confirms the People's right to receive an education "equally, in response to their abilities," and that Article III of the Fundamental Law of Education stipulates the "equality of educational opportunity." It should not be overlooked that "equally" and "in response to their abilities" are expressed as a set.

The postwar reform of Japanese education attempted to promote the development of human character under conditions of equality without the imposition of any improper forms of discrimination with regard to the opportunity for learning. The fundamental aim here was to concretely realize both the right to receive an education and the equality of opportunity. Thus, if we look, for example, at the controversy in the early postwar Educational Reform Council concerning the Constitution's phrase "equally in response to their abilities," those like Ashida Hitoshi who argued that this allowed discrimination on the basis of ability were in the minority. The majority view was that of Mutai Risaku and Kido Bantarō, who held that the constitutional principle to be upheld was individualization under equality of conditions. This was expressed in a more developed form as "in response to their needs of development." (For a detailed account of this controversy, see Yamazumi Masami and Horio Teruhisa, *Kyōiku Rinen* [*The Ideals of Education*], University of Tokyo Press, 1976, Volume 2 in a series entitled *Sengo Nihon no Kyōiku Kaikaku* [*The Postwar Reform of Japanese Education*].)

In the administration of educational content as well, the postwar change from a nationalized system of textbooks (in which a single text was used in all schools for the same course) to a screening system (in which a number of texts were approved for each subject) meant that teachers could construct curricula on their own initiative. The Course of Study was designed to be used as a "handbook." Compulsory standardization was rejected, and an attempt made to allow greater room for individualization. We can even go so far as to say that equalization and individualization themselves constituted the ideals of postwar democratized education.

Article 42 of the School Education Law proclaims the following objectives for high school education:

> The upper secondary school must work to help the student define his path for the future, raise the general level of culture, and aid the student to attain mastery of specialized skills. . . . It must work to cultivate within society a wide and deep understanding, healthy critical abilities and the establishment of individuality.

This section from the School Education Law was quoted in its entirety in the Course of Study for Upper Secondary Schools, as well as in Article I of the Fundamental Law of Education, as defining the aims and objectives of secondary education. But, sadly, after 1955 these ideals disappeared once and forever.

IV. The Right to Develop while Choosing

The principle underlying the spirit of respect for individuality which the postwar democratizing reforms sought to instill at the heart of a new educational system, and which those of us who believe in such values have continually struggled to support, has been characterized by Ōta Takashi as "the right to develop while choosing." Ōta has argued that it is critically important to place the focus of educational planning upon the needs of individuals who are still developing, and to make their educational needs the touchstone for all such organizational activity. In this formulation, guaranteeing these rights is conceived of as an obligation shared by all of the members of society, and in particular as a duty of the older generation to the younger. In this light, the "policy of diversification" reveals nothing more than the desire of those controlling Japanese society to rob our youth of their inherent possibilities as human beings, while our insistence upon the principle of individualization, in contrast, is intended to provide a real basis for "opening up the possibilities of the young and allowing them to flower to the fullest."

Therefore, as soon as we begin to rethink the aims of today's education from the point of view of the principle of individualization, it becomes clear that there are a number of vital tasks which we should be seriously thinking about how to accomplish, particularly through the institutions of the lower and upper secondary schools. These include the fostering of a shared national culture, while at the same time helping individual young people to choose the lives they want to live and, by ascertaining their own possibilities, to establish a firm and independent self-identity.

With these ends in mind it becomes necessary for us to rethink the contents of each subject area, to construct both an elective system and an advisory system that truly respects the values of individualism. Only by proceeding in this way can we hold out any hopes of fully realizing each individual student's right to develop while choosing to become the kind of person he or she wants to be.

Of course these ideals cannot be accomplished simply by reforming the schools. To the extent that this transformation is predicated upon a genuine equality of conditions, and given the reality of the working environment into which young people are cast after leaving school, unless there is a corresponding transformation of the principles of social organization and the consciousness of values, these ideas will degenerate into mere flights of educational utopianism. Thus, in order to appreciate how difficult these tasks really are, we need to ask ourselves how we can construct a logically consistent system that will enable us to surmount the dehumanizing division of labor that has taken over our society. In doing so we must also ask ourselves if socialism as it currently exists has really made any progress towards unraveling these problems and providing alternative structures.

The shift outlined above towards a society organized on the so-called principle of ability-first, and the excessive reliance upon academic pedigree that it has generated, have become markedly apparent in a number of countries. Similarly, as the school system has been made to function as a "rationalized" mechanism of social selection, the closely related problems of equality and diversity (or overall development and individualization) have become the focus of much attention in a growing number of societies. Thus, in addition to theoretically reconceptualizing the principle of equality of educational opportunity, it has become critically important to take into consideration the ways compulsory education also functions as an active system of social discrimination.

In Japan it has become amply clear that there are basic correspondences between differences in quality among upper secondary schools and the academic pedigrees and economic situations of those whose children graduate from them. The appearance of surveys showing the high income levels of the families who send their children to top-ranking national universities has also forced people to take another look at the claims made about the equality of opportunity that our schools are reputedly making possible. In all honesty, however, it should be noted that these problems are not unique to Japan and that efforts have been made throughout the world to generate educational reforms which grapple with the issues of equalization and individualization. These efforts have come to occupy a major place in contemporary educational thought.

The Langevin-Wallon Educational Reform Plan, which was prepared during the anti-Nazi struggle as a scheme for French education after liberation, is one example of this concern. The keystone of that plan was its emphasis on the *principle of justice* as the force required to uphold the spirit of reform. While aiming at the creation of a system in which the principles of *equality* and *diversity* could coexist, it presented a method for establishing a system for national enculturation *and* greater individualization.

The Langevin-Wallon Plan described the principle of justice as follows:

> All children have an equal right to be aided in the development of their characters to the greatest possible extent, regardless of their familial or racial background. They must not be placed under any limitations outside the natural limits of their own abilities. Accordingly, education should make the possibilities for human development available to all people equally, and it should open the paths to culture to all members of society. It must not select and set apart from the masses those blessed with talents and gifts, but should constantly endeavor to raise the cultural level of all the people, so as to make democratization more and more possible.

This plan is premised on an approach that views all kinds of work as having equal social value, and its merit lies in the attempt to present principles for guaranteeing the rights of all citizens to develop their abilities and aptitudes as fully as possible.

In regard to the problem of the relation between the creation of a national culture and the need for specialization, we find the following argument:

General cultural training should provide an initiation into all the various forms of human activity, not merely an opportunity to ascertain variations between the abilities of particular individuals; nor should it simply provide a way to impart information about an occupation to someone before he starts working so as to test and select him in relation thereto. More importantly, it should provide a way to generate and preserve the cohesiveness of social relations and, while encouraging all the members of society to understand the interests of others, help them to fairly evaluate the results of both their own actions and those of others, and help them become able to harmonize the total range of their own activities. . . . In distinction from general cultural training, which when properly organized brings people closer to one another and provides them with valuable opportunities for joining together, "employment"is something which in most cases sets them in opposition to one another. Thus a general culture should be conceived as the foundation for work-related specialization, and should be continually taught throughout the period of apprenticeship. . . . In a democratic state where all workers are also citizens, a widely based and deeply rooted general culture should liberate man from the narrow framework of technical labor.

And on the duties of the school:

The total organization of the school system should facilitate the establishment of personality and character, and must aid and spur on to the greatest possible extent those feelings which are conducive to the development of willfully spontaneous activities and efforts.

In this fashion Langevin and Wallon firmly insisted upon the necessity of an individualizing form of education. Between the ages of 11 and 15, they maintained, students should not only be taught about a broadly based general culture but should also be encouraged to develop the beginnings of a meaningful occupational orientation. Appropriate guidance should be provided concerning the actual conditions surrounding the various types of work available in society, and help should be offered so that the adolescent can honestly evaluate his or her own aptitudes, in preparation for the period from 15 to 18 when young people must choose the lives they want to pursue and develop their individuality through their own efforts.

The process of observation leading to a free and responsible choice of one's path through life was equated with the discovery of the "future citizen" and "future worker" in the present-day student population. For these purposes, it was insisted, "education must be based on objective research into adolescent psychology and adolescent individuality." This was closely connected to a proposal that schools should be staffed with trained psychologists.

The Langevin-Wallon plan was partially incorporated in France's 1959 Bertrand Law, and thus its spirit has become part of the reality of today's French education. It has become customary for French educational reformers to return to this plan as the most dependable source of educational authority. The ideas of "equality and diversity," which support the Langevin-Wallon plan, have helped to redefine the central problems facing us today, and for that reason alone this plan remains a pioneering attempt to clarify the most serious problems plaguing education in our modernized societies. It is still a source of great inspiration to those of us in Japan who are struggling to reform the conditions in which education is currently undertaken.

The Comprehensive School movement that is trying to reform middle-level education in England and the Gesamte-Schüle movement in Germany represent other attempts to grapple with the problems of "equality and diversity." The criticisms found in the 1974 Report of the Japan Teachers' Union Committee on Educational Reform[8] were similarly focused on the problem of "nationalism" and the ideology of "ability-first." This report advocated the "principle of justice" for dealing with these problems, and insisted upon "education in accordance with ability" as a response to the needs of the developing child. Here too we find the claim that the drives towards equalization and individualization should be the moving forces behind educational reform. The report attempted to define a program for reforming the entire educational apparatus from the nursery school to the organs of higher education, and can itself be viewed as a valuable treatise on the "principle of justice."

Nonetheless, it is certainly not easy to foster a shared national cul-

[8] *Nihon no kyōiku kaikaku o motomete* (Keisō Shobō, 1974), published in English in 1975 by the Japan Teachers' Union as *How to Reform Japan's Education.*

ture while at the same time providing an education that facilitates the flowering of the abilities of all students. In answer to the question "How should the contents of education be reformed?" the Japan Teachers' Union Committee for Investigating the Educational System proposed the introduction of a large-scale elective system (particularly for students who have entered upper secondary school) which would make the principle of individualization a reality. Unfortunately, however, this plan met with strong resistance from teachers, who argued that while the call for an individual elective system seemed reasonable at first glance, before students can make the appropriate choices they need more information, and this necessitates a wide range of required— as opposed to elective—subjects. This argument was supplemented with the opinion that since it is experience that arouses interest, the development of individuality must follow from a rigorous program of prescribed studies. As a result, stress on the importance of an elective system was deleted from the final report.

As this incident showed, the problems of establishing a balance between the drives towards equalization and towards diversification, and between the ideas of a shared culture and of individualization, are important and troubling ones, beset with inner contradictions and antagonisms.

The difficulties embedded in any attempt to balance these conflicting demands is attested to by the fact that even the socialist countries, which should theoretically be in a better position to deal with them, have not been able to make much headway towards their resolution. A careful consideration of the failure of the massive social experiment known as the Chinese Cultural Revolution more than amply testifies to this.

In his thoughtful work *The Diploma Disease*, R. P. Dore, who also held great expectations for the Cultural Revolution, exudes a very pessimistic tone regarding the possibility of resolving these difficulties:

The sad fact is that the claims of equality, of individual dignity, are not easily reconciled with the increasing need—as society becomes more technologically complex, or begins a late-twentieth-century development drive as in the Third World—to take account of that diversity in deciding who does what. . . . [A]bilities vary across a spectrum with most of us clustered around the average. And so the tension between equality and diversity becomes increasingly apparent. [*The Diploma Disease: Education, Certification, and Unemployment*, University of California Press, 1976, pp. 197–98]

V. Towards a Reformation of Our Value Consciousness

However difficult it may be, we must begin to come to terms with these painful problems. In order to do so, we must affirm the following points.

Today's advocates of egalitarianism are not claiming that human abilities are all the same. In other words, by now it should go without saying that the principle of individualization is not synonymous with equality of ability. The "principle of equality of ability" is a false one that the opponents of egalitarianism have maliciously invented in order to distort and denigrate reformist aspirations because they cannot criticize them fairly and objectively.

Even if we should successfully reform our society to the extent that everyone has an equal opportunity to realize his or her capacity to the fullest possible extent, it is only natural that there will be disparities in the ways the abilities of individuals will be expressed and recognized. Therefore, it is most desirable that the fundamental principle underlying the reform of education be rooted in a recognition of the variety of developmental needs of different individuals. Thus we are not aiming to institutionalize an arrangement in which only outstanding people receive a rich and abundant education, while stragglers are given an education in kind. The latter is the very essence of "throwaway education,"[9] which takes the existence of stragglers for granted and seeks to do nothing for them. However, as I believe we have made clear, this should definitely not be the aim of a standardized and thoroughly uniform style of education.

We certainly do not look forward to a society where the people who are indeed blessed with special talents are not able to demonstrate them, but neither do we want a society in which those less well intellectually endowed are simply and brutally cast aside. The problem we must overcome, then, is how to realize all these individual abilities and put them to use for the general good of society. This comes down to the question of how society and its various types of people conceive of themselves. To reform present-day society, where the overwhelming emphasis is placed on self-interest, we have to get away from a system where the abilities of each person are mobilized strictly for his or her own individual advantage, and move towards the creation of a system in which priority will be given to the social meaning and value of the

---

[9] The expression "throwaway education" (*kirisute kyōiku*) refers to the attitude that legitimates the behavior of teachers who ignore or disparage students who do not earn high grades, as if they were not worthy of serious pedagogic attention.

individual's labor. The difference in fundamental attitude between these two life-style approaches is great and demands our further consideration.

The growth and development of the value orientations of our youth are from an early age closely related to the organization of our system of school education (see Chapter 1). Locked into a framework which encourages them from an early age to view each other as rivals, and which places the highest value on the capacity to outwit those rivals and thereby triumph over them in the intense examination competition that is central to our dehumanizing system of social selection, is it any wonder that our children are growing up with a distorted sense of values? Therefore a fundamental reform of our educational system must be seen as lying at the heart of the transformation of social values and consciousness which we desire. Unless and until this transformation is effected, there is little reason to look forward to any meaningful changes in the value consciousness of Japanese youth.

Wouldn't it be better for our society in the long run if our children, right from the beginning of their socialization in primary school and continuing on through their experiences of higher education, were able to engage in a wider range of socially meaningful activities, sharing both the joys and sorrows of learning with their classmates? Wouldn't it be more advantageous to the solidarity of our society if education nourished the values of kindness and cooperation rather than those of vicious competition and if our children were encouraged to adopt a helpful attitude towards those who are weaker or disabled for whatever reason? And is this not as desirable for Japanese international relations as it is for our domestic ones? In short, we must transform our educational system so that the values of human respect and freedom are instilled in our youth.

It is dangerous to believe that the problems plaguing Japanese society and education today can be remedied simply by reforming the existing university entrance examination system and the way it has made the school into a mechanism for competition and selection, without transforming the values that underlie this system. If we rearrange our perspective so that the focus is shifted to the adolescent's right to choose the life he or she wants to live, then we can begin to replace the existing system, which separates youth at the age of 15 through the entrance examination and which exerts destructive influence on the rest of our lives, with an educational system which will work to bring people together. Only then will we be in a position to provide our youth with an education that is worthy of the name.

The central tasks of education will then become the formation of a human value consciousness. Of course this work cannot be accomplished by education alone, but without an education that aims at these goals, this important work cannot even be spoken of with any serious hope of realization.

In order for there to be justice in the social world, we must work to realize a humanism predicated on both equalization and individualization. If there is to be a future for humanity, it must be sought in the "naturalization of man and the humanization of nature." We will have to turn our backs on the age in which social inequality is rationalized by appeals to an ideology of natural inequality. Thus we will have to make new efforts to promote the values of social equality if we are to reduce the destructive influence of natural inequalities. This means creating a society that treats all of its members as equally important, and one which seeks to make the diversity and individuality founded on natural differences the grounds for the fullest flowering of the riches inherited by all the bearers of human cultures. It is only then that the dream of a real harmony between freedom and equality, the age-old ideal of a complete human development, can be truly revived.

13 The Ideology of Ability-First and the Distortion of Meritocracy

I. Introduction

In a widely reported incident during the summer vacation of 1976, a student from a prestigious high school in Yamagata Prefecture stabbed to death a friend whom he feared as an academic rival. This abhorrent affair came as no surprise to many of us in the educational world, who had long feared that something like it would eventually happen. What made this incident particularly upsetting, however, was the fact that the deranged adolescent came from a home in which both parents were teachers. It was most distressing to consider how these parents' personal sacrifices to enable their son to advance to the University of Tokyo were rewarded by his actual behavior.

We can see in such incidents much more than the suffering of the afflicted families, for what we are really confronted with are the conditions that are driving young people into neurosis, homicide, and ever-increasing numbers of suicides. What is the primary factor in Japanese social life that is producing these conditions? High school and university entrance examinations that threaten to take over the entirety of adolescence, as examination results become the basis for determining just what our children's futures will be.

Shortly after the Yamagata incident occurred, the *Asahi Shimbun* ran an editorial entitled "Exam Preparation as a Symptom of Our National Decay," which called attention to the "polarization of teenagers" by the monstrous wedge known as the entrance examination system. The editorial described, at one end of the spectrum, the *moyashikko* (grinds; literally "beansprout kids") who never read anything but reference materials for exam preparation and, at the other end, the *bōsōzoku*, young toughs who have been driven from the classroom and loiter about on the streets. Both types, the editorial writer pointed out, were growing up without learning how to think as responsible adults:

> If things continue on their present course there will be no way to rescue our young people from the spiritual desolation they are being driven into. These absurdly idiotic conditions simply

must not be allowed to go on. There must be a major change in our basic ways of thinking about education.

Schooling in Japan today has fallen under the domination of a logic which makes it possible to select human beings on the basis of examinations and the measurement of standard deviation. In this anti-educational environment it is becoming increasingly difficult to provide our youth with a meaningful form of education. Education, an activity whose original meaning lies in the cultivation and nourishment of the full range of possibilities inherently available to human beings, has thus, ironically, been transformed into a tool for greatly reducing the range and scope of those possibilities.

That the above-mentioned incident was neither accidental nor exceptional can be understood from the reaction of my students in the Liberal Arts Department at the University of Tokyo. Looking back at their own sense of shock when hearing of this incident and reflecting upon the examination-taking stage of life in Japan, which they themselves had only recently passed through successfully, these students spoke of the spiritual emptiness and inner poverty of those years.

Even though the majority of our high school students have serious doubts about the educational value of the competition which compels them to view success as something which must be sought at the expense of their friends, their sensitivities are gradually worn down as they learn how to tolerate such a life, as they become inured to these conditions.

Today's educational environment is plagued by a large number of serious problems. The most prominent of these are associated with the anxieties that well up in February and March each year during the entrance examination season. While on the one hand the mass media criticize the overheated conditions surrounding exam competition (as in the previously cited *Asahi* editorial), at the same time they repeatedly throw more oil on these fires with sensational coverage of the nation's "examination fever" simply in order to sell more copies. The very serious problems of *ochikobore*—students who fall behind in their attempts to keep up with the fast pace of exam preparation—and of delinquency, suicide, and homicide are continually being compounded by the workings of a school system that has been given over to competition and the heartless sorting of young human beings.

Nobody in Japan today professes to be pleased with this state of affairs. But when it comes to analyzing the underlying causes, and generating policies designed to counteract it, the political and ideological differences found in Japanese society in general reappear in a highly exaggerated form. While there is common agreement that something must be done to remedy these patently unacceptable conditions, the profound divergences in the way these problems are viewed only serve to exacerbate the basic situation. Therefore it must be recognized that the fundamental problems associated with the ideological construction of ability in our society are closely related to the existence of these complicating factors.

From my perspective, the main cause of the disease devastating the schools of Japan today is the dominant influence exerted upon the practice and pursuit of education by the representations of ability formulated and sponsored by the government in cooperation with industry. Of course there are also those who want to argue that the only true solution to our educational problems lies with an even more thoroughgoing reorganization of educational life in accordance with the policies which the government has formulated on the basis of its ideology of ability. But, as I will attempt to show here, pursuit of this way of thinking will only serve to intensify our educational crisis.

The flexibility of our young people's minds is gradually being undermined by the dehumanizing reality of examination competition. This competition did not originate in the recent past: even in the prewar period there were people decrying the so-called examination hell. Nonetheless, since the objectives of postwar reconstruction were realized in the mid-1960s, the importance of examination competition has become more pronounced, especially as part of the government-initiated policies designed to produce rapid economic growth. In this context the government-manufactured theories of ability must be understood as having played a major role in the ongoing reorganization of Japanese social and educational life.

It is the goal of this essay to explore a number of the major problems implicitly related to the way the notion of ability has been ideologically constructed within the framework of contemporary Japanese education. Proceeding from a discussion of the history of "ability" as a political construct in the modern world, I will then turn to an analysis of the formulations of ability ruling educational life in Japan since the 1960s.

II. Historical Vicissitudes of the Principle of Ability in the Modern World

The "principle of ability" first appeared on the stage of modern world history as a manifestation of the spirit that rejected the validity of social formations based solely on preexisting special privileges. This principle was forcefully enunciated, for example, in Article 6 of the French Declaration of the Rights of Man and the Citizen, which stipulates that all are equal before the law:

> All citizens, being equal in its eyes, are equally eligible to all public dignitaries, places, and employments, according to their capacities, and without other distinction than that of their virtues and their talents.

Similarly, we find in Article 5 of the Constitution of 1793:

> All citizens are equally able to take up a public office. A free citizenry will in choosing its public officials show no preferences beside moral character and talent.

Thus we can see that right from the beginning of the modern era the values of "ability" and "talent" played important roles in the attack upon status-oriented social systems which were based on the privileges of blood and lineage. However, as the development of capitalism substituted the principle of property for the principle of pedigree, ability gradually came to be subordinated to property. Thus, for example, in many cases even those who had natural ability were, because of their economic indigence and lack of educational opportunities, unable to fully develop their abilities. And even those who were able to develop their capacities in spite of adverse circumstances were only rarely given proper social respect and esteem.

At the end of the nineteenth century the principle of ability was pushed to the fore once again both in response to movements for the democratization of society and in response to the necessity of state unification. At this juncture the classic harmony between liberty and equality was destroyed. Equality was subordinated to liberty, and thereby reduced to the principle of equality of opportunity. It was functionally transformed, in short, into a principle of social selection in the guise of freedom of competition and uniformity of opportunity.[1]

The principles of ability and achievement played important roles in sustaining this conversion, having been reassigned to positions within the discourse on social control as constitutive elements of competition and selection. These principles then came to have major im-

---

[1] See Horio, *Gendai Kyōiku no Shisō to Kōzō* (Iwanami Shoten, 1971), for a fuller discussion of this transformation.

portance as principles of social organization and human evaluation.

From this time on, the principle of ability was divorced from its original context as a basis for abolishing all forms of discrimination apart from ability, and was transformed into *the* principle of modern discrimination. The unequal distribution of wealth and social esteem was thereby ideologically legitimized as a natural consequence of differences always explained in terms of "natural" ability.

The English sociologist Michael Young has brilliantly explored these transformations in his book *The Rise of Meritocracy, 1870–2033* (London, Thames and Hudson, 1958). He has identified the decade of the 1870s in England as a pivotal point in the course of this transformation, because it was at that time that ability and achievement came to have clearly recognized meaning as the dominant principles of social organization. Young predicted that this principle would become acutely problematic in the latter half of the twentieth century and that during the following century merit would increasingly come to be the organizing and controlling principle of advanced social formations. In this imaginary foretelling of the future, Young portrays a world in which there will be two classes of people: those having the abilities officially recognized as being worthy of meritorious social esteem, and those without them. This class division would become especially pronounced as those having ability would marry and produce children only with others of ability while the have-nots would also continue to reproduce themselves.

One cannot overemphasize the importance of the transformation of the principle of ability into the problem of meritocracy, which since the end of the nineteenth century has been the ruling principle of modern social life. It is also necessary to be mindful of the danger of viewing this problem as somehow unique to Japan and the pathological phenomena associated with the policies designed to produce rapid economic growth during the 1960s and 1970s.

In his discussion of the historical vicissitudes of the principles of success and achievement in *Man and Society in an Age of Reconstruction*, Karl Mannheim observed that the transition from the principle of blood in traditional societies to the principle of property in modern capitalist formations is constantly being supplanted by the transition to the principle of achievement operating in the democratically organized societies of today.

Young gives two reasons why this transformation was significantly accelerated during the 1870s. The first was the popularization of compulsory education in England. The other was the institution of a system of public examinations as the basis for recruitment into the civil service, a move which signaled the repudiation of family background and other personal connections as the principle of social advancement. According to Young, equality of educational opportunity and the systematization of competitive recruitment of civil servants are the two takeoff points for the transformation to a social organization rooted in the logic of meritocracy.

In England during the 1870s, middle-level education was repositioned as an essential step in the ladder that now led from primary to secondary education. In fact, the modern idea of secondary education only became conceivable because this ladder had been erected in the first place. Historically speaking, middle-level education had very different origins, and served very different purposes, from those served by the new system designed to make more than the rudimentary forms of education available to the masses. The traditional concept of middle-level education was as a form of preparatory training for an elite class who by virtue of their birth and social standing had been pre-selected to inherit the primary positions of leadership in society. Passing through the privileged world of middle-level education, these individuals then advanced to the universities, where they acquired further refinement. However, through the reforms of middle-level education which were initiated at the end of the nineteenth century and which continue in the present day, efforts have been made to make a more unified and comprehensive form of education available to all segments of society.

It was at this same time that England became deeply embroiled in overseas competition and in imperialistic struggles over the partitioning of colonies. Accordingly national unification became increasingly necessary in order for Britain to pursue its colonialist ambitions. The combination of these internal and external political demands created conditions that were highly favorable to the spread of competition and meritocracy.

Social Darwinism, as the ideology most suited to these perceived imperatives of time, exerted an overwhelming influence over social life and thought. Arguments that the "law of the jungle" and the "survival of the fittest" were both natural and social principles contributed to the growth of social and intellectual conditions which were conducive to the institutionalization of a meritocracy.

This tendency was, of course, not limited to English life, and it can well be thought of as reflecting the drift of affairs in European societies in general. In France, for example, ideas about merit came to have great significance at this time as the foundation for new principles of social organization. This was manifested in particular in the cutthroat competition to enter the *grandes écoles* and the extremely rigorous preparation that it necessitated.[2] As a consequence of this super-heated competition, adolescent suicides became a pressing social problem. Durkheim's interest in the phenomenon, and his attempt to formulate a theory of anomie, emerged from this social background.

In his book *Elite against Democracy* Walter Struve examined Germany in the period from 1880 to 1933 in order to explore the antagonistic relations between elitism and democracy in the years before the Nazis came to power. Although Struve began his research believing that the problems of elitism and racism were special characteristics of Nazi Germany, he was led to conclude that this was simply not the case. In the preface to this book Struve argued that the elitism and racism usually associated with the Nazi movement were in fact a reflection of a spirit commonly seen throughout all of Europe. In a similar vein, I believe elitism today poses a danger which threatens to unhinge all of the contemporary meritocracies in Europe.

Nor is the United States immune from these problems. While it is true that from the perspective of nineteenth-century Europe America appeared as the world's most democratically progressive state, its democratization was still riddled with unresolved difficulties: the vaunted equality was often little more than a formalistic equality of opportunity, and the principle of meritocracy was used to provide a cover for the preservation of elitist privileges which were not seriously challenged until the middle of the twentieth century.

It is true that in the United States the idea of meritocracy gained respectability earlier than in Europe as the cardinal principle of social life. To the extent that American society was unencumbered by traditional notions of status and pedigree, the principle of ability was able to appear earlier and be accepted more fully than was the case elsewhere. Indeed America was the first society to organize itself as a meritocracy. Young, in fact, has called America the progenitor of modern meritocracy.

The principle of meritocracy which has underwritten the development of modern educational life has been seriously challenged by the continued presence of elites whose powers are legitimated by ideologically dominated constructions of ability. In this sense it is critically important for all social formations that pride themselves on being democratically rationalized to resolve the contradictions spawned by the incomplete realization of the principles of meritocracy. But it must be pointed out

---

[2] The *grandes écoles* were specialized schools within the French university system that educated the elite group of students who would enter government service at the higher levels.

that even if the problems highlighted here are based on an analysis of the conditions found in the most advanced capitalist societies of the West, the socialist societies I am familiar with have not fared much better in their attempts to resolve these vexing difficulties. The Soviet system, for example, is equally riddled with the problems spawned by an elitist system of education, and those students who aspire to the most privileged positions in society spend as much time in cramming academies as do their counterparts in Japan. Thus it is clear that even if they have made more progress than their capitalist antagonists in realizing the spirit of meritocracy, the nations which proclaim themselves committed to the values of socialism still have a long way to go before they can legitimately offer themselves as models of a fully realized meritocratic society.

Therefore, I want to argue, the problem of meritocracy, or what I want to call the problem of the ideological construction of ability, must be recognized and attacked head-on as one of the most pressing problems confronting educational thought and practice in the contemporary world. Moreover, it must be seen as a problem whose ramifications extend beyond the walls of our schools, a problem which in fact calls into question the principles of social organization and the bases upon which human beings are evaluated. Resolution of these issues has profound implications for the future well-being of man and the fairness of our social lives.

III. The Ideological Construction of Ability in Japan

By the time the national educational system was inaugurated in the early 1870s, Japanese values had already fallen under the sway of those constructions of ability and meritocracy which I characterized above as the dominant ones in the leading capitalist societies of the modern West.

From the very beginning of this process strong control was exercised by the State. Through its declaration of the equality of the four classes previously established under Tokugawa feudalism,[3] and through its efforts to equalize the opportunities available to the members of society, the new Meiji State attempted to open the pathways to success and distinction in the world to all those publicly recognized as having ability. But since those who had seized State power in the Meiji Restoration were inclined to favor those who came from the same domains

---

[3] The four classes were, in decreasing order of prestige, warriors (*samurai*), farmers, artisans, and merchants.

and clans which they themselves came from, it was only natural that those pathways were more open to some than they were to others. Historically speaking, both the Japanese State and its modern educational system were steeped in these origins.

Equality of educational opportunity and its promised benefits do not become a reality simply through the rhetorical power of arguments about their desirability. The contestation in Japan over the powers to define the meaning of ability and its appropriate place in social life has evolved into a conflict between those who support and those who challenge the claim that the State has a privileged right to determine exactly what constitutes ability. The position of the former group was given its first systematic expression in the educational administration of Mori Arinori (see Chapter 2). Challenges to the hegemony of the State were first voiced in the 1870s and again in the 1920s during the period of "Taishō Democracy"—but essentially remained unorganized until the establishment of the People's Education Movement in the postwar environment. As a consequence of these struggles, the ideological formulation of ability has been continuously reworked and readapted; if there is anything unique about the ideological forms within which ability has been encased in Japan, it is by virtue of the oddities of this struggle rather than on account of some peculiarity of the Japanese people's national character.

Thus we should not attempt to comprehend these problems as uniquely Japanese or as the result of a spiritual pollution caused by contact with the West and its ideologies. Our problem rather is how to make sense of the realities engendered by the distorted development of meritocracy within our society. Men and women in modern societies have suffered under the weight of this problem for the past one hundred years and will most likely continue to do so well into the next century. That we have been slow in coming to terms with the true nature of the problem only accentuates the need for greater thought and research undertaken to discover ways to overcome it.

The problem of ability and meritocracy in Japan is directly tied to the abuses caused by the State's long control over education. We can take pride in saying that the development of the People's Education Movement has led to the articulation of a much deeper theoretical understanding of the citizenry's educational rights. Indeed, we have begun to perceive the directions in which we must proceed, but as yet I do not believe that anyone can declare with total confidence that the problems associated with the ideological formulation of ability in our country can be readily resolved simply by "doing such and such." This underlines the urgent need for more intensive forms of cooperative research.

It has been said that diligence and the desire to achieve are particularly strong in the Japanese people. This viewpoint has been advanced for example in the work of the American cultural anthropologist George De Vos. In his *Socialization for Achievement* (University of California Press, 1973) De Vos compares Japanese-Americans with other groups in the U.S. and observes that the strength of their desire to achieve is particularly evident in the enthusiastic zeal they bring to school education.

If, however, one is going to speak of the uniquely Japanese dimensions of the struggle to succeed, careful attention must be paid to the conditions under which this struggle is allowed to proceed. In other words, one must address the ways participation in this severe competition is premised on the forms of control the State exerts through its unification and standardization of education.

Ishida Takeshi argues in his *Nihon no Seiji Bunka* (*Japan's Political Culture*) (University of Tokyo Press, 1970) that the distinguishing characteristic of Japanese political culture resides in what he has called "synchronized competition" (*dōchōteki kyōsō*). I believe it can be said that the problems involved here are equally observable in other provinces of Japanese social life. Thus, if the values publicly recognized in Japanese society were to become truly pluralistic, the power of competition would disintegrate within a diversity of values and its controlling effects would be mitigated.

The axis of moral judgment in prewar Japan was provided by the Emperor system, under which distance from the Emperor determined the standard of all moral evaluations. Although this criterion of value was changed after the war, firmly established internal values have yet to take root, so our nation's evaluative scales continue to be imposed on the People from the outside. It is on the base provided by these imposed scales that the State continues to control social competition in postwar Japan.

Present-day educational policymakers frequently speak of diversification, but the underlying reality of this diversity is a standardized and unified measure of values. In the simplest of terms this means that, for example, there is only one scale for evaluating universities, and the model for this is the University of Tokyo, the most prestigious among Japan's universities. What is passed off as "diversification" is really nothing more than the ranking of other institutions relative to the fixed and unchallengeable position of top-ranked "Todai." This certainly does not even faintly resemble true diversification, in which each university would have its own individual character and be organized to cultivate the individuality of each of its students.

This most pressing educational problem in Japan today has emerged from the forced yoking together of an ideology legitimating standardization with a policy designed to promote a superficial "diversification." The challenge we face lies in the tasks of equalizing, to as great an extent as possible, the conditions under which education is conducted. We must work to organize our schools and universities as institutions that can offer their own individualized types of education. If our ideals are not brought to bear upon the concrete resolution of these problems, then they are of little value either to us or to the country as a whole. This standardization—what Ishida called "synchronized competition"—means that Japan's social climate has once again become dominated by extreme conformism. Herein we find one of the identifying marks of the aggravated competition that has virtually taken over Japanese education.

Ishida also discusses the ways in which the Japanese wage system has been adapted to the unusual conditions surrounding competition in this country. In particular, he has observed how the so-called piecework payment system has limited competition within strictly controlled boundaries. Of course piecework is also found in Europe, but what is unique to the Japanese case is the priority given to the ranking of workers' production rather than a simple and straightforward concern with the amount of work they turn out. In other words, the worker's wages are set according to the ranking he or she receives relative to the other workers. The rate of pay given for piecework is made the object of the worker's competitive drives. This system was adopted, for example, in prewar textile factories in order to spur on the productivity of the women who operated the textile factory machinery. The problematic nature of the organization of Japanese competition is seen in the control exerted through strict adherence to a ranked ordering of competitors.

The postwar reforms of Japanese education were clearly intended to break the dehumanizing stranglehold of the Imperial system, and to liberate the determination of human values from the monopoly which the State had officially created for itself. They were designed, in other words, to establish individuality as the central principle of Japanese social life. In this sense the postwar reform of education implied a promise that the principles ruling the definition of ability would be quite different from those which had reigned in the prewar environment. This promise was premised on a diversification of values and led to a legitimation of the principle of individuality. In that sense ability was thought of quite differently from today's standardized normative consciousness and the economic agenda it is premised on.

We see in today's world of educational law a considerable struggle over how to interpret the phrases found in Article 26 of the Constitution and Article III of the Fundamental Law of Education concerning the People's right to receive an education "equally" and "according to their ability." Those who support the officially sponsored ideology of ability make a great deal out of the words "according to their ability" as they press their arguments for "diversification." This is, however, as far as they go in acknowledging the spirit of the Constitution and the Fundamental Law of Education; on other occasions these same individuals call for altering both of these legal cornerstones.

At the time these laws were enacted there were individuals like State ministers Kanamori Tokujirō and Ashida Hitoshi, whose public pronouncements were not unlike the ideological declarations of those who today support the officially sponsored formulation of the expression "according to their ability." However, there were also people, such as Kido Bantarō and Mutai Risaku, who pointedly insisted that enunciation of the principle of ability meant recognition of the importance of individuality. In fact, the general trend of the postwar reform period was such that the expression "according to their ability" was originally understood as an expression of the principle of individuality, not as a justification for differentiation. Kawamoto Unosuke, for example, understood the expression "according to their ability" as meaning "according to their developmental needs." This interpretation is very close to the position advocated today by our Education Movement.

Historically speaking, the problem of interpreting the meaning of "an education according to ability" as provided for by the Constitution and the Fundamental Law of Education is directly tied to the problems posed by the existence of modern concepts of success that are not constrained by the privileges of status or family background. At the same time that this bespoke a commitment to the principle of individuality, it contained, right from the outset, the danger of permitting a construction that would legitimate discrimination on the basis of ability. Since we cannot very well relinquish these phrases, it is particularly important for us to work to gain acceptance for a reading of their meaning as "according to the needs of their development."

If there comes a time in the future when the Fundamental Law of Education is revised and its meaning deepened, I believe we will be compelled to choose more appropriate expressions for dealing with these problems. At that time we will be required to examine much more closely the issues involved in attempting to provide an education in response to the developmental needs of the students. To the extent, however, that we can speak of the postwar educational reforms as the institutionalization of a pluralistic *Weltanschauung*, it should become clear that these reforms resulted from a conscious choice to reproduce a normative basis for social organization different from that which characterized life in Japan prior to August 15, 1945. As we behold the severe and sometimes violent competition regulated by the unified set of values which finds its center in the desire to be admitted to the University of Tokyo, we cannot help but be aware of the regressive realities of postwar education.

The emergence of today's ruling ideology of ability on the center stage of social and educational life was closely connected to government and industry policies designed to encourage rapid economic growth. Although it can well be argued that definitions of "ability" had always been rigorously controlled through the ideological formulations promulgated by the prewar State apparatus, the problems posed by the present-day configurations had yet to fully surface as a threat to the integrity of education as a unified whole.

I believe we must go back to the 1963 Report of the Economic Deliberation Council for the first public declaration of what was then clearly proclaimed "the imperative to reorganize both society and education on the basis of a new formulation of ability":

> In order to resolve the problem of securing the talents and capacities required to successfully realize the aims of high economic growth, educational planning must be firmly subordinated to these objectives.

The Central Council on Education acted on this imperative and began to articulate a thoroughgoing agenda designed to reorganize the Japanese educational system in its totality. If we ask why competition became so extreme in the 1960s, we must surely recognize its roots in the Central Council's repeated interventions.

As Japan entered the 1970s, the moral bankruptcy of the policies designed to produce economic growth was becoming widely recognized. Nonetheless official educational policy remained firmly committed to this course of reorganization. Both in the declarations of those responsible for formulating educational policy and in the reportage of their journalist supporters we find a firm commitment to the proposition that the standardization crippling Japanese education is a by-product of "egalitarianism" and that the ideology of ability-first will provide the necessary solutions to these problems.

Thus in its 1975 "Proposals for the Reorganization of High Schools" the Education and Culture Committee of the ruling Liberal Democratic Party strongly advocated the reorganization of education according to the government's ideology of ability:

> The principle of competition is the principle of human existence. In its absence progress is inconceivable. Societies that fail to adopt constructions of ability in accord with these truths are doomed to stagnate and perish.

As for the root causes of the by this time already overheated "examination hell," the party position paper declared:

> The abnormality of these conditions does not reside in the examination system itself. Without carefully thinking about their own abilities and capacities it appears that anybody and everybody devotes pointless energy to taking the entrance examinations for universities. It is this that is abnormal.

For the advocates of this educational reorganization "ability" is grasped as something genetically determined. Thus we find LDP ideologues such as Arita Kazuhisa fortifying their arguments through reliance on the theories of psychologists Arthur R. Jensen and Richard J. Herrnstein, who maintain that up to 80 percent of an individual's capacities and talents are genetically preordained.[4] Ruling party spokesmen like Arita incessantly repeat their attacks on a more humane approach to "ability development" through reference to the supposedly scientific incontrovertibility of the work of discredited ideologues like Jensen and Herrnstein. If nothing else, this acceptance of what is in fact controversial research work underlines the importance of dedicating our efforts to produce a more penetrating understanding of what might be termed "the science of human development."

Conditions in Japan would be bad enough if this way of thinking were limited to members of the ruling Liberal Democratic Party, the bureaucracy, and industrial planners, but when it is embraced even by classroom teachers, things have indeed become frightening! In his

---

[4] Arthur R. Jensen, "How Much Can We Boost IQ and Scholastic Achievement?" *Harvard Educational Review*, Vol. 39, No. 2 (1969); Richard J. Herrnstein, *IQ in the Meritocracy*, 1971.

book *Our Schools Are Dead!* Kawakami Gentarō has criticized the genuine advances in postwar education from the standpoint of the official ideology of ability. A teacher who was deeply moved by Kawakami's work sent him a letter, which Kawakami proudly quoted in the August 1974 issue of the journal *Seiron*:

> Conditions in present-day Japan are replete with all kinds of foolish absurdities, the most ridiculous of which is the constant insistence upon "rights." What is stupid must be identified as such. However, few, if any, of our people realize the extent of their foolishness. Therefore, in our schools the instructor should at least be able to say to such a student [who is claiming to have "rights"]: "You are an asinine idiot!" Since the parents of such fools tend to be the same way themselves, it is impossible to expect them to correct their children. When students who are incompetent are forced to recognize this, they will give up their vain desire to participate in the severe examination competition found in our society, accept their limitations, and give up their unrealistic aspirations. This problem is complicated, however, by the fact that even within the ranks of our teachers there are too many foolish individuals who are intimidated by students. We can no longer stand idly by and allow this absurdity to continue.

Kawakami proclaimed, "As long as such teachers as the letter-writer are still to be found in Japan's schools, these institutions are not yet completely dead."

In accordance with this way of thinking, those who are officially judged as possessing ability are awarded a richer and more substantial form of education, while those who are not recognized as possessing the requisite abilities receive a less rewarding and much more impoverished education. This discriminatory treatment is justified on the grounds of genetic endowment.

The advocates of this ideology argue that even if less gifted students were allowed to attend better schools, it is pure fantasy to believe that their abilities and talents would thereby be increased. According to this ideologically charged representation of ability, competition has gotten out of hand and produced the vexing conditions of "examination hell" only because so many parents are pushing their children to participate in the race to advancement through admission to good schools.

In contrast with this way of thinking, the members of our Education Movement have found it more educationally meaningful to interpret the concept "according to their ability" in terms of the principle "according to their developmental needs." By making this our highest educational principle, we have tried to show respect for each student's individual abilities and have worked to enrich the educational experience of all children by directing our efforts to their particular talents. It has become quite natural for us to think that "in response to their developmental needs" is the proper theoretical conceptualization of "in response to their abilities," at least when considered from an educational perspective.

Inasmuch as we firmly believe in the possibilities that children are born with, our approach to the problem of recognizing and responding to ability is very different from that advocated by the ideologues of the State. Our movement has prospered in fact precisely because we have taken the trouble to ask ourselves how we can most fully contribute to the development of all the children we come into contact with as teachers. In the midst of all the pressures exerted upon us to conform with the officially formulated ideological formulation of ability, we should take pride in the success of our arguments as reflected in the decision handed down by Justice Sugimoto (see Chapter 6). The judicial recognition of our claims that education must be autonomously organized and that it is the teacher's responsibility to develop the child's potential will undoubtedly stand as a source of inspiration and a position from which to advance our cause for many years to come.

If we limit our activities merely to criticizing the official ideology of ability-first, and make no significant efforts towards replacing it with a new and more humane approach to the problems of human development, then it must be said that in the last analysis we are no better than those we criticize. We cannot rest content, in other words, simply because we have voiced such criticisms; our real task is to invent a new form of pedagogic practice. For this we need fewer government bureaucrats with statute-making power and more educators equipped with scientifically developed practices. Thus, if we are going to free education from the dead weight which the State imposes upon it and create the conditions wherein it can be returned to popular control, then we must begin to formulate answers to questions such as the following.

What are the possibilities waiting to be awakened in a child? How can they be discovered, nourished, and developed? What should be the roles of parents and teachers? What should the relations between children's groups and the broader social environment be like? Questions like these must be addressed on the basis of autonomous educational research and the free inquiries of our teachers. If, however, "ability" is grasped as something fixed by heredity, then the work of "scientific" inquiry is reduced to ranking and measuring predetermined amounts of arbitrarily chosen competencies. When conceived in this manner, the testing and evaluation of children, rather than contributing to their development, strangles their potential to grow and develop humanely. And as testing is tied to ever-increasing amounts of homework, education becomes more and more odious and oppressive to our youth.

In recent years we have seen our educational system being manipulated and transformed into a mechanism for officially separating children into "those who can" and "those who can't." The standards on the basis of which this selection is made have been set in accord with the labor power requirements enunciated by industry, and the social requirements formulated in light of the interests of the State. The members of our Education Movement have taken upon themselves the responsibility to resist these encroachments upon the freedoms which should be guaranteed to the citizens of a democratic nation.

An examination of the history of education in Japan makes it possible to distinguish two clearly conflicting types of educational thought. On one side education has been grasped as a process of "socialization" designed to internalize a preestablished set of social values. In this framework education has been thought of as a duty the members of society must fulfill towards the State. The other approach sees the role of education as that of enhancing the child's potential to unfold and grow. Here education is understood as being intrinsically related to the individual's right to live and freely develop. In the former the social function of education is seen as reproducing an already existing sociopolitical and economic order and the constellation of values it represents. It is basically conservative and seeks to use the educational system as a way of maintaining the status quo. In the latter the social function of education is perceived in relation to the rights of a new generation which will carry our society into the future. This viewpoint is progressive; it wishes to make the educational system an important instrument for the reform of Japanese social and cultural values.

In the government and financial circles that are remaking education into what is referred to as a "system of ability development" there is cynical talk of a "transformed society." But the banners that proclaim "calls from the future" are in fact ingeniously disguised calls that reverberate with the echoes of Japan's unfortunate past.

It must be recognized that this attempt to control education does not have the development of the child as its objective; rather, its goal is to subvert education to the social demands of the State and the manpower requirements of business and industry. In attempting to realize the objectives of "ability development" in response to the requirements of industry, governmental policies have sought to gain entrance to the inner reaches of the Japanese people's lives and to utilize all human values as sources of labor power. Thus we must not lose sight of the fact that the government's proclamation of support for the "total flowering" of ability is strictly limited to only those abilities it has already preselected as appropriate for and required by our society. This is part and parcel of the process by which the logic of monopoly capital has penetrated into and exerted its domination over all facets of Japanese social life.

In recent years "ability" has been given a privileged position in the government's policies for high economic growth and manpower development as the central link between economics and education. Within the purview of the government-sponsored discourse, the concept of ability has been formulated in close conformity with industry's stated demands for labor power and has become the focal point of all officially proclaimed educational policies. The "Image of the Desired Japanese" that has emerged from the cozy alliance between government and business is really an image of the desired attitudes of citizens as workers and members of State society. As this State-manufactured ideology has been introduced into every phase of educational life, it has struck a powerful blow against the integrity of our educational system. The true agenda of the Central Council on Education (Chūō Kyōiku Shingikai)[5] was to make the schools serve as the locus for the classifying and sorting out of young human beings.

Beginning in Toyama and Kagawa prefectures and spreading through the entire country, "guiding efforts" were made to establish the government's new "system of ability development." Of course these activities were undertaken in strict conformity with the State's officially approved constructions of competency and aptitude. Stretching from "early childhood development" through "lifelong education," and hand in hand with a restructuring of testing and other evaluative practices, the government has introduced a variety of "educational tools" to regulate and control the lives of our citizens.

Education officials have also been motivated by their desire to suppress the autonomous educational movement that we have been struggling to establish. We have worked to grapple with the problem of ability from the perspective of "*human* development and education" as opposed

[5] The Council issued the report entitled "The Image of the Desired Japanese" in 1965.

to the official perspective of "*economic* development and education."

In the remaining sections of this essay I will examine the ways in which *nōryokushugi* (the official ideology of ability) has been given a pivotal position in the government-sponsored discourses on ability management and educational reform. I will expose the policies that have darkened our educational environment and hindered the work of teachers. In so doing I will also discuss how we should adjust our educational practices in order to promote the independence of educational values as an intrinsic component of the human values appropriate to life in a democratic society.

IV. The Discourse on Managing Ability

What kinds of arguments about ability form the foundations of the government-sponsored discourse on *nōryokushugi* and "competency development systems"? To understand these arguments it is necessary to reconstruct the discourse within which they were generated, a discourse that attempted to repudiate the viability of a logic whose underlying values are primarily educational. In other words, this discourse rejects the notion that education can possess its own objectives, arguing rather that it must always be subordinated to the demands of society as they are interpreted by the government-industry alliance.

Let us proceed by examining one of the many publications issued by the Japan Federation of Employers' Associations (Nikkeiren) entitled "The Management of Ability: Its Theory and Practice" (Nikkeiren Kōhōbu, 1969). According to this book, the doctrines of ability management arose as a response to a number of important changes:

> Major changes such as the emergence of a labor shortage, large-scale improvements in wage standards, radically new technologies, the growth of an open economy, and transformations in worker consciousness obliged our country's industrial managers to respond dramatically to the changed conditions accompanying our rapid economic development. "Ability management" is a generic term designating the various policies designed to facilitate the control and administration of labor. These policies seek to identify those employees who ably contribute to further development of their abilities and the more effective use of their labor power. In short, the principle underlying these policies is to promote a small number of the very best workers.

Nikkeiren identifies the "ideal" of ability management in what is

THE IDEOLOGY OF ABILITY-FIRST   339

referred to as the "harmonizing of economic rationality and human respect in commercial enterprises." Concerning the relation between these two values, it declares: "Of course the ideal of human respect is to be comprehended within the context of the pursuit of economic rationality in business." The subordination of human values to economic rationality is clearly advocated in the following statement:

> Respect in enterprises is to be limited to recognition from above of workers' competencies. It should be based on discovery of those workers who are successful in fulfilling their job-related duties, more fully developing and realizing those abilities, and creating opportunities, places, and an environment in which these individuals can flourish. Managing ability consists in tying the treatment of workers to this way of thinking.

Concerning the "aims" of ability management, we are told:

> To best cope with changes in the immediate economic environment and in the conditions surrounding the management of enterprises, the competencies of each and every employee must be precisely discovered, developed to the maximal extent, put to practical use, and used to motivate workers. Through these measures productivity is improved, the company's competitiveness is strengthened, and the prosperity of the enterprise as well as its employees is assured. This doctrine shows us how it will be possible to promote the continued growth of the Japanese economy, and defines the path leading to a speedy elevation of our national standard of living.

These quotations clearly reveal a growing concern on the part of our industrial leaders that identifiable deficiencies in Japanese workers will leave the country in a position from which it will be unable to continue making the rapid economic strides seen in recent years. Identifying these deficiencies and then correcting them, which is the essence of the new manpower and ability management policies, has thus been seen both as a way to "remedy the shortcomings in traditional personal management styles" and as a way to mobilize human capacities to the fullest possible extent in order to guarantee continuing Japanese economic accomplishments. Arguing against what they called an "unacceptable disharmony between experience and ability," the Nikkeiren authors called for a new industrial structure more suited to the needs of corporate management:

The prevailing tradition of personnel management hitherto utilized by enterprises in our country has been centered on seniority,
academic pedigree, and the suppression of individuals within the
confines of the group they belong to. However in the wake of the
rapid and dramatic changes which appeared around 1960, these
practices were found to be both inadequate and unsuited to a new
environment.

Based on a recognition of the degree of "disharmony between experience and ability," a new industrial structure was advocated in accordance with "the needs of corporate management."

These and other like-minded formulations clearly express the thinking which underlies the manpower policies currently advocated by
Japan's industrial circles. What is particularly new and significant here
is the importance attached to terms like "competency, spontaneity,
and creativity."

The worker-evaluation practices utilized by Japanese industry in
its lifetime employment system have been based on traditional
models of proper human relationships and on severely outdated
notions of desirable behavior and character. Therefore, a new
system of personnel management, one rooted in the concepts of
ability that are being developed by today's corporate leaders, requires a clear idea of what it means to be a human being. The
standard for this new set of relationships and desired forms of
behavior should therefore be based on the contributions workers
are able to make to the well-being of the firms they work for.

While on the surface this does suggest a repudiation of the traditional
notions of seniority ranking and academic pedigreeism, it certainly
does not signal the complete abandonment of traditional Japanese
forms of practice, nor does it represent, for example, the pursuit of
an American-style "managerial society."

Let me cite an example that calls attention to the persistence of the
family-oriented group ideology and traditional paternalism that still
pervades managerial methods and practices in Japan.

In response to our new economic situation (as a rising economic
superpower), we require a system of personnel management in
which workers can be judged on the basis of their individual aptitudes and contributions to the firm, rather than strictly in accord
with the traditional approach which placed primary emphasis on

the individual worker's contributions to the group. In other words, while preserving the integrity of the group writ large (the nation or the Japanese race), we should try to encourage the development of smaller groups of more individually oriented workers.

But it is also necessary to use prudence in promoting a system that encourages the independent and enthusiastic participation of all employees in helping to realize the objectives of management. The abilities required for these ends should be nurtured in an environment of small groups. In this regard our formulation of ability differs from Western notions founded on the unity between rights and duties.

Concerning the system designed to reduce the employee's enthusiastic participation in the objectives of the organization as determined by management, Shinohara Hideo, president of Mitsubishi Chemical Corporation, published an article entitled "On the Control of All Employees" in the Nikkeiren house organ *Keieisha* (*Industrial Manager*). In the essay he called attention to the role of human respect:

> In referring to the principle of human respect within the confines of the enterprise, I am primarily thinking about how to create opportunities for all members of the company to exhibit their abilities. Expressions such as "I want to be freed as much as possible from labor" or "I want to have more elbowroom at work" do not represent the thinking of workers who deserve to be shown respect. It is the attitudes revealed by expressions such as "I want to be given ample opportunities to exhibit my capacities as a worker" or "At all times I will strive to work for the good of the company through my efforts at self-improvement" which should provide the foundations for corporate management based on human respect.
>
> The path leading to the realization of one's ideals as a member of the organization comes into view when employees act so as to contribute to the "public good" rather than serve their private interests. It is when one works to make the organization he belongs to stronger and better that his ambitions and ideals are attained.

Of course phrases like "total participation" and "enthusiastic participation" mean that the worker is one hundred percent under the jurisdiction of the company. This is the new way of management that seeks to control the definitions of responsibility and dedication.

How then is the notion of competency grasped within this discourse on the management of ability? Nikkeiren defines it as follows:

> Competency in the case of the members of an enterprise means the ability to contribute to the attainment of the organization's objectives through one's work. It must be concretely manifested in the form of recognizable achievements. While in one sense ability is an individualized thing whose meaning depends upon the demands inherent in different job-related functions, in general its essential components are physical strength, aptitude, knowledge, experience, character, and desire. These elements vary in quantity and quality in response to effort and environment.

Accordingly, within this ideological landscape the central problem of management is generating the incentives and motivations necessary to arouse in workers the desire to do what management wants them to do.

The "human respect" so passionately proclaimed by the ideologues of management is in the end nothing more than a means to industrial prosperity. This becomes particularly clear when we consider the following passage:

> The ideal of ability management is to harmonize human respect and the pursuit of economic rationality. Of course the primary objective of enterprise management resides in the latter, but this becomes an impossible pursuit if there is no respect shown to employees as human beings. And as has been recognized by the majority of top managers, these two values are not opposed; in fact human respect is directly involved in the quest for economic rationality. In concrete terms, what is human respect? According to our investigations it is understood by top managers as treating employees in a way that allows for the development of their abilities, giving them hope for the future and arousing their desire to work or creating the space in which the individual employee can most fully demonstrate his or her abilities and then be judged on these abilities without regard to seniority or academic background.

When uttered by the semi-official ideologues of ability management, the term "human respect" really means respect for those who have the desired abilities and discarding those who don't. It is another name for the ideological formulation of achievement, and is clearly unrelated to the notion of "human respect" as a fundamental right shared by all humanity.[6]

V. The Ideology of Ability and Manpower Development Policies

It is vitally important not to let these ideas about developing "systems for managing ability" go unchallenged as matters inherent in the organization of industry, because they are increasingly being used to legitimate a dangerous reorganization of education. In fact, it is already becoming clear that every aspect of the educational system will be subordinated to industrial requirements and made into parts of a system for selecting and developing ability.

If the Economic Deliberation Council (Keizai Shingikai) can be thought of as the government body which formulates industrial policies tailored to satisfy the requirements of our large-scale business organizations, then the Central Council on Education (Chūō Kyōiku Shingikai) can be viewed as the body which formulates policies that concretize these demands in the realm of education. Let me trace the history of the connection between the activities of these two officially constituted bodies.

The slogan "education in response to ability and aptitude" has played a central role in the claims of those who have argued that our postwar educational system should be reorganized into a "diversified" (meaning double-track) system. This expression was first enunciated in the 1951 Report of the Seirei Kaisei Shimon Iinkai.[7] The work of this body bore a close relation to the choice of Japan's course under the arrangements set in place through the San Francisco Treaty system. Following the Korean War and the resurgence of Japanese capitalism, demands for the reorganization of education also emerged from the economic world.

Five years after the publication of the Nikkeiren-sponsored "Our Demands for Re-examination of the New Educational System," on December 25, 1957, a document was issued under the title "Opinions Concerning the Promotion of Scientific and Technical Education." It declared:

[6] Sakamoto Tadashi, in *Gendai Kyōiku Shisō Hihan (Criticism of Today's Educational Thought)* (Aoki Shoten, 1971), examines the issue of respect and rights.
[7] The Seirei Kaisei Shimon Iinkai was a Cabinet-appointed deliberative council charged with the task of examining the need to revise the postwar reforms and the Constitution. It was convened with the encouragement of the Occupation authorities, who were already feeling the Cold War-inspired pressure to undo many of their liberalizing reforms of Japanese society.

We insist that in order to make education more effective and efficient, the single-track system found in lower and middle-level schools should be replaced with a dual-track system. In the middle and higher-level schools, we believe there should be a division between academic and vocational programs. (It is also necessary in the academic programs to distinguish between humanist and scientific courses of study.) The separation of students into academic and vocational tracks should be engineered in accordance with each student's abilities, specific characteristics, and appropriate lifelong agenda.

The intentions voiced in this Nikkeiren position paper were reflected in a report entitled "On Renovation of Primary and Lower Secondary School Curricula," issued the next year (1958) by the Ministry of Education's Council on Primary and Lower Secondary School Curricula:

We need to be clearer about the reasons why lower secondary school is the final stage of our children's compulsory or free education. During the third year [the ninth and last year of compulsory schooling] much more time should be made available for teachers to give guidance on appropriate courses for future study and on the proper career paths for the individual student to pursue.

The view articulated here proved to be the first step in a process that has led to the destruction of our school system's educational integrity. This was accomplished by dividing our lower secondary schools into separate tracks for those going on to higher schools and those going directly into the labor force. The character of the Course of Study was altered (see Chapter 8), and special courses in "moral education" were established, moves which supported the inauguration of a system of discrimination based on the educations received in different school tracks or programs of study.

During the 1960s the demands for educational reorganization coming from Japan's financial circles were reinforced by the policies for high economic growth that were made possible by the U.S.-Japan Security Treaty. In June of 1959 the Economic Deliberation Council created a Long-Term Economic Development Division and in November of that year established its National Income Doubling Planning Division. These two bodies investigated the question of how to reorganize the school system so as to make it more conducive to both the government's policies for high economic growth and the business world's requirements for specific types of labor power. Their reports, "Long-Term Prospects of the Japanese Economy" and "Plans for Doubling the National Income" (both published in December 1960), advocated an approach to educational problems that underscored the relation between economic growth and employment policies.

The viewpoints expounded in these reports were included in a report entitled "Tasks and Counterpolicies for Developing Human Abilities in Pursuit of Economic Expansion," issued by the Economic Deliberation Council on January 14, 1963. This report set the keynote for subsequent economic and educational policy formation. It proceeded from the observation that

> the scale of our entire economic structure will be greatly expanded in the wake of technological innovations and the changes in our industrial structure that will inevitably follow. This will necessitate a new economic and occupational structure, one within which the quantity and quality of the labor power required by industry will no doubt change more than it has up to this time. Accordingly, the structure and scale of educational training will have to be reformed and balanced by future manpower requirements for the cultivation of all types of workers.

The labor economist Sumiya Mikio touched upon the significance of this report in his 1970 work *The Economics of Education*:

> The demands placed upon education have been presented for a long time mainly from the side of those who want to receive an education. However, in recent years the authority to speak about these concerns has gradually shifted to the side of society's demands.
> The bonds between education and industry have now become virtually indissoluble, and as the industrial world assumes the leading role in publicly enunciating society's manpower requirements, its demands upon education will continue to grow. In other words, economic demands have directly found their way into every corner of the educational world.

In 1962 the Ministry of Education issued an educational white paper called *Japanese Growth and Education*. As this title indicates, educational bureaucrats were also approaching education from the perspective of its potential links with policies designed to stimulate economic growth. This white paper opens with the following statement:

It is unnecessary to reiterate the importance of the role education must fulfill with regard to social prosperity. In particular, it has recently come to be widely accepted both inside and outside Japan that education is one of the most potent factors producing economic development.

These remarks make it clear that the Ministry of Education had enthusiastically aligned itself with the initiatives of the Economic Deliberation Council and the demands of the industrial world that lurk in their background. Adoption of the Nationwide Uniform Scholastic Achievement Tests proceeded in tandem with the national income-doubling policy; these tests were carried out to help those "drafting plans for manpower development."

Shimizu Yoshihiro, the University of Tokyo educational sociologist who participated in the Economic Deliberation Council's long-term policy formation, has been one of the most vocal critics of the postwar educational system from the standpoint of those advocating the industrialists' policies for "talent development" and "educational diversification." For Shimizu the basic shortcoming of our postwar Japanese education is that

we have forgotten how to utilize a wide range of educational opportunities in response to ability and aptitude in middle-level education. Too much importance has been given to the notion of *equality* and too little to that of *in response to ability* as stipulated in Article III of the Fundamental Law of Education. ("All citizens must be given equal opportunities to receive an education in response to their abilities"). [*Education and the Economy 20 Years Hence*, Tōyōkan Shuppansha, 1961, p. 46]

Professor Shimizu also argued in the same work that

there is nothing which equals the postwar educational system's failure to meet the needs of our industrial society. Certainly it is not proper for employment planning to only serve the interests of large-scale industrial organizations. However, postwar education has forgotten the idea of *service* to both large and small-scale business enterprises. There is room to discuss whose interests education should serve, but is it even possible to conceive of an educational establishment serving no interests other than its own? This calls into question the *raison d'être* of our entire educational enterprise.

Concerning the aims of education, Shimizu claimed:

> Education does not possess its own objectives. What determines educational objectives are the forces actually existing in society.
> Under the framework of high economic growth, national educational policy should be formulated in accord with the shifting of concern from quantitative to qualitative issues and from political to industrial interests. . . . Speaking straightforwardly, the pursuit of Japan's economic growth through educational policy formation means cultivating superior-quality labor power. Educational policies must work to make the school system serve as the supplier of the desired work-oriented competencies.

The previously cited Report of the Economic Deliberation Council called for the diversification of education in response to the demands of the economic world vis-à-vis the working class. At the same time that this revealed a desire to make the schools function as organs for selecting potential workers on the basis of abilities and aptitudes, it also bespoke a growing tendency to think of this as the natural, necessary, and only genuine function of schools:

> We must devote our efforts in the direction of reforming the nation's educational *Weltanschauung* as well as the People's consciousness of work. They must be led to accept the idea that they are only entitled to receive an education in conformity with their abilities and aptitudes and that it is only through the evaluations rendered by the school system that they are entitled to employ their recognized competencies in their roles as workers.

We see here precisely the terms in which the "reform" of Japan's educational system was advocated from the perspective of the economically articulated ideology of ability.

The Central Council on Education inherited the task of educational reorganization in line with the demands of the financial world. This led to the introduction of an all-encompassing investigation of the educational system which yielded "The Image of the Desired Japanese" and the "Report on the Expansion and Adjustment of Education in the Final Stages of Middle-Level Schooling" (October 31, 1966). The latter document states:

> The form and content of education shall be diversified to more fully accommodate every individual student's aptitude, ability, life prospects, and environmental circumstances. Careful consideration shall be given to social demands in this process.

The same disposition was displayed in a statement issued by the Council on Educational Curriculum, under the title "Concerning Reform of the Lower Secondary School Curriculum":

> Ample consideration shall be given to methods of guidance in relation to the actual Course of Study so as to provide direction in keeping with the student's individuality, ability, and distinctive characteristics. This requires paying attention to the principles involved in the selection of curricular content, and to curriculum organization and management.

The Report of the 25th Central Council on Education, delivered in 1970, went further:

> The success of a diversified [meaning multi-track] educational system can best be measured in terms of its ability to produce students whose interests and qualities cover a broad spectrum; it is contingent upon the proper selection and separation of students into different courses of study on the basis of careful calculations of ability. This also requires smooth and effective educational guidance.[8]

VI. Regional Development and Educational Planning: The Case of Toyama Prefecture

The ideologically charged transformation in the concept of ability which was generated by the leaders of the Japanese government in cooperation with the leaders of Japanese industry was profoundly felt at the prefectural level as well. Taking their cue from the plans formulated to spur regional industrialization, Ministry of Education

---

[8] For a critique of these manpower exploitation policies, see Ogawa Toshio and Fujioka Sadahiko's "Capitalism and Education," in *Kōza: Gendai Minshushugi Kyōiku*, Vol. 1 (Aoki Shoten, 1970).

bureaucrats, working closely with local educational officials, have instituted new policies to "diversify" education and expand vocational training programs. As these strategies were experimentally worked out in Toyama Prefecture, let us proceed by examining some of the more serious problems which emerged there.[9]

The reorganization of education in Toyama Prefecture which was undertaken in accord with national industrial policy was thoroughly consistent with the general course of developments outlined elsewhere in this book, movements that began in 1952 following the signing of a peace treaty in San Francisco. In 1957 a Revised Four-Year Plan was announced, and in 1961 a second phase of comprehensive developmental planning was inaugurated. Its stated objectives were to reposition comprehensive educational planning and give it a new status as one link in the chain of policies designed to produce an enhanced level of economic growth. Policies were announced

to establish the appropriate contents of, and methods for, guidance that will facilitate the thoroughgoing institutionalization of vocational education. Hereafter, decisions about what constitutes the appropriate course for any particular student will be predicated in response to society's requirements and the demonstrated capacities of the student.

These policies were epitomized in the proposals calling for the so-called 3–7 System, in which 30 percent of the students are selected for a course of studies leading to college and 70 percent receive technical and vocational training. The keynote of the 3–7 System was "industrial high schools built by the cooperation of industry and education officials."

In 1963 Takaoka City in Toyama Prefecture was designated by the government as a New Industrial City. The third phase of comprehensive developmental planning began in 1966 with the official proclamation of "human competency development policies." The activities and findings of the Central Council on Education, as well as reports by the Science Education and Industrial Education committees, provided a further impetus for the realization of these policies. These efforts represented an attempt to carry out policies originally designed to diversify the school system so as to produce what was widely called "the unification of schooling and industry."

[9] The account below relies largely on a detailed report issued by a group of researchers associated with the People's Educational Research Institute: "Ability Development Education and Its Impact on Children and Their Teachers: Conditions and Problems in Toyama Prefecture."

It was frequently argued that in the absence of an appropriate system for distributing talents and abilities, both the State and the economy would incur unacceptable losses. Diversification of upper secondary schools was thus seen as a necessary step in the process intended to make them function smoothly as a vital part of a system for "pre-distributing" manpower. In this spirit it was concluded that there was a pressing need to develop a more rationalized system for discovering human abilities and distributing their possessors more effectively throughout the educational machinery. It was just at this time that a system designed to "supervise and guide abilities and aptitudes" appeared on the scene of Japanese educational life.

As part of this effort the Teachers' Guidance Division of the Toyama prefectural government decried the prevailing attitude that stressed the importance of what was seen as "intellectualized education":

There is no nation of people who equal the Japanese in mistaking intellectual ability for human ability. Under this misbegotten view too much importance has been attributed to academic pedigree and intellectual occupations. As a consequence physical and technical occupations have come to be viewed as vulgar and low-minded ways to make a living. . . . Human competencies and abilities are many. Of course intellectual powers are important, but it must not be forgotten that social competency as well as technical, artistic, and physical powers are vital to our national well-being. . . . The most blissful capacities are discovered and given room to grow so that [one] can exhibit these competencies with all his strength in the work environment. It is societies which possess many such individuals that can be thought of as sound and healthy.

Notwithstanding the multiplicity of human competencies, present-day school education has been swept away by the distorted view of work that captivates public opinion with the allure of academic pedigreeism. The flow of opinion has gone much too far in the direction of overvaluing the importance of intellectual training. This has resulted in an environment where there is a dearth of realistic guidance designed to help the individual student choose his life path in conformity with those skills and competencies already discovered and developed. As a consequence students falter in choosing their paths and become unhappy as individuals. We cannot even begin to evaluate the extent of the losses suffered by society. [Toyama Prefectural Board of Education, Board Newsletter, Issue No. 25, November 1966]

As can be readily understood from the above quotation, the educational consciousness of the prefectural authorities was rooted in a deceptive critique of intellectually centered and academically oriented education. The distinguishing characteristic of their underlying ideology rested in the quest to transform the occupational environment of the people of Toyama. From the declared vantage point of the Toyama Prefectural Board of Education, the educational disarray that accompanied the institutionalization of an overly rigorous testing system did not result from a policy of diversification wedded to the demands of industry, but were explainable rather in terms of the overextended and unreasonable educational ambitions parents held for their children. Matsumoto Shōzō, vice-chairman of the prefectural board of education, commented on these conditions as follows:

There are too many "problem parents" today who because of their hopes and expectations for the future of their children lose sight of reality when they begin to think about how to help those children select their paths for the future. Whether it be due to vanity or foolishly excessive expectations, parents show a reluctance to think realistically about their children's abilities and ambitions. We find them nurturing a zealous desire to see their children enter top-ranked schools, advance academically, and find work as employees of major corporations. In the end we observe children who have been overwhelmed by excessive pressure and anxiety. There are also stubborn fathers who oppose their children's aspirations on the grounds that they would be injurious to the family's reputation and standing in the community. [Board Newsletter, Issue No. 23, September 1966]

In many cases, Matsumoto went on, children themselves are at fault in their aspirations; and these unrealistic goals, he declared, must also be "adjusted."

At the junior high school level it is difficult for children to independently choose life paths. Their powers of self-evaluation and social discernment are also unreliable. Regarding these important choices for the child I strongly feel that the guidance actually given in the schools today should be viewed as the most important factor. Accordingly we must expend the greatest possible efforts to completely realize the teacher's responsibilities to provide appropriate guidance.

Thus the case was made that in order to provide guidance which would "relieve unhappy individuals and protect the State and society against unnecessary losses," all educational activities had to converge on guidance as the central duty of the schools.

However, the ability of those working in the prefecture's schools to actually provide such guidance was directly called into question by children and parents themselves. As a result it was declared that the child's selection of a future course should be based on his or her unrestrained judgment and independent choice. Quoting from the Central Council on Education's report on secondary education, the prefectural board authorities addressed the question of educational diversification and supervision and guidance at the junior high school level:

> Ways of thinking and basic directions should not be set only within the educational world. It has become all the more necessary that social and industrial considerations determine educational thinking and direction. An education which encourages the full play of each and every citizen's abilities to the greatest possible extent is intimately linked to national prosperity. Devising diversified methods of supervision and guidance means leading students to choose on their own, in response to the awareness they have been led to concerning their capacities. It means cultivating those competencies that will serve them in their future life and work. [Prefectural Board of Education, "Desirable Supervision and Ways of Providing Guidance," 1967]

It was announced that, to most effectively realize these objectives in Toyama's schools, learning would be reorganized "on the basis of a careful analysis of each and every child's abilities and aptitudes." The work of the school was summarized as the "individualization of educational guidance, the diversification of the academic curriculum, and the particularization of learning."

However, the reality of "education in response to ability and aptitude" has been a form of discriminatory education grounded in unproven assumptions about inherent differences in capacities for academic achievement. Of course what constitutes students' "academic ability and achievement" is strictly controlled within the context of the Ministry of Education's official Course of Study. The Toyama Prefectural Board of Education proposed that "the contents of the objectives for each school year set forth in the Course of Study be grasped in terms of measurable abilities" and that "academic achievement tables be drawn up upon detailed classification of the divisions found in the Course of Study" (Prefectural Board, "Supervision and Guidance of Abilities and Aptitudes"). Prompted by the authorities who stood behind this proposal, local boards of education, in cooperation with government-controlled regional educational research institutes, drew up model "academic achievement tables."

In this manner academic ability came to be frozen and rigorously defined in strict conformity with the government's official Course of Study. And as academic achievement was given a definitive meaning for those involved in the schools of Toyama, the directions in which teachers could "properly analyze and investigate the Course of Study" were strictly circumscribed. Supervision and guidance were routinized and duly recorded through the officially provided academic achievement tables. The diversification of educational content to make it more appropriate to conditions in Toyama has proven to be the means for institutionalizing an educational praxis that classifies, rates, and discriminates among different measurable quantities of ability solely on the basis of a prearranged system of conceptualization. Of course the principles of preselection witnessed here are rooted in the manpower requirements of industry and the social requirements of the State.

VII. The Actual Conditions of Children

A. Lethargy, Apathy, and Indifference

The officially mandated system of supervised guidance based on the policy of "diversification" as described above reached maturity in the 1960s when it came to constitute a vital link in the industrial development plans worked out by the leaders of Toyama Prefecture. Schools were ranked in a clearly demarcated hierarchy, and thereafter made to function as if they were factories to which the work of sorting out and classifying human beings had been subcontracted. And as academic testing became the means by which all human values were measured, education was thoroughly insulated from the cries of any concerned citizen who called for more spontaneous or creative forms of human development. Thus, to the extent that educational praxis was absorbed by the imperatives associated with the desire to stuff children's minds full of empty but easily testable knowledge and information, it was transformed into an essentially anti-educational undertaking.

How has the weight of this system made itself felt amongst the students of Toyama? Let us listen to some of their troubled voices and expressions of despair.

During my primary school days I thought that maybe there were treasures concealed in my studies. Upon entering junior high school I was hit in a flash by an endless barrage of tests. How I hate having to show the test scores to my parents and walking the school's corridors when everyone knows what grade I received. How can this be when Fukuzawa Yukichi said, "Heaven creates no man superior to another"? I think it is really strange to attach numerical ranks to us when after all we are still unknown quantities as human beings. Study at school, study at home, and still it is not enough. There are even people who try to outstare their books during vacations. It is altogether a war fought by studying. . . . I feel as if day after day I am being mechanically manipulated. [Student essay in "*Toyama no kodomo no sakubun*" (*Compositions by Toyama Students*), compiled for presentation to the Second National Educational Research Assembly, 1970]

Students have written these poems on the testing system they are captives of:

Wishing I'd Been Born in the Primitive Age

End-of-month test—45 points.
Showed it to mother.
In a twinkling of the eye her face changed,
"What is this, such a terrible score."
Without warning into the closet
I am thrown.
"What, because of a piece or two of test paper?"
I, locked in the pitch-dark closet,
Cry out in a roar,
"If it's to be like this
I'd rather have been born in a primitive age
With no tests,
Where even Tarzan could do well."

*

My Head

I score below 20 points on tests.

My friends call me "Zero-point Yamada."
At such times having friends is bitter.
I want to say to the teacher
Who gave me such a score,
"You are a gorilla's father."

Another student has written:

Two-thirds of my first year as a junior high school student has
already passed. During these months we have been assaulted by
tests every 20 days. . . . Everyone only thinks about himself. It's
total egoism. I have come to understand that the greatest cause
of the destruction of friendship among junior high school students
is our relations with our test scores.

Education which sorts out and discriminates among still-growing
human beings is not peculiar to Toyama Prefecture. It is becoming the
norm for Japanese education as the demands of the industrial world
for educational reorganization spread throughout the country.

I am always thinking about the tests that are upcoming. Should
I hear some other students making mistakes on a problem that
I have already solved, I keep my mouth shut. When people are
frantically trying to memorize information, to say anything at
all is an intrusion. I am burning with the spirit of one who refuses
to be defeated by one's rivals. When there is something I can't
do I wish the others would fall sick, and I always struggle to get
better scores than everyone else no matter what. I'm quite accustomed to this competitive consciousness and assault as I have
these thoughts at least once a day. If it weren't for this I would
not understand what it is human beings live for.

These words are taken from the composition of a second-year student
at a prefectural high school in Kōchi. The alienation that young people
suffer under the school's systematization of competition and selection
is revealed in all its pathos here.

A few years back the novelist Ōe Kenzaburō held a conversation
with students from Hibiya High School that appeared in a weekly
magazine. I am often haunted by the cold and cavalier way in which
one student said, "It's good enough for incompetent students if they
go to vocational high school."

B. The Official Ideology of Ability
and Its Disregard for the Spirit of Childhood

A number of high schools and colleges have begun to experiment with a new admissions system, one that places great importance on what is referred to as a confidential report on the student's activities (*naishinsho*).[10] The intentions that lay behind the attempt to institutionalize this system were quite straightforward and laudable: to liberate students from "examination hell" and send them on to a school life more humane in its orientation than one totally given over to being successful in academic tests.

However, the discontinuation of high school entrance tests and the attempt to lay greater value on the *naishinsho* did not remedy the basic problem. Quite to the contrary: what actually happened is that every hour of every day became a potential occasion for this confidential reporting. The result has been that supervision cards are filled out in great detail and the everyday activities of schools have become ensnarled in vehement forms of competition.

At the 1970 National Research Assembly of the Teachers' Union, reports were presented to the Committee on Supervision and Guidance about the situation in Hyōgo Prefecture, where efforts were made to replace the system of selection tests with one rooted in the *naishinsho*. One of the most telling examples of how this affected educational life in Hyōgo's schools is found in the statement by a teacher to a group of new junior high school students in music class and their response:

> Teacher: Let's sing a song that everyone likes.
> Students: Are our performances going to count on the *naishinsho*?

In this fashion the official construction of ability has been ideologically coupled with the testing system and the school has been reduced to an organ for distributing human abilities and competencies. Through the daily activities of selection that go on under the name of the "teacher's supervision and guidance," Japanese youth have been divided into two distinct classes. On the one hand there are a small number of arrogant and unsympathetic elitists who believe they have been specially selected because of their ability to perform in conformity with the official Course of Study. On the other there are a mass of lethargic young people who have resigned themselves to being academically

[10] See Chapter 11, "Student Evaluation and Personal Control: The *Naishinsho* Decision."

discriminated against and made into the reserve force of an army of laborers.

VIII. From Discussions at Research Assemblies

A. Supervision and Guidance, Report Cards, and Classroom Composition on the Basis of Ability

Reports presented to the research assemblies of the Japan Teachers' Union (*Nikkyōso*) contain ample evidence reflecting the influence the social reorganization based on the official ideology of ability has exerted on education.[11] While in a sense this was only to be expected, it is nonetheless quite deplorable.

There is much in the reports concerning the scheming that went into the strategies for revising supervision and guidance, evaluation and report cards, and classroom composition on the basis of differentiated abilities. Under the new formalism that totally avoids scrutinizing the quality of the educational practices which make up instruction, the schools have in the blink of an eye fallen prey to the danger of being made totally subservient to so-called social requirements.

Supervision and guidance, for example, should of course constitute an important part of educational work. The reports presented by our members from Ōita and Nagano prefectures, however, suggest that detailed investigations into every aspect of the child's life have merely provided fodder for the compilation of career guidance programs based on preexistent notions of ability, and that their usefulness can only be "appreciated" in the context of the government's officially sponsored industrial reorganization. Thus the child's study, health, and performance in school activities are broken down and made to fit the detailed supervision planning tables approved by administrative authorities.

The reports presented to our research assemblies show that in spite of the increased energy and time teachers expend composing "supervision planning charts," and then recording the relevant data, their performance as educators is hardly improved. Rather than revealing the dedication and joy of those whose efforts are expended in grappling with the problems of youth, these reports give the impression of teachers as cold and indifferent observers. In the words of one teacher from Nagano: "Supervision and guidance should not be understood as imposing supervision on the child, but as providing helpful direction."

---

[11] This part of the essay is adapted from a speech by the author to the 20th National Educational Research Assembly.

There clearly are dangers involved in teachers' observations when they end in the compilation of supervision tables, practices that can lead to the dehumanization of teachers and education. The apprehensions of teachers themselves are evident in reactions such as: "Isn't this akin to computerized education?" "Isn't this analysis for the sake of analysis?" "These practices call to mind the diagnostic charts of psychiatric classification." "Is it really possible to observe and evaluate the child's internalized sentiments and feelings?"

The problems involved here have been aptly pointed out by a teacher from Akita Prefecture:

> Even if we use supervision tables that cover a detailed array of items, when we check the appropriate categories, at the very best we only discover the child's particular characteristics in a negative way. What comes across from these tables is not the ordinary activities of the child, but only his or her "undesirable" activities. This is not to deny the importance of observation and supervision but rather to call into question the dangerous changes that have been effected in our role as the providers of guidance to children. The problem is in the attitude of teachers when they make their observations and offer supervision. It is crucial that observation not be conceived as the work of a disinterested third party but rather as a natural outgrowth of the human bonds that unite students and teachers.

We have learned from our Tokyo representatives that extensive efforts have been made by the government to show that it is necessary to provide supervision and guidance in strict conformity with the notions of ability, aptitude, and environment as set forth in the Central Council on Education's "Image of the Desired Japanese"[12] and "Education in the Latter States of Middle-Level Schooling." It has also been reported that there was a sudden surge in activities directed to creating "supervision tables" on the basis of these arguments. At first glance this all seems very scientific and efficient. However, even where the intentions displayed in individual schools were honorable, there remains ample room for worrying about how these test results will ultimately be used. Repeated "psychological" testing, rather than promoting practices that expand upon the students' good points (no matter how few they may be), are actually very dangerous inasmuch

[12] See Chapter 5, "Education and Law in Postwar Japan," for further discussion of this report.

as they are tied to ranking and discrimination based on the intellectual abilities and personal characteristics of the child.

Finely detailed supervision tables have inverted the relation between means and ends. They do not encourage the teachers to be helpful guides but limit them to the imposition of prescribed and routinized supervision. These carefully itemized supervision tables are all too easily controlled within the framework of an ideology that authorizes the identification and recording of the child's defects and imperfections. Rather than focusing attention upon children's strengths and virtues, they direct it to their faults, shortcomings, and blemishes.

Speaking objectively, these practices bear no fruit whatsoever regarding the real work of education, and only have value as means for producing data useful when filling out *naishinsho* reports.[13] We cannot afford to overlook the dangers that arise when they are thought of as a "reliable" means for discriminating and selecting human beings.

Concerning the existing report card system, too, there is a growing awareness of danger. The effort to replace the current five-stage ranking system with a ten-tiered one is still rigidly premised on the notion that abilities can be measured by a standard distribution curve. Inasmuch as these "reforms" are still yoked to the *naishinsho* system and its codified forms of guidance, this limited rationality has only led to the classifying of human beings. These measures have actually worsened the conditions surrounding educational life in present-day Japan.

We have heard more promising reports from Chiba Prefecture about efforts to discontinue the five-stage evaluation system and reorganize the report card system on the basis of teachers' independently directed formulation of educational content. Under this new method of *educationally* oriented evaluation, emphasis has also been placed on the child's behavioral development. The results of these experiments have been most encouraging as children come to feel more at ease, and as parental interest shifts from test scores to their children's development.

We have learned of efforts in Nagasaki to refashion the report card as a communication sent from the school to the home. Believing that what should be communicated to the home is a matter for the teacher to decide, teachers in Nagasaki have labored to freely organize the report cards that they want to send. Not surprisingly, however, the city board of education has opposed these efforts by issuing an official order that the same report card format must be used in all schools within the city board's jurisdiction. We have heard from teachers in

---

[13] Chapter 11 presented a more detailed discussion of these reports on secondary students' school performance and behavior.

Nagasaki about their struggle to defend the reforms they have worked so hard to realize.

We have also been presented with reports from Kyoto on the development of practices designed to eliminate end-of-term reports. Proceeding from the position that report cards should only be used to notify parents and children about the state of the latter's learning and study, the teachers in Kyoto have sought to utilize report cards as a way to heighten the child's desire to learn:

> If the report card is routinely conceived as necessary for furthering the parent's understanding of the child's educational development, then there is no need whatsoever for issuing end-of-term report cards.

In this vein it has been argued that "evaluation" should be reconceived as one link in the process of educational (rather than economic) development. Rather than ranking human beings through a process that "rates" students' test accomplishments, concern should be given to positively evaluating as much as possible the student's educational accomplishments. The need for such an approach to evaluation is made all the more pressing by the fact that there are already students who tamely submit to the discrimination that they have become accustomed to through the ranking produced by repeated testing. However, even in Kyoto (which has traditionally prided itself on its independence from the central government authorities in Tokyo) it has proven impossible to do away with the *naishinsho* and all of the detailed recording that the system requires. The Kyoto Board of Education mandated a bell-curved grading system in which the top 10 percent of students receive the highest grades and the bottom 10 percent receive the lowest. This of course has added to the difficulties facing conscientious teachers in Kyoto. The conclusion of the report delivered by the representatives from Kyoto left a deep impression on all those who were present when it was read:

> It is an inescapable reality under the present system that the child's future is largely determined on the basis of the ratings provided by the school. This system does violence to the child, the teacher, the school, and education itself. We must seek to validate the principle of respect for the child's real desires and aspirations.

Ōta Takashi, as the representative of those who organized the forum, summarized these discussions:

At the time that teachers appealed to parents to help them resist the Teacher Evaluation System, the argument was advanced that through the report card system the teacher's ratings would be made to function as the basis of discrimination against students. At the time of the university disturbances in the late 1960s the problems of evaluation and classification were again thrust before us. We must not be deceived by the form of the report card. The things that are of great importance for human beings cannot be grasped in an itemized list of skills and attitudes evaluated in the manner our educational authorities would have us do. If we eliminate the presently existing report card system and replace it with communications sent to the home, then these communications should be of a nature to promote the mutual understanding of teachers and parents. It should be our work to bring methodological clarity to the desire to reform our nation's educational life in this direction.

14 Conflicting Approaches to the Reform of Japanese Schooling: Economic Liberalization versus Educational Liberation

I. Introduction

A. The Need for Educational Reform

Up to this point I have examined the history of postwar Japanese education, focusing upon the ways in which the spirit of reform embodied in the Constitution and Fundamental Law of Education has repeatedly been attacked. In doing so I have tried to show why today's educational system offers a very faint echo of the hopes and desires that underscored the reorganization of schooling in our country some forty years ago. The most recent blow in this ongoing attack upon the spirit of intellectual and political liberation has come from the activities of the Nakasone Cabinet's Extraordinary Council on Education (*rinji kyōiku shingikai*), a body established in 1984 as one link in Prime Minister Nakasone's attempt to "settle the score" on the postwar reforms of Japan.

As the reader of this book should well understand by now, the conditions in which our children are growing up have reached the crisis stage, and there can be no doubt that our educational system is in a terrible mess. And, as already documented in these pages, the problems of delinquency, truancy, cruel physical punishment by teachers, bullying of weak students and teachers by other students, and diminished academic performance are continually becoming more serious while at the same time tightened censorship of textbooks, increased bureaucratic interference, and restrictions of teachers' freedoms are collectively contributing to a situation in which our schools are being transformed from the locus of education into the site of struggle for social selection. Thus it is not surprising that we hear more and more voices calling for drastic reforms. Moreover, it is clear that these problems are all closely related to the increased pressure attendant upon our overheated university entrance examination system.

These disruptions of the educational process are visible outside the school as well, as can be seen for example in the startling growth of the cram school (*juku*) industry. It is even becoming difficult under these conditions for our schools to resist the pressures which are transforming them into mere appendages to the cram school industry. Thus

362

it is increasingly evident that the opportunities to receive what passes for an education in Japan are becoming more and more dependent upon the amount of money parents are willing and able to shell out for private tutors and exam preparation schools. We have indeed come a long way from the time when the Fundamental Law of Education proclaimed the ideal that all citizens are guaranteed the right to receive the best education possible regardless of the financial or social status of their families. In the light of these conditions, anyone who looks carefully at what our schools are doing to his or her children cannot help but agree that drastic reforms must be enacted, and very soon.

B. Conflicting Approaches to Educational Reform

Nor should it come as any surprise to the reader that there are two diametrically opposed approaches to the problem of how we should be reforming our schools. This cleavage reflects the fault lines that first appeared a century ago during the early Meiji era between those who advocated an "enlightenment from above" administered by the State and those who pushed for an "enlightenment from below" which could only be worked out by the People themselves. This dichotomy has appeared in a number of guises over the past hundred years, but the nature of the conflict remains the same and is readily apparent in the bitter controversies going on today regarding the most desirable kind of educational reform.

In recent years the arguments of those advocating reform from above have followed the positions worked out by the Ministry of Education in the 1960s and 1970s under the direction of the ruling Liberal Democratic Party in response to the manpower development demands of business and industry. These calls for reform are referred to by their supporters as "the third reform of education."[1] Needless to say, those proclaiming the need for a "third reform" of education see it as a way to bring back the spirit of strict order and tight discipline which was instilled by the educational system of the prewar Imperial State. In other words, the discourse on the need for a "third reform" of education is an intrinsic part of the attempt to eradicate the liberalizing influences of the postwar reforms.

But there are also important differences between the attempts to instigate reforms initiated by the government most recently and those launched in the 1960s and early 1970s. These differences do not result from a transformation of fundamental value orientations; rather, they

[1] The first reform being that in which the Meiji statesmen established the Imperial educational system; the second, that in which the Occupation authorities attempted to democratize education after World War II.

reflect the response to the changed economic conditions Japanese business and political leaders found themselves in after the first "oil shock" in 1973. Recognizing that Japan's unprecedented rapid economic growth could no longer be sustained, they decided to reorganize the Japanese economy in line with the more modest aim of moderate growth. In this changed climate it gradually became clear to the shapers of national policy that a form of education suited to the country's altered economic agenda was required. Thus as Japan entered the 1980s new calls for reform emerged as an important part of the Nakasone government's attempt to enact comprehensive reforms of national administration.

One of the fundamental objectives of this program for administrative reform has been an attempt to lighten the government's financial burden. To this end the National Railways have already been privatized, and the government is beginning to sell off the telephone and telegraph monopoly. Education is the next area the government has targeted for privatization. Concretely this means shifting the burden of educational expenses from the public budget to that of private individuals; however, it does not mean limiting the State bureaucracy's interference with the inner workings of the educational process.

It is worth noting that the original impetus for the recently proposed reforms did not arise within the government itself but emerged from a series of initiatives undertaken within Japan's economic and financial circles. Thus, for example, the Discussion Group on Problems Related to Education and Culture set up by the Nakasone Cabinet had originally been organized as a private group closely allied with the Kyoto Round Table for Thinking about the World, a body established by the industrialist Matsushita Kōnosuke to formulate long-range economic, social, and educational policies for the twenty-first century. These efforts were supplemented by a number of reports issued by other organs connected with industry. It must also be pointed out that the Nakasone government recruited the members of its Extraordinary Council on Education largely from the groups mentioned above. In short, it is not hard to tell whose interests were more than amply represented in this officially sanctioned body, and whose were totally ignored.

The other major impetus for educational reform has come from the non-governmental, non-industrial sector of society. These views are represented most clearly in reports issued by the Japan Teachers' Union Committee for Educational Investigation.

There have been other attempts to formulate the bases for educational reform, such as the program advocated by the Japanese Society for Education, which attempts to mediate between the conflicting positions of those in the government–business alliance and those within the People's Education Movement. But given the extreme polarization between these two approaches, the wish to reach a compromise is little more than a vain hope.

II. Neo-Conservative Reform

A. The Extraordinary Council and Japan's Educational Problems

The main pillar upholding the thinking of the Extraordinary Council on Education is the idea that Japan requires an educational reform that will prepare it to face the challenges of the twenty-first century. In particular this has been viewed in terms of the nation's need to reorganize education so that the members of society will be able to adapt to a form of life increasingly dependent upon new kinds of information. It has also been framed in terms of Japan's need to "internationalize" and to prepare for an increasingly aging society. These three objectives have been at the forefront of the Extraordinary Council on Education's deliberations about the kind of educational reform Japan currently requires.

The members of this council have sought to dramatically alter the meaning of "Japan's modernization," to shift the focus of attention from a program designed to help Japan "catch up with the West" to one which will make it possible for the nation to finally overcome and surpass the West. Shifting the focus of attention in this manner certainly serves to place even greater emphasis upon the cultivation of those elites who will be responsible for leading the Japanese into the forefront of the post-industrialized world, because it is only these elites, the argument goes, who will be able to manage society's needs for new and ever greater amounts of information. By proceeding in this fashion, it has been claimed, Japan can both consolidate the economic gains it has won over recent years and increase its already powerful advantages in the global economy. In this sense, educational reform constitutes a vitally important part of the plans Japan's industrial leaders have for reaching an even higher and more dominant position in the world marketplace. Thus it must be remembered that the various debates on school reform which seek to "liberalize" or "diversify" education are in reality little more than attempts to streamline the cultivation of elites as the cornerstone of our nation's educational system.

There is one other major component in the Extraordinary Council on Education's proposals that requires careful analysis, namely, the emphasis placed upon Japan's "eternal, unchanging traditions." This theme, running throughout the work of both the Discussion Group on Problems Related to Education and Culture and the Kyoto Round Table for Thinking about the World, reveals that another agenda lies concealed beneath all the talk about internationalizing Japan and preparing it for the twenty-first century. This is nothing other than the desire to restore to their previously privileged positions within prewar Japanese life the mythic dimensions of Japanese nationalism and a tightly controlled form of moral education. The dangerous implications of this appeal to the values of chauvinistic Japanism are succinctly visible in the proposals of the Extraordinary Council on Education that called for a reinvigorated pursuit of Japanology and which insisted upon the need to force the rest of the world to show more respect for Japan's unique national character and its unequaled traditions. Here we can see tangible signs of the birth of that culturally constituted form of nationalism which the Nakasone government has been promoting throughout the 1980s.

Inasmuch as the work of the Extraordinary Council on Education has proceeded on the basis of these two major pillars, it is clear that its proposals will contribute nothing to the resolution of the real educational crises we are now confronting such as the physical punishment of students, delinquency, truancy, dropouts, and the overextended administrative control of students and teachers alike. Moreover, it is equally apparent that the distinguished members of the council are not at all troubled by the distress of our children because they have chosen to proceed in directions in which these concerns are not even registered as matters worthy of genuine concern. In fact, in twenty-first-century Japan as they have envisioned it, these problems will have become so widespread that the situation will be considered normal.

Originally the Extraordinary Council on Education did not plan on addressing these problems, but in response to repeated criticisms from the Japanese public, it finally agreed to set up a special panel to examine the problem of bullying. Its conclusion was that since the roots of this problem reside in the character of contemporary society and civilization, there is nothing in particular which can be done to treat or remedy these most grievous problems. This is an example of the kind of lame excuses offered to ultimately justify what have come and continue to be intolerable conditions. In the end we can only infer that in the future society desired by the council's members, the social conditions which make the phenomenon of bullying an everyday part of our lives will become more and more severe, and the structure of abuse will become more and more complex.

Thus it is clear that, rather than formulating policies which will enable us to resolve the contradictions currently destroying the vitality of our schools, the Extraordinary Council is only attempting to reorient our educational system so that it will more effectively produce workers who will be thoroughly responsive to the demands of Japan's industrial and financial circles. The most painfully ironic aspect of this is that if all these proposals are in fact put into effect, not only will the Japanese people and their children have to endure the new abuses now being prepared for them; they will also have to suffer the additional insult of being required to pay for this with ever greater out-of-pocket expenditures.

B. Educational Liberalization and Educational Liberation

There was much discussion in the meetings and reports issued by and about 'the Extraordinary Council on Education regarding the need for "educational liberalization" and "greater individualism" in education. In one sense this represented a criticism of the Ministry of Education and reflects some of the reasons why this council was established as an organ attached to the Prime Minister's cabinet and not to the Ministry of Education, as is typically the case with such blue-ribbon deliberative bodies. But one should not be deceived by all the commotion raised in relation to this point, particularly the claim that the council's proposals constituted an attempt to denigrate the Ministry of Education and take away many of its powers. After all, it should be remembered, by the time the council was disbanded in September of 1987, it had already become quite clear that the work of seeing its proposals through to realization was the major new task facing the Ministry of Education.

The calls for "liberalization" voiced within the deliberations of the Extraordinary Council emerged from the earlier debates of the Kyoto Round Table regarding the character of a desirable educational reform. Against this backdrop it can be seen that these ideas clearly reflect the desires of our financial and industrial leaders. Moreover, when these would-be reformers speak of liberalization (*jiyūka*), they are most definitely not referring to the kinds of freedom and liberty which the postwar reforms of education attempted to make into the basic human rights of all citizens in the new Japan. What liberalization has been viewed as meaning here rather is *deregulation*. In this highly limited sense, it can be said that the work of this council was somewhat critical of the Ministry of Education's usual way of doing business, but the reader should not be deceived about the depth or extent of this antagonism. Indeed it is closer to the truth to say that the members of the Prime Minister's Extraordinary Council on Education saw the challenges they construed in terms of the need for liberalization not as a response to the need for a spiritually freer form of schooling but rather as a way to respond to the need to extend the "unparalleled virtues of our educational system" well into the next century.

At the heart of these proposals one finds an attempt to apply the logic of administrative reform which has been the hallmark of the Nakasone Cabinet's efforts to streamline government in general and education in particular. In other words, one of the primary aims of the reforms proposed by the council is to reduce the amount of public funds used for education while increasing the educational expenses directly shouldered by the People out of their private household budgets.

This approach to our educational problems was clearly enunciated as early as 1977 in a report issued by a study group of eminent economic managers, entitled "Advancing Liberalism":

If we really want to act upon the wish to establish a liberal society and free economy which will be both strong and enduring, it is now necessary to liberalize all elementary and lower secondary schools by putting their management into private hands. Their privatization is the necessary condition for any successful attempt to resolve the many problems spawned by our postwar system of universal compulsory education.

Here we can see how "educational liberalization" was made to stand for "educational privatization." This has subsequently come to be associated with proposals such as that for a system of tuition vouchers which parents can use "freely" when selecting the schools they decide are the most appropriate ones to send their children to. This system has been put before the Japanese people as providing the best way to "rationalize educational expenditures" and to keep them from imposing unjustified strains on the national budget. Here we see an updated version of the ideology discussed in earlier chapters, which subordinates the logic of education to the logic of bureaucratic rationality.

Therefore those who want to use arguments about fiscal responsibility to justify educationally arbitary forms of administrative rationalization never stop long enough to ask themselves what effect these changes will have on education itself. Failing to do so, they obliterate the autonomy of education as an important *public* social enterprise, and allow it to be transformed into a purely *private* one, dependent upon fluctuations in the job marketplace rather than upon developments in the worlds of knowledge and educational science. In this manner education, and the forms of knowledge it makes available, will be transformed into consumer goods, so much so that the commodification of learning will in the end become an all-encompassing process. I fear that there will be nothing left which we can properly call "education" after this transformation is completed. The principles of "learning" will be entirely replaced by the principles of "competition," and children no less than their parents will become the consumers of whatever products "schools" have to offer. In other words, the freedoms which will result from this proposed "liberalization of education" are only the freedoms of choice which the consumers of all mass-produced goods are able to enjoy. The unique values of education will cease to exist, and the critical spirit which it can nourish will be hard to find.

Other major problems can be attributed to this kind of thinking. Not only would it lead to a drastic reduction in the number of public schools, and a marked growth in what has already become a private "educational industry"; under the guise of educational freedom, it would also destroy the neighborhood system of schools, and reduce the parent's input into the educational process to the mere act of signing his or her "school-use coupons." Thus, far from guaranteeing "parents' freedoms of educational choice," these proposals, if indeed enacted, would eliminate one of the most important dimensions of educational liberty itself.

It is also important to understand why this plan won't remedy our worst educational problems, in spite of the assurances provided by its most ardent supporters. One cannot deny that adoption of this system would make it much easier for a parent to transfer his or her child out of a school in which there is a great deal of bullying and violence, and those families which choose to enroll their children in private schools could use these vouchers to help defray the cost of tuition. But such measures certainly cannot be thought of as representing an enduring solution to our educational problems; they merely offer a way in which some parents and children can escape from public education on an emergency basis. Moreover, what is really proposed here is a way to "reform education" without holding those who make educational policy responsible for solving the difficulties they have gotten us into.

Finally, it must be reiterated, the freedom to choose which this system would ostensibly make available is only the freedom to choose from a preselected list of options, one over which parents would have even less control, and into which they would have far fewer opportunities to make meaningful input than they currently do. Thus the greatest irony in all of the recent talk about liberalization is that it would leave us with an educational system even more standardized and uniform than the one we now have. The freedoms it would make available are limited to those of the consumer in a tightly regulated marketplace. They are most definitely not the freedoms of educational creativity which we have argued should be recognized as belonging to the citizens of a truly democratic nation. And they are clearly not the freedoms which should be expected from an educational system that purports to respect the value and dignity of individuals.

C. The Principle of Competition and the Principle of Individuality

The reorganization of our schools which began in earnest in the 1960s following the introduction of unconstrained competition as the major principle of education has had two important consequences. First, it has made educational activities totally subservient to economic ones; and secondly, it has prompted the growth of an educational industry in which teaching and learning are transformed from a social enterprise into a money-making one. In recent years, the argument has been put forward by those who believe that the principle of competition is the key to a good education that in order to make it possible for the private educational entrepreneurs who run these academies to provide even more kinds of "high-quality educational services," it is now necessary for the government to license and officially supervise the cram school (*juku*) industry.

The operators of these cram schools and private tutoring academies know full well that parents in Japan today will assume major additional financial burdens if they think that as a result their children will have even a slightly better chance of success at entrance examination time. However, education and scholarship lose their universal and public character when they fall under the domination of the logics of management and efficiency. Moreover, once the principle is established that the beneficiaries of education should predominantly shoulder its costs, it is hard to resist the tendency to view education and scholarship solely in terms of its personal or private payoffs. In such an environment education can no longer respond to any aspirations of the People other than those for financial success. In short, if the thinking of the Extraordinary Council on Education fully finds its way into law, the People will no longer be masters of their learning and studies.

These arguments rest upon the contention that schools only become more individualized as a consequence of privatization and increased competition between them for students. However, individualizing our schools on the basis of the principle of free choice is fundamentally different from doing so on the basis of the principle of competition. In fact it is closer to the truth to say that the values underlying these principles are fundamentally opposed to and in irremediable conflict with one another. In other words, because the principle of competition stimulates the standardization of education, it can never encourage the principle of individualization.

In addition to the publicly declared objectives of these "educational liberalists," i.e., encouraging the growth of a "private" but "officially certified" educational industry, there are a number of unstated but no less important aspects of their thinking which must be analyzed as well. These can be recovered from the following chain of reasoning. If private schools receive official support in their competition with public ones, they will begin to triumph over them in a resoundingly apparent fashion,[2] and before long, students will simply stop going to publicly organized institutions. Thus, as the march towards a totally privatized system of education picks up irreversible momentum, the vitality of the public school system will be destroyed. The other major outcome of this process as envisioned by our erstwhile liberalists will be the final and inexorable triumph of the economically oriented values of examination competition over the educationally oriented values of learning, discovery, and enriched understanding. At that time the publicly recognized markers of being educated will, even more so than is true now (if that is possible), become the prestige and ranking of the universities and colleges students succeed in entering as rewards for their competitive efforts and valor. The individuality of human beings will be totally supplanted by the "individuality" fictitiously attributed to the schools which they attend.

This raises a number of troubling questions of both theoretical and practical significance. How far can the commodification of education actually go? How much pressure can be inflicted upon the financial resources of the Japanese people and upon the spiritual resilience of their children before the vitality of all those concerned quite simply snaps? Likewise, how far can the pathological phenomena swallowing up our schools degenerate before the system becomes unsustainable?

[2] Success for a school is measured not only in terms of numbers of students but also—and more importantly—in terms of how well its students perform in the competition to enter prestigious universities and upper secondary schools.

Unfortunately, it seems as if the economic maxim which states "Bad money drives out good" is applicable here. Assuming therefore that the proposals formulated by the Extraordinary Council on Education are actually adopted, we can look forward to disheartening answers to these vexing questions in the years to come.

One of the most revealing contradictions in the liberalism of the council's members can be seen in their treatment of our textbook problems. If their proclaimed commitment to less government intervention were more genuine, or for that matter even logically consistent, we could expect them to have come out against the existing screening system. But by the time they concluded their deliberations, it was clear that this was certainly not to be the case.

This turn was prefigured by the debates of Matsushita Konosuke's Kyoto Round Table, in which it was first suggested that the Ministry of Education's textbook system was no longer needed, and should become the object of administrative reform. But as the deliberations of that body progressed, this proposal was retracted. When the Round Table subsequently issued a pamphlet entitled "Why Is Educational Liberalization Necessary?" it declared unambiguously that the screening of textbooks should be conducted "aggressively and rigorously."

How, then, can we make sense of the argument earlier advanced by the members of the Round Table that textbook control by the State was no longer required? Rather than seeing this as a repudiation of the principle that the State must organize and exert firm control over society, one of the most revealing aspects of the thinking which has dominated the work of the Extraordinary Council on Education can be seen in its attitude towards the values embodied in the Fundamental Law of Education. As the reader will recall from the analyses of postwar educational history presented in Chapters 4 and 5, the Fundamental Law was established after the war to repudiate the totalitarian values embedded in the Imperial Rescript on Education and to replace them with the democratic values of freedom and liberty. Because the ministers of education who over the past 30 years have served under successive Liberal Democratic Party governments have almost without exception expressed their opposition to the Fundamental Law of Education, we assumed that one of the objectives of the Extraordinary Council on Education would be to propose a new law to replace it. Thus it came as quite a surprise when, rather than adopting the strategy previously employed in which this law was roundly denounced, the members of the council chose to praise it. This new approach began with Prime Minister Nakasone's declaration: "It is not necessary to alter the Fundamental Law of Education." This approach was further elaborated by the Extraordinary Council on Education when it called for a reinterpretation of this law from a perspective it called that of "living law." Here we can observe one of the major differences between the conservatism of the Nakasone government and that of its friends in Washington who insist that laws should be interpreted from the standpoint of their framers. What we find here is a desire to look back behind the Fundamental Law to the Imperial Rescript, which, curiously enough, are now being spoken of as if they were not in basic contradiction and opposition. In short, the perspective of "living law" is being used to justify, in the name of liberalization, a violation of the legal foundations of postwar Japan's system of democratic education.

I think it is more appropriate to view this attitude as an expression of the new optimism and confidence of those on the Japanese right, an ease generated by their recognition of the conservative trends which are coming to dominate national consciousness. Convinced that as free competition increasingly comes to define the norm in Japanese educational affairs, left-leaning textbooks will no longer be written (and, even if authored, not chosen by parents), the members of the Kyoto Round Table at first believed that the time had come when vigorous Ministry of Education censorship was no longer needed. But upon further consideration they decided that "too many left-wing teachers are employed in our school system," and concluded that checks are still called for. Thus, in addition to textbook screening, it was argued that firm measures be taken such as careful political screening by boards of education at the times teachers are initially hired, dismissal of teachers judged by their peers "not to be good," and periodic teacher aptitude testing. In short, the sphere of activities deemed appropriate for forms of deregulation proposed by these new advocates of "educational liberalization" was carefully circumscribed so that deregulation would not be allowed to endanger the basic structure of educational control developed and jealously guarded in postwar Japan.

D. The Economics of Liberalization

In the background of the current discourse on educational liberalization is a strong element of economic theory, in particular, public sector economics. But rather than drawing upon the Keynesian theories according to which funds should be invested in the public sector in order to stimulate economic activity, the fundamental outlook employed here stresses reducing public expenditures as much as possible.

This school of thinking in Japan has been very heavily influenced by works such as *Free to Choose*, co-authored by the American economist Milton Friedman (Harcourt, Brace Jovanovich, 1982). In this book one finds a highly impassioned criticism of the inflexibility of American public education and a plea for increased freedom of choice. The impetus behind Friedman's critique came from a desire to repudiate the policy of "reverse discrimination" which was developed by the Democratic Party in the 1960s to improve the conditions of minority groups. Although this policy led to highly successful programs such as Project Head Start which was instituted by the Johnson administration to provide equal educational opportunities for black children from nursery school age, it has been the object of repeated criticisms by Republican administrations from the time of Nixon to that of Reagan as part of their attacks upon the welfare policies championed by the Democrats. Friedman's economic writings have been used to provide the theoretical foundations for these retrogressive policies.

In 1984 Friedman's *Tyranny of the Status Quo* appeared in Japanese, translated by Professor Katō Hiroshi of Keiō University, who in recent years has also served as one of the leading members of the Kyoto Round Table, in particular as the chief of its education subcommittee. Thus we can see how the ideas of Friedman were directly incorporated into the current discourse on educational reform. In fact, in the foreword to this translation, Katō specifically called upon Prime Minister Nakasone to make these ideas into the theoretical foundation for his program of administrative reform.

The keystones of this program for reform rest upon the economic philosophy which states that government should be made both smaller and cheaper, and that public expenditures, especially for education and social welfare, should be markedly reduced. Friedman exempts military expenditures from his austerity recommendations, however: his book devotes one central chapter to demonstrating why, in his view, "national security is the precondition for economic liberalism." In the United States, this line of reasoning has come to be associated with a policy designed to produce what the Reaganites call a "strong America." Not surprisingly, the contradictions generated by the conflicting goals of achieving a cheaper, more streamlined form of government and at the same time increasing national defense expenditures are plaguing public policymakers in Japan as severely as in America. Thus it should be quite clear that the currently proposed forms of educational liberalization will not lead to greater intellectual freedom *from* the State, but rather to greater financial freedom *for* the State.

E. The Neo-conservative Discourse on the State

The Japanese financial world has characteristically identified the State with its bureaucracy, and long ago accustomed itself to fawning obsequiously upon those government officials who they believed could be helpful to them. But in recent years, as Japan's economic standing in the world has steadily risen, our business leaders have come to view the endless rules and regulations issued by the State bureaucracy as unnecessary and undesirable forms of interference, and have issued calls for deregulation of the private sector. These arguments invariably rest upon the belief that to more fully unleash Japan's already impressive economic might, it is now necessary to remove all those unnecessary shackles upon private economic activity which the State has traditionally relied upon to dominate and control national life. Our industrial leaders are increasingly confident when making these claims because they are convinced that it is the accomplishments of the business sector which have made the Japanese nation as powerful as it in fact is today. Therefore, they insist, it is the State bureaucracy which should be responsive to their needs rather than the other way around. Here we can detect the emerging foundations for a new structure of power within Japan itself, and a new form of Japanese nationalism in the larger world environment. This new nationalism is itself coming into existence through a dynamic integration of the recently emergent forms of industrial or enterprise nationalism and the more traditional or established forms of State-centered nationalism. Herein lie the foundations of the currently popular theories of the State alternatively referred to as neo-liberalism or neo-conservatism.

From this perspective it can be clearly seen that too much significance is being read into the frequently touted antagonisms between the Ministry of Education's ideology of strict control and what is described as the Extraordinary Council on Education's emphasis on educational liberalization or deregulation. This is to deny neither that major changes are in the works, nor that the balance of power is shifting away from the Ministry of Education towards industry; my point rather is that viewing recent developments solely in terms of the conflict between these two parties blinds us to the increasingly serious danger that if the Extraordinary Council's recommendations are fully enacted, then the bureaucratic apparatus of the Ministry of Education will in time become the agency executing the will and desires of the Japanese industrial world. We will return to this point and examine it in greater detail in the following section.

For the moment, however, let us consider some of the major differences between the way proposals for educational reform were formulated in the 1960s and the way this is being undertaken in the 1980s; in other words, let us consider the significance of the fact that the locus of this activity has shifted from the Central Council on Education (a deliberative body organized under the jurisdiction of the Ministry of Education) to the Extraordinary Council on Education (a deliberative body organized under the jurisdiction of the Prime Minister and his Cabinet). This transformation is based on the thinking of those "educational liberalizationists" who have argued that Japanese schooling is becoming increasingly distorted under the extreme forms of administrative control exerted by the Ministry of Education. It reflects both (a) the conditions in which the leaders of Japanese business and industry have concluded that the Education Ministry's bureaucratic management is interfering with their own desires for a more efficient form of manpower development and (b) the fact that they have attempted, through the Extraordinary Council on Education and in cooperation with the leadership of the Liberal Democratic Party, to take the power to fix the goals of national educational reform away from our deeply entrenched State bureaucracy.

This assault upon the authority of the Ministry of Education is not an isolated one. It is an expression of the self-assertive boldness characterizing industry's new attitude towards the national government, an attitude in which the unquestioned supremacy of the State's bureaucratic managers is being subjected to unprecedented doubts and previously unimaginable challenges. But to the extent that these new voices only represent the interests of industry, rather than pointing to an effort to liberate the education of the Japanese people, they merely reveal the attempt of a different segment of society to become its unassailable master. What is involved here is an attempt to release educational values from the domination of State nationalism, only to reorient them in the direction of enterprise nationalism. Thus, when the proponents of these educational reforms speak about showing greater respect for the values of individualism, it must be understood that they do not mean the kind of individualism which the early postwar reformers of our schools had in mind. Their thinking is based upon the same motif of an "educational reform administered from above" that has historically been the hallmark of the various forms of anti-democratic and anti-populist educational reform seen in Japan since the Meiji era. Thus it should be clear that these "reforms" will do nothing to relieve the inhuman conditions in which our youth are presently being "educated."

I would like to add one more observation here in regard to the relation between diversification and standardization. As the reader will recall from the discussions in Chapters 12 and 13 of the myths and realities of egalitarianism and individualism in Japanese education, the Ministry of Education's policies for diversification were formulated in the 1960s on the basis of what its bureaucrats criticized as the uniformity of postwar schooling. Of course what they were really attacking were the newly introduced values of egalitarianism. What they presented as an antidote to this was not a form of diversification which contributed significantly to the cultivation of each and every student's individuality, but rather something which made it even easier to make the economic values of the financial and industrial world the central values of our entire society. The direct consequence of this has been a subordination of educational values to the values represented by the ideology of ability-first, which legitimates the ranking of human beings on the basis of test scores and standard deviation. Thus diversification proved to be a ploy for the elimination of all non-economic values that stood in the way of a total commodification of the Japanese people and of Japanese society. The proposals for educational liberalization being offered up today will, if enacted, drive the final nails in the coffin of individualism, and reduce our schools to vicious arenas in which students struggle to rise above one another at whatever cost, regardless of whether the price to be paid is financial or spiritual.

F. The Pact between Industry and the Ministry of Education

It would be a big mistake to draw the conclusion that the members of the Extraordinary Council on Education Reform saw the loosening of State control over the educational process as a necessary correlate of their efforts to lighten the State's financial burden. To promote the further development of a highly competitive school system, one which places the utmost importance on the cultivation of coldly efficient elites, the members of this deliberative body worked to streamline the mechanisms which the existing school system has already provided for controlling the thoughts and aspirations of the People.

At first the Ministry of Education was very much opposed to the tone of the Extraordinary Council's discussions on "educational liberalization." Recognizing that these ideas could very easily be expanded upon to provide the opponents of their administrative domination with the grounds they needed to challenge both the continued legitimacy and desirability of that control, the Ministry's spokesmen countered that their management of the nation's educational and cultural policies was vitally important for preserving the framework of social control which Japan's economic system ultimately rests upon. As a consequence of these arguments the initial tensions between the Extraordinary Council's thinking and the Ministry of Education's thinking gave way to a new form of cooperation in which the foundations were laid for reducing the government's financial burden while at the same time increasing the Ministry of Education's actual capacity to control the inner workings of the educational process.[3] In this fashion the manpower concerns of Japanese industry were neatly harmonized with the financial fears of politicians facing mounting deficits and the prospects of lower rates of economic growth.

Thus, at the same time that the politicians who rule the Liberal Democratic Party were undermining the notion that the State has a responsibility to underwrite the costs of public education in Japan, the Ministry of Education was succeeding in shrewdly preserving the traditional idea that the State has a direct responsibility to involve itself in the organization and management of national education. By bowing to the power of Japan's economic elites, the Ministry of Education was essentially able to maintain its power to control what actually goes on in Japan's schools.

The terms in which this compromise were worked out and the new policy initiatives they have resulted in offer a clear view of the character of power in Japan today. Fearing that if the principle of unrestrained competition which underlies the neo-conservatives' arguments for "educational liberalization" are not balanced by an effective counterforce, then a socially dangerous and destructive state of affairs will inevitably arise in which everyone will view everyone else as his or her enemy, both those sitting on the Extraordinary Council and their nominal antagonists in the Ministry of Education agreed that serious measures were urgently called for. Not surprisingly, these took the form of proposals which pointed to the desirability of strengthening moral education and placing greater emphasis on inculcating the ideologies associated with the virtues of "traditional" Japanism. Thus, for example, we find much talk in the council's various reports on the need to accentuate the symbolic value of the Imperial system and the regalia which have characteristically been associated with it such as the *Kimigayo* (prewar Japan's national anthem) and the *Hinomaru* (the Rising Sun) in order to better control the People's sentiments.

Interestingly enough, this has also been framed in terms of Japan's need to internationalize. But internationalization here means nothing other than Japan's ambition to rise to a position of singular importance and power in the twenty-first century. Needless to say, this also represents a concerted attempt to subsume all of our children's hopes and dreams within the vision of a new, but no less dangerous, form of

---

[3] The point of these budgetary restrictions was not to reduce the expenses involved in administrative control, but to reduce the expenses incurred in making compulsory education available to the Japanese people.

Japanese imperialism than that which led to Japan's militaristic adventurism in the 1930s and 1940s.

Finally, we should pay attention to the way these impulses are working themselves out at the level of administrative control. First of all, with regard to the problem of the bureaucratic domination of teachers, it must be pointed out that the proposals put forth for strengthening the Ministry's control over the in-service training of new teachers, far from giving them greater opportunities to talk freely and openly with their colleagues in the teaching profession, are actually intended to make young instructors more fearful of the consequences they will face if they do not eagerly and willingly uphold the directives issued to them by the Ministry of Education.

Second, we must look at the way the council dealt with the problem of textbook screening. Even the original system appears to have some real merit compared to the one now being proposed. While textbook authors at present have the opportunity to negotiate with Ministry inspectors at three different stages in the screening process, if the form of rationalization advocated by the Reform Council is adopted, the occasions for these exchanges of opinion will be eliminated altogether. Arguing that this makes the process unnecessarily complex, the Extraordinary Council has suggested that the work being put up for certification as a textbook should simply be approved or rejected at once. Of course what they are really pushing for is a system wherein the textbook publishing companies do all the censorship of "unacceptable" ideas before the work ever finds its way to the Ministry of Education's inspectors. This would have the effect of strengthening the power of the Ministry's own Course of Study. Here is a clear example of the way the logics of economic liberalization and rationalization can be used to adversely circumscribe educational liberty.

Another informative example is provided by the council's recommendations with regard to the rationalization of educational content. In the curriculum mandated for use in the lower levels of compulsory education, it was declared desirable to eliminate social studies and science and replace them with a comprehensive life-style course. There is nothing in itself objectionable with the idea of relating these heretofore distinct areas of study within a larger context, and those of us in the People's Education Movement have long been arguing about the desirability of doing precisely that. The problem, however, arises when one considers where this will lead in the future. An answer to this question is provided by the recent declaration by the Curriculum Deliberation Council (under the Ministry of Education's control) that, beginning in the 1990s, social studies, the linchpin of postwar democratic education, will no longer be taught as a required subject in Japan's high schools. Already we have seen the Ministry reduce the amount of time given to these subjects in lower and upper secondary schools. Nor is it an accident or a strange coincidence that the classroom time thus freed up is now being used for more moral education instruction. Moreover there is much less opportunity now for teachers to decide how to use this time for creative educational purposes.

III. People-Based Reform

A. The Standpoint of the Japan Teachers' Union

Notwithstanding the centrality of the rhetoric of liberalization within the debates of the Extraordinary Council on educational reform, it is clear that this discourse is directly opposed to all serious attempts to free education from the clutches of the State. In fact, the meaning of this discourse is incomprehensible apart from the assumption that the "public" in public education refers to the State, and not the People. To combat this dangerously deceptive discourse, we must rededicate our efforts to formulating an alternative approach to educational reform, one in which the People will no longer be conceived merely as passive consumers of knowledge but as the active creators and masters of knowledge. In other words, the time has now come when we must take decisive steps to free education from the forms of control imposed by the State and industry, and realize the vision of a nation in which the People enlighten themselves.

This spirit of popular-based reform from below has underscored the efforts of the Japan Teachers' Union's (Nikkyōso's) Council for Educational Reform. Its 1974 report, "How to Reform Japanese Education," attacked the administrative overregulation of our schools and its deleterious effects upon the development of our young into autonomous human beings. It was based on two fundamental value orientations: (a) the principles of equality and individuality as discussed in Chapter 12 of this book, and (b) the principle that education is one of the People's most fundamental human rights. That report examined a wide range of problems in the current conditions such as the situation with regard to education for handicapped children, rigid government control of curricular development, and violations of teachers' professional rights. Moreover, as these and related problems became more serious in the 1980s, a second Council for Educational Reform was formed as an affiliated but independent organ by the J.T.U. in 1981. This group's proposals for the improvement of Japanese education appeared in two documents issued in 1984, "Educational Reform in Present-day Japan" and "A Plan for Reforming Popular Education." These reports have been widely read and are exerting a not inconsiderable influence upon the character of the debates within the non-governmental, non-industrial sector of our society on the best way to overcome the educational crises analyzed throughout this volume.

B. Reconstructing the Public Character of Public Education

By this point it should be eminently clear to the reader that the Ministry of Education has tried throughout the postwar period to resurrect the prewar idea that the public character of public education can only be determined by the State as part of its management of the nation's business. In their attempt to recapture a privileged position within the new legal framework of Japanese democracy, the Ministry's bureaucrats have been forced to invent a wide range of arguments which allow them to navigate their way around the notion that in a free society the State has no business telling teachers what to teach, textbook authors what to write, or students what to learn. These arguments have tended to revolve around the notion that only the State can provide the authoritative voice capable of defining and upholding the nation's need for uniform standards. Under this pretext, these agents of Japan's bureaucratic State have reinstalled the Ministry of Education as the one and only legitimate arbitrator of the public's genuine educational needs. However, those of us who believe that the true aims of education must reside both in the development of each and every child's capacities as a human being and in the guarantee of their rights as the autonomous subjects of a democratic society have long maintained that the meaning of "public" in public education *cannot and must not* be determined unilaterally by the State and its agents.

Therefore, in order to help children fully realize their naturally given rights to learn and develop as human beings, our school system must be reorganized to make it more responsive to the authority of parents. Moreover, the pooling of parental authority is critically important for: (1) the establishment of a democratic or popularly controlled system of schools; (2) an expansion of the rights of individuals; and (3) the creation of a new sense of what "the public" means, and can be made to mean. In other words, in order to revitalize our system of public education, it is necessary to create a new sense of the public character of society as something which belongs to everyone equally and to which everyone equally belongs.

This is intimately related to the issues of how children are understood, and who is viewed as having the primary responsibility for educating them. Today's liberalists argue that children should be regarded as the private property of their parents. Therefore the only authority they recognize as legitimate is that belonging to the parent, and as a consequence they threaten to insulate and isolate parental authorities and responsibilities from the very real social and educational concerns I am trying to call attention to. It is necessary to insist that in addition to the fact that children belong to their parents, they also belong to the society they live in and to mankind in general. With this in mind it becomes possible to correct the excesses in contemporary thinking about the appropriate character and organization of educational authority and responsibility.

In our attempt to formulate a new foundation for public education, it is also necessary to go beyond the idea that education is primarily the responsibility of the student's parents. This means building upon the notion of what constitutes the public's interest in order to make education responsive to other voices in society. There is one other reason why it is important for us to think about public education in terms of its communal or cooperative character: because education is the means by which knowledge and culture are transmitted to the members of new generations, it has the potential for nurturing the capacities the young need to overcome the problems and contradictions they inherit from their elders. In this sense the public consequences of education impinge upon the lives and interests of all members of society, not just the State, parents, or students themselves.

Even though today's would-be educational deregulators argue that the aim of their proposed reforms is to free our schools from existing forms of excessive bureaucratic control, it must not be overlooked that even if they succeed in dissolving what remains of our public system of education, and manage to replace it with a totally privatized form of instruction, inasmuch as the work of our schools will still be geared to standards unilaterally fixed by the Ministry of Education, their reforms will do nothing to introduce the spirits of intellectual and academic freedom into the world of Japanese education. Moreover, we must raise the question of whether it is even possible to transform publicly established schools in the image and spirit of privately organized ones.

Underlying the populist reforms of our schools which I am advancing in opposition to the elitist reforms advocated by the neo-conservative liberalists on the Extraordinary Council on Education is the notion (legally proclaimed in the Fundamental Law of Education) that the primary aim of education should be the cultivation of a citizenry that demands freedom, justice, peace, and their basic human rights. From this standpoint it should become quite obvious that the creation of a new consciousness of "the public" in public education is inseparable from the liberation of popular education from all forms of control imposed by the State from above. This is also closely tied to the need to develop a new discourse on the relation between "human rights and the public welfare."

Finally I want to point out that within the revitalized system of public education being called for here, children must be respected as autonomous personalities, and never treated merely as means to someone else's ends. From this perspective the right to education can and should be grasped as inseparable from the right to develop and learn in a manner befitting free human beings. Likewise, our school system must be reorganized so that neither parents, teachers, nor administrators are able to violate or trample upon these basic educational rights. This requires the nurturing of a new educational consciousness within the hearts and minds of the Japanese people, a consciousness which will support our efforts to rededicate our schools to the values of democracy and human rights. Until this new consciousness becomes accepted as common sense in our society, all our efforts—for example to improve the teaching methods utilized in our schools—will have little lasting significance. Until, in other words, the foundations of educational practice are reconceived in relation to the need for a new sense of "the public," and a new commitment to the values of truth, justice, and peace, there is little reason to believe that the educational mess analyzed in this book can or will be corrected.

C. The Various Forms of the Right to Learn

I would now like to discuss in greater detail the significance of the idea that people possess the inalienable right to learn throughout the different phases of their lives. To this end I will explore the meaning of the right to learn in four different senses: the citizen's right to learn in general, the right to learn of local inhabitants, workers' right to learn, and the child's right to learn.

The Citizen's Right to Learn

If the People's right to learn is inconceivable apart from the idea of popular sovereignty, then popular sovereignty is unthinkable apart from the right to learn. In fact, as soon as one begins to think of education as the activity which protects the vitality of popular sovereignty, it should become abundantly clear that the right to learn must be guaranteed so that the People can autonomously achieve full consciousness of their status as the rulers of our democratic society. Hence the right to an education must be included among the rights of citizens in a popularly controlled society because it cultivates the sensibilities necessary for upholding a free form of political life.

Under the ancien régime, not only were the People treated merely as objects to be controlled, they were thoroughly alienated from access to genuine forms of knowledge and the truths of their own social life. Control was exercised by keeping the People politically dependent and socially ignorant. Thus in Japan no less than in Europe it was difficult to disentangle tyrannical government of the nation from the ignorance of the People in general.

As I demonstrated in Chapter 2, this was fully understood by Fukuzawa Yukichi, who argued that if people want to avoid tyrannical government, they must immediately set their minds to the pursuit of learning so as to elevate their talents and virtues. Fukuzawa called upon the People to maintain their commitment to learning and study across the entire course of their lives. To the extent that he understood this was necessary for producing subjects who could bear the weight of national independence, Fukuzawa was indeed one of the forebears of our movement for a free form of educational life.

It was this kind of thinking which originally fueled the modern impulse to establish systems of universal public education. In spite of these attempts to transform the relation between people and knowledge, however, in states such as Japan the propagation of universal schooling has actually worked to consolidate the political power of the privileged few who have bureaucratically administered knowledge from above.

The political philosopher Sigmund Neumann was forced to re-examine the classical thesis that tyrants come to power through the ignorance of the People after the Nazis assumed power in a Germany which had already witnessed the development and diffusion of a modern system of compulsory education. Even if this system banished illiteracy, it was responsible for the birth of a new form of domination, one based on what he called the cultivation of mass "political illiteracy." In this manner Neumann was able to solve the riddle of how a dictatorship could be established in a modern nation-state having a high standard of education. His analysis holds as well for the Imperial system of education imposed on the Japanese people before World War II.

The American sociologist C. Wright Mills was troubled by this problem and tried to account for it in terms of the mechanisms established to achieve mass manipulation in modern democracies. Mills called attention to "alienation from the truth" as one of the primary factors making this possible. Organized education, he intuited, is useful for producing intellectual mediocrity, and schools are easily transformable into worship halls in which the spirit of loyal devotion to the State can be cultivated. As the holders of state power use the organs of the mass media to secretly set the directions in which they want to see public opinion move, they increasingly become able to exercise what Mills saw as new modes for achieving virtually total social control.

The appropriateness of this analysis was made apparent to all in the U.S. in the 1970s through the Pentagon Papers and Watergate incidents. Or is there any room for doubt about how successful the American government was in defrauding public opinion both internally and externally during the Vietnam War? The Washington correspondent of the *Asahi Shimbun* summarized these conditions following the signing of the Vietnam Peace Accords (January 26, 1973):

> Practically all newspaper reporters in the Western camp placed confidence in announcements from the White House at the time of the Tonkin Gulf Incident, and used them uncritically in their reporting. After all, it was virtually unthinkable that an American President could be party to such blatantly shameless forms of falsification.

These revelations gave us a double-barreled shock. First we were forced to confront the reality of an American President trying to make black appear white, and then we realized that the very reporters whom we rely upon to be professionally skeptical were in fact unbelievably credulous. In response to these circumstances the importance of citizens' rights to inquire and their freedom to know the truth have been widely recognized, and one can only hope this will eventually lead to the development of new demands for the "right to know" with regard to political and other forms of publicly relevant information.

The confessions of this *Asahi* journalist go on to tell a story that clarifies some of the underlying reasons why news reporters were virtually compelled to believe statements coming from the White House.

> From the outset there were many American reporters who repeatedly sensed that something was wrong. Tom Wicker, former Washington bureau chief for *The New York Times*, shared this bitter recollection: "In the fall of 1966 I attended a Washington dinner party where in front of all the guests present I was attacked by a high-ranking U.S. government official who after asking 'Why does your newspaper only print lies?' placed a telephone call to a military commander in Vietnam. 'Is it true, as *The New York Times* has reported, that the radio station where you are

has been taken over and occupied by Buddhists?' From across the ocean came back a voice answering 'No.' Some months later I was in Hue and met the military man who had been called that night. He lowered his head in shame and said, 'The truth was exactly as your paper reported. But it was impossible to say so in answer to a question from Washington.'" Herein lies revealed the true nature of the Vietnam War: from top to bottom it was held together and carried forward on the basis of lies.

This example clearly shows the extent to which the leaders of democracies are willing to go to distort and hide the truth even in excessively information-oriented societies. The People, who as the citizens of a democratic society should be the masters of its political life, are thereby reduced to mere objects of the most cynical and callous forms of control. Of course this is not limited to political life in foreign countries. We already know of too many cases, such as the Lockheed bribery scandal, where strong pressures were exerted to prevent disclosure of official malfeasance. There have even been cases where members of the Diet have been subjected to punitive action in response to their perfectly legitimate questioning of the government's leaders.

Thus, it should be clear to all concerned that the citizens' rights to freely inquire and to know the truth are intimately tied to the realization of a genuine form of political sovereignty. It is our duty as educators to make these rights a vital part of our people's self-consciousness as citizens. We must therefore work to (a) win acceptance of the idea that *the People's rights to know* are constitutionally guaranteed ones, and (b) further their concrete development in the everyday life of the nation.

The Right to Learn of Local Inhabitants

Because citizens dwell within and make their livings as the residents of a particular area, it is important to recognize their rights as its inhabitants. In recent years, as the destruction of the different regions of Japan has been accelerated by the government's industrial development policies, local residents have become more aware of the need to assert their regional rights and to strengthen their claims to regional autonomy. In the years to come it can be expected that this will lead to increased tensions between those who support and those who want to restrain the growth of local residents' movements and the principle of regional autonomy they rest upon. The future success of these populist movements will depend in large measure on the extent to which regional inhabitants become aware of and exercise their rights to learn.

Miyamoto Ken'ichi, an economist at Osaka Municipal University who has played a major role in articulating the theoretical foundations and objectives of local residents' movements, has argued:

> It will become increasingly urgent for the People to regulate the role of large-scale capital and to influence the ways it is used to transform the regional environments within which they live.

Regional industrial development exerts a powerful influence on nature, human health, the economy, and culture. To make comprehensive judgments concerning these influences, and to apply the brakes to uncontrolled industrial development, residents' cultural consciousness must be significantly enhanced.

These movements achieved their first successes in Mishima, Numazu, and Shimizu. They were stimulated by hundreds of study assemblies in which primary importance was given to the experiences of the local residents. The methods employed there were not based on abstract arguments, but rather came out of the concrete experiences of the citizens of these local areas. Teachers and professional scientists also played important roles in these assemblies, but not as enlighteners from above who arrogantly set the residents straight. Thus it can be said that these meetings were guided by the principle that when it comes to the efforts of citizens in the regions to educate themselves, ordinary residents, professional researchers, and teachers all stand on an equal footing. Within this framework it became possible for the residents to alter the directions in which researchers do their work, and in doing so they gave new meaning to Bachelard's reformulation of the dialectic of learning and teaching.

Although these local citizens' movements were begun in response to the problems posed by industrial development and environmental pollution, they have not limited themselves to those issues. Groups have also been formed throughout the nation to study textbooks and defend the principles of democratic education. These popularly organized associations have matured to the point where today they play a major role in upholding the foundations of our education movement. The energies which have coalesced in support of Professor Ienaga's courtroom struggles to free textbook production and certification from the tentacles of the State's bureaucratic apparatus (see Part II, Chapters 6 and 7) have in most cases been nurtured precisely in these independently organized forums. Moreover, these associations have made an important contribution to the development of regional inhabitants' deepening understanding of their right to learn.

Workers' Rights to Learn

Work is mankind's most fundamental form of self-realization. Its driving force is tied to the conceptual powers that emerge from concrete experience and study. This recognition stands at the heart of the modern labor movement, and is reflected in the idea that in order for workers to become the masters of their own free (unalienated) labor, they must be guaranteed the right to continue learning throughout the entire course of their lives.

Our current consciousness of the educational rights of workers has its roots in nineteenth-century England, in particular in the Chartist Movement, which sought to bring about democratic social and political reforms. In France this awareness was historically deepened through the experiences of the February Revolution, the Paris Commune, and the Second International. In recent years new emphasis on the right to learn has been incorporated into the agendas of labor movements both inside and outside Japan. The joint communiqué issued by the International Symposium on Occupational Training sponsored by Sōhyō (the Japan Labor Unions General Council) in 1971 declared:

We affirm the basic right of all workers to demand a reorganization of school education, job training, and adult education in accordance with their needs, and insist that their rights to receive such education and training be steadfastly guaranteed.

The impetus to organize the educational rights of workers had already been manifested in Japan by the early 1960s. In the Second Appeal of the Research Assembly on Occupational Training and Education sponsored by Sōhyō and Chūritsu Rōren (the Unaffiliated Unions Liaison Conference) we find this formulation:

All workers have a right to receive occupational and technical education at the public's expense without regard to age or sex. The State should provide the necessary resources. Particular emphasis should be given to the rights of young workers.

Consciousness of the bonds uniting labor and educational rights was born both inside and outside the working-class movement. This consciousness has led to a rigorous and critical scrutiny of the training and education promoted in Japan as one link in the systems designed to enhance managerial efficiency and control in the industrial world. For example, the National Railways workers who protested officially organized enterprise training on the grounds that it failed to uphold the principles enunciated in the Fundamental Law of Education revealed an expanding awareness of the inherent connections between educational and labor rights.

The Child's Right to Learn

Among the various rights to learn which must be recognized as belonging to the People in a democratic society, none are more important than those which should be enjoyed by children. For young people, who are still replete with untapped possibilities, the right to study and learn is inseparable from the right to a humane form of growth and development. In other words, as long as these rights are not adequately guaranteed, the rights children are entitled to take advantage of as adults—the rights to exist, work, and participate in political society—can never be fully realized. Indeed, it can be said that the child's right to learn is the cornerstone of all our human rights, and the one which gives them their social lifeblood.

Since the child's right to learn is not one that can be directly guaranteed by each child individually, it already presupposes the existence of people who will work to support and encourage children in their attempts to make sense of the world. Seen in this light, parents and teachers in particular, and society in general, have an obligation to guarantee children's rights by providing them with the opportunities for an appropriate form of education. This way of thinking is indeed very different from that advocated by the Prime Minister's Extraordinary Council on Education, in which the child is viewed as the parent's private property, deserving only the kind of education parents see fit to provide them on the basis of their needs and desires. Only when this attitude is truly taken to heart does it become possible to protect education from "improper forms of control," be they of parents, society, or the State. Only then can education assure the intellectual, developmental, and political rights of the new generation of society.

IV. From Passively Protecting to Actively Demanding Human Rights

The preceding discussion of the People's educational rights was driven by a desire to reapprehend the place of learning and inquiry within the organization of contemporary social life. Underlying this is my concern to provide an expansive interpretation of our modern intellectual rights and freedoms. In other words, I have sought to encourage people in Japan to move beyond the generally accepted perspective in which these rights are viewed as things to be passively defended so that they can begin to re-envision them as values which must be actively and creatively demanded.

I would now like to conclude this book by exploring some of the most important implications of this way of thinking.

A. The Right to Learn as a Basis for Reconstructing the Freedom of Information

Article 21 of Japan's postwar Constitution states:

> Freedom of assembly and association as well as speech, press, and other forms of expression are guaranteed. No censorship shall be maintained, nor shall the secrecy of any means of communication be violated.

These freedoms are rooted in the time-honored idea that the citizens of a modern nation have certain inalienable rights of expression, centered around the liberties I want to call the right to learn and the freedom of information. Unfortunately, however, in entirely too many cases the freedom of information has been understood not as an everyday right but as a special privilege. Moreover, inasmuch as these freedoms have been subjugated to the authority of the State and the power of large-scale money-making organzations, the status of information as a form of knowledge has been severely limited and in many cases perverted. This is visible in those instances where the "freedom of information" argument has been invoked to legitimate attempts to deprive the People of access to public truths which should be seen as belonging to everyone. When, however, the freedom of expression comes to be viewed from the perspective of the People's rights to learn, it can be spoken of as an expression of their "right to know."

Okudaira Yasuhiro attempted to clarify the legal framework of the right to know from the standpoint of the People in an article that appeared in the journal *Juristo* (*Jurist*) in 1970. According to Okudaira, this right has been seriously blighted by the social interventions of large-scale capital. As a consequence, he argues, the pluralism and diversity of different forms of knowledge have been severely eroded and in many cases forfeited altogether:

> Present conditions are such that those working in the mass media think that the freedom of expression belongs only to them. In other words they think that this freedom has been specially provided for them and does not belong to all the People. Therefore

it is more appropriate to speak in terms of the "right to know."

This viewpoint shares the same fundamental values as my arguments on the meaning of the People's right to learn. The thinking which underscores this transformation of priorities aims to help the People see why it is their duty to force the government to make political and other forms of public information available to everyone equally. It also suggests that the values guiding those in the media should be altered so that they will take it upon themselves to aggressively and accurately report to the People all the information they need to act responsibly as citizens in a society based on the principle of popular sovereignty.

I think this demonstrates why the People's "right to learn" and their "right to know" are expressions of the same democratic spirit. However, in the field of constitutional law as presently constructed, the People's right to know has essentially been viewed in two contrasting ways. On the one hand (the standpoint of the State) it has been defined as being limited to a "personal" or "private" right granted solely to facilitate the growth and development of the individual. In opposition to this, others have argued that the People's right to know must be seen as "the precondition for formulation of the popular will." From this perspective this right has been understood as having "a public nature intended to guarantee full political participation in the political process." For the constitutional scholar Ashibe Nobuyoshi the importance and significance of this modern right rests with the interpretation that stresses its public and political character. He has constructed a legal theory which sees the "principal purpose" of this right as "guaranteeing the freedom of educational and political knowledge."

On the basis of this formulation, it can be argued that the right to know must not be limited to passively receiving information from those with special intellectual privileges. The perspective that sustains our thinking about the People's right to learn is therefore one which allows us to unify the rights "to learn" and "to know" in terms of the right to freely obtain knowledge, whether of a political or any other kind of public nature.

Thus I want to restate the central point of this thesis about the inseparability of the right to know and the principles of popular sovereignty and political liberty: notwithstanding the fact that they originate in long-established ideas about human rights, they have to be reasserted as "new rights" in response to the forms of alienation developed in contemporary mass society.

An editorial in *The New York Times* of January 23, 1945, referred to a speech given by Kent Cooper, who for many years was employed by the Associated Press. Cooper was singled out for attention by the *Times* for his advocacy of "the right to know."

> Kent Cooper used a good phrase for an old freedom. The citizen is entitled to have access to news, fully and accurately presented. There cannot be political freedom in one country, or in the world, without respect for "the right to know."

As the Watergate and Iran-Contra scandals have made so frightfully clear, when the guardians of public authority are unwilling or unable to trust the People, they take it upon themselves to determine what the "right to know" in fact means. This is tantamount to a denial of the People's political liberties and their freedoms to inquire into things they want to know about. It means keeping vitally important knowledge and information from the People and forcing them to swallow all fallacious representations of existing realities. In fact, it can even be argued that this is what keeps today's mass democracies afloat. Thus we can see how important it is to tie the "People's rights to know and learn" to the larger project of breathing life into the ideal of popular sovereignty.

B. The People's Right to Learn as a Basis for Reconstructing Academic Freedom

Article 23 of the postwar Constitution declares: "Academic freedom is guaranteed." If read in an unbiased fashion, there is no way this can be viewed as saying anything other than that the intellectual rights and liberties of each and every Japanese citizen are legally protected. Within the context of the official interpretation handed down by the State, however, academic freedom is still viewed in the way it was in prewar Japan—namely, as a special privilege of elites in the universities. This interpretation has proven to be a useful tool for those who have wanted to short-circuit the aims set out by the postwar reform of our schools.

By including academic freedom in the section on human rights, the authors of our Constitution made it clear that this liberty belongs to all citizens equally, and must no longer be thought of as a special privilege conferred on specific individuals by the State. Thus we must work to make sure that in the future academic freedom will be treated in Japan as an expression of the People's intellectual freedoms—their rights to inquire freely, to learn, and to discover new truths. Only in this way can the People become the masters of scholarly research, and only in this way can our universities be lifted above their present status as self-complacent ivory towers. Besides which, it is necessary to attack the corruption resulting from cooperation between universities and industry.

Uehara Senroku defined this challenge as the "popularization of learning" (*gakumon no kokuminka*), by which he meant that the needs of the People should form the nucleus of scholarly concern and activity. Likewise this teaches us to recognize that the freedom to conduct research enjoyed by professional scholars is not delegated to them by the State but entrusted to them by the People. Accordingly, the contents of their research should be determined in response to the needs of the People.

There is thus a pressing need to reorganize our system of national education so that it will guarantee the integrity and indivisibility of the bonds between education and scholarship. To this end our universities should be seen as one link in our system of national education, not as its apex. In other words, we must pursue a rebirth of "the university for the sake of the People."

The American political scientist Alexander Meiklejohn has written about the academic freedom of professional researchers in his *Political Freedom: The Constitutional Powers of the People*:

> Academic freedom is a special form, a subform, of popular freedom. We who engage in research and teaching do so as agents of the people of the nation. In virtue of special abilities and training, we are commissioned to carry on for the people forms of intellectual activity which belong to them, are done in their interest, but which, in some specific forms, they cannot carry on for themselves. Just as some men make shoes and other men grow food, so it is our business to discover truth in its more intellectualized forms and to make it powerful in the guidance of the life of the community. And since we are thus acting as the agents of the people, they grant to us such of their freedom as is needed in that field of work. In a word, the final justification of our academic freedom is to be found not in our purposes but in theirs. In the last resort, it is granted not because we want it or enjoy it, but because those by whom we are commissioned need intellectual leadership in the thinking which a free society must do. May I state the principle bluntly and frankly? Our final responsibility, as scholars and teachers, is not to the truth. It is to the people who need the truth.

Uchida Yoshiko has argued in a similar vein that since the social sciences we have today were developed as part of an attempt to develop the means for "manipulating the People," redressing this situation requires that the People take a more active interest, even if as amateurs, in the activities that make up academic praxis. Thus it can well be said that a perspective which allows us to speak of the People and their needs as the only legitimate point of reference for scholarly research must not be restricted to a discourse on education and educational rights. This perspective must be extended so as to include, for example, the concerns of local citizens' protests against regional industrial exploitation and environmental pollution. By concentrating our concern in these directions, I believe we can improve the quality and character of our right-to-learn movement, and at the same time increase the political competency of the Japanese people in general. Thus we can show that the popularization of scholarship (*gakumon no kokuminka*) is dialectically inseparable from intellectual cultivation of the People (*kokumin no gakumonka*). This is absolutely crucial if we are going to succeed in transforming academic freedom from a special privilege to the right of each and every citizen, and if we are going to increase the social awareness of those doing research and the intellectual awareness of society in general.

C. Educational Freedom and the Right to Learn

History shows that the struggle to liberate education in Japan from the tentacles of State control has repeatedly been energized by new ideas about the necessity of intellectual freedom and the importance of an independent form of pedagogic authority. In fact, this struggle is now being fortified by fresh ideas about why the freedoms of thought and belief are so vital to the success of the educational process.

Acknowledgment of the "educational rights of the child" can lead to no conclusion other than that the child must be regarded as the sovereign or master of his or her intellectual fate. In addition to establishing that parents and society have an obligation to guarantee an education appropriate to the child's particular developmental stage, this new perspective makes it possible to view "educational freedom" as indistinguishable from the "right to an education" (*droit à l'enseignement*). In addition, as the inseparability of the ties linking popular sovereignty and the right to an education come to be more universally recognized, support continually grows for the movement to fulfill the child's educational rights. This growing consciousness has been manifested most forcefully in the Sugimoto decision discussed in Chapter 6.

Our new formulations of the child's right to learn have made it possible to fuse the concept of "the right to an education" with already well-established ideas concerning the character of "educational freedom." Our calls for the popularization of higher learning have been directed towards a realization of these values. In particular, our discourse on the educational rights that belong to children by virtue of the developmental possibilities contained within them itself represents an attempt to awaken popular consciousness to the necessity of guaranteeing these most basic of all human rights in as concrete a manner as possible.

The idea of educational liberty demands that educational practice be autonomous and independent from the State. This means that guarantees must be provided to assure the freedom of the teacher's educational research and praxis and that parents' freedom not only to choose the school but also to criticize and influence the kind of education their children receive must also be protected.

Jean Piaget has written about the "right to an education" in his commentary on Article 26 of the Universal Declaration of Human Rights that was adopted by the General Assembly of the United Nations on December 10, 1948. Piaget saw this right as "neither more nor less than the right of an individual to develop normally, in accord with all the potential he possesses, and the obligation that society has to transform this potential into useful and effective fulfillment."

> Affirming the right of all human beings to an education is to take on a far greater responsibility than simply to assure to each one reading, writing, and arithmetic capabilities; it is to guarantee fairly to each child the entire development of his mental faculties and the acquisition of knowledge and of ethical values corresponding to the exercise of these faculties until adaptation to actual social life. Moreover, it is to assume the obligation—keeping in mind the aptitudes and constitution that each person possesses—of not destroying or spoiling those possiblities he may have that would benefit society first of all, or of allowing the loss of important abilities, or the smothering of others.

From this vantage point, it is quite clear that thinking about the "right to an education" should be premised on the freedom of educational choice, but should not stop there.

From the perspective of educational freedom, the right to an education should be conceived as containing the rights to expect and receive an education as well as the right to reject one that is judged to be unsuitable. This perspective has played an instrumental role in helping us wage our struggle against the State's system of textbook censorship; it underlies our arguments that the authorship and adoption of textbooks should be undertaken in a free manner.

This flies directly in the face of the arguments put forth by the Ministry of Education that textbook authors do not suffer any infringement of their right to free expression because even if their works are judged unfit for publication as texts for use in publicly supported schools they still can be published like any other book. However, textbook freedom is not a corollary of the freedom of expression; rather it is part of the right to learn. In this sense the struggle for textbook freedom is an indispensable element in our effort to reconstitute educational authority within the context of a system that stresses popular sovereignty as the only legitimate foundation for educational practice.

D. The Right to Learn, the Freedom of Occupational Choice, and the Right to Self-Fulfillment through Work

By shattering all social systems rooted in status and hierarchy, the establishment of modern states made it possible for men to assert the principles of occupational freedom and equality of opportunity. Article 22 of our postwar Constitution acknowledges these principles by declaring:

> Every person shall have freedom to choose . . . his occupation to the extent that it does not interfere with the public welfare.

However, as Japanese society is presently constituted, there is little room in the workplace for the free development of the worker's individuality. This results from the fact, as discussed in Chapter 13, that the development and manifestation of each and every individual's unique characteristics as a human being has been retarded, if not totally suppressed, by the subjugation of educational development to economic development.

To connect occupational freedom with true individuality, and to transform the workplace into an environment in which genuine individuality can be developed, education must be actively premised on the notion that the rights to grow and develop are not limited to one's life during the stages of childhood and adolescence, but also extend into and throughout one's working life. At the same time, we must also struggle to make work a necessary part of the process of learning and inquiry.

At the same time, the rights to grow and develop, which we have associated with education, should also be considered a vital part of our inalienable right to the pursuit of personal happiness. Thus the freedom of occupational choice will only cease to mean the "freedom to be unhappy" after each and every member of the nation becomes the autonomous subject of his own freely entertained inquiries—only when this right is recognized as something more than a merely formal (but unrealistic) one, and one constantly and actively demanded by all the People.

E. The Right to Learn as a Way to Guarantee the Substance of Popular Sovereignty

In order to reverse the conditions in which the political freedoms guaranteed to the People have essentially been reduced to legal fictions, and in which the right to rule has been transformed into the right to be controlled, the movement for educational reform must work to increase the Japanese people's desire to exercise—and thereby reclaim—their rights to self-governance. One of the best ways to encourage the People to actively assert themselves as the supreme authority in Japanese social life is by getting them to become directly involved in the struggle to wrest the power to control education away from the State bureaucracy.

The right to self-determination is inseparable from the rights to learn and freely inquire. The ability of people to make the kinds of judgments regarding society that they must make in order to defend their naturally given political rights depends upon their exercising those rights to learn and inquire.

This process has already begun. In the schools, participation in PTA activities, parent-teacher study groups, and committees of inquiry on various school problems have shown parents that they need not be only passive recipients of State educational policies. At the community level, political activism is growing: in residents' and voters' pressure groups, people are learning to take community affairs into their own hands.

Condorcet long ago observed that the power to usurp popular sovereignty is made possible by the adeptness with which rulers are able to deprive the People of the right to formulate their own thoughts and opinions. Our task today is to eliminate this possibility by making politics the object of everyday discussion and criticism as well as the focus of popular demands for reform. Establishing the autonomy of the citizens who make up our self-governing bodies is therefore the key to revitalizing the foundations of popular sovereignty. Accordingly, when we succeed in making the citizens of Japan realize that they also have rights as the residents of their towns, cities, and regions, then it will become possible to help them expand their horizons as the ultimate defenders and upholders of a democratic culture.

The ideas I have been discussing in relation to "the People's right to learn" represent an attempt to generate a new starting point for mobilizing these concerns. When the significance of these ideas is fully grasped, it becomes possible to expand the arena of discussion from the narrowly defined one of defending rights from encroachment to the broader one of enhancing people's potential. The freedom of expression, viewed from a wider perspective, becomes "the People's right to know." Academic freedom is expanded into "the popularization of scholarship." Educational freedom becomes "the right to an education"; occupational freedom, "the right to self-realization through work." Political liberty, viewed in a broader context, is the "right of a sovereign people to self-governance." Therefore an unwavering commitment to the values and possibilities contained in the notion of the People's right to learn also reveals the path by which human rights can be transformed from passive into active forces within our shared social life. These ideas teach us how to go beyond tranquilly defending human rights to forcefully demanding them.

The values embedded in the idea that the People have a right to learn also provide us with a vantage point from which we can re-examine the foundations of the freedoms that are already recognized as belonging to those who pursue specialized occupations with particular relevance to the liberties and rights of the People: journalists and others in the mass media, researchers, and teachers. From this perspective it can furthermore be seen that definite social responsibilities go along with these liberties, and that these must be understood as being rooted in the "People's right to know the truth" and their freedom of inquiry. In short, this standpoint teaches us to see that the source of all such special rights is not the State, but the People who entrust those practicing these professions with special responsibilities. In this fashion it can well be said that the "People's right to learn" is indeed the foundation of all our human rights.

Appendix I

The Imperial Rescript on Education (1890)

Know Ye, Our Subjects:

Our Imperial Ancestors have founded Our Empire on a basis broad and everlasting and have deeply and firmly implanted virtue; Our subjects ever united in loyalty and filial piety have from generation to generation illustrated the beauty thereof. This is the glory of the fundamental character of Our Empire, and herein also lies the source of Our education. Ye, Our subjects, be filial to your parents, affectionate to your brothers and sisters; as husbands and wives be harmonious, as friends true; bear yourselves in modesty and moderation; extend your benevolence to all; pursue learning and cultivate arts, and thereby develop intellectual faculties and perfect moral powers; furthermore advance public good and promote common interests; always respect the Constitution and observe the laws; should emergency arise, offer yourselves courageously to the State; and thus guard and maintain the prosperity of Our Imperial Throne coeval with heaven and earth. So shall ye not only be Our good and faithful subjects, but render illustrious the best traditions of your forefathers.

The Way here set forth is indeed the teaching bequeathed by Our Imperial Ancestors, to be observed alike by Their Descendants and the subjects, infallible for all ages and true in all places. It is Our wish to lay it to heart in all reverence, in common with you, Our subjects, that we may all thus attain to the same virtue.

The 30th day of the 10th month of the 23rd year of Meiji [1890].

—Official Translation

The Fundamental Law of Education (1947)

Having established the Constitution of Japan, we have shown our resolution to contribute to the peace of the world and welfare of humanity by building a democratic and cultural state. The realization of this ideal shall depend fundamentally on the power of education. We shall esteem individual dignity and endeavor to bring up people who love truth and peace, while education which aims at the creation of culture, general and rich in individuality, shall be spread far and wide. We hereby enact this Law, in accordance with the spirit of the Constitution of Japan, with a view to clarifying the aim of education and establishing the foundation of education for new Japan.

ARTICLE I. Aim of Education. Education shall aim at the full development of personality, striving for the rearing of the people, sound in mind and body, who shall love truth and justice, esteem individual value, respect labor and have a deep sense of responsibility, and be imbued with the independent spirit, as builders of a peaceful state and society.

ARTICLE II. Educational Principle. The aim of education shall be realized on all occasions and in all places. In order to achieve the aim, we shall endeavor to contribute to the creation and development of culture by mutual esteem and co-operation, respecting academic freedom, having a regard to actual life and cultivating a spontaneous spirit.

ARTICLE III. Equal Opportunity in Education. The people shall all be given equal opportunities of receiving education according to their ability, and they shall not be subject to educational discrimination on account of race, creed, sex, social status, economic position, or family origin. The state and local public bodies shall take measures to give financial assistance to those who have, in spite of their ability, difficulty in receiving education for economic reasons.

ARTICLE IV. Compulsory Education. The people shall be obligated to have boys and girls under their protection receive nine years' general education. No tuition fee shall be charged for compulsory education in schools established by the state and local public bodies.

ARTICLE V. Coeducation. Men and women shall esteem and cooperate with each other. Coeducation, therefore, shall be recognized in education.

ARTICLE VI. School Education. The schools prescribed by law shall be of public nature and, besides the state and local public bodies, only the juridical persons prescribed by law shall be entitled to establish such schools. Teachers of the schools prescribed by law shall be servants of the whole community. They shall be conscious of their mission and endeavor to discharge their duties. For this purpose, the status of teachers shall be respected and their fair and appropriate treatment shall be secured.

ARTICLE VII. Social Education. The state and local public bodies shall endeavor to attain the aim of education by the establishment of such institutions as libraries, museums, citizen's public halls, et cetera, by the utilization of school institutions, and by other appropriate methods.

ARTICLE VIII. Political Education. The political knowledge necessary for intelligent citizenship shall be valued in education. The schools prescribed by law shall refrain from political education or other political activities for or against any specific political party.

ARTICLE IX. Religious Education. The attitude of religious tolerance and the position of religion in social life shall be valued in education. The schools established by the state and local public bodies shall refrain from religious education or their activities for a specified religion.

ARTICLE X. School Administration. Education shall not be subject to improper control, but it shall be directly responsible to the whole people. School administration shall, on the basis of this realization, aim at the adjustment and establishment of the various conditions required for the pursuit of the aim of education.

ARTICLE XI. Supplementary Rule. In case of necessity appropriate laws shall be enacted to carry the foregoing stipulations into effect.

Supplementary Provision

This law shall be enforced on and from the day of its promulgation.

Law No. 25
31 March 1947

—Official Translation

Sources

Chapter 1

Adapted from:
1. "Kodomo no jōkyō to kodomoron," in *Kodomo o Minaosu: Kodomokan no Rekishi to Genzai* (Tokyo: Iwanami Shoten), pp. 1–33.
2. "Kodomotachi no jōkyō," in *Kodomo no Kenri to wa nanika: Jinken Shisō no Hatten no tame ni*, Iwanami Pamphlet No. 72. Tokyo: (Iwanami Shoten), pp. 2–5.

Chapter 2

"Meiji 'keimō' no gakumon, kyōiku shisō," originally published in *Kagaku to Shisō* No. 14, 1974; reprinted in *Tennōsei Kokka to Kyōiku: Kindai Nihon Kyōiku Shisōshi Kenkyū* (Tokyo: Aoki Shoten, 1987), pp. 3–43.

Chapter 3

Adapted from:
1. "Tennōsei kyōiku taisei no seiritsu," originally published in *Zasshi Kyōiku*, February 1967; reprinted in *Tennōsei Kokka to Kyōiku: Kindai Nihon Kyōiku Shisōshi Kenkyū* (Tokyo: Aoki Shoten, 1987), pp. 45–64.
2. "Nihon ni okeru kyōiku to kyōikuhō," Part 1, Section 1: "Tennōsei Kyōiku Taisei no Tokushoku," in Horio Teruhisa and Kaneko Masashi, *Kyōiku to Jinken* (Tokyo: Iwanami Shoten, 1977), pp. 104–119.
3. "Kokumin kyōiku ni okeru 'kyōyō' o meguru mondai," in *Gendai Kyōiku no Shisō to Kōzō: Kokumin no Kyōikuken to Kyōiku no Jiyū no Kakuritsu no tame ni* (Tokyo: Iwanami Shoten, 1971), pp. 344–380.

Chapter 4

Adapted from:
1. "Nihon ni okeru kyōiku to kyōikuhō," Part 1, Section 2: "Sengo kyōiku kaikaku to kyōiku kihonhō taisei no seiritsu," in Horio and Kaneko, *Kyōiku to Jinken* (Tokyo: Iwanami Shoten, 1977), pp. 120–143.
2. "Kyōiku kihonhō o yomu," in *Kyōiku Kihonhō wa doko e: Risō ga Genjitsu o Kirihiraku* (Tokyo: Yūhikaku Shinsho, 1986), pp. 42–135.

Chapter 5

"Nihon ni okeru kyōiku to kyōikuhō," Part 2: "Sengo 30 Nen ni okeru

Kyōiku to Hō no Dōtai," Sections 1, 2, 3, 4; in Horio and Kaneko, *Kyōiku to Jinken* (Tokyo: Iwanami Shoten, 1977), pp. 144–191.

Introduction to Part II

Adapted from:
"Yuragu Kyōiku Kihonhō," in *Kyōiku Kihonhō wa doko e: Risō ga Genjitsu o Kirihiraku* (Tokyo: Yūhikaku Shinsho, 1986), pp. 137–178.

Chapter 6

"Sugimoto hanketsu no ronri: 'Kyōshi no kyōiku no jiyū' to 'kyōikuteki hairyo' o chūshin to shite," originally published in *Hanrei Jihō* No. 604, October 1970; reprinted in *Kyōiku no Jiyū to Kenri* (Tokyo: Aoki Shoten, 1975), pp. 76–83.

Chapter 7

"Takatsu hanketsu no ronri: Gakushū no kenri to kyōiku no jiyū ni chōsen suru mono," originally published in *Zasshi Kyōiku* No. 307, September 1974; reprinted in *Kyōiku no Jiyū to Kenri* (Tokyo: Aoki Shoten, 1975), pp. 84–94.

Chapter 8

"Gakuryoku tesuto to wa nan de atta ka," originally published in *Rōdō Hōritsu Jumpō*, Issue No. 894, December 1975; reprinted in *Gendai Nihon no Kyōiku Shisō* (Tokyo: Aoki Shoten, 1979), pp. 92–98.

Chapter 9

"Kyōikuken no kōzō to kyōiku naiyō hensei," originally published in *Kikan Kyōikuhō*, Issue No. 21, Sōgō Rōdō Kenkyūjo, Fall 1976; reprinted in *Gendai Nihon no Kyōiku Shisō* (Tokyo: Aoki Shoten, 1979), pp. 120–150.

Chapter 10

"Kyōshi ni totte kenshū to wa nani ka," originally published in *Kikan Kyōikuhō*, Issue No. 2, Sōgō Rōdō Kenkyūjo, December 1971; reprinted in *Kyōiku no Jiyū to Kenri* (Tokyo: Aoki Shoten, 1975), pp. 147–175.

Chapter 11

"Kyōiku hyōka to kyōiku tōsei: Naishinsho saiban," *Kikan Kyōikuhō* Issue No. 52, Sōgō Rōdō Kenkyūjo, Summer 1984, pp. 88–94.

Chapter 12

"Kyōiku ni okeru byōdō to koseika: Kachi ishiki no henkaku ni mukete," originally published in *Zasshi Kyōiku* No. 364, November 1978; reprinted in *Gendai Nihon no Kyōiku Shisō* (Tokyo: Aoki Shoten, 1979), pp.265–285.

Chapter 13

Adapted from:
1. "Kyōiku no mondaisei," *Kikan Kyōikuhō*, Issue No. 22, Sōgō Rōdō Kenkyūjo, Autumn 1976.
2. "Kyōiku no 'nōryokushugi' teki saihen hihan," *Kokumin Kyōiku* No. 8, Rōdō Junpōsha; Spring 1971.
3. "'Nōryokushugi' kyōiku to kodomo no gakushūken," *Nihon Kyōiku Hōgaku Nenpō*, Yūhikaku, February 1978.
All three are reprinted as Section III of *Gendai Nihon no Kyōiku Shisō* (Tokyo: Aoki Shoten, 1979), pp. 152–230.

Chapter 14

Adapted from:
1. "Kyōiku kaikaku to kyōiku kihonhō," in *Kyōiku Kihonhō wa doko e: Risō ga Genjitsu o Kirihiraku* (Tokyo: Yūhikaku Shinsho, 1986), pp. 179–210.
2. "Gendai shakai to kyōiku kaikaku no ideorogii," in *Gendai no Kyōiku Kaikaku: Igirisu to Nihon*, ed. Brian Simon and Horio Teruhisa (Tokyo: Eideru Kenkyūjo, 1987), pp. 122–143.
3. "Gendai shakai to kyōiku kaikaku: Kyōiku no jiyūka to kōkyōiku o megutte," *Zasshi Kyōiku* No. 456, Special Edition, August 1985, pp. 18–33.
4. "Hendō suru gendai shakai ni okeru kyōiku kaikaku no sujimichi," *Asahi Jānaru*, March 1, 1987, pp. 102–106.
5. Interview with Horio Teruhisa, in *Kodomo to Kyōiku*, November 1987, pp. 52–57.

Index

Natsume Sōseki, 89, 92, 254, 266
neo-conservatism, 374
Neumann, Sigmund, 119, 272, 384
New Journal on Education (*Kyōiku Shinshi*), 33, 34, 84
Nihon shoki, 201
Nikkeiren (Japan Federation of Employers' Associations), report on manpower policy, 338–48
Nishimura Shigeki, 25, 27, 71
Nitobe Inazō, 96
Nixon, Richard M., visit to Japan, 148
Northern and Southern Dynasties controversy, and academic freedom, 77, 100, 175
nōryokushugi (ideology of ability-first), 3, 301–5, 338
Occupation period, 8, 106–29, 131
Ōe Kenzaburō, 355
Ōishi Yoshio, 155
Okamura Tsukasa, 102
Okudaira Yasuhiro, 390
Onishi Hajime, 74
opportunity, equality of, 219
Organization for Economic Cooperation and Development (OECD), 303–4; Report on Japanese Education issued by, 210
Oshikawa Katayoshi, 73
Ōsugi Sakae, 94
Ōta Takashi, 307, 311
Ōuchi Hyōe, 150
Ōuchi Tsutomu, 13
An Outline of a Theory of Civilization (Fukuzawa Yukichi), 52, 62, 87
Ozaki Saburō, 83

Pacific War, 4
Paine, Thomas, 8–9, 138
parents, duty to educate children, 34–35, 225, 228–29, 273–74
Parent-Teacher Association (PTA), 162, 235–36, 397

Peace Education Movement, 172
Peace Preservation Law (1925), 94, 119
People's Education Movement, 18, 39, 161–62, 166, 328
Piaget, Jean, 395
Pittau, Joseph, 304
political education, 60–61
politics, separation of education from, 57–59
popular sovereignty, 129, 130, 159, 397–98
Potsdam Declaration, 106
press, freedom of, 29
Primary School Edict, 86
privatization, 364
Project Head Start (U.S.), 374
punishment, corporal, 280
Regulations for Primary School Instructors (1882), 254–55
Rekishi Kyōiku Kyōgikai (History Education Council), 264
religion, freedom of, 73, 118–119
right to learn, 4, 6, 9, 85; of children, 16, 229–31, 389; of citizens, 383–86; of local residents, 386–87; of workers, 388–89
rights, political, 32–33
Rōyama Masamichi, 96

Sagara I'ichi, 250–51, 273
Saitō Kihaku, 266–67
Sakai Toshiaki, 94
San Francisco Peace Treaty, 142
Sasaki Susumu, 300–1
Sayama Kisaku, 14
Scholarship, distinguished from education, 48, 52, 76, 171
Scholastic Achievement Test for lower secondary schools, 164, 166, 180–82, 213–21, 281; court rulings on, 222–45, 300
School Edicts (*gakkōrei*), 69, 80